OXFORD MONOGRAPHS ON MUSIC

*Music and Women of the Commedia dell'Arte
in the Late Sixteenth Century*

Music and Women of the Commedia dell'Arte in the Late Sixteenth Century

ANNE MACNEIL

OXFORD
UNIVERSITY PRESS

Great Clarendon Street, Oxford OX2 6DP

Oxford University Press is a department of the University of Oxford.
It furthers the University's objective of excellence in research, scholarship,
and education by publishing worldwide in

Oxford New York

Auckland Bangkok Buenos Aires Cape Town Chennai
Dar es Salaam Delhi Hong Kong Istanbul Karachi Kolkata
Kuala Lumpur Madrid Melbourne Mexico City Mumbai Nairobi
São Paulo Shanghai Taipei Tokyo Toronto

Oxford is a registered trade mark of Oxford University Press
in the UK and certain other countries

Published in the United States
by Oxford University Press Inc., New York

© Anne MacNeil 2003

The moral rights of the author have been asserted
Database right Oxford University Press (maker)

First published 2003

All rights reserved. No part of this publication may be reproduced,
stored in a retrieval system, or transmitted, in any form or by any means,
without the prior permission in writing of Oxford University Press,
or as expressly permitted by law, or under terms agreed with the appropriate
reprographics rights organization. Enquiries concerning reproduction
outside the scope of the above should be sent to the Rights Department,
Oxford University Press, at the address above

You must not circulate this book in any other binding or cover
and you must impose this same condition on any acquirer

British Library Cataloguing in Publication Data
Data available

Library of Congress Cataloging in Publication Data
Data available

ISBN 0–19–816689–3

1 3 5 7 9 10 8 6 4 2

Typeset by SNP Best-set Typesetter Ltd., Hong Kong
Printed in Great Britain
on acid-free paper by
Biddles Ltd., Guildford & King's Lynn

Vedendo Isabella Andreini recitare una Tragedia

Tace la notte, e chiara à par del giorno
Spiegando per lo Ciel l'ombra serena
Già per vaghezza oltre l'usato affrena
Di mille lumi il bruno carro adorno.

Caggia il gran velo homai, veggiasi intorno
Dar bella Donna altrui diletto, e pena,
Che 'n sù la ricca, e luminosa Scena
Faccia à Venere, e Palla invidia, e scorno.

Febo le Muse, Amor le gratie ancelle
Seco accompagni; e da l'oblio profondo
Sorga il Sonno à mirar cose sì belle.

A sì dolce spettacolo, e giocondo
Dian le sfere armonia, lume le Stelle,
Sia spettator' il Ciel, Teatro il Mondo.

                Giovan Battista Marino

Seeing Isabella Andreini recite a tragedy

The night is silent and, light as day,
Spreading over the heavens her serene pallor
Already beautiful beyond accustomed measure, she stops
Her dark chariot adorned with a thousand lights.

Let the great curtain fall at last, let all see
A beautiful woman give others pleasure and pain,
So that from the sumptuous and luminous Stage
She may engender envy and scorn in Venus and Pallas Athena alike.

Let Phoebus lead the Muses, and Cupid his handmaidens,
The Graces; let Sleep arise from deep oblivion
To witness such beautiful deeds;

Let the Spheres lend harmony to such a sweet
and happy performance, and the Stars light;
Let the heavens be its audience, and the World its theatre.

                Giovan Battista Marino
                (translated by Massimo Ossi)

Preface

No work of research goes forward without the compassion and assistance of library and archive staff the world over. I am deeply indebted to the people who work at the many institutions whose materials contribute to this study: the American Academy in Rome, the Biblioteca Nazionale Marciana, the Museo Correr, the Ca' Goldoni, the Fondazione Cini, the Biblioteca Burcardo, the Biblioteca Apostolica Vaticana, the Archivio Capitolare in Rome, the Biblioteche Comunali of Padua, Mantua, and Como, the Biblioteca Comunale dell'Archiginnasio, the Archivio dell'Accademia Filarmonica di Verona, the Bibliothèque Nationale de France, the Biblioteca Trivulziana, the Biblioteca Ambrosiana, the Biblioteca Braidense, the Regenstein Library of the University of Chicago, the Houghton Library of Harvard University, the Newberry Library, the British Library, and the State Archives in Mantua, Milan, Florence, Venice, Padua, Modena, Bologna, and Rome.

Especial thanks go to the Biblioteca Nazionale Centrale in Florence, the Biblioteca Comunale dell'Archiginnasio in Bologna, the Blacker-Wood Library of Biology at McGill University in Toronto, the Biblioteca Burcardo in Rome, the Bibliothèque Nationale de France, the Musée Carnavalet, and the British Museum for permission to reproduce materials from their collections.

Portions of this book first appeared in 'The Divine Madness of Isabella Andreini', *Journal of the Royal Musical Association*, 120 (1995), 195–215; 'A Portrait of the Artist as a Young Woman', *Musical Quarterly*, 83 (1999), 247–79; and 'Weeping at the Water's Edge', *Early Music*, 27 (1999), 406–18, all reproduced by permission of Oxford University Press.

I am further grateful to the financial institutions that have generously funded my work on this project: the American Academy in Rome, the Gladys Krieble Delmas Foundation, the University of Chicago, the American Musicological Society, the University of Texas at Austin, and the University of North Carolina at Chapel Hill.

This book contains the work of many people, although only one name appears on its cover. Some are family, whose unconditional love and support have sustained me throughout my life. And some are old friends, to whom I owe debts of patience, motivation, encouragement, and love in addition to their more tangible contributions to these pages. Others I know only slightly, and their unlooked-for generosity signals a greatness of heart that both honours and humbles me. My esteem and gratitude go especially to my parents Georgia and Sam MacNeil, to Steven Brooke, Jeanice Brooks, Tim Carter, James Wyatt Cook, Suzanne Cusick, Andrew Dell'Antonio, Filiberto Donzelli, Annegret Fauser, Alison Frazier, Christine Getz, Philip Gossett, Leofranc Holford-Strevens, Ellen Harris, Lester Little, Massimo Ossi, Franco Pavan, Ellen Rosand, Brian Rose, Sergio Rossi, Ingrid Rowland, Patricia Sachs, Romano Sarzi, Thomas Schumacher, and Christopher and Michael Siciliano. My colleagues at the University of North Carolina, Chapel Hill have been unstinting in their support of this project, and for this I thank them all. Finally, I am grateful to Bonnie Blackburn, whose wisdom and careful editing have made this a much better book than otherwise possible.

To those who have not lived to see this work completed, I dedicate it. Their absence as I write these words casts a shadow over my heart that no satisfaction in the accomplishment of publication can dispel. To Nino Pirrotta, Franca Camiz, and above all to Howard Mayer Brown: may this gift be worthy of you.

A.E.M.

Contents

List of Illustrations — x
List of Music Examples — xi
List of Abbreviations — xii

1 Prologue — 1
2 Turn About is Fair Play — 32
3 Behold, now there are Amazons of Learning — 77
4 The Politics of Description — 127
5 Epilogue — 163

Chronology — 187
Documents — 265

Bibliography — 325
Index — 343

List of Illustrations

1.1	'La musica della sonata con l'intavolatura di leuto del Canario', from Cesare Negri, *Le gratie d'amore* (1602)	23
1.2	Dionisio Minaggio, *The Feather Book*, 'Schapin'	25
1.3	Engraving of Francesco Gabrielli by Carlo Biffi	26
1.4	'Per la Varietà degli Instrumenti Musici di Scapino', showing Francesco Gabrielli on stage	28
1.5	Commemorative medallion of Isabella Andreini	31
2.1	SS Annunziata, Florence, fresco showing Isabella, Francesco, and Giovan Battista Andreini amid the Medici court	50
2.2	Conclusion of the canzone 'Quando scendeste ad'illustrare il Mondo' by Isabella Andreini	65
3.1	Portrait of Isabella Andreini from the frontispiece to her *Rime* (Milan, 1601)	117
3.2	Portrait of Isabella Andreini, after the engraving by Raffaello Sadeler	118
3.3	Anonymous portrait of Isabella Andreini derived from the frontispiece of her *Rime* (Milan, 1601)	119
3.4	Portrait of Isabella Andreini	120
3.5	Satyr flogging a Nymph, engraved by Agostino Carracci, from the 'Lascivie' series	124
5.1	Giulio Caccini, *Tu c'hai le penne Amore*, from *Le nuove musiche et nuova maniera di scriverle* (1614)	171
5.2	Dionisio Minaggio, *The Feather Book*, 'Florinda'	183

List of Music Examples

1.1	L'Aria di Scapino, *I più rigidi cori*	29
2.1	Monteverdi, *Si come crescon alla terra i fiori*, with Andreini's text from *Mirtilla*, Act III, Scene v, lines 1748–53	45
2.2	Eleuterio Guazzi, *Io credèa che tra gli amanti*	72
3.1	Pietro Paolo Torre, *Ove sì tosto voli sogno?*	105
3.2	Donat'Antonio Spano, *Quella bocca di rose*	109
3.3	Giaches de Wert, *Tirsi morir volea*, bars 40–51	112
4.1	Monteverdi: (*a*) beginning of the *Lamento d'Arianna*, 'Lasciatemi morire'; (*b*) Lamento dell'Ingrata, 'Ahi troppo è duro'	131
4.2	Monteverdi, *Amorosa pupilletta*	136
4.3	Giulio Santo Pietro del Negro, *Movèa dolce un zefiretto*	138
4.4	Monteverdi, *Lamento d'Arianna*, 'Non son, non son quell'io'	143
5.1	Claudio Saracini, *Care gioie che le noie*	179

Abbreviations

Ambrosiana	Milan, Biblioteca Ambrosiana
ASB	Bologna, Archivio di Stato
ASF	Florence, Archivio di Stato
ASM	Milan, Archivio di Stato
ASMN	Mantua, Archivio di Stato
ASMO	Modena, Archivio di Stato
ASP	Padua, Archivio di Stato
ASR	Rome, Archivio di Stato
BAV	Vatican City, Biblioteca Apostolica Vaticana
BCB	Bologna, Biblioteca Comunale dell'Archiginnasio
BCC	Como, Biblioteca Comunale
BCMN	Mantua, Biblioteca Comunale
BCP	Padua, Biblioteca Comunale
BNC	Florence, Biblioteca Nationale Centrale
BNF	Paris, Bibliothèque Nationale de France
Braidense	Milan, Biblioteca Braidense
Burcardo	Rome, Biblioteca e Raccolta Teatrale Burcardo
Capitolare	Rome, Archivio Capitolare
Cini	Venice, Fondazione Cini
Correr	Venice, Museo Correr
Filarmonica	Verona, Archivio dell'Accademia Filarmonica di Verona
Goldoni	Venice, Ca' Goldoni
Marciana	Venice, Biblioteca Nationale Marciana
New Grove	*The New Grove Dictionary of Music and Musicians*, ed. Stanley Sadie, 20 vols. (London, 1980)
Trivulziana	Milan, Biblioteca Trivulziana

I

Prologue

Virtù, fama ed onor: ne fer i Gelosi
Virtue, fame, and honour: of these are the Gelosi made

So reads the impresa of the longest-standing commedia dell'arte company to hold the Renaissance stage. Formed in imitation of the intellectual academies of northern Italy, the Gelosi took for their own this proud motto and the sign of the Janus face, which looks both back to the classical past, with its ancient harmonies of intoned poetry and mystical powers of representation, and forward to a new golden age of theatre in which women mount the stage with men to sing and speak with sibylline authority. This golden age endured for fifty years, although its classical foundations and inclusion of women in the profession continue into the present, and the three generations of the Compagnia dei Gelosi, together with the first flowering of its heir, the Compagnia dei Fedeli, comprehend its entirety. This book narrates the story of the Gelosi and the Fedeli in this first era of the commedia dell'arte, focusing in particular on the representation of women on stage and on the role of music-making in their craft.

The Milanese printer Pandolfo Malatesta marks a precise beginning of this golden age of theatre, ascribing the genesis of the commedia dell'arte to an era of peace in Italy, when thoughts of survival gave way to dreams of life and compassion. His dedication to Alessandro Striggio of Giovan Battista Andreini's comedy *Lo schiavetto* in 1612 associates the new practice with the political calm granted by the Treaty of Cateau-Cambrésis, signed by Henri II of France and Philip II of Spain in 1559: 'From those years, when beautiful Italy began to enjoy a tranquil peace, almost as a restorative to the hardship of such continuous wars, the most valiant persons began to rediscover the ancient forgotten practice of performing comedies.'[1]

---

[1] G. B. Andreini, *Lo schiavetto* (ed. Falavolti), dedication, 57: 'Da quegli anni, che la bella

As important as is his chronological contextualization of commedia dell'arte practice, Malatesta associates the performance of comedies with politics, characterizing the art form as a reprise from, and even an antidote to, war. Numerous documents confirm this relationship, from the declaration by the historian Pietro Mattei that one comedienne's performances were commonly used by princes to exorcize the turbulent moods of the French populace, to the Count of Fuentes's request in 1601 that Vincenzo Gonzaga send his comedians to Milan to perform for the conclave of the papal legate Cardinal Pietro Aldobrandini and the Duke of Savoy.[2] Bound to politics and civic life by Aristotelian philosophies of art in the service of the state, commedia dell'arte performances thus mirror the societies for which they were created in a manner that is both profound and perverse. Humour, with all its distortions, lies at the core, but as an adjective, modifying the critiques, commentaries, and satires comedians made of the world around them.

It is the dramatist Angelo Ingegneri who, in 1598, distinguishes stagecraft in this era by its imitation of ancient Greek and Roman ideals and the introduction of 'virgins and honest women' to the stage.[3] While the appearance of women on stage might at first seem to invoke a simple sense of realism in an otherwise fantastical art form, the resulting exercise of female authority virtually requires the invocation of classical reasoning in order to justify women's expression, although the relationship is hardly one of cause and effect. This is, in my view, the central precept of the commedia dell'arte, which distinguishes it from *commedia vulgare* and *commedia erudita*. As will be seen in the pages that follow, classicizing themes arise over and over again as Renaissance writers strive to define the authoritative voice in new ways to encompass the speech of women. Conceptions of Aristotelian *virtù*, Neoplatonic divine madness, and sibylline prophecy—at times wonderfully contorted and often intertwined—form the foundation of nearly all descriptions of comediennes in performance, allowing for the expression of emotional excess and its subsequent regulation by social norms. The ubiquitous staging of contests between actresses similarly rests on ideas of enacting transcendence from

---

Italia cominciò pur a godere una tranquilla pace, quasi a restoro de' travagli di tante continuate guerre, cominciarono valentissimi personaggi a ritrovare l'antico tralasciato uso del rappresentar comedie.'

[2] Pietro Mattei, *Della perfetta historia di Francia*, trans. Alessandro Sanesio (Venice, 1625), 227; ASM, Autografi, cart. 95, fasc. 19bis.

[3] Ingegneri, *Della poesia rappresentativa* (ed. Doglio), 4–8.

discord to concord, and the performance of music, especially singing, is often given as proof of a comedienne's attainment of celestial virtue and god-like authority.

Contributing to both Ingegneri's and Malatesta's formulations of this first era of the commedia dell'arte are the fortunes of the noble houses that patronized comedians and their troupes. Foremost among them stood the Medici and, in particular, the generations comprising Eleonora, Ferdinando, and Maria. Medici patronage, by definition, had a strong French cast due to the long history of interwoven relations between the two courts (not for nothing does the Medici coat of arms bear the fleur de lis), and this intertwining of French and Tuscan affairs was further strengthened by the weddings of Ferdinando de' Medici to Christine of Lorraine in 1589 and of Maria de' Medici to Henri IV in 1600. Many commedia dell'arte performances during this period thus enunciated a dialogue between French and Florentine politics and styles. Medici influence radiated also to Mantua with the wedding of Eleonora de' Medici to Vincenzo Gonzaga in 1584, and the Mantuan court gained prominence thereafter as a centre of commedia dell'arte production. Indeed, by the end of the century, and especially after the devolution of Ferrara to papal rule, when Vincenzo Gonzaga undertook a programme reminiscent of the Caesars of bestowing citizenship on his prized actors and musicians, Mantua became the undisputed epicentre of theatrical activity in Italy.

But when, within the space of three years from 1609 to 1612, Ferdinando de' Medici, Henri IV, Eleonora de' Medici, and Vincenzo Gonzaga died, the commedia dell'arte suffered a blow from which it never recovered, and these events mark the final close of its first, golden age. The subsequent era of commedia dell'arte production centred initially, as one would expect, around the court of Maria de' Medici, as comedians spent more time in the French capitol. Beyond this geographical shift, however, the commedia dell'arte in this second era was characterized by the increased production of composed plays—including the nascent genres of *dramma per musica* and 'opera reale' in addition to comedy, pastoral, tragedy, and tragicomedy—and the publication of fully texted dramas, often with instructions on how to perform them, became an increasingly important part of the profession. What had been an era of avant-garde performance turned quite suddenly into a time of documentation and commemoration.

The Compagnia dei Gelosi, whose impresa opens this chapter, came into existence at the beginning of Malatesta's tranquil peace and endured until the year of the second treaty of the Pax Hispanica.[4] From the start, as if in proof of Ingegneri's portrayal of the craft, the troupe was primarily identified with its leading actresses, the first surviving notice of the Gelosi's activities dating from a contest held in Mantua between the comediennes Vincenza Armani and a Roman called Flaminia in 1567. Armani was the troupe's first *prima donna innamorata*, and her talents for oratory, singing, and musical and poetic composition made her the most lauded actress of the 1560s. Vittoria Piisimi reigned over the Gelosi's next incarnation, and she too brought a lively talent for music, and especially for dancing, to her art. The third generation was that of Isabella Andreini (née Canali), whose magnificence came to define the company that died with her in Lyons on 10 June 1604.

When the Gelosi disbanded, some of their members retired, as did the bereaved Francesco Andreini, while others looked to Isabella's and Francesco's son and daughter-in-law to lead them. Thus, most of the Gelosi brought the era to a close as members of the Compagnia dei Fedeli, the troupe established by Giovan Battista Andreini and his wife Virginia. Cast in the mould of the Compagnia dei Gelosi, the Fedeli came under the patronage of Eleonora de' Medici and Vincenzo Gonzaga in Mantua, and they spent much of their time performing in the Mantuan capital—most significantly for the wedding celebrations of Francesco Gonzaga and Margherita of Savoy in 1608. Virginia Andreini (née Ramponi), once a member of the Gelosi and *prima donna innamorata* of the Fedeli, represents the last generation of the era and she, like her predecessors Vincenza Armani, Vittoria Piisimi, and Isabella Andreini, received high praise for her musical skills. In particular, Virginia Andreini was known as a fine singer and a virtuosa of the five-course Spanish guitar.

Together with the Gelosi's leading actresses, the comedians who formed the core of the ensemble quite rightly called themselves 'comico geloso' or 'comica gelosa'. The appellation was a proud one, which had effect even after the troupe disbanded in 1604, and individual members reminded patrons of their quality by invoking the almost mythical name. In addition to the Gelosi's leading actresses, among the longest-standing members of the company were Adriano Valerini and Silvia Roncagli, Giovanni Pellesini (*in arte* Pedrolino), Giulio Pasquati da Padova

---

[4] The Pax Hispanica was negotiated in three major treaties: the Treaty of Vervins in 1598, the Treaty of London in 1604, and the Treaty of Antwerp in 1609. See Paul Allen, *Philip III and the Pax Hispanica*, pp. vii–xi.

(Pantalone), Lodovico de' Bianchi (Dottor Graziano), Flaminio Scala, and Francesco Andreini. Other comedians known to have performed with the troupe at various times in its history include Giovan Battista and Virginia Andreini, Orazio de' Nobili, his wife Vittoria, and their son Flaminio, Simone Basilea, Gabrielle Panzanini, Giovan Paolo Fabbri, Lutio Fedele, Girolamo Salimbeni, Nora fiorentina, and Aurelia romana.

The troupe's membership, however, like that of any commedia dell'arte company, rarely remained fixed for long and various members performed with other companies as well. Illustration of the ease with which individual comedians entered and exited the troupe is perhaps best served by the examples of Isabella Andreini and Vittoria Piisimi, two of the Gelosi's *prime donne*. Both performed with the troupe in the festivities for the Medici wedding of 1589, but in the Milanese licence dated 15 October the following year, neither Isabella nor Francesco Andreini was named.[5] Perhaps Isabella was pregnant and temporarily needed to avoid the rigours of work, or perhaps she and Francesco travelled from Florence directly to Rome, where they attended the inauguration of the new Pope, Urban VII.[6] In any event, they left the Gelosi for a while, and the Andreinis' licences in 1591 refer to 'Isabella and her company'.[7] At the time of Cosimo II de' Medici's baptism on 26 April 1592, however, the Gelosi and the Andreini were together again in Florence on the recommendation of Emilio de' Cavalieri, and payments for the troupe were made to Francesco Andreini.[8] At about the same time, Piisimi began performing with the Confidenti. But in 1595 Piisimi again requested a licence in Milan for herself and the Gelosi, while Francesco Andreini sought permission for the Compagnia degli Uniti to perform in Bologna. The composition of the Gelosi thus changed regularly, and sometimes significantly, although the basic identity of the troupe remained intact.[9]

Patrons, too, often worked to form new companies, putting their favourite performers together for a season or for a specific occasion.[10] But

[5] ASM, Registri delle Cancellerie, serie XXI, no. 23, fo. 119^{r-v}.
[6] Isabella Andreini dedicated a sonnet, 'Quando i tuoi chiari, e gloriosi honori', to the new pope Giovan Battista Castagna for the occasion.
[7] ASF, Mediceo del Principato, filza 2941, 7 Jan. 1591; 29 Mar. 1591.
[8] ASF, Filze strozziane, serie I, fasc. 27, fos. 2^r, 6^r.
[9] See the Chronology, 16 June and 15 Oct. 1595.
[10] The calendar year is typically divided into four seasons of commedia dell'arte production. The carnival season, when comedians tend to perform publicly, extends from Epiphany to Ash Wednesday. It is followed by Quaresima or Lent, when comedies are generally

this is not to say that the social fabric of the commedia dell'arte was chaotic. It was instead a highly energized and fluctuating system of artists who sometimes dealt individually and sometimes collectively with each other, with their patrons, and with the owners or managers of public performing spaces, making both permanent and temporary alliances. The resulting hierarchy of allegiances was complicated, and many comedians exercised a diplomacy worthy of ambassadorial rank in maintaining good relations with all concerned. When, for example, in 1583, Vincenzo Gonzaga wanted to create a virtuoso comic ensemble to perform for his wedding to Eleonora de' Medici, Francesco Andreini politely refused the summons on behalf of himself and his wife, explaining to the Mantuan prince that they were obligated to the Gelosi and to the patron of the *stanza delle commedie* in Venice:

Most serene sir. I understand from your highness's musician Sig. Antonio your desire and good intentions regarding the New Company that you would like to assemble. And because I hold myself very much obliged to your highness's most good graces, I cannot, without great displeasure, thank you for your most courteous intention, in having made me worthy, together with my wife, to be numbered among such a worthy company, since, finding myself bound by faith to the Gelosi, and in particular to Sig. Alvise Michiel, patron of the hall in Venice, I am constrained to decline the offer. [Nor can I fulfil] your highness's wish, since, to put together this company requires breaking up three, which is difficult, even though to your highness every most difficult thing is very easy to do. Moreover, because I am in Ferrara by myself, I lack the ability to offer the Gelosi to your highness's service without the agreement of the others in the company. With which I pray that you will keep my wife and me among the number of your least servants and in your good graces. I kiss your most worthy hands, together with my wife, praying to Our Lord for your happiness and exaltation. From Ferrara, 13 April 1583. Your highness's most humble servant, Francesco Andreini, *comico geloso*.[11]

Andreini's letter is an extremely important document. It not only contains an illustration of the webs of obligation governing commedia dell'arte performers in the late sixteenth century, but it provides us also with a sense of comedians' stature within the hierarchy of the Renaissance

---

prohibited. The summer season tends to run from just after Easter to around 15 Sept., during which time a company will usually accompany a ruler to the summer residence of his or her court. The commedia dell'arte troupe will then usually relocate to another court for the winter season, which includes the December holidays and New Year.

[11] Doc. 9.

court. For although comedians were itinerant, performing for various rulers and in public spaces as well as private, they most certainly entered into the sociology of the court and occupied clearly defined positions within it.

Francesco Andreini's polite refusal to Vincenzo Gonzaga, together with other documents, indicates that comedians and musicians shared similar status at the Mantuan court and that some of their duties were interchangeable. The Antonio Ricio to whom Andreini referred was a Mantuan musician who had been sent in April 1583 to visit the Este court in Ferrara, not only to treat with Francesco, but to also assess the quality of the *concerto delle donne*.[12] At the same time, another musician named Filippo Angelone, a *cantore* in the chapel of Giaches de Wert, was the official purveyor of comedians' licences in Mantua, a position conferred on him on 14 March 1580. This post later devolved to the comedian Tristano Martinelli, who replaced Angelone nineteen years later, on 29 April 1599. Further evidence of activities shared among comedians and musicians at the Mantuan court dates from the earliest years of the seventeenth century, when Giovan Battista and Virginia Andreini collaborated on several projects with the composer Claudio Monteverdi and his brother Giulio Cesare, including the performances of *Arianna* and *Il ballo delle ingrate* in Mantua in 1608 and of *Il rapimento di Proserpina* in Casale in 1611, and the composition of *La Maddalena*, published in 1617.

Francesco Andreini's enunciation of comedians' allegiances opens up a world of elaborate ties, formal and informal agreements, and standing versus temporary obligations. He mentioned two specifically and alluded to a third: first came the bond of faith to his company, which might be honourably broken only in consultation with the other members of the troupe, and second was his contractual obligation to the owner/manager of the Gelosi's performing space in Venice. Andreini's third obligation, peeking through the obsequious language of his letter, was his continuing relationship with Vincenzo Gonzaga as the ruler of one of a number of courts on which Andreini, his family, and his troupe depended for their livelihood.

The fact that Andreini was alone in Ferrara at the time of writing should not be taken to indicate that he had broken with the Gelosi, although his reluctance to speak on behalf of the company he clearly led is noteworthy. Both the tone and date of the letter suggest that the troupe

---

[12] Cavicchi, 'Lettere di musicisti ferraresi', 196.

had simply agreed to resume their performing schedule in Venice after the Lenten season and Easter holiday, during which time the performance of comedies was typically prohibited.[13] Still, comedians straddled an inconvenient fence in maintaining relationships with noble patrons at the same time as they entered into contractual agreements with others, as Andreini's reference to Alvise Michiel indicates. One such negotiation, between Vittoria Piisimi and Alfonso II d'Este, shows how disasterous the results could be. Obligated by contract to the owner of another of Venice's *stanʒe delle commedie* during carnival in 1581, Piisimi politely refused a summons from Alfonso II to return to Ferrara together with her colleague Pedrolino. In spite of a consoling letter of explanation written on 4 January by the owner of the theatre, which accompanied a similar letter from Piisimi, the duke's anger was not assuaged, and Piisimi again begged his forgiveness for both herself and Pedrolino after carnival ended.[14] Clemency was not granted until the following year, however, and the next time Piisimi performed in Ferrara was on 18 June 1582.

Both Piisimi's and Francesco Andreini's negotiations involving performances at the *stanʒe delle commedie* in Venice allude to a great watershed in the history of theatrical production in Italy and especially of the commedia dell'arte: the openings of the Teatro Michiel and the Teatro Tron in the parish of San Cassan. In 1581, during a meagre carnival season that lasted only a month from 6 January to 8 February, the Teatro Michiel and the Teatro Tron for the first time offered theatrical productions to a ticket-buying public. Owned and operated by the sons of noble Venetian families, both theatres contracted with elite commedia dell'arte companies for the use of a regular hall, with permanent or semi-permanent audience seating and stage, lavish decoration, sets, and lighting.[15] Actors and actresses like the Gelosi, used to performing in the galleries of ducal palaces, found a familiar, luxurious ambience in the *sestiere* Santa Croce's two *stanʒe delle commedie*. Francesco Sansovino's guidebook to 'Venice, noble and singular city', published that same year, gives a modest

---

[13] It should be noted that commedia dell'arte troupes often continued to perform through the first few weeks of Lent, stopping just short of the fourth Sunday in Quaresima. The week before Easter and the octave of the feast, however, were held sacred.

[14] ASMO, Archivio per materie, Comici, letters from Vittoria Piisimi to Alfonso II d'Este, 4 Jan. and 5 Mar. 1581; Ettore Tron to Alfonso II d'Este, 4 and 26 Jan. 1581.

[15] Examples of late 16th-c. technology regarding stage sets and theatrical lighting are well preserved in the Teatro Olimpico in Vicenza, which was built in 1585 by the Accademia Olimpica to designs by the renowned architect Andrea Palladio. See Rigon, *The Teatro Olimpico in Vicenʒa*.

announcement of the theatres that provided permanent, indoor stages to professional comedians and which made impresarios of the noblemen who owned them: 'Not far from this Church of San Cassan are two theatres, very beautifully built at great expense, one in the form of an oval and the other round, with a capacity for a great number of people, for reciting comedies during the carnival season, according to the customs of the city.'[16]

The Teatro Michiel stood on the opposite side of the Grand Canal from Ca' d'Oro, tucked in just behind the Palazzo Brandolin on the Rio di San Cassan. The hall was built in the shape of an amphitheatre; Sansovino called its interior measurements capacious at approximately 20 × 21 m. Owned by the Michiel family and run by the then 36-year-old Alvise and his brothers, the Teatro Michiel was open only a short time, and documentation of its activity ceased by 1608.[17]

Christoforo Ivanovich, writing one hundred years after the Teatro Michiel's opening, recorded its inauguration with performances by the Bolognese comedian Francesco Gabrielli (*in arte* Scapino). Ivanovich's chronicle must be discounted, however, because Scapino, born in 1588, could hardly have graced the Venetian stage seven years earlier. The writer simply may have confused Gabrielli with his father, Giovanni (*in arte* Sivello), also a famous comedian and, like his son, the owner and player of a magnificent collection of exotic musical instruments. Or, he may have been altogether wrong, for a letter written by the Mantuan comedian Drusiano Martinelli (the brother of Tristano) on 17 October 1580 suggests that it was in fact the Gelosi who performed for the Teatro Michiel's opening season.

In his letter, Martinelli offered the services of his company to Duke Guglielmo Gonzaga for the carnival season of 1581, 'since the Gelosi and the Confidenti will be in Venice'.[18] Franco Mancini and the other editors of the monumental series *I teatri del Veneto* have taken this to signify that the Gelosi performed for the opening of the Teatro Michiel, since it is known that the Confidenti, then led by Vittoria Pissimi and Giovanni Pellesini (Pedrolino), inaugurated the other of Venice's new theatres, the

---

[16] Sansovino, *Venezia città nobilissima*, 175. Cfr. Mancini et al., *I teatri di Venezia*, 94: 'Sono poco distanti da questo Tempio [di San Cassan] due Teatri bellissimi edificati, con spesa grande, l'uno in forma ovata et l'altro rotonda, capaci di gran numero di persone; per recitarvi ne' tempi del Carnevale, Comedie, secondo l'uso della città.'

[17] See Mancini et al., *I teatri di Venezia*, p. xviii.

[18] ASMN, Gonzaga, Autografi, b. 10, fo. 130ʳ.

Teatro Tron. But Martinelli, too, was mistaken, for the Gelosi did not go to Venice. The company were in Bologna throughout the carnival season of 1581, as may be seen in the account books of the Monasterio Corpus Domini, to which they made weekly payments of L.100 in alms.[19] And on 25 April, Jacopo d'Osmo in Bologna wrote to Guglielmo Gonzaga to say that the comedians were on their way to Mantua, where they had been summoned to perform for the wedding festivities of Prince Vincenzo and Margherita Farnese.[20]

In the end, nothing certain is known of the Teatro Michiel's inaugural performances, although I suspect that Isabella and Francesco Andreini, leading a company other than the Gelosi, performed there in 1581. This would make sense of Martinelli's assumption that both the Confidenti and the Gelosi were in Venice for the carnival season, while allowing for the Gelosi to be, in fact, in Bologna. The Andreinis' whereabouts in this period are not known, in that their names are not specified in any of the extant documentation, and so it is both possible and probable for them to be performing independently of the Gelosi. Francesco Andreini's letter of 1583, outlining the troupe's obligation to the owner of the Teatro Michiel, is the first extant notice of him and Isabella after the birth of their eldest son Giovan Battista in 1576, as well as the earliest known documentation of the theatre's operations.

The Teatro Michiel's sister theatre, the Teatro Tron, located at the intersection of the Rio di San Cassan and the Rio della Madonnetta, just off the Campo San Polo and directly opposite the Palazzo Albrizzi in what is now a public garden, opened its doors during carnival, 1581 with performances by Vittoria Piisimi, Giovanni Pellesini (Pedrolino), and company.[21] This marks the initial period of activity of the theatre, which lasted

---

[19] ASB, Assunteria di Munizione, Recapiti, b. 3, fasc. 18. Suprisingly, the Gelosi's donations to the Monasterio, which were a requirement of their contract to perform, continue past Ash Wednesday, abating only with the fourth week of Lent. Similarly, Vittoria Piisimi's letter of reconciliation to Alfonso II is dated the fourth Sunday of Lent. Bolognese contracts customarily require comedians to pay alms. See Documents, no. 8.

[20] Vincenzo Gonzaga was married twice: the first time to Margherita Farnese in 1581, a marriage that was annulled when Margherita failed to become pregnant, and the second time to Eleonora de' Medici, in 1584. For both occasions, the Prince negotiated with the Gelosi to perform for the nuptial celebrations. No descriptions of their performances, however, are known to survive.

[21] A prolonged battle for performing rights at the Teatro Tron in 1619 demonstrates its financial appeal. From June to Dec., Flaminio Scala tried valiantly to oust Virginia and Giovan Battista Andreini and the Fedeli from the favoured venue. See Scala's letters to Giovanni de' Medici, dating June to Dec. 1619, in ASF, Mediceo, f. 5150. For excellent trans-

until 1629, when it was destroyed by fire. After the terrible plague that ravished Venice in 1630 and 1631, which years saw the deaths of Virginia Andreini, Tristano Martinelli, and Alessandro Striggio, the Teatro Tron reopened for the carnival season in 1633, only to burn again on 20 December of that year. Its second restoration did not begin until May 1636, when it was designated by the Council of Ten as a music hall and finally opened its doors again with a performance of Benedetto Ferrari's opera *L'Andromeda*.[22] Although not specifically heralded as a 'teatro di musica' before 1636, the Teatro Tron in its earliest incarnation saw much music-making and deserves recognition as a site where the Venetian public paid to enjoy music and spectacle fifty-five years in advance of 'the first public opera house'.

In contrast with the propagandistic programme representing a court's wealth through staged spectacle, public theatres generally lack descriptive documentation. This is unfortunately true for Piisimi's and Pellesini's performances for the innauguration of the Teatro Tron. But diaries of other spectacles do survive that give us an idea of the comedians' individual styles of acting and of the role of music in their productions. Analysis of the documents surrounding their performances in Venice in 1574 and in Milan in 1594 allows for a more comprehensive understanding of the commedia dell'arte as well, by offering an introduction to the various theatrical genres that made up the Gelosi's repertory and to the characteristics that distinguished men's and women's performances.

Piisimi and Pellesini stood at the height of their profession in the last quarter of the sixteenth century. Piisimi performed with the Gelosi for Henri III in 1574 in Venice when he travelled from Warsaw to Paris to take up the crown, and again in 1594 for the wedding of the Count of Harò in Milan—an event for which Pedrolino also took the stage.[23] For the representation of Cornelio Frangipani's *Tragedia* in Venice on 24 July 1574, Piisimi and her colleagues

criptions of Scala's notoriously sloppy hand, see *Comici dell'arte: corrispondenẓe*, 540–66. These and other notices of performances by Scapino, Cecchini, the Andreinis et al., and of negotiations concerning the Teatro Tron in this period, may be found in Mancini et al., *I teatri di Veneẓia*, 126–30.

[22] Correr, MS Cicogna 3234, no. 6, *Sommario degli avvenimenti accaduti nella parrocchia di S. Cassano*, 'Teatro Tron ridotto in cenere'; Mancini et al., *I teatri di Veneẓia*, i. 97–100.

[23] ASV, Collegio IV, fol. 50; ASV, Senato III, Secreta, Lettere del Residente a Milano, 13 July 1574; BNF, ital. 1494, fo. 49; Frangipani, *Tragedia* (1574 edn.); Nolhac and Solerti, *Il viaggio in Italia di Enrico III Re di Francia*, 133–4, 144, 231. The last notice we have of Piisimi is 15 Oct. 1595; the dates of her birth and death are unknown.

recited in the manner derived from the form of the ancients: all the performers sang in the softest harmonies, sometimes singing alone, sometimes together; and at the end, the chorus of Mercury was of instrumentalists, who had the most various instruments that were ever played. The trumpets heralded the entrance of the gods on stage, which was done with a tragic machine that was impossible to regulate because of the great tumult of people who were there. Neither was it possible to imitate antiquity in the musical works, which were composed by Sig. Claudio Merulo, of such quality that the ancients could never aspire to it, nor of that of Monsig. Gioseffo Zarlino, who was occupied with the music played for the King on the Bucintoro, which set some of my Latin poetry, and with the [music for the] church of S. Marco. And he was the director of those [compositions] that were made continually at His Majesty's command.[24]

Frangipani's description extends the compass of our understanding of comedians' talents and performing repertories. It tells us not only that the Gelosi performed tragic texts set to music, but that they sang music composed by Claudio Merulo in both solo and accompanied settings. Moreover, it relates that their style of singing was suited to the neoclassical manner favoured by Renaissance humanists like Giovanni de' Bardi in Florence, whose camerata similarly began to imitate the ancient manner of combining music and rhetoric in the 1570s.

Merulo's settings for Frangipani's *Tragedia* unfortunately share the fate of much music performed on the commedia dell'arte stage in that they are not known to survive, and the above passage describing the 1574 performance—the sole known report of that entertainment—appears only as an addendum to the second edition of Frangipani's text.[25] The lyrics published in that edition, however, offer tenuous clues to their musical settings and to the performing styles of those who sang them. The resulting analysis becomes a kind of archaeology of musical performance, divining the shapes and character of entire vessels on the basis of a few random shards. In spite of its title, *Tragedia* appears to have been a set of intermedi—this because the entire text was sung and because it begins

---

[24] Frangipani, *Tragedia*, afterword to the second edition (see Documents, no. 4); cited in Nolhac and Solerti, *Il viaggio in Italia di Henri III*, 133–4.

[25] Indeed, the printed editions of *Tragedia* contain only musical lyrics, leading Nolhac and Solerti to hypothesize that the work more closely resembled a cantata than a play, which would make the employment of Piisimi and company as its performers extraordinary. It is not clear, however, that the work consisted only of the published text, and its performance by professional comedians suggests that additional spoken text may have been improvised, while the music and musical lyrics were composed. If not, Frangipani's *Tragedia* would be one of the earliest dramatic works set entirely to music.

with a prologue and ends with an encomiastic chorus. Most of the text is set in *ottava rima*, although Mars and the choruses sing in *versi sciolti* of varying stanza lengths and rhyme formations, freely alternating seven- and eleven-syllable lines and concluding each stanza with a rhyming couplet. The musical settings for Mars and the choruses were thus undoubtedly madrigals, some set for solo voice, as indicated above, and some sung in parts, as in the choruses of Amazons and Soldiers. The *ottave*, too, may have been set as madrigals, although the variation in poetic form suggests a corresponding difference in musical setting— perhaps they were sung over a ground bass or other recurring formula, in the manner of the *cantastorie*.[26]

What is remarkable about this performance is its timing. On 10 July Aloisio Mocenigo in Venice wrote to Ottaviano Maggi in Milan to request that the Gelosi be sent with all speed in order to perform for the king. Three days later, the comedians requested permission of their patron Don Giovanni d'Austria to leave the city. And on the 21st, one week after they left Milan, Vittoria Piisimi and the Gelosi performed Frangipani's *Tragedia* in Venice. That the comedians learned the music composed for the performance in less than a week's time is impressive indeed. It also tempers the shock of Antonio Costantini's remark during the winter of 1608 that Virginia Andreini similarly learned the role of Monteverdi's *Arianna* in six days.[27] Whereas one might suspect Costantini of exaggerating about Andreini's facile memory, Piisimi's feat is circumscribed by physical fact, and the unassailable truth of it thus lends credence to the later report. Clearly, comedians were quick on their feet and could learn new material, be it music, poetry, or prose, at a speed we now find astonishing.

In some cases, as with Giovan Battista Andreini's comedy *Lo schiavetto*, the written composition of theatrical material followed after any number of performances, and so the issue of memorization does not arise.[28] These compositions are most accurately characterized as codifications of an oral process, although as artefacts they do not appear to differ from works first conceived in writing. But to say that Merulo composed

---

[26] Haar discusses the possible musical genres for setting *ottava rima* in his book *Essays on Italian Poetry and Music*, 76–100.

[27] Costantini's letter is transcribed by Solerti, *Gli albori*, i. 95, and translated in Fabbri, *Monteverdi*, trans. Carter, 83.

[28] As Andreini writes in his preface to *Lo schiavetto*, 'Having exercised the comic arts for many years, such that I would be the inexpert gardener of such a flowering and fruitful orchard, I am nevertheless persuaded to put into print some of those subjects that I composed in performance ("composi recitando").'

the music for *Tragedia* or that Monteverdi composed the music for *Arianna* implies that composition precedes performance in these works. And to show that comedians were able to learn and perform their parts in a matter of a few days suggests not only that their powers of memorization were acute, but confirms what we know from the existence of *scenari*— that their comprehension of texts was fundamentally structural, resulting in a dense intertwining of memorization and improvisation. Indeed, comedians may have constructed for themselves hermetic theatres of memory like that of Giulio Camillo, which combined memory theory with concepts of proportion, imagination, celestial harmony, and the dramatic arts. As Camillo wrote in his *Discorso in materia del suo teatro*,

> I have read, I believe in Mercurius Trismegistus, that in Egypt there were such excellent makers of statues that when they had brought some statue to the perfect proportions it was found to be animated with an angelic spirit: for such perfection could not be without a soul. Similar to such statues, I find a composition of words, the office of which is to hold all the words in a proportion grateful to the ear ... Which words as soon as they are put into the proportion are found when pronounced to be as it were animated by a harmony.[29]

One needn't mythologize the comediennes who performed with the Gelosi to note how often ideas of facile memory, proportional perfection, an angelic spirit, and harmonious animation were invoked to describe them. The cleric Tomaso Garzoni, writing in *La piazza universale*, published in 1585, attributed to Vittoria Piisimi such non-sequiturs as 'proportionate gestures' and 'harmonious and concordant movements', and when Vincenza Armani sang, 'souls that no longer heard that true harmony which makes the stars move, melted in the ineffable sweetness [of the sound], remembering their celestial home'. In his discussion of Piisimi, Garzoni emphasized the nobility and refinement of the actress's manner, not only in this 1574 entertainment, but throughout her career. Using neoclassical terms of proportional beauty and enchantment, Garzoni accorded her the highest praise and suggested that her inspiration was conveyed by a harmonious voice that was sweet, soft, and penetrating:

> But above all, the divine Vittoria, who metamorphoses herself on stage, seems to me worthy of the highest honours; that beautiful witch of love who entices the hearts of a thousand lovers with her words; that sweet siren who bewitches the souls of her devoted spectators with soft incantations, and who without doubt

[29] Camillo, *Discorso in materia*, in *Tutte le opere*, 33, as cited in Yates, *The Art of Memory*, 156.

deserves to be heralded as the summation of the art, having proportionate gestures, harmonious and concordant movements, majestic and welcome acts, affable and sweet words, lovely and cunning sighs, witty and gentle laughter, noble and generous deportment, and in her entire person a perfect decorum that is due to and belongs to a perfect comedienne.[30]

Imagine the delight of Henri III in having such an enchantress perform for him. Pallas Athena, the leading female role in *Tragedia*, and therefore the role Vittoria Piisimi would have performed, sang a substantive and affective address to the French King ('Poi che veggio de' Dei questo soggiorno') and then, in the finale, a duet with Mars ('Spargiam piante felici allori, e mirti'). The duet was followed by a chorus, which concluded the work. Piisimi's appearance as a goddess in the entertainment implies that her entrance was heralded by a trumpet fanfare, as stated in Frangipani's description, and that she sang Merulo's melodies with the proportional perfection and harmonious manner due to music that surpasses the quality of ancient music. The rhetorical tropes contained in her opening aria betray its formula, which bears marked similarities to other sung introductory soliloquies of its kind:

> Poi che veggio de' Dei questo soggiorno
> Così illustrarsi, e come de' bei lumi
> Celesti adorno farsi tutto Cielo,
> Vò discoprirmi, e uscir da quella nube
> Che me ha celato a gli occhi de' mortali
> Indegni di guardar celesti numi,
> Per parlar teco che tuoi detti rei
> Potriano tormi tutti gli honor miei.[31]

(Since I see this abode of the gods so disclose itself, and how the heavens adorn themselves with beautiful celestial lights, I wish to unveil myself and to step down from the cloud that has concealed me from mortal eyes, which are unworthy of looking at the celestial gods, in order to speak with you, for your wicked words could take away all my honour.)

---

[30] Garzoni, *La piazza universale* (1595), 737: 'Ma sopra tutto parmi degna d'eccelsi onori quella divina Vittoria che fa metamorfosi di se stessa in scena; quella bella maga d'amore che alletta i cori di mille amanti con le sue parole; quella dolce sirena che ammaglia con soavi incanti l'alme de suoi divoti spettatori, e senza dubbio merita d'esser posta come un compendio dell'arte, avendo i gesti proportionati, i moti armonici e concordi, gli atti maestevoli e grati, le parole affabili e dolci, i sospiri leggiadri ed accorti, i risi saporiti e soavi, il portamento altiero e generoso, e in tutta la persona un perfetto decoro quale spetta e s'apartiene a una perfetta comediante.'

[31] Frangipani, *Tragedia*, fo. [3ᵛ].

Fifteen years later, Vittoria Archilei's opening aria for the intermedi sung at the wedding festivities of Ferdinando de' Medici and Christine of Lorraine would deliver a similar rhetorical formula:

> Dalle più alte sfere
> Di celeste sirene amica scorta
> son l'Armonia, ch'a voi vengo, ò mortali,
> poscia, che fino al Ciel battendo l'ali
> l'alta fiamma n'apporta,
> che mai sì nobil coppia il sol non vide
> qual voi nuova Minerva, e forte Alcide.[32]

(From the highest of the spheres, gently escorted by celestial sirens, I am Harmony, and I come to you, O mortals, after beating my wings up to the heavens to bring back their flame. For never did the sun see such a noble couple as you, the new Minerva and powerful Hercules.)

Both 'Poi che veggio de, Dei questo soggiorno' and 'Dalle più alte sfere', one an *ottava*, the other composed in *versi sciolti*, transcend the physical space between earth and heaven. Both feature a goddess or a female allegory descending to earth on a cloud, and both offer a direct mode of address between the singer and her audience, wherein she describes heaven and equates the audience members with gods and heroes. This is as standard a trope as the ball and sceptre.

In Athena's aria, as in Harmony's, words that carry obvious madrigalistic potential, like 'celesti' ('celestial') and 'celato' ('hidden'), together with the wonderfully vivid depiction of the gods and mortals looking at each other from distant realms—embodied in Frangipani's parallel references to eyes, 'bei lumi celesti' ('beautiful celestial lights') and 'gli occhi de' mortali' ('the eyes of mortals')—invite interpretation with brilliant flights of diminutions and the muted, sombre tones of flatted *ficta*. The precise notes and rhythms Merulo used, however, to fill the formulaic mould of Athena's address—much less the notes and rhythms sung by Vittoria Piisimi towards the same end—we cannot know, but the composer's cooperation in the performance, together with the texts he set and Frangipani's all too brief description, provide a strong foundation for our developing comprehension of the Gelosi's music-making and the nature of their performative tropes in the early years of the company.

In its representation of Piisimi as a siren, Garzoni's encomium presages

[32] Walker, *Les Fêtes du mariage*, i: *Musique des intermèdes de 'La Pellegrina'*, p. xxxvii.

another performance by the actress that took place in Milan five years following the Medici wedding of 1589. The nuptial celebrations of the Count of Harò in October 1594 offer us another intriguingly hazy glimpse of one of the finest singing actresses of the sixteenth century, thanks to an atypically detailed description of the intermedi performed on that occasion.[33] In Milan, Piisimi again sang the prologue for a set of intermedi depicting the Fall of Phaethon:

First intermedio.
The signal given, a curtain depicting the ocean fell, adorned with diverse sorts of fish, revealing a scene representing Naples. In the middle of the stage, a curtain portraying the ocean was drawn, above which the comedienne Vittoria appeared in the guise of a Siren. From there she made the prologue and, when it was finished, the scene suddenly was covered by a curtain painted with pleasant trees, woods, mountains, and hills, where Phaethon and Epaphos appeared, in dialogue together. . . .[34]

The description of these intermedi is extraordinary. It offers us a second example of Vittoria Piisimi singing the prologue to an entertainment and, together with testimony given by Lodovico de' Bianchi in 1585 and by Francesco Andreini in 1615, it demonstrates that the Gelosi performed not only the plays that offered a pretext for the scenic and musical indulgence of intermedi, as suggested by Nino Pirrotta, but the intermedi themselves.

Bianchi's letter to Vincenzo Gonzaga of 16 December 1585 is an extremely valuable document, although it elicited no response from the comedian's patron. It was sent just a year after Vincenzo's marriage to Eleonora de' Medici. Writing from Bologna in an untutored hand and signing himself 'servitore lodovicho di bianchi da bolognia deto il dotor graziano comicho geloso', Bianchi informed the then Prince of Mantua that he would no longer suffer working with the importunate and overbearing actress Delia [Camilla Rocha Nobili]. If she forms part of the company in Mantua, he writes, he will remain in Bologna! On top of

---

[33] I say 'atypically detailed' because this is one of the very few descriptions of wedding entertainments that mentions comedians by name. Witness that, among the plethora of publications describing the Medici wedding of 1589, only one—the privately written *Diario* of Giuseppe Pavoni—mentions the performances of Vittoria Piisimi, Isabella Andreini, and the Gelosi, even though the comedian's plays were accompanied by the famous and extravagant intermedi.
[34] Gentile Pagani, *Del teatro in Milano avanti il 1598*, cited in D'Ancona, 'Il teatro mantovano', pt. 3, p. 333 (Doc. 22).

everything, he exclaims, because of Delia, whom everyone in Bologna calls the hunchback, the troupe must omit from their number Adriano Valerini and Silvia Roncagli, who are essential members of the company and who are necessary for performing intermedi.[35]

Francesco Andreini's smug dedication to the readers of his *Bravure* bolsters Bianchi's documentation of the Gelosi performing intermedi, and demonstrates that the context of Piisimi's performance in Milan in 1594 was anything but unique: 'That famous and never enough lauded company of the Gelosi endured many, many years, demonstrating to future comedians the true manner of composing and reciting comedies, tragicomedies, tragedies, pastorals, visibile intermedi, and other dramatic inventions, that are seen daily on the stage.'[36]

Visible intermedi, or *intermedi apparenti*, are most closely identified with the grand spectacles produced for the Medici court in Florence after the commencement of the *principato*. Prior to their advent, comedic structures were articulated by *intermedi non apparenti*, which usually took the form of madrigals sung between the acts (or sometimes between scenes) of a play. Notable examples include Nicolò Machiavelli's *La mandragola* of c.1518[37] and *Clizia* of 1525, and Anton Francesco Grazzini's *La gelosia* of 1550. These types of intermedi were, as their name suggests, sung without staging or costumes, and their subject matter may have been only tenuously related to the comedy they accompanied, if, in fact, it was related at all. As early as 1539, however, Francesco Corteccia, together with Giovan Battista Strozzi, created a set of intermedi for the wedding of Cosimo de' Medici and Eleonora de Toledo that may be clearly characterized as both visible (that is, staged) and distinct from the comedy they accompanied, Antonio Landi's *Il commodo*. After *Il commodo*, it was nearly thirty years before the Medici court again would mount grand spectacles with intermedi. In 1567, they did so for the baptism of Francesco de' Medici's and Giovanna d'Austria's first child, and in 1569 for the entry of the Archduke

---

[35] ASMN, Gonzaga, b. 1162, fos. 743ʳ–744ᵛ (Doc. 13). Delia's activities are not heavily documented, but see the title page of Bruni, *Dialoghi scenici*, which states that he composed the prologues in the collection at the suggestion of his colleagues Flaminia [Orsola Cecchini], Delia [Camilla Rocha Nobili], Valeria [unknown], Lavinia [Diana Ponti], and Celia [Maria Malloni]. It is possible, although I have not investigated the matter, that Rocha Nobili is the hunchback of whom Carlo Rossi writes in his letter dated 14 Mar. 1608. See Fabbri, *Monteverdi*, trans. Carter, 83; and Solerti, *Gli albori*, i. 95.

[36] Andreini, *Le bravure* (ed. Tessari), 7.

[37] For a detailed discussion of the dating of *La Mandragola*, see Radcliff-Umstead, *The Birth of Modern Comedy in Renaissance Italy*, 116–18.

of Austria into Florence, on both occasions with music by Alessandro Striggio.[38]

The most lively period of grand court spectacles in Florence, however, began in 1583 with the performance of Giovanni Fedini's *Le due persilie*, with intermedi by Stefano Rossetti, Giovanni Legati, Gostantino Arrighi, Jacopo Peri, Cristofano Malvezzi, and Alessandro Striggio. By this time, the Gelosi had been performing intermedi for nearly a decade, although none of the Florentine performances before 1589 is known to have included comedians in either comedies or intermedi. This lacuna makes the intermedi performed for the wedding of the Count of Harò in 1594 all the more important for the history of music theatre and the history of the commedia dell'arte.

The Count of Harò's wedding and the description of its intermedi, in addition to opening up a wide field of inquiry regarding the production of staged musical events and comedians' participation in them, enhances our nascent understanding of one of the most important facets of commedia dell'arte performance: the prologue. Typically sung by the leader of the troupe, the prologue served to explain the reasons for the performance and to contextualize its plot and metaphors. As such, its text was often excerpted and printed with the text of the play, if the play was published. The prologue for the Count of Harò's wedding was performed, as one would expect, as part of the first intermedio, and it shares a generic designation with sung introductory soliloquies like Piisimi's 'Poi che veggio de Dei questo soggiorno' (1574), Archilei's 'Dalle più alte sfere' (1589), and Musica's 'Dal mio permesso amato a voi ne vegno' from Monteverdi's *Orfeo* (1607), which is called 'Prologo' in the score.

The Fall of Phaethon, together with the other prologues listed here, reveals that women, as often as—and perhaps more often than—men, sang the opening soliloquies to a variety of dramas, and that they might do so in costume rather than always in the archetypal toga and laurel wreath stipulated by Leone de' Sommi in his treatise on theatrical performance, the *Quattro dialoghi in materia di rappresentazioni sceniche*.[39] The resulting

---

[38] Stefano Rossetti and Scipione della Palla also contributed music to the 1567 celebrations; see Pirrotta and Povoledo, *Music and Theatre from Poliziano to Monteverdi*, 202–6.

[39] Sommi, *Quattro dialoghi*, ed. Marotti, 55. The dating of Sommi's treatise is uncertain, although his mention of the Roman actress Flaminia and of Dottor Graziano suggests a date of composition *c.*1567. The original manuscript of the treatise was lost in the fire that consumed the Biblioteca Nazionale in Turin on 26 Jan. 1904, and the only surviving copy is an 18th-c. transcription housed in the Biblioteca Palatina in Parma. See p. xvi, and Blanchard-Rothmuller, pp. xiv–xv.

feminized contextualization of the dramas that followed these prologues stands in marked contrast to the masculine gendering of other theatrical frames, such as the more closely circumscribed narratives that accompanied Monteverdi's laments of Arianna and the Nymph.[40] The performance of prologues by women emphasizes the aggressive representation of gender in music theatre of this period and,[41] when combined with the omnipresent references to acting companies by the names of their *prime donne*, demonstrates the strength of feminine representation within the profession.

The characterization of men's performances in the commedia dell'arte was very different from that of women's. Like Piisimi, Pedrolino too performed in Milan for the Count of Harò's wedding, although his style of performance contrasted sharply with hers, and no neoclassical encomia like Garzoni's are known to have been written for him. In the 1594 festivities, Pedrolino appeared notably at the end of the second intermedio, together with the Mantuan comedian Tristano Martinelli (*in arte* Arlecchino), in a scene designed to show off the acrobatics and dancing that distinguished these two comedians throughout their careers:

Phaethon, passing over the chariot, lamenting the great toil and peril in which he found himself, Jove struck him down and made him fall from the sky, and his mother appeared, lamenting the loss of her son; and his sisters, for their great weeping, were turned into poplar trees. And they heard roaringly loud thunder from the heavens, after which, with continued thunder and lightning, confetti rained down on the stage, which caused great delight in Arlecchino and Pedrolino, and much laughter in the audience . . .[42]

This version of the Fall of Phaethon is an odd story for its juxtaposition of sorrow and joy. Here, the audience is uncharacteristically aligned with the designated mortal response to the action on stage, and one can only imagine their delight in seeing these two famous actors—comedians who would work together for another twenty years—capering about joyfully amid a cloud of confetti as the heavens opened up with thunder and lightning. Pedrolino's lifelong acrobatic acumen was attested to in a letter written by Martinelli on 15 August 1612, in which he informed Ferdinando

---

[40] See Susan McClary, *Feminine Endings*, 80–111.

[41] I deliberately use the term music theatre here to avoid the cumbersome and at times overly pedantic distinctions employed in discussions of genre as it applies to opera and its related forms.

[42] D'Ancona, 'Il teatro mantovano', pt. 3, p. 333. See Doc. 22 for a transcription of the account in its entirety.

Gonzaga that the aging Pedrolino had lost his 'natural vigour'.[43] But in 1594 Pedrolino was in his prime, and his skill as a dancer was commemorated by a style of dancing that bore his name, as mentioned in a famous letter written by Emilio de' Cavalieri in Rome to the Florentine secretary Marcello Accolti.

The letter was written on 18 January 1594—nine months prior to Pedrolino's performance in Milan and less than two years after Cavalieri's recommendation of the Gelosi to Ferdinando de' Medici for the entertainments organized for the baptism of his son. Cavalieri described a musical evening held in the room of a Mr Filippo on the 17th, which featured a woman named Vittoria. Warren Kirkendale and Claude Palisca have identified Mr Filippo as Filippo Neri and Vittoria as Vittoria Archilei. After Vittoria sang, and before she received a friendly slap from Mr Filippo, a Vallicellan priest danced in the style of Pedrolino:

Yesterday, Vittoria was in the room of Mr Filippo, where Cusano was. And she sang—a Benedictus—but they wanted to hear *spagnole* and *galanterie*, [of which] there were many. And at the end Mr Filippo made a Vallicellan priest dance a *canario* and in the manner of Pedrolino. And Vittoria told me that [he did] stupendously, so he must practise often. Mr Filippo then gave the benediction to some, and particularly to Vittoria, and so that she would remember him, he gave her a good-natured slap. And he made her promise to return another time . . .[44]

What movements comprised Pedrolino's style of dancing are not known, although the tone of this letter, together with the vigorous physicality of the evening it describes—a priest, stereotypically restrained in movement by his robes, danced and must have exercised himself at it often; a woman was slapped—and the exotic athleticism of the *canario*, implies that the priest's dance in the manner of Pedrolino was something equally energetic and cavalier.

The pairing in Cavalieri's letter of a *canario* and the style of Pedrolino

---

[43] ASMN, Gonzaga, b. 10, fos. 162ʳ–163ʳ; also *Comici dell'arte: corrispondenze*, 379–80.

[44] ASF, Mediceo, f. 3622, fos. 32ʳ–33ʳ, transcribed and translated by Palisca, *Studies in the History of Italian Music*, 397. My translation differs from Palisca's in several respects. 'Vittoria ieri stette in camera di Messer Filippo, dove fu Cusano; et cantò, un benedictus, ma volsero sentir spagnole, et galanterie, vi furno di molti; et in ultimo Messer Filippo fece ballare un prete della Vallicella, canario et da pedrolino; et mi dice Vittoria che stupendamente sichè deve esercitarsi, spesso; Messer Filippo poi dà la benedizione ad alcuni, et particolarmente a Vittoria, et perchè si ricordasse di lui; gli diede un bono schiaffo; et si fece promettere che ritornasse un altra volta . . .'.

merits some attention because the histories of the *canario* and of Pedrolino brush against each other in intriguing ways over a period of some twenty years. If nothing else, the popularity of both waxed and waned together, and Cavalieri's letter suggests that it was Pedrolino who made the dance famous. The *canario* was a relatively recent dance in 1594, its choreography having appeared for the first time in Fabritio Caroso's *Il ballarino* of 1581, a treatise published in Venice in the same year that Pedrolino performed there for the inaugural season of the Teatro Tron. It is intriguing to think that Pedrolino might have danced the *canario* there for the first time. Julia Sutton, editor of the revised edition of *Il ballarino*, which Caroso retitled *La nobiltà di dame* in honour of the wedding of Ranuccio Farnese and Margherita Aldobrandini in 1600, has described the rise in popularity of the *canario* as 'explosive, if one is to judge by the number of canary variations in all the manuals. It exists both as a separate dance consisting of a series of variations, or as the last dance of a balletto suite.' The dance features a sequence of unique stamping movements or *battuti*, performed to a short and simple ground in either triple or compound duple metre with distinctive dotted rhythms. The style of the *canario*, according to Caroso, is in imitation of a dance or dances originating in the Canary Islands, which are located off the north-west coast of Africa and which, in the late sixteenth century, were governed by Spain.[45]

Music and choreography for the *canario* are given not only in Caroso's *Il ballarino* and *La nobiltà di dame*, but also in Cesare Negri's *Le gratie d'amore*, published in 1602. *Le gratie d'amore* is a compendium of diverse chronicles and descriptions relating to the festivities staged in Milan in 1599 in honour of the double alliance of the dynasties of Austria and Spain—festivities at which Pedrolino and his company performed.[46] Negri's version of the *canario*, a court dance dedicated to the Marchesa Giulia de' Vecchi e Cusana, who is perhaps related to the Cardinal Cusano in Cavalieri's letter, comprises a sequence of variations, performed alternately by the cavalier and the lady (although in the case of the Vallicellan priest, the dance must surely have been executed by one person alone), each calling for combinations of stamping (*battuti*), leaping (*saltini*), and sliding (*schisciati*) steps, performed to the music shown in Pl. 1.1.

The last notice we have of Pellesini is an account by the poet Malherbe,

[45] Caroso, *Courtly Dance*, 45 and 110–11.
[46] Pedrolino and his company were paid 150 ducatoni for comedies performed for the Infanta Isabella of Spain and her husband, Archduke Albert of Austria. See ASM, Registro delle Cancellerie, serie XXII, no. 42, fo. 232^r.

PL. 1.1. 'La musica della sonata con l'intavolatura di leuto del Canario', from Cesare Negri, *Le gratie d'amore* (1602), 201–2

who saw Pedrolino perform with Virginia Andreini, her husband Giovan Battista, and the Fedeli at Fontainebleau in 1613. His review of the ageing Pedrolino's and Arlecchino's performances is waspish, and he suffered them only at the desire of the Medici queen:

> On Saturday evening I shall be at the Italian Comedy at the express bidding of the Queen, without which I would not have gone to see it before we returned from Fontainebleau. Arlequin [Tristano Martinelli] is certainly very different from what he once was, as too is Patrolin [Giovanni Pellesini]: the former is 56 years

old, and the latter 87, neither of an age any longer appropriate to the stage, where one needs lively temperaments and firm minds, and those one rarely finds in such old bodies as theirs.[47]

The end of Pedrolino's career coincides precisely with the end of the first era of commedia dell'arte production. Only a year before his performance in France, Martinelli had sought to replace him with another, younger comedian: the Bolognese comedian Francesco Gabrielli, *detto* Scapino, who in his turn became the leading *zanni* of his time (see Pl. 1.2). Gabrielli's speciality helps to show the hierarchy of musical performance on the commedia dell'arte stage, and his publications—all of which postdate the period in question—offer some codification of the practices of the *zanni*.[48]

Athletic dancing, rude songs, and the playing of exotic instruments were the purview of the *zanni*, male actors like Scapino, Arlecchino, and Pedrolino whose roles focused on the bizarre and the ridiculous. Refined styles of singing, however, either a cappella or accompanied by 'soft' instruments such as the lute, flauto dolce, or Spanish guitar, together with more modest forms of dance, were performed by the *innamorati*, male and female actors whose roles mirrored the ideal courtier. Gabrielli had a notorious reputation for composing and singing *tagliacanzoni* and *villanelle*, and his extensive musical instrumentarium was one of the wonders of the commedia dell'arte stage. Moreover, his collection of instruments was a source of intense interest to Claudio Monteverdi and his correspondent in Rome, widely believed to have been Giovan Battista Doni, in 1634. An engraving of the comedian made by Carlo Biffi the year before gives an indication of the plenitude of Scapino's instruments, as well as their ornate designs (see Pl. 1.3).

Doni, evidently ignorant of Biffi's engraving, wrote to Monteverdi in Venice to ask the composer to obtain drawings and descriptions of Scapino's instruments. Monteverdi, enlisting the assistance of friends because Scapino was performing in Modena rather than in Venice during the carnival season of 1634, sent Doni as much information as he was able to cull from his friends' memories. His letter, like Biffi's engraving,

---

[47] Malherbe, *Œuvres*, ed. Lalanne, iii. 337, as cited in Richards and Richards, *The Commedia dell'arte*, 272.

[48] ASMN, Autografi, b. 10, fos. 162ʳ–163ʳ, letter from Tristano Martinelli, Milan, to Ferdinando Gonzaga, Rome, 15 Aug. 1612; transcribed in *Comici dell'arte: corrispondenze*, 379–80.

PL. 1.2. Dionisio Minaggio, *The Feather Book*, 'Schapin'. Blacker-Wood Library of Biology, McGill University

PL. 1.3. Engraving of Francesco Gabrielli by Carlo Biffi. Bologna Biblioteca Comunale dell' Archiginnasio

suggests that Scapino's instrumentarium was more exotic to the eye than to the ear:

I have seen a drawing of the instrument on the piece of paper you sent me, which—far from diminishing my eagerness—has on the contrary made it grow. And since in the aforesaid second letter you ask me to engage the services of Scapino in order that I may send Your Worship drawings of the many extraordinary instruments that he plays, because of my great desire to find an opportunity of serving you, and being unable to do this as he is performing in Modena, not in Venice, I therefore feel very disappointed.

Nevertheless I have used a little diligence with certain friends so that they can at least describe to me the ones they are able to remember, and so they gave me the enclosed sheet of paper which here and now I am sending off to Your Worship. Nor did I neglect to write to a friend about trying to obtain drawings of those most different from the ones in use. I have never seen them myself, but from the little information I am sending, it seems to me that they are new as regards shape but not in sound, since all fit in with the sounds of the instruments that we use.[49]

Innovative in sound or not, Scapino used his instruments well for the performance of side-splittingly funny *villanelle*, *villanesche*, and *canzoni* (see Pl. 1.4), such as the lowbrow and stuttering 'Ho ho ho, la la la, spu spu spu, za za za, la la la, mer mer mer, da da da' ('He- he- hey, sh- sh- shit st- st- stinks!'), sung at the end of a comedy performed for the fantastical wedding of Lipotoppo and Madonna Lasagna. And although Scapino's celebrity was founded as much on satire as on his instrumentarium and songs, he was also capable of less vulgar efforts, such as the strophic song 'I più rigidi cori', otherwise known as the *aria di Scapino*, which he published under the title *Infermità, testamento, e morte di Francesco Gabrielli* in 1638. Not lacking in humour, the publication evokes notarial pedantry and the narcissism of one who dictates how his friends and colleagues will mourn him when he dies. The only other piece in the print is a *ciaccona*. The first stanza of Scapino's signature piece, as it appears in the 1638 publication, to which I have added modern chord symbols above the *alfabeto* notation for Spanish guitar, is shown in Ex. 1.1.

As may be seen in the example, the *aria di Scapino* contains a modulation into the dominant key area at lines 4 to 6 and a harmonic ornamentation of the basic progression I–IV–V–I. Twenty-eight stanzas long, Scapino's *aria* suffers harmonic variation well, as he first names many of the commedia dell'arte characters with whom he has performed and then lists the cities to which he will leave his various musical instruments. To Cremona goes the violin, to Piacenza the bass; Milan will inherit the viola, Venice the guitar, and Naples the harp; Rome receives the bonacordo, Genoa the trombones, and Perugia the mandola; Bologna, mother of Scapino's invention, is given the theorbo, Ferrara the lute, and all the rest go to Florence. The publication of such a text cheek-by-jowl with a *ciaccona* increases the humour in its interpretation for, as the dying Scapino ekes out his last twenty-eight stanzas of living breath, one or more of his colleagues might very well caper at the foot of his deathbed to the lively,

---

[49] Monteverdi, *Letters*, trans. Stevens, 427.

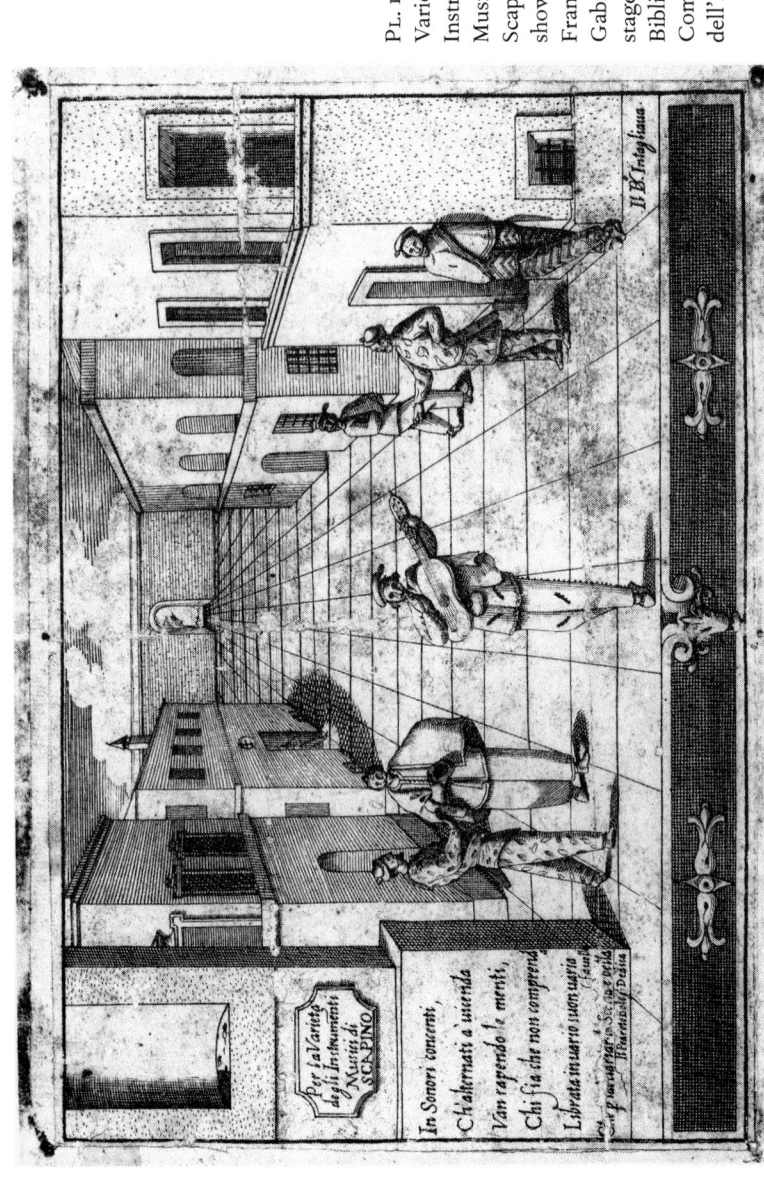

PL. 1.4. 'Per la Varietà degli Instrumenti Musici di Scapino', showing Francesco Gabrielli on stage. Bologna, Biblioteca Comunale dell'Archiginnasio

Symbols immediately above the text indicate intabulation for Spanish guitar. The letter symbols above give the modern harmonic equivalents. Capitals indicate major chords, lower-case letters minor chords.

CIACCONA.

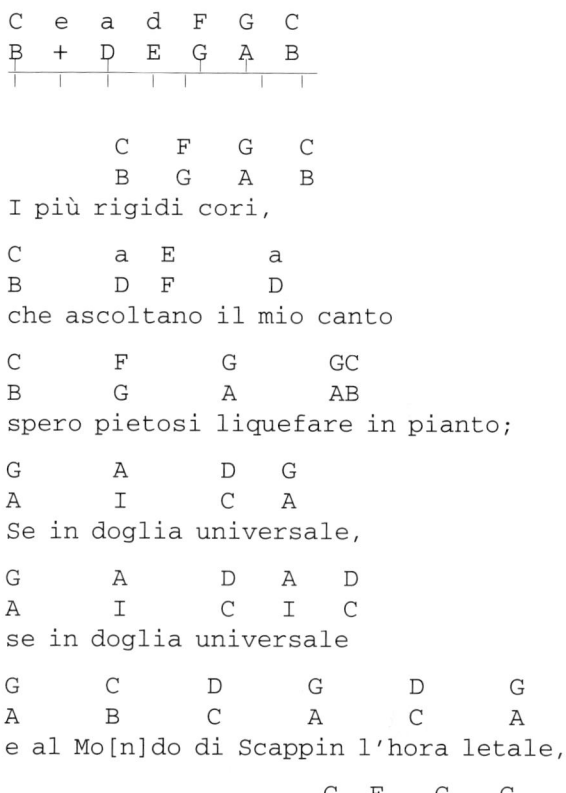

```
Rhythm:    C   e   a   d   F   G   C
           B   +   D   E   G   A   B
           |   |   |   |   |   |   |

                       C       F       G       C
                       B       G       A       B
                   I più rigidi cori,

           C           a       E           a
           B           D       F           D
           che ascoltano il mio canto

           C           F       G           GC
           B           G       A           AB
           spero pietosi liquefare in pianto;

           G           A       D       G
           A           I       C       A
           Se in doglia universale,

           G           A       D       A       D
           A           I       C       I       C
           se in doglia universale

           G       C       D       G       D       G
           A       B       C       A       C       A
           e al Mo[n]do di Scappin l'hora letale,

                               C       F       G       C
                               B       G       A       B
                               l'hora letale.
```

Ex. 1.1. L'Aria di Scapino, *I più rigidi cori*, from *Infermità, testamento, e morte di Francesco Gabrielli* (1638)

syncopated rhythms of the Spanish dance, thereby gainsaying the profound mourning ascribed to the comedian's friends in the aria's lyrics. Seneca's death scene in Monteverdi's *L'incoronazione di Poppea*, which had its premiere across town in Venice's Teatro Grimani in 1642, similarly conflates gleeful music and mournful lyrics, although in more subtle measure than Scapino's scalding aria. In both works, the juxtaposition of opposing themes of life and death engenders a pathetic humour that stains the scene with a pungent irony and enables auditors to laugh at their own mortality. Mid-century ideas of life and death, following in the wake of the Thirty Years War, seem gruesomely jaded when viewed through lenses like these.

Forty years before the publication of the grandiloquent aria that prophesied Scapino's death, Angelo Ingegneri foretold the mortality of Italian theatre writ large and of those whose performances gave it meaning. His treatise, *Della poesia rappresentativa e del modo di rappresentar le favole sceniche* (1598), he avowed, would capture the spirit of theatrical performance before it vanished with the wind.[50] His motivation, in fact, was the death of Alfonso II d'Este in Ferrara, a city and court where music and drama thrived. With the collapse of Este rule, and the subsequent disequilibrium of European political structures, both comedians and playwrights intuited the demise of past theatrical practices, and they began to preserve their art, not only in treatises, but in collections of play scenarios, speeches, dialogues, and scenes. Thus, only at the end of the era do we encounter a self-conscious attempt to document what had previously been jealously guarded as the stuff of living performance. Francesco Andreini, whose sense of artistic mortality was perhaps greatest in the years following Isabella's death in 1604, freely published his wife's soliloquies and his own dialogues featuring the characters Capitano Spavento and his servant Trappola, secure in the knowledge that neither he nor Isabella would ever speak those lines again. The anthology of the Gelosi's *scenari*, written in cooperation with the troupe's *innamorato* Flaminio Scala and published in 1611, share the same fate.

Although the Gelosi's molten inspiration continued in the work of Francesco's and Isabella's son, his wife, and their company, something ineffable ended when the troupe disbanded that June in Lyons following Isabella's death. The candle-lit procession through the streets of the city, the commemorative medallion cast in Isabella's honour (Pl. 1.5), and her

---

[50] Ingegneri, *Della poesia rappresentativa* (ed. Doglio), 7: 'Di maniera che grand'obligo (torno a dirlo) parmi che s'abbia ad avere a chi ci ha per questa via restituito l'uso della scena e l'utile e 'l piacere che da lei si tragge, ravvivando insieme nei dotti e pellegrini ingegni lo studio delle poesie dramatiche colla speranza di veder quando che sia i lor poemi rappresentati e le fatiche loro non gettate al vento.'

PL. 1.5. Commemorative medallion of Isabella Andreini. Paris, Bibliothèque Nationale de France

burial in the church of St-Croix mark the end of an era. Giovan Battista's and Virginia's careers, like Scapino's, were more 'composed' than those of their parents, and the documents of their artistry leave us a comparative wealth of scripted plays, musical scores, and letters from which to extrapolate an understanding of their performances. Giovan Battista Andreini published over forty plays, many of which contain musical lyrics and performing instructions, sometimes in sufficient detail to join them with a musical print or manuscript. And several of Virginia's performances—of both her husband's material and that of others—are preserved in the scores of composers like Claudio Monteverdi and Giulio Caccini. As a continuation of the craft of the Gelosi, this documentation is invaluable, for it gives us an anchor with which to secure the scattered descriptions of the Gelosi's earlier performances. And yet, in the end, Francesco Andreini was right when he suggested that, although we have evidence of the Gelosi's and the Fedeli's performances, and even some of the words they spoke and the songs they sang, we will never hear the sounds of their voices or be enchanted by their movements. At best, we may try to imagine the qualities that characterized the virtue, fame, and honour that were the Gelosi.

2

Turn About is Fair Play

IN the spring of 1589 Vittoria Piisimi, Isabella Andreini, and the Gelosi travelled to Florence to perform for the wedding of Grand Duke Ferdinando de' Medici and Christine of Lorraine. Their presence is noted in none of the official descriptions of the festivities, and Giuseppe Pavoni, an envoy to the Vizani family of Bologna, is the only eyewitness known to have recorded notice of the Gelosi's comedies for the Florentine wedding. His diary provides one of the very few detailed descriptions of a commedia dell'arte performance, yielding important information about not only the troupe's stagecraft but also, in more general terms, the performance of commedia dell'arte plays at court and, in particular, the practice of performing 'in concorrenza' or in competition. Pavoni's account speaks of the rivalry of the two prima donnas and of the Grand Duke's wishes to hear them perform in competition. Like the ancient orators who vied for superiority in contests at the festival of the Great Panathenaea in Athens, the Gelosi thus presented two comedies for the Medici/Valois wedding festivities: *La cingana*, starring Vittoria Piissimi, and *La pazzia d'Isabella*, featuring Isabella Andreini.

Saturday, which was the sixth, the Duke finding himself at a performance of the Gelosi with those two most famous women Vittoria and Isabella, it occurred to him that for entertainment it would be a good idea if they recited a comedy of their own choosing. Upon which, the said women nearly came to a quarrel because Vittoria wanted to recite *La cingana* and the other woman wanted to perform her *pazzia*, entitled *La pazzia d'Isabella*, *La cingana* being the favourite of Vittoria and *La pazzia* the favourite of Isabella. They agreed, however, that the first to be recited would be *La cingana* and that *La pazzia* would be performed another time. And thus they recited the said *La cingana* with the same intermedi that were performed with the high Comedy. But whoever has not heard Vittoria perform *La cingana* has not seen or heard a rare and marvellous thing, which certainly in this Comedy left everyone most satisfied. At another time they will perform *La pazzia*, and it will be Isabella's turn to be the madwoman. There is no need to describe her valour and the loveliness of her conceits, for her virtues are already noted and manifest to all Italy.[1]

Performing in competition was nothing new in 1589, for the Gelosi had made a practice of pitting actress against actress from the earliest days of the company. The first prima donna of the troupe, Vincenza Armani, entered into a contest in Mantua during the summer of 1567 with a comedienne known today only as Flaminia, and Isabella Andreini included a song competition for two nymphs in her pastoral play *Mirtilla* only a year before the famous 'concorrenza' with Piisimi in Florence.

These examples allude to a general aesthetic of commedia dell'arte performance that is based on emulative displays of feminine virtue, each contest having its roots in shared generic soil. The crux of each competition centres on the performer's fulfilment of neoclassical ideals: her wisdom and wit in selecting and imitating either classical or contemporary models, and her ability to harmonize with the Music of the Spheres in reciting and singing affective verse. Vincenza and Flaminia challenged each other in the tragic arena and in intermedi, with observers making special note of their representations of heightened texts, such as laments and other passages set to music. In Florence, Andreini and Piisimi vied in the medium of comedy, and Pavoni remarked especially on Andreini's performance of canzonettas, sung in the French style. The nymphs in Andreini's *Mirtilla* compete in the alternating singing of *terzine*.

I do not mean to confuse this aesthetic with the emulative impulse described by Howard Mayer Brown in his landmark study, 'Emulation, Competition, and Homage: Imitation and Theories of Imitation in the

---

[1] Pavoni, *Diario*, 29–30. 'Sabbato, che fù alli sei, ritrovandosi in Fiorenza a li Comici Gelosi con quelle due famosissime Donne la Vittoria, & l'Isabella, parve al Gran Duca, che per trattenimento fosse buono far, che recitassero una Comedia à gusto loro. Così vennero quasi, che à contesa le dette Donne fra di loro, perche la Vittoria voleva si recitasse la cingana, & l'altra voleva si facesse la sua pazzia, titolata la pazzia d'Isabella, sendo che la favorita della Vittoria è la cingana, & la pazzia, la favorita d'Isabella. Però s'accordarono in questo, che la prima à recitarsi fusse la cingana, & che un'altra volta si recitasse la pazzia. Et così recitarono detta cingana con gli Intermedii istessi, che furono fatti alla Comedia grande: ma chi non ha sentito la Vittoria contrafar la cingana, non ha visto, ne sentito cosa rara & meravigliosa, che certo di questa Comedia sono restati tutti sodisfatissimi. Un'altra volta faranno poi la pazzia, & toccarà à l'Isabella à far la Pazza; il valor della quale, & la leggiadria nell'esplicare i suoi concetti, non occorre hora esplicarlo, che è già noto, & manifesto à tutta Italia le sue virtudi.' Although the beginning of this passage suggests that the comedians only arrived in Florence on 6 May, the *Memoriale* of Girolamo Seriacopi alludes to the upcoming performance of *La cingana* on 4 May; see Testaverde Matteini, *L'officina delle nuvole*, 236.

Renaissance'. For although the Gelosi's performances featured imitation as well as emulation, the competitive thrust of their performances engaged not the comedienne and her compositional model (or, often, models), but the invention and *varietà* of the rival performers. Thus Armani and the Roman Flaminia contended with each other rather than with the authors of their sources, and the nymphs in Andreini's *Mirtilla* vied for the love of a shepherd, independent of Andreini's compositional impulse in regard to her Virgilian archetype. *La pazzia d'Isabella* shows how delightfully Andreini's choice of models might coincide with the classical agenda of Bardi's intermedi, although her rivalry was with the protagonist of *La cingana*. Indeed, the models invoked in such contests were chosen to be unassailable: selection of a poor one revealed a performer to be lacking in the judgement, intellectual valour, and, inevitably, the virtue necessary to choose her sources well.

Vincenza Armani's contest with Flaminia in 1567 began with representations of tragedy. The precise subject of the Gelosi's offering is unknown because Armani's topic was said to be poor and the chronicler Luigi Rogna declined to discuss it further. But Flaminia and her company performed a tragicomedic version of the tale of Dido from Ariosto's *Orlando furioso* (canto 37).[2] This choice of text makes apparent a reflective stance on the part of comedians that speaks to their understanding of the dual nature of the commedia dell'arte as an art that revivifies classical ideals and dares to represent heroic women on stage. The canto begins:

If those accomplished ladies who have striven night and day with the most diligent application to acquire some gift that Nature bestows only upon the industrious—and some brilliant work will have been the happy product—if those ladies, I say, had devoted themselves instead to those studies which confer immortality upon mortal virtues, and had been able by themselves to achieve undying reputation without having to beg it from authors, their fame would soar to heights perhaps beyond the reach of any of the male sex.[3]

All of Mantua hummed with activity as everyone from courtiers to pages argued over which was the better actress. They commended Flaminia for her fine laments and for the nobility of her tragedy and they praised Armani for her music-making and beautiful clothes ('lodata per la musica, per la vaghezza degli habiti et per altro'), although the quality of her

[2] See the various letters written by Luigi Rogna from May 1567 to Feb. 1568 cited in the Chronology; Rogna's correspondence is summarized in D'Ancona, 'Il teatro mantovano', pt. 2, pp. 9–18 and in Burattelli, *Spettacoli di corte a Mantova*, 181–3.

[3] Ariosto, *Orlando furioso* (trans. Waldman), canto 37, ottave 1–2.

drama was acknowledged to be the weaker of the two.[4] With the debate still raging, on 5 July the companies entered into a contest of intermedi: Vincenza sang the role of Cupid, who freed the nymph Clori from her Ovidian metamorphosis into a tree, and Flaminia's company introduced into their intermedi satyrs and sorcerers who danced morescas. Flaminia played the part of a nymph.[5]

Although Rogna seems to have liked Armani's intermedi better than Flaminia's (his preferences determined by his recognition and esteem of the models employed), by 15 July Armani and the Gelosi had left for Ferrara. Flaminia and her company stayed on in Mantua into the autumn, performing a pastoral comedy on the story of Jupitor and Io for the baptism of Massimiliano Gonzaga on 10 July and then a comedy in the Palazzo della Ragione for which they were preparing on 3 August.[6] To all appearances, Armani lost the encounter with Flaminia, but her fame endured long past that of her rival, due to the praises of Tommaso Garzoni and her fellow *comico geloso* Adriano Valerini. Garzoni's acclaim, published nearly twenty years after the Mantuan competition, is especially germane, in that he painted Armani as a winner of contests: 'I will not speak of the wise Vincenza who, imitating Ciceronian fluency of speech, has put the comic art in competition with oratory and, partly with admirable beauty and partly with ineffable grace, has erected a great triumph of herself for the world to see, revealing herself as the most excellent comedienne of our age.'[7]

---

[4] Valerini's description of Armani singing the *licenza* to a tragedy in his *Oratione* may be based on her Mantuan performance in 1567; she died by poisoning only two years after the event, and Valerini published his epithet immediately thereafter. Whether his account regards this or another of Vincenza's tragedic performances, he wrote that she clothed herself in black to sing several stanzas on the subject, as a summary of the plot (p. 33): 'Si vestia, finita la favola, in abito lugubre e nero, rappresentando la istessa Tragedia, e cantava alcune stanze che succintamente del Poema tutto conteneano il soggetto, ed era come di quello un Argomento; e così data la licenza al popolo, e finito il canto, si sentiva un alto grido, un manifesto applauso che andava sin alle stelle, e le genti stupide ed immobili non sapeano da quel luogo partirsi.'

[5] Luigi Rogna, Mantua, to [Pietro Martire Cornacchia], 6 July 1567 (Doc. 2). See also D'Ancona, 'Il teatro mantovano', pt. 2, pp. 14–15.

[6] Luigi Rogna, Mantua, to [Pietro Martire Cornacchia], 11 July 1567 and 3 Aug. 1567; see ibid. 16–17.

[7] Garzoni, *La piazza universale*, in Marotti and Romei, *La professione del teatro*, 12. 'Della dotta Vi[n]cenza non parlo, che, imitando la facondia ciceroniana, ha posto l'arte comica in concorrenza con l'oratoria e, parte con la beltà mirabile, parte con la grazia indicibile, ha eretto uno amplissimo trionfo di se stessa al mondo spettatore, facendosi divulgare per la più eccellente comediante di nostra etade.'

All the Gelosi's prima donnas—Vincenza Armani, Vittoria Piisimi, and Isabella Andreini—were lauded for their musical talents, and the success of the troupe rested in large part on their music-making. Valerini placed music high among Armani's talents, together with rhetorical eloquence, decorum, improvisation, and *varietà*. He noted that she sang sonnets and madrigals with the best singers of the time and played a variety of musical instruments with a celestial hand. Would that any of her musical compositions were extant! When she accompanied herself singing, Armani caused even the stars to align in the heavens:

> In music, she was so talented that not only did she sing her part securely with the finest singers of Europe, but composed miraculously in this profession, putting into song those same sonnets and madrigals that she wrote herself, in the manner of a musician and a poet. She played a variety of musical instruments with such grace that it seemed an angelic hand touched their concordant wood, and it appeared almost as if she spoke with her fingers. She accompanied the sweet sound of her melody with such beauty that every sense, whether however sickly and sad, remained happy and content. And the Souls, who felt an unheard semblance of that true harmony that the stars create in their movement, melted with ineffable sweetness, remembering their celestial home.[8]

High praise indeed. Armani was especially well known, as was Isabella Andreini after her, for her scholarship, rhetorical fluency, and the studied breadth of her style. Garzoni's reference to her composition of songs 'in the manner of a musician and a poet' suggests a compositional technique based on improvising tunes to her own poetry, which in turn, recalls the contests of orators in ancient Athens. These traits inspired Valerini in 1570 to describe Armani in terms that the Belgian academician Erycius Puteanus would echo a quarter century later in regard to Andreini: that she surpassed her sex with intellectual virility.[9] Valerini's and Puteanus'

---

[8] Valerini, *Oratione*, in Marotti and Romei, *La professione del teatro*, 33: 'Nella Musica poi fece profitto tale che non pure cantava sicuramente la parte sua con i primi cantori d'Europa, ma componeva in questa professione miracolosamente, ponendo in canto quell'istessi Sonetti e Madrigali, le parole de cui ella anco faceva, di modo che veniva ad essere e Musico e Poeta; sonava de varie sorti de stromenti musicali, con tanta soavità che d'angelica mano pareva che fosser tocchi gli accordati legni, e parea quasi che con le dita ella parlasse; al dolce suono accompagnava poi con tanta vaghezza il canto, che ogni senso, quantunque egro fosse e dolente, rimanea lieto e contento, e l'Alme, che di quella vera armonia che fanno movendosi le stelle sentivano non più udita sembianza, d'ineffabil dolcezza si struggeano, rimembrandosi del suo celeste albergo.'

[9] Ibid.: '. . . passò in questi onesti essercizii i teneri anni suoi puerili, e perché ben s'avide che questi non eran bastanti a farla risplendere nel suo sesso, come poi non solamente nel suo,

praises make sibyls of Armani and Andreini, whose intellectual valour and authority to make music gives them an aura of the masculinity that Michelangelo depicted on the ceiling of the Sistine Chapel with muscled shoulders and robust hands.

Both Armani and Andreini knew Latin, and both spiced their performances with allusions to classical authors as well as modern and to current intellectual trends. But perhaps it is the other way around: that they peppered classical and literary scenes with improvised dialogue and comic twists. The latter is certainly the case in the singing contest Andreini included in her pastoral play *Mirtilla*, published only a year before her acclaimed performance for the wedding of Ferdinando de' Medici and Christine of Lorraine. The scene is patterned on Virgil's third eclogue in both action and form, although with a gender reversal that nicely casts nymphs rather than shepherds in the roles of sexual pursuers who are to prove their valour through song. This extended Virgilian imitation lends a decidedly Mantuan flavour to the drama, for the ancient bard was born in the region surrounding that city and Mantuans to this day take pride in claiming him as their own. Moreover, Andreini's implicit reference to Dante's *Inferno* (especially canto 20, where Virgil tells the story of Manto) reflects the self-consciousness of her choice to let Virgil be her guide.

The power of song to demonstrate truth harks back to a widely imitated Neoplatonic motif based on the *Timaeus* and the *Phaedrus* dialogues and larded with hermetic allusions, wherein the voice of a true lover resounds in sympathy with the Harmony of the Spheres. In that the main characters of any commedia dell'arte troupe are *innamorati* and Andreini a *prima donna innamorata*, her rehearsal of variations on this Neoplatonic theme endured her life long. An affective soliloquy on 'La forza d'Amore' from Andreini's *Lettere* interweaves images of the god of love, the pastoral landscape, the awakening of consciousness, and the Harmony of the Spheres:

Only for Love do the woods become green and the meadows adorn themselves with flowers; in which, to our greatest delight, we see them uncover their beauty. Love drew from the woods those first rustic and uncultured people, who took the

ma nel virile ancora, mercé gli onorati studii a cui si diede quasi un lucido Sole splendeva d'ogn'intorno. Si rivolse all'imparar a leggere ed a scrivere, il che con la Grammatica insieme facilmente apprese, ed in poco spazio di tempo; né avendo i tre lustri dell'età sua toccati appena, possedeva benissimo la lingua latina, e felicissimamente vi spiegava ogni concetto, leggeva tanto appuntatamente e scriveva così corretto nel latino e nel materno idioma, che più non vi scriverebbe chi dell'Ortografia diede i precetti e l'arte.'

same food and drink as did the beasts, living without rules and without laws, and he gave them beautiful cities to live in, teaching them the way to live well. Love taught the world to reconcile the grave with the acute and to imitate with voices and instruments the harmony of the Heavens; because of him all the arts, and especially poetry, were born and held in the highest regard. One sees that this is the truth because the true Poet is always in love.[10]

The nymphs in Andreini's *Mirtilla* put this philosophy to the test when they arrange a singing contest to prove the validity of their love. Filli and Mirtilla both dote on the shepherd Uranio and compete with each other for his attentions. Uranio, of course, loves neither, but carries an unquenchable yet unrequited torch for the narcissistic Ardelia. Ignorant of this, Filli and Mirtilla agree to a musical contest to win the shepherd's affection because they share the belief that a true, virtuous love manifests itself in celestial song. They ask the old shepherd Opico to judge them, for it is he who recommends they try the traditional pastoral method for resolving disputes. And thus they sing as Damoetas and Menalcas did before them under Palaemon's watchful eye in Virgil's third eclogue.

The formal similarities between the singing contests in *Mirtilla* and in Virgil's eclogue are noteworthy. Each is bounded by a judicious frame, wherein an elder shepherd calls for the contest to begin and announces its conclusion. Like the narrative frame that encompasses a lament, the shepherd-judge, by virtue of his age and experience, represents a controlled context within which the irrational is allowed free reign.[11] At the same time, however, and more importantly, he serves as an ambassador of the

---

[10] Andreini, *Lettere*, 'La forza d'Amore', 22–3: 'Solo per Amore verdeggiano i boschi e di fiori si smaltano i prati, ne i quali vediamo con grandissimo nostro diletto scuoprirsi la bellezza. Amor trasse dalle selve quella prima gente roza e 'ncolta, ch'aveva con le fiere commune il cibo e la bevanda, vivendo senz'ordine e senza legge, e le diede le bellissime città per abitazione, insegnandole il modo di ben vivere. Amore al mondo ha insegnato d'accordar il grave con l'acuto e d'immitar con le voci e con gli stromenti l'armonia de' Cieli; per lui nate sono e son tenute in pregio le scienze tutte, particolarmente la Poesia, e che ciò sia vero vedesi per isperienza che 'l vero Poeta è sempre innamorato.' Andreini's argument bears more than a passing resemblance to a dialogue in Pietro Bembo's *Gli Asolani*. Whereas Andreini makes the bond between love and music explicit, it is Bembo who provides the link between love and virtue. As cited by Guido Ruggiero, 'Nor, ladies, does love merely bring human beings into existence, but it gives a second life as well—or I should rather call it their principle life—that is the life of virtue.' Bembo goes on to say that without love, men would still be like the beasts (Ruggiero, *Binding Passions*, 133).

[11] For further information about lament structures, see McClary, *Feminine Endings*, ch. 4; Carter, 'Weeping Ariadne?'; MacNeil, 'Weeping at the Water's Edge'; and Cusick, 'Re-voicing Arianna'.

wild wood, whose long understanding of the forest's semi-celestial nature enables him to mediate between the earthly and the divine and even to guide the lovers' initial steps towards Parnassus. In their turn, the contestants plumb the depths of their emotions in their quest for celestial song, secure in the knowledge that someone older and wiser watches over them.

In addition to fulfilling his role as guide through the uncharted waters of the soul, the sage old shepherd also bears the responsibility of setting the pastoral scene and ordering the strophic, antiphonal form of the song. Following the implications of the pastoral landscape in Andreini's 'La forza d'Amore', setting the locus for a singing contest in a woodland glade offers a visual cue to the preconscious natural impulses governing all that happens there. Thus the music is to be simple, made with the human body, and delicately infused with the sounds of nature. And singing in alternation, so say both Virgil's Palaemon and Andreini's Opico, is loved by the Muses, whose own song contest with the Pierides forms the subject of the second intermedio for the 1589 wedding festivities. The Muses' contest, similarly located in a lush, verdant grove, is framed by a tribunal of sixteen woodland nymphs, whose womanhood demonstrates that the contextualization of a song contest's judge within the forest takes precedence over a masculine gendering of the frame.

Andreini's rendition of the song-contest trope exceeds its source by intertwining Virgil's pastoral metaphors with directions for musical performance. Whereas Palaemon's speech describes the blooming spring,

Sing on, now that we are seated on the soft grass. Even now every field, every tree is budding; now the woods are green, and the year is at its fairest. Begin, Damoetas; then you, Menalcas, must follow. Turn about you shall sing; singing by turns the Muses love.[12]

Opico goes beyond the command to sing, alluding to the instrumental parts that will accompany Filli and Mirtilla:

> Now give life to the sound, the song tuned to it,
> since we are in a beautiful spot in the shade
> where Flora among the flowers
> in the arms of her husband reposes,
> And he for sweetness
> breathes a soft wind into these grasses,
> and the murmuring of the waves
> will make the tenor to the sound

[12] Virgil, *Eclogues* (trans. Fairclough), 21.

> of this hollowed wood.
> Now you start, Fillide
> and then you follow, Mirtilla;
> Sing then in competition,
> for the Muses love singing in turns.[13]

Opico's references to instruments are not crystalline, but the nymphs' dialogue in Scene 4 offers some assistance in interpreting them. Here, Filli complains that the old shepherd is late for their appointment and expresses her surprise that he tarries so long 'to come see us with his instrument, which he plays with such a masterly hand' ('a venirci a trovar co 'l suo stormento, / tocco da lui con sì maestra mano'). The phrase, and especially the verb *toccare*, enable us to discern a lute, as we see Opico now, entering the stage bearing the hollow wooden instrument that he plays with the skilful touch of his hand. And if we are not to believe our minds' eyes, earlier literary sources, including Garzoni's adulation of Vincenza Armani cited above, describe singing to the lute and tuning one's song to its sound in precisely these words. When Domenico Venier wrote his sonnet in praise of the singer Franceschina Bellamano in 1565, he portrayed both the beauty of her hand (her 'bella mano') and its music-making as it touched the hollowed wood:

> Con varie voci or questa, or quella corda
> tocca da bella man sul cavo legno
> mirabilmente il canto si al suon accorda.

(With various notes, now this, now that string does the lovely hand touch on the hollowed wood, miraculously tuning her song to its sound.)[14]

Opico's exhortation alludes to another instrument as well, which Flora's husband plays by breathing against the grasses and causing an undulation along their tips. And this will be an important instrument, because it plays the tenor part of the song. The key to its riddle lies in knowing that Flora's husband is the westwind Zephyrus—the same Zephyrus of whom Monteverdi complained when asked to write vocal music for the breezes in 1616: 'How, dear Sir, can I imitate the speech of the winds, if they do not speak? And how can I, by such means, move the passions? Arianna moved us because she was a woman, and similarly Orpheus because he was a man, not a wind.'[15] Andreini's verses do not

---

[13] Andreini, *Mirtilla* (1588), ll. 1714–33 (ed. Doglio), 101.
[14] Lines 9–11. See Feldman, 'The Academy of Domenico Venier', 409.
[15] Fabbri, *Monteverdi* (trans. Carter), 97.

suggest that Flora's husband either sings or speaks, but rather that he plays a flauto dolce or the panpipes, both instruments in common use among commedia dell'arte players. Indeed, the scene is almost incomplete without a flute of some kind, for Francesco Andreini, in the preface to his *Bravure*, symbolizes the comedian's craft with a rustic pipe. Entitled 'The shepherd Corinto to his dead Fillide and to his rustic flute' ('Corinto pastore alla defunta sua Fillide ed alla sua boscareccia sampogna'), Andreini's essay relates how Corinto will give up his panpipes now that his Fillide is gone. After describing the joys he had of playing them when Fillide (that is, Isabella) was alive, Francesco hangs them for ever on a verdant branch. With his nymph dead, Corinto will accompany her no longer, and the instruments the old shepherd once played to accompany her celestial song will remain mute: 'I leave you here, then, for ever on this green and honoured tree, and with you remain for ever on these green and honoured trunks all my other pastoral instruments, turned to the glory and honour of my dear Fillide.'[16]

The orchestration of the nymphs' song contest, then, becomes quite clear, although its visual tableau remains hazy. The musical composition comprises three parts: a canto tune, sung in alternating verses by two women, a tenor melody played on a blown instrument such as a flauto dolce or a panpipe, and a bass part played by an old shepherd on the lute: four musicians in all. Andreini's text makes no mention, however, of a fourth person on the stage, and no character other than Filli, Mirtilla, and Opico has dialogue in this scene. And yet the song would be without its tenor without the sound of the wind against the waving fronds.

In the absence of written stage directions, one answer may be gleaned from Angelo Ingegneri's treatise on drama and its performance practices, *Della poesia rappresentativa e del modo di rappresentare le favole sceniche*, published in Ferrara in 1598. *Mirtilla* is noted in the opening paragraphs as one of the noteworthy pastorals performed in recent years, upon which the author bases his observations.[17] In the second part of the treatise,

---

[16] F. Andreini, *Bravure* (ed. Tessari), 5: 'Rimanti adunque per sempre appesa a questa verde ed onorata pianta, e teco rimangano per sempre appesi a questi verdi ed onorati tronchi tutti gli altri miei pastorali stromenti solo invertiti a gloria ed onor della mia cara Fillide.' Andreini was celebrated, in fact, for the role of Corinto in pastoral dramas, and in that guise he played diverse musical instruments, including a variety of flutes; see the often-cited fourteenth *ragionamento* in his *Bravure* (ed. Tessari), 70.

[17] Ingegneri also exchanged sonnets with Andreini: to Ingegneri's 'In ischietto vestir vera bellezza' Andreini responded with 'Un bel sembiante in habito negletto'; see Isabella Andreini, *Rime*, 86–7.

within the context of a general discussion of musical performance in comedies and pastorals, Ingegneri recommends that instrumental musicians might be hidden within the scenery. 'And it would not be bad, on occasion', he writes, 'to place some company of instruments behind the scenes.'[18] Let us imagine, then, that Andreini represented the west wind in *Mirtilla* with the perfect verisimilitude that Monteverdi demanded almost three decades later: without visual aspect and without speech, the instrumentalist hidden behind a tree, but sounding the wind's presence among the grasses with his pipe.

The orchestration of their contest complete, Filli and Mirtilla begin by singing exhortations to the gods, in which they call on various deities to inspire and hear their song. Although the text of *Mirtilla* as a whole remains remarkably unaltered over the course of its numerous editions, these introductory stanzas do change, and the modification appearing in the 1599 Veronese edition recommends a parallel alteration in musical setting. In both stanzas, the sense of the text does not vary, but the metre, and specifically the metre of the first lines, mutates from seven to eleven syllables. Modifications to subsequent lines bring the rhyme schemes into conformity with the new opening verses, but otherwise alter as little as possible. Thus Filli's stanza reads,

1588:	1599:
Dotta Calliopea,	Calliope al biondo Apollo amica tanto
madre di quel buon Trace,	madre di quel buon Trace
ch'ogn'animal più fero e più fugace	ch'ogn'animal più fero e più fugace
con la sonora voce a sé traea,	a se trahea, col suo lodato canto
inspira, o diva, a questa voce mia,	inspira, o diva, a questa voce mia,
soave melodia.	soave melodia.

followed by Mirtilla's,

O de le Muse padre,	Tu ch'arrestasti la non ferma Delo
vien oggi nel mio canto e nel mio core,	vien hoggi nel mio canto, e nel mio core,
nel mio cor che si sface	nel mio cor, che si sface
de' tuoi studi non men che de la face	di tuoi studi, non men che de la face
del mio nemico Amore.	del mio nemico Amore.
Così le prime sue membra leggiadre	Così 'l terrestre suo leggiadro velo
vesta la figlia di Peneo sdegnosa	vesta la figlia di Peneo sdegnosa
per esserti pietosa.	per esserti pietosa.

[18] Ingegneri, *Della poesia rappresentativa* (ed. Doglio), 31: 'e non sia per aventura male a proposito il dar loro alcuna compagnia d'istromenti posti dalla parte di dentro della scena . . .'.

The lack of symmetry in these stanzas denies their setting to a rigorous musical form like the canzonetta and instead suggests either that this portion of the contest was composed in full, with each nymph singing a separate solo madrigal to the accompaniment of the lute and flauto dolce, or that the introductory verses were set to a kind of recitative, sung over a formulaic bass.[19] Given the evidence of the Gelosi's 1574 performance for Henri III, where Claudio Merulo composed the musical setting for Frangipani's *Tragedia*, together with the alteration in poetic form in the 1599 edition of the text, the former choice seems the more likely of the two—that is, that the musical setting for these stanzas was composed. The style of music or the identity of the composer is anyone's guess, although the general Mantuan tenor of the play, as seen through its models as well as its style, suggests music of similarly Mantuan origin.

After the nymphs conclude their exhortations, they perform an alternating series of tercets in hendecasyllabic metre with an *aba* rhyme scheme. The rhymes do not interlock as in *terza rima*. Musical settings of *terzine* were quite popular at northern Italian courts in mid-century, and in the 1580s a number of composers took to publishing collections of these light, witty songs. By the time of Isabella Andreini's death in 1604, the publishing market was virtually flooded with them.[20] Masters of the genre lived and worked mainly in the north: Luca Marenzio, Claudio Monteverdi, Giaches de Wert, Orazio Vecchi, and the chameleonic Orlando di Lasso. These composers' canzonettas appear sometimes in three-, four- and five-voice settings, but also in one- or two-voice settings with instrumental accompaniment and in intabulations for various instruments.[21] From among these, the type of canzonetta most suitable to the performance dictated by Andreini's *Mirtilla* is the simpler, three-part variety like those featured in Monteverdi's Cremonese publication of *Canzonette à tre voci* of 1584. In this collection, ten of the twenty-one canzonettas included set texts of the same form as Andreini's (although not the same rhyme scheme). And, as shown in the text of Giovan Battista Andreini's *Lo schiavetto* in 1612 (discussed in Chapter 5), it would not be

---

[19] Feldman suggests that the musical genres used to accompany exhortative stanzas outside the theatrical tradition arose from the repertories of the *cantastorie* or other musical improvisers; see 'The Academy of Domenico Venier', 501–2.

[20] See Wert, *Opera omnia*, xiv (ed. MacClintock); Prizer, 'The Frottola and the Unwritten Tradition'; Haar, 'The *Madrigale arioso*'.

[21] See especially Cardamone's edition of *canzoni villanesche* and *villanelle* by Lasso et al. in Recent Researches in the Music of the Renaissance, vols. 82–3.

unreasonable to think that the performers of *Mirtilla* might poach an existing musical composition to serve their means. This too, of course, would enter into the realm of models imitated, and the performers would be judged on the merits of their musical choices.

Monteverdi's canzonettas in this form are remarkably formulaic and suffer contrafacta well, as may be seen in *Si come crescon alla terra i fiori*. In Ex. 2.1 I have replaced Monteverdi's text with the first two tercets of Filli's and Mirtilla's singing contest, setting only the canto line and using almost exclusively syllabic declamation. Note how the canto carries a tuneful melody, shadowed at the interval of a third by the obviously secondary inner voice, whose range of a sixth is easily encompassed by either a treble or alto flauto dolce. The lowest part, although careful to maintain contrary motion with the upper voices, never carries the tune and often sacrifices melodic contour to harmonic progression. A lutenist would only want to fill out the implied sonorities—'con sì maestra mano'—to conform the line to the harmonic potential of his instrument.

Andreini's pairing of stanzas by way of textual repetition not only emphasizes the emulative conceit that underlies the canzonetta, but offers numerous opportunities for ornamentation and competitive interpretations of specific words or images. While the last two stanzas of the contest, with the repetition of the initial word, 'Dimmi', seem particularly suited to competitive vocal strategies, earlier strophes bear equally suggestive wordplay. Apart from Petrarchan phrases like 'Quanti spargo sospiri', 'la mia angosciosa pena', and 'lieta gioir d'ogni tormento', which call to mind blazing moments of sweet consonance and acrid dissonance and an affective use of rests, the nymphs' banter about numbers of things seems also to cry out for ornamental variation. Filli begins the arithmetic badinage with 'four and six apples' in the first *terzina*, followed in the second by Mirtilla's 'single catapult'. Not to be outdone, Filli rejoins with 'so many sighs and so many lays' in the third stanza, to which Mirtilla replies, 'who knows how many times . . . ?'. In the very next stanza, Filli boldly speaks of Igilio's gift to her of 'two nightingales', which Mirtilla matches with the 'two baskets of flowers' that Alcon gave her. From here, the contestants move on to other motifs. Surely, apples, catapults, sighs, lays, nightingales, and baskets of flowers might be metaphors for varying types of vocal ornamentation.

Filli's and Mirtilla's antiphonal song concluded, Opico calls the contest a tie and advises the nymphs to cease their antagonism and to search for those who will return their love:

Ex. 2.1. Monteverdi, *Si come crescon alla terra i fiori*, with Andreini's text from *Mirtilla*, Act III, Scene v, lines 1748–53

> No more, loving nymphs; it suits me
> to end this, your
> amorous contest.
> There should be no quarrel between you, where there is
> such parity of valour; and I swear to you
> by the high gods that to my judgement you are
> equal in beauty, equal in song.

The contest between Isabella Andreini and Vittoria Piisimi in Florence the following May was not such an even match, although the same actresses surely performed the roles of Filli and Mirtilla in Andreini's play. Once he saw the performances in Florence, Pavoni clearly favoured Andreini's *La pazzia d'Isabella*. He described her portrayal of the madwoman in detail, giving the plot, an account of her acting, singing, and parlance in diverse languages, and summarizing the audience's reactions to the performance. *La pazzia d'Isabella* was evidently the court's as well as Pavoni's favourite, and the 27-year-old Andreini the more intriguing of the two actresses: a noteworthy feat, given the praises heaped on Piisimi by Garzoni, as cited in the previous chapter. Andreini expressed her insanity in 'elegant and wise style' and thereby demonstrated her 'sane and learned intellect'. She left her audience abuzz with the marvel of her performance, and inspired Pavoni to confirm the praise written by Garzoni four years earlier, that 'while the world endures, her beautiful eloquence and valour will be praised'.[22] In contrast, *La cingana* received little attention from Pavoni's pen, although the words used by the Grand Duke to describe Vittoria's performance call to mind her intellectual valour: 'a marvel, let alone the intellect of a woman'.[23]

The Gelosi staged their comedies on consecutive Saturdays, sandwiched between the two performances of Bargagli's *La pellegrina*. *La cingana*, as stated above, was given on 6 May and *La pazzia d'Isabella* on 13 May at 'the twenty-second hour' or two hours before sunset.[24] All four performances took place on the stage of the Uffizi theatre, accompanied by the lavish intermedi designed by Florentine courtiers under the direc-

---

[22] Pavoni, *Diario*, 46. See also Garzoni's prognosis of Andreini in Marotti and Romei, *La professione del teatro*, 12: 'La graziosa Isabella, decoro delle scene, ornamento de' Teatri, spettacolo superbo non meno di virtù che di bellezza, ha illustrato ancor lei questa professione in modo che, mentre il mondo durarà, mentre staranno i secoli, mentre avran vita gli ordini e i tempi, ogni voce, ogni lingua, ogni grido risuonarà il celebre nome d'Isabella.'

[23] Pavoni, *Diario*, 43: 'una meraviglia, non che intelletto di donna'.

[24] *La pellegrina* was performed on Tuesday, 2 May and again on Monday, 15 May.

tion of Giovanni de' Bardi. Pavoni's location of the performance venue for the Gelosi's comedies and of the accompanying intermedi is unique among the numerous sources documenting the 1589 events: 'And thus, the Grand Duke having made his wishes known to the Gelosi, at the twenty-second hour, on the same stage where *La pellegrina* was recited, they performed *La pazzia* with the same intermedi I have already described.'[25]

Presentation of *La cingana* and *La pazzia d'Isabella* with Bardi's intermedi on the stage of the Uffizi theatre discloses an impressive architecture of performance that helps us to understand the Gelosi's style of homage to their Medici patrons and their contributions to the wedding festivities in 1589. In the absence of a text for either comedy and of any mention of them in Bastiano de' Rossi's commemorative *Descrizione*, a close reading of Pavoni's account yields the only avenue of interpretation for the comedies, for the songs Andreini sang as part of *La pazzia d'Isabella*, and for the reasons that Andreini might have won the contest with Piisimi. Contextualization of Andreini's performance (unfortunately, Pavoni did not describe Piisimi's) within the Gelosi's repertory and consideration of the symbols that defined Medici patronage provide the backdrop in front of which my interpretation unfolds.

Andreini's familiarity with the symbols of Medici patronage was extensive by the time the Gelosi performed at the Medici wedding of 1589. Florentine support of the Andreini family had its origins in the time of Ferdinando's grandfather Cosimo, who was Francesco Andreini's 'natural' patron, the comedian having been born in Pistoia sometime around

---

[25] Pavoni, *Diario*, 43–4: 'Et così havendo il Gran Duca fatto sapere alli Comici Gelosi questo suo pensiero, su le vintidoi hore nella Scena istessa, ove si è recitata la Pellegrina, fecero anco la pazzia, con quelli istessi Intermedii, che si sono altre volte detti.' Not knowing Pavoni's *Diario* and basing his argument on the evidence of the manuscript diary of Francesco Settimani (transcribed in Solerti, *Gli albori del melodramma*, ii. 17–18), Nino Pirrotta concluded that the Gelosi's comedies were performed in three acts and in the Great Hall of the Palazzo Vecchio. But this would have put all the inconvenience of the court in the service of an itinerant band of commedia dell'arte players, whose comedies were just as easily adaptable to the Uffizi stage. The arrangement would have caused the machinery for the intermedi to be moved twice and, in the second instance, over the space of only two days. It also would have necessitated performing only four of the six intermedi or otherwise arranging the entr'acte interludes so that they might be presented in the four intervals allotted in the course of a three-act play. See Pirrotta and Povoledo, *Music and Theatre from Poliziano to Monteverdi*, 213. Pirrotta's conclusions in this case are invalid, for in addition to the conflicting evidence of Pavoni's *Diario*, Settimani's diary has been shown to be an unreliable source, in that it constitutes an 18th-c. copy of various pre-existing manuscripts. And like many copyists, Settimani got things wrong. See Benedetti, *Notizie e documenti intorno la vita di Francesco Settimani*, and Hill, *The Life and Works of Francesco Maria Veracini*, 441.

1544. As a young man, Andreini fought under the Medici banner during the wars with the Turks. Eight years in a Turkish prison turned him from military service to a life on the stage, but his filial relationship to the Medici household continued, and his first son Giovan Battista was born and baptized in the Tuscan capital.[26]

By April 1587 Isabella Andreini had secured patronage for two of her daughters from among the Medici household: the eldest in the service of Eleonora de' Medici, recently wed to Vincenzo Gonzaga in Mantua, and the younger in Florence under the auspices of the Grand Duke and the Grand Duchess.[27] Although Lavinia Andreini left Mantuan court service after ten years to enter the monastery of the Madri della Cantelma in that city, Eleonora de' Medici's patronage of the child endured, and she paid the required dowry.[28] And when, in 1606, Giovan Battista Andreini published a collection of poetic obsequies in memory of his mother, Eleonora's name appeared as the beloved dedicatee, together with the axiom 'great love is not unbound by death'.[29] Maria de' Medici's benevolence at the French court, inspired by her sister's support of the Gelosi and of the Andreini in particular, resulted in handsome payments made to Isabella Andreini when the troupe travelled to Paris in 1602, and extended even to the use of the Queen's writing paper. The comedienne's gilt-edged enquiry to Belisario Vinta in 1603 regarding her account with the Monte di Pietà ended months of the Florentine secretary's neglect of Andreini's concerns.[30]

Finally, the fresco that once graced the cloister of the Santissima Annunziata in Florence of Isabella, Francesco, and Giovan Battista

[26] For biographical information on Francesco Andreini, see *Comici dell'arte: corrispondenze*, ed. Ferrone et al., i. 97–8; and Falavolti, *Attore*, 89. Documents concerning Giovan Battista Andreini's birth and baptism are found in Florence, Archivio dell'Opera del Duomo, Registro dei battezzati maschi dal 1571 al 1577, letter G, fo. 172^v.

[27] ASMN, Gonzaga, Autografi, b. 10, fos. 54–5.

[28] A complaint made by the nuns of the monastery on 13 Feb. 1625 against Giovan Battista and Domenico, heirs of Francesco Andreini (who died on 21 Aug. 1624) requests payment for all of Lavinia's (suor Fulvia's) expenses from the time she entered the monastery, excluding the 300 lire given by Eleonora de' Medici. ASMN, Notarile, notaio Battaleoli Cristoforo, 1627, 26 July.

[29] G. B. Andreini, *Il pianto d'Apollo*, 3: 'Grande amor non si scorda co 'l morire'.

[30] A receipt dated 8 Oct. 1603 records that Andreini was paid 1,500 livres tournais on behalf of her company, and her letter to Belisario Vinta in Florence dated 7 Dec. 1603 states that she is earning 200 ducatoni per month. See BNF, Généalogies d'Hozier, pièce originale 59, 'Andriny'; and ASF, Mediceo, f. 920, fos. 513^{r-v}, 555^{r-v}. Andreini's gilt-edged letter to Belisario Vinta, dated 26 Aug. 1603, may be found in ASF, Mediceo, f. 917, fos. 777^{r-v}, 791^{r-v}.

Andreini among the members of the Medici court gives visual testimony of the esteem in which the family was held by the Medici rulers. The scene (see Pl. 2.1) shows Isabella Andreini in the right middleground among the ladies of the court. She is in profile and the bright light of inspiration shines on her. In the foreground, heads bowed in mourning (the fresco dates from c.1611), stand Francesco (left) and Giovan Battista (centre). All three wear the fine clothes of the courtier, and Isabella's hair is coiffed in the style of imperial Rome. The same Roman figurations, together with the high lace collar and pearls typical of sixteenth-century French noble style, grace the medallion of Isabella Andreini that was cast in bronze, silver, and gold in commemoration of her death in Lyons. The reverse of the coin, as may be seen in Pl. 1.5 above, displays the image of Fame, wreathed in laurel and carrying two trumpets, one of which she plays. The lettering that circumscribes the medallion reads 'Isabella Andreini: Aeterna Fama'. Nor is the reference to fame a casual one used only to mark the actress's passing, for the Gelosi's self-fashioning rested on concepts of virtue, fame, and honour.

The language of Pavoni's diary, and especially his description of Andreini's madness and its cure, alludes to the omnipresent Neoplatonic metaphors of Medici monumentalism, as well as to the Ciceronian ideals of virtue, valour, and eloquence that govern comediennes' performances 'in concorrenza'. Demonstrating her intellectual prowess in a number of languages and imitations of other characters, Andreini made cunning sense out of her nonsensical rantings. And her overabundance of passion when in the guise of the madwoman spilled out inevitably in song.

Isabella, in that she found herself deceived by Flavio's insidiousness, and not knowing how to remedy the harm he had done, gave herself over completely to sorrow and thus was overcome by passion. And allowing herself to succumb to rage and fury, she went out of herself and, like a madwoman, went running through the city, stopping now this one, now that one, and speaking now in Spanish, now in Greek, now in Italian, and many other languages, but all without reason. And among other things she set to speaking French and also singing certain canzonettas in the French manner, giving such delight to the most serene bride that she could hardly express it. She then mixed in imitations of the languages of all her comedians, like that of Pantalone, of Gratiano, of Zanni, of Pedrolino, of Francatrippa, of Burattino, of Captain Cardone, and of Franceschina so naturally and with so many eccentricities that it is not possible to put into words the valour and virtue of this woman. Finally, by the art of magic, with certain waters they gave her to drink, she returned to her original state and thus,

Pl. 2.1.
SS Annunziata,
Florence, fresco
showing Isabella,
Francesco, and
Giovan Battista
Andreini amid
the Medici court.
Private collection

with elegant and learned style explaining the passions of love, and the travails of those who find themselves in similar predicaments, she made an end to the comedy. Demonstrating in the performance of this madness her sane and learned intellect, Isabella leaving such a murmur and marvel in her audience, that while the world endures, her beautiful eloquence and valour will always be praised.[31]

Pavoni's description demonstrates the interpretative depth capable of performances that might otherwise have been cast as simple amusements for the Florentine audience. His words portray Andreini as an actress familiar with a style of courtly discourse that impressed her listeners with its rhetorical flair and urbane references to humanistic conceits. The chronicler's use of the words *virtù* and *valore* hint at Andreini's erudition and her ability to 'order her mind with respect to reason'.[32] The songs she sang are audible testimony to this mental organization, for the individual notes harmonized with each other, and the harmonies resonated with the order of the universe. Virtue, in addition to resulting from the organization of one's thoughts and emotions, is formed, so wrote the Accademia della Crusca in its *Vocabolario* of 1610, by submission to authority, and sometimes it may be ingested in a drink ('essendo la virtù del beveraggio consumata'). This last characterization is particularly apposite to Andreini's performance of the madwoman, for her insanity was cured with magic water. Ariosto, too, conceived of virtue as a liquid property, healing Orlando's fury in the *Orlando furioso* with water, and Andreini, like the Roman Flaminia before her, exhibited virtue upon virtue in her imitation of such a worthy source.

---

[31] Pavoni, *Diario*, 45–6: 'L'Isabella in tanto trovandosi ingannata dall'insidie di Flavio, ne sapendo pigliar rimedio al suo male, si diede del tutto in preda al dolore, & così vinta dalla passione, e lasciandosi superare alla rabbia, & al furore uscì fuori di se stessa, & come pazza se n'andava scorrendo per la Cittade, fermando hor questo, & hora quello, e parlando hora in Spagnuolo, hora in Greco, hora in Italiano, & molti altri linguaggi, ma tutti fuor di proposito: e tra le altre cose si mise a parlar Francese, & a cantar certe canzonette pure alla Francese, che diedero tanto diletto alla Sereniss. Sposa, che maggiore non si potria esprimere. Si mise poi ad imitare li linguaggi di tutti li suoi Comici, come del Pantalone, del Gratiano, del Zanni, del Pedrolino, del Francatrippa, del Burattino, del Capitan Cardone, & della Franceschina tanto naturalmente, & con tanti dispropositi, che non è possibile il poter con lingua narrare il valore, & la virtù di questa Donna. Finalmente per fintione d'arte Magica, con certe acque, che le furono date a bere, ritornò nel suo primo essere, & quivi con elegante, & dotto stile esplicando le passioni d'amore, & i travagli, che provano quelli, che si ritrovano in simil panie involti, si fece fine alla Comedia; mostrando nel recitar questa pazzia il suo sano, e dotto intelletto; lasciando l'Isabella tal marmorio, & meraviglia ne gli ascoltatori, che mentre durerà il mondo, sempre sarà lodata la sua bella eloquenza, & valore.'

[32] *Vocabolario degli Accademici della Crusca*, s.v. 'virtù'.

Humanistic allusions like these, which bolster ideas of the culture and civility of the Medici court, may also be seen in the intermedi designed by Bardi and the other members of the Florentine camerata. Although the camerata is best remembered for its members' radical new alliance of music with Aristotelian rhetoric, the matrimonial festivities devised by members of that group for the court from 1539 to 1637 maintained well-worn conventions of Neoplatonic, hermetic, and Aristotelian imitations in their subject matter and imagery. Indeed, the association of Neoplatonism with the Medici rulers was so firmly entrenched in Florentine art and scholarship that Eric Cochrane described the century and a half from the restoration of the Republic of Florence in 1527 to the publication of Orazio Ricasoli Rucellai's Platonic dialogues in the late 1660s as an era of reaction to that established philosophic norm.[33]

Neoplatonic and hermetic allegory served the Florentines again in 1589 in the presentation of the intermedi for *La pellegrina*, which depicted the now well-known themes of the Music of the Spheres, the singing contest between the Muses and Pierides, Apollo's victory over the serpent Python, the Inferno and its harpies, Arion's rescue from the sea, and the Gifts of Harmony and Rhythm.[34] The opening perspective, as described by the secretary of the Accademia della Crusca Bastiano de' Rossi, provided an introduction to the neoclassical conception of the entertainment by invoking the image of a Roman amphitheatre. Within this great edifice, it would be shown that the theatrical entertainments of the Medici stand on a par with the revered dramas of the ancient Romans. The semicircular architecture of the audience area in the newly renovated *sala delle commedie* in the Uffizi theatre was to serve as one half of the Corinthian structure, with the perspective created by the stage set as the other half.[35]

The entertainment's allegorical frame, embodied in the first and final intermedi, outlines the transcendent potential of humanity through music, and it operates as a structural parallel to Opico's speeches that

[33] Cochrane, *Florence in the Forgotten Centuries 1527–1800*, 69, 145–6, 156–7, 242.

[34] For a deep and complex analysis of the fourth intermedio in terms of its humanistic and astral components, see La Via, '*Concentus Iovis adversus Saturni Voces*'.

[35] Rossi, *Descrizione dell'apparato e degl'intermedi*, 7. The preface of Rossi's publication is dated 14 May 1589, at which time the wedding festivities were still in progress. Rossi probably composed most of his narration while the scheduled wedding entertainments were still in rehearsal, since he does not mention either of the comedies performed by the Gelosi, and his is the only account to describe the symbolism of the Roman amphitheatre—a stage effect that may not have been realized in performance. A detailed reconstruction and analysis of the Uffizi renovations may be found in Saslow, *The Medici Wedding of 1589*.

frame the song contest in *Mirtilla*. Like Filli's and Mirtilla's contest, the frame for the intermedi provides a rational and, in this case, omniscient perspective that confines the emotional depth explored within. For this is the Platonic definition of catharsis, that it plumbs the depths of emotion, stirring the passions of its auditors in order to purge them of destructive humours.[36] Andreini's performances achieved this neoclassical end, as Pietro Mattei wrote in 1624: 'Her comedies inspired admiration and universal delight. And in truth these performances benefited communal affairs and commonly were needed by Princes in order to rule the populace, as they say the Buffoon said to the Emperor Augustus, they purge their rebellious tendencies.'[37]

Framing Andreini's exploration of passions in 1589, the first intermedio, as Bernardo Buontalenti's watercolours so beautifully show, unveils a depiction of the Harmony of the Spheres, with musicians in cloud machines placed among the celestial Sirens and other planets. After Harmony's opening soliloquy, discussed in reference to the performance of prologues in Chapter 1, all sing in the elegant and delightful figurative harmonies of *musica mundana*. Arising from numerous commentaries on Plato's *Timaeus* from Porphyry's to Ficino's, the theory of the Music of the Spheres gave the Florentine courtiers an irresistible visual as well as audible image with which to magnify the glory and virtue of the Medici court. The last intermedio complements the first by presenting the same gods descending to earth to honour mortals with the gift of *musica humana*.

The final scene appears, ornamented in gold, showing seven cloud machines. Two clouds remain in the heavens where the pagan gods may be glimpsed watching over the event. The five remaining clouds—three carrying the Graces, Cupid, and the Muses, and the others transporting Apollo and Bacchus with gifts of Harmony and Rhythm—descend slowly into the pastoral scene below. With the descent of Apollo and Bacchus from the heavens, Bardi conceded divine knowledge, grace, and power to the Medici rulers by virtue of their favour among the gods. The image of Apollo offered the Grand Dukes a symbol of beneficent strength and knowledge, and that of Bacchus the victory of culture over nature, as

---

[36] See Plato, *Politics*, bk. 8; Aristotle, *The Poetics*, ch. 6 (trans. Hutton), 50.
[37] Mattei, *Della perfetta historia*, 227: 'Le sue comedie venivano godute con ammiratione, e con diletto universale. Et per il vero queste rappresentationi giovano a i costumi, e comunemente sono necessarie a i Principi, per trattener i popoli, come si recita che dicesse quel Buffone all'Imperatore Augusto, incantano ogni turbulento partito.'

otherwise signified in the celebrated tale of his taming and yoking a pair of wild tigers.[38]

Bardi carefully arranged the pastoral set for the final intermedio to depict the utopian scene that accompanies Neoplatonic transcendences like the one invoked for the song contest in *Mirtilla*. Rossi related the imitation to his readers as follows: 'The poet made these deities enter the stage in the most pleasing and most beautiful scene that he could, because he wanted it to represent that which Plato writes in the books of his *Laws*.'[39] Plato took up the idea of the pastoral landscape as the locus of interaction between heaven and earth when he created the First Academy, and this concept is mirrored not only in the *Laws*, but in the *Phaedrus*, by Socrates' journey from the city into the countryside. Members of the First Academy were said to walk through sylvan gardens, inspired in their discussions by communion with the gods. For Ficino, whose goal was to recreate the First Academy in late fifteenth-century Tuscany, the pastoral scene with its humanistic associations was one of many characteristics adopted in imitation of Plato's earlier institution: 'Not least of these deliberately cultivated parallels was the garden or parkland setting. Plato enthusiasts raked the ancient notices and apocrypha for clues to its exact extent and situation, its statues, flora, and topography, and where they could find no sherds from the past, they felt at liberty to invent Platonically appropriate details.'[40]

The pastoral setting continued to function as a visual cue for divine inspiration throughout the sixteenth century, especially at the Medici court. Not only did Bardi take pains to construct his own Platonically appropriate details in the form of a pastoral setting for the sixth intermedio in the 1589 entertainment, but Barbara Russano Hanning has shown that the pastoral landscape, combined with images of Apollo, formed a foundation for the imagery and metaphors at work in the first operas.[41]

Glosses of Plato's works and the commentaries they inspired by the early medieval authors Macrobius, Chalcidius, and Martianus Cappella

---

[38] Putnam, 'Virgil and History', outlines these Apollonian and Bacchian attributes in his reading of the intersignificance of history and literature in the *Aeneid*.

[39] Rossi, *Descrizione dell'apparato*, 61: 'Fece il poeta queste deità venire in iscena nella più lieta, e più bella vista, ch'egli potè, perchè ci volle quel fatto rappresentare, che scrive Platone ne' libri delle sue leggi.'

[40] Allen, *The Platonism of Marsilio Ficino*, 6–7.

[41] Hanning, 'Glorious Apollo'; ead., *Of Poetry and Music's Power*; ead., 'Apologia pro Ottavio Rinuccini'.

were among the most consequential sources for the dissemination of Neoplatonism to the Latin West. Macrobius' *Commentary on the Dream of Scipio* and *Saturnalia*, especially, had a profound influence on medieval and Renaissance music and theatre and specifically on comedians like the Gelosi. The catholicity of Macrobius' subject matter and the extensive distribution of his works ensured a broad readership, and the uniquely comprehensible style of his prose allows for its interpretation by simple readers as well as scholars. Macrobius' writings served, for example, as principal models for Boethius' interpretation of the mathematical proportions governing music and the planets, thereby providing a tacit foundation for late medieval and Renaissance music treatises written in imitation of the sixth-century author's *De institutione musica*.[42]

References to Plato and Macrobius appear in the treatises of the comedians Domenico Bruni and Nicolò Barbieri, as well as in the third book of Garzoni's *La piazza universale*, entitled 'De' comici e tragedi'. Each describes Macrobius as a widely imitated authority in the development of comedic plots and dramatic imagery, whom comedians were keen to quote in defence of the comic arts.[43] As Garzoni writes in 1585, 'Thus, it happens that Macrobius, in the third book of his *Saturnalia*, defends the histrionic art from baseness with the example of Roscius Amerinus [*sic*: Quintus Roscius Gallus] and Aesop, actors who were familiar with Cicero, who defended their works as wise and singular speeches.'[44]

Macrobius' *Commentary on the Dream of Scipio* invites a specific construction of divine madness as an imitation of Plato's *Phaedrus*, for in Book 2 of the *Commentary*, the early medieval writer includes among his glosses on the *Timaeus* and the Music of the Spheres an extensive passage from Cicero's translation of Plato's dialogue. Isabella Andreini's treatment of the Phaedran allegory, in addition to the passage from 'La forza d'Amore' cited above, may be gleaned from the first sonnet from her *Rime*, given in Chapter 3, which displays a brash, satirical version of the trope: 'with lies, no less, with false words, I have portrayed the Muses'

---

[42] Macrobius, *Commentary on the Dream of Scipio* (ed. Stahl), 3–66; Palisca, *Humanism in Italian Renaissance Musical Thought*, 35–54, 164–90.

[43] I. Andreini, *Lettere*; ead., *Fragmenti d'alcuni scritture*; Barbieri, *La supplica* (ed. Taviani), 150–2; ibid. in Marotti and Romei, *La professione del teatro*, 592; Bruni, *Fatiche comiche* in Marotti and Romei, 366; Garzoni, *La piazza universale*, fo. 319ᵛ; id., *De' comici e tragedi* in Marotti and Romei, 11. For more information concerning attacks against comedy, especially those made by Carlo Borromeo, and comedians' defences of it, see Taviani, *La fascinazione del teatro*.

[44] Garzoni, *La piazza universale*, in Marotti and Romei, *La professione del teatro*, 11.

high madnesses'. The poet Giovan Battista Marino describes Andreini's Neoplatonic imitations with more empathy:

> Piangete, orbi Teatri: invan s'attende
> più la vostra tra voi bella Sirena;
> ella orecchio mortal, vista terrena
> sdegna, e colà donde pria scese, ascende.
>   Quivi, ACCESA d'amor, d'amor accende
> l'eterno Amante; e ne l'empirea Scena,
> che d'angelici lumi è tutta piena,
> dolce canta, arde dolce e dolce splende.
>   Splendono or qui le vostre faci intanto,
> pompa a le belle esequie; e non più liete
> voci esprima di festa il vostro canto.
>   Piangete voi, voi che pietosi avete
> al suo tragico stil più volte pianto;
> il suo tragico caso, orbi, piangete.[45]

(Weep, bereaved theatres. In vain one still awaits your beautiful Siren among you; she scorns mortal ear, earthly sight, and there, where once she descended, she ascends. Thus, inflamed with love,[46] with love she ignites the eternal Lover; and on the celestial Stage, filled with angelic light, sweetly she sings, loves sweetly, and sweetly shines. They shine now here, your torches, pomp to the beautiful exequies; no longer do happy voices express your festive joy. Weep, you: you who pityingly have often wept at her tragic style; for her tragic fate, orbs, weep.)

A Neoplatonic interpretation of *La pazzia d'Isabella* offers the potential for an intertextual reading with Bardi's intermedi. Together, the entertainments construct an overwhelming representation of the Medici court's achievement of Apollonian ideals through allegories of love and divine inspiration. And perhaps this confluence of meaning helped win the contest for Andreini, for who could argue with her choice of model if the same choice was made by Bardi and his fellow courtiers? She may even have decided the subject of her comedy after seeing the intermedi. As far as we know, Andreini had the opportunity to witness Bardi's grand spectacle prior to her performance at least once, between the acts of *La cingana*. And, although there is no positive indication that the Gelosi were in Florence prior to 4 May, they may have seen the first staging of *La pellegrina* and, potentially, its rehearsals.

---

[45] In I. Andreini, *Lettere*, as cited in Marotti and Romei, *La professione del teatro*, 167.

[46] 'Accesa' was Andreini's pseudonym among the members of the Accademia degli Intenti of Pavia.

La pazzia d'Isabella begins in Padua, where Isabella, only daughter of Pantalone de' Bisognosi, is shown to be in love with the gentleman Fileno, as is her servant enamoured of his. Fileno asks Pantalone for Isabella's hand in marriage, but the older man refuses, stating that Fileno is too young. Intent on thwarting Pantalone's wishes, Fileno and Isabella agree to meet in secret outside Isabella's home at an assigned hour so that they may elope and leave Padua. Unknown to the lovers, the student Flavio [probably played by Flaminio Scala] carries a secret passion for Isabella. He overhears their conversation and appears at the rendezvous a few moments ahead of time, disguised as Fileno. As soon as Isabella appears, they go off together. Fileno then arrives at Isabella's home and, concerned that she is not waiting for him, alerts the maid, who searches the house for her mistress. When Isabella is nowhere to be found, Fileno despairs of his beloved and loses his senses. Meanwhile, Isabella realizes too late that she has been abducted by an imposter. Having sustained the ruin of her reputation, she goes mad for her true love, Fileno, and wanders the streets, speaking in tongues.[47]

[47] Pavoni, *Diario*, 44–6: 'Il soggetto principale di detta Comedia fu questo, che Isabella figliuola unica di M. Pantalone de' Bisognosi s'innamorò di Fileno Gentil'huomo molto virtuoso, e lui di lei. La serva d'Isabella s'innamorò ancora lei del servitore del Sig. Fileno, & il servitore di lei; per il cui mezo li loro patroni si servivano dell'ambasciate. In questo mentre Flavio, studente in detta Città, che Padova per nome si chiamava, s'innamora d'Isabella, ma non trova riscontro, perche lei era di già presa dell'amore di Fileno. Avenne, che il detto Gentil'huomo la fece da un suo amico domandar al padre per moglie, il vecchio rispose non volerne fare altro, sendo che Fileno era troppo giovanetto, sopra di che ne passò per mezo d'amici molti ragionamenti, ne mai fu possibile a poter concluder nulla. Perilche li giovani innamorati vedendo il lor negotio andar tutto al contrario, vennero in tanta disperatione, che non sapevano che partito pigliare al fatto loro, e stando le cose in questi termini, Isabella si risolse alla fine di torsi di casa del padre una notte, & andarsene con Fileno in altri paesi, e così posero l'ordine per la sera, dandosi i cenni l'un l'altro del riconoscersi. Simile accordo fece la serva con il servitore di star'uniti, e seguir la fortuna de i lor patroni.

Avenne, che mentre ponevano l'ordine di questa fuga, Flavio, che stava in disparte nascosto, udi tutti li ragionamenti passati tra l'amata, & il suo rivale; & ne prese tanto cordoglio, quanto si può imaginare chi habbi provato simili tormenti. La onde si dispose servirsi di questa occasione, e per tal via conseguire la sua amata Isabella, come fece. Così venuta l'hora dell'accordo: ma un poco prima, comparve Flavio, & con li cenni, che Fileno dovea dare ad Isabella si fece udire: la quale subito n'uscì di casa, & fu raccolta con tanto contento di Flavio, che più non si può imaginare: & così alla muta se n'andarono: ne appena hebbero volte le spalle, che comparve Fileno col servitore, & fatti li cenni ordinati, non comparve mai nessuno. Alla fine la serva si fece fuori dell'uscio, & disse a Fileno, che non trovava la Patrona, & cercando di nuovo per casa, non la seppe mai ritrovare: la onde il misero, & infelice Fileno venne in tal dispiacere, che cominciò a farneticare, col discorrere fra se ove se ne potesse essere andata, & tanto immerso stette in questi pensieri, che come insano, over pazzo

Comparison of Andreini's comedy with Plato's *Phaedrus* reveals a shared thematic thread centring on the relationships between love, music, and madness. Plato's dialogue relates the story of Socrates and his student Phaedrus, who one day walk together outside the city of Athens, discussing the qualities of love. Socrates is unused to the suburban environment and comments on it, saying that he ordinarily confines his activities to the city. Upon reaching an enclosed pastoral bower, near the place where the north wind Boreas had abducted the young girl Oreithyia, Socrates is struck with a homoerotic attraction to his beautiful young student and a madness overcomes him. The hot afternoon is spent with the two scholars reclining in the shade as Socrates expounds on the virtues of love. As part of his discourse, the teacher reveals an allegory wherein a winged charioteer and his two horses ascend towards the heavens, casting off mortal sanity and causing the gods and Muses to descend to earth with gifts of poetry and music.[48] Ficino's interpretation of the dialogue places special emphasis on the musical characterization of Socrates' madness. As related by Gary Tomlinson,

> The ultimate causes of the poetic furor, Ficino said, are the divine musics found in the mind of god and in the motions and order of the heavens. When we perceive the echoes of these musics, our souls burn with the desire to loose their bonds to the body and fly back to them; thus the poetic furor is a first stimulus for the soul to journey forth from the body. But at the same time our perception of the divine musics causes us to strive to imitate them. This imitation takes two forms. Its superficial form involves the echoing of celestial harmonies by normal musicians, those, it would seem, not in the grip of poetic furor. Its more profound form is revealed instead by those frenzied poet-musicians who 'through an influx of divine spirit pour forth with full voice the most solemn and excellent song'.[49]

Several of the tropes mentioned draw *La pazzia d'Isabella* and the *Phaedrus* dialogue together. Boreas's rape of Oreithyia mirrors the abduction of Isabella by Flavio, and the dementia that overcomes Socrates in

divenne, uscendo fuori di se stesso. L'Isabella in tanto trovandosi ingannata dall'insidie di Flavio, ne sapendo pigliar rimedio al suo male, si diede del tutto in preda al dolore, & così vinta dalla passione, e lasciandosi superare alla rabbia, & al furore uscì fuori di se stessa, & come pazza se n'andava scorrendo per la Cittade . . .'.

Identification of the character Flavio as Flaminio Scala stems from Scala's *Favole rappresentative* (Venice, 1611), in which his stage name is given as Flavio.

[48] Plato, *Euthyphro, Apology, Crito, Phaedo, Phaedrus* (trans. Fowler), 405–580. For a detailed analysis of the allegory of the winged charioteer, see Allen, *Marsilio Ficino and the Phaedran Charioteer*; id., *The Platonism of Marsilio Ficino*.

[49] Tomlinson, *Music in Renaissance Magic*, 172–3.

contemplation of his student has its counterpart in Isabella's madness for love of Fileno, both of which result in learned speeches on the topic of love. Each divinely inspired oration is depicted as a mediation between the earthly and the celestial, symbolized by a subsequent descent from the heavens of gods bearing musical and poetic gifts. As suggested in Tomlinson's paraphrase, the proof of Andreini's virtue—the substance by which she would have won the contest with Piisimi—would emerge in the quality of her songs, for the ordinary musician might imitate divine madness, but the truly inspired would be known by the divine resonance of her harmonies.

Abduction and domination are conjoined in *Phaedrus* as components of divine inspiration, represented in both the allegory of the charioteer and the rape of Oreithyia. Each describes an event in which two individuals are paired in a dyad balancing submission and domination. Within the story of the charioteer, the winged horses represent two opposing wills, bound together by virtue of the yoke. One is the good horse, obeying readily all the charioteer's commands; the other is the unruly horse, tormented by the growth of feathers beneath the skin, who must be beaten, bleeding, into submission. Once the second horse has been subdued, the chariot soars to the heavens, and the gods respond with divine gifts. The rape of Oreithyia, in contrast with the allegory of the charioteer, lends more emphasis to the images of abduction and removal of the submissive partner from his or her native physical surroundings, although abduction also carries with it the strong implication of a submissive/dominant pairing.

Ficino wrote about the correspondence of abduction with dementia in his *Commentary* on the writings of Plato in 1496. He interpreted the rape of Oreithyia as an allegory of divine madness, in which Boreas represents 'the breath of inspiration ravishing a virgin soul' in the figure of the young girl.[50] The abduction or removal of the submissive partner from his or her usual surroundings is, in itself, an allegory of the displacement of the individual's mind from sanity to lunacy. This corresponds to Plato's dictum that divine madness 'takes hold upon a gentle and pure soul, arous[ing] it and inspir[ing] it to songs and other poetry'.[51] Here, the word 'pure' implies 'inaccessible places, mountainsides, streams, and groves, undefiled by the passing of man'.[52] Thus, the submissive partner, wrapped in a

---

[50] Allen, *The Platonism of Marsilio Ficino*, 5.
[51] Plato, *Euthyphro, Apology, Crito, Phaedo, Phaedrus*, 469.
[52] See Allen's discussion of this point in *The Platonism of Marsilio Ficino*, 3–5.

metaphorical pastoral cloak, may be seen as untainted by sin and innocent of worldly (that is, urban) wisdom. In both the allegory of the charioteer and that of Boreas and Oreithyia, metaphors of opposing wills and of the binding of individuals within a single harness imply the very structure of competitive performances, which link antagonists together within the shared yoke of a dramatic or musical genre.

While Plato's *Phaedrus* might suggest an exclusively masculine gendering of divine madness and its resulting musical and poetic creativity that clashes with Andreini's representation of it, Ficino adopts a somewhat different perspective that introduces a marked feminine gendering of the subject. He assigns to the medium the characteristics of a sibyl—a female figure betraying masculine attributes that symbolize her chastity and ability to prophesy—as illustrated in the sections of the Sistine Chapel ceiling noted earlier in this chapter. The archetypal Cumaean Sibyl—the most masculine-seeming of all Michelangelo's sibyls—comes into being when she spurns the love of Apollo who, in return, grants her the longevity of a thousand years, albeit without enduring youth. She therefore comes to represent the wisdom of old age and prescience of the heavens.[53] In sixteenth-century religious dramas, where sibyls appear as bearers of the word of God to Charlemagne, they carry a Christian connotation in addition to their ancient Roman heritage. Michael J. B. Allen's summary of Ficino's writings on divine madness gives form to the latter's vision of its sibylline associations:

In the preliminary moments of rapture any subject of divine madness may indeed resemble the Delphic Pythia or the Dodonan Sibyl or Aeneas' Cumaean Sibyl writhing under the goad of Apollo; but the subsequent 'release' in the heightened utterance of poetry and song transforms the ecstatic subject, however partially or momentarily, into a poet. For all the divine madnesses, Ficino says, have recourse for their articulation to the poetic madness, since its poetry and song, its poetic song, 'demand concord and harmony.' By this he means both metrical and musical organization, the observation and incorporation of Pythagorean mathematics and harmonies, and above all the structures of 'well-composed' as opposed to ordinary 'simple' speech.[54]

The alliance of sibylline prophecy with divine madness discloses a tacit socialization of gender roles that extends to notions of propriety in musical and poetic performance. On the one hand, the sibyl's masculine traits

[53] Grafton, *Defenders of the Text*, 162–77; Bulfinch, *Myths of Greece and Rome*, 292–8.
[54] Allen, *The Platonism of Marsilio Ficino*, 61–2.

define her powerful stature as a teacher and vessel of celestial wisdom; on the other, the Neoplatonic process of achieving communion with the gods necessitates a complete and sometimes violent oppression of the errant, feminine-gendered subject in favour of a dominant partner. In both senses the sibyl is 'possessed' either in mind or in body. Moreover, the word 'possessed' implies that the subject of divine madness achieves yet another form of virtue through the act of submission, as suggested in the definitions of that term published by the Accademia della Crusca.

The sibylline image resulting from the careful draping of this veil of cultivated masculinity over Andreini's natural self lays unquestionable claim to her valour. Pavoni's praise of her high moral fibre persists in direct conflict with contemporary social mores equating a woman's public appearance on stage with sexual promiscuity, but Andreini's intellectual transcendence of her sex transforms her into an exceptionally virtuous actress.[55] Seen in this light, her actions in the mad scene of *La pazzia d'Isabella* take on far greater meaning than the vacant rantings of the ruined woman represented in the drama's plot. The songs and poetry born of her insanity may be understood rather as the immortal teachings of the gods conveyed through a pure and innocent medium who has attained sibylline virtue through subjugation of her natural sexuality. Andreini's homage to Christine of Lorraine therefore takes on significant overtones: first, that the virgin bride would be the subject of chaste and virtuous devotion rather than suffering the doubtful merits of an actress's praise; second, that Andreini's tribute to her would be received as celestial homage to the new Grand Duchess of Tuscany; and third, that the Medici court would be depicted as an oasis of culture amid its otherwise natural—implying wild and barbarous—environs.

The celestial gift granted to Christine of Lorraine via the envoy of Isabella Andreini took form, Pavoni tells us, in both music and oratory. This concurs with Ficino's view of divine madness, that it results in a combination of poetry and song symbolizing the concord and harmony of the universe. Pavoni's description of Andreini's musical outpourings and concluding speech, however, proposes not only their virtue, but in more concrete terms, their form and style. To begin, his phrase *canzonette pure*

---

[55] On the immorality of actresses, see Taviani and Schino, *Il segreto della commedia dell'arte*, 337; Barbieri, *La supplica* (ed. Taviani), pp. i–lxxxv. Authors who have praised Andreini's high moral character include Garzoni, *La piazza universale*, fo. 320'; Andreini's fellow academician of the Intenti, Spelta, *La curiosa, et dilettevole aggionta*, 169; and Bartoli, *Notizie istoriche de' comici italiani*, i. 32–3.

alla francese, if we are to read into the chronicler's meaning more than a generic reference to 'little songs in the French style', offers an indication that Andreini in her madness sang, as did the nymphs in her pastoral play *Mirtilla*, canzonettas. This simple musical form, which heightens the recitation of strophic poetry with a naturalistic use of melody and harmony, makes audible the pastoral landscape of its origin. Pavoni's phrase further dictates that the style of Andreini's poetry, its musical setting, and performance practice evoked French mannerisms, as would resonate well with a wedding joining the houses of Tuscany and France.

Inclusion of French-style canzonettas in Andreini's performance of *La pazzia d'Isabella* in 1589 only accentuates the neoclassical interpretation of the entertainment, since reference to this form and style in late sixteenth-century Italy implies the influence of Pierre de Ronsard and of Jean-Antoine de Baïf's Académie de Poésie et Musique in Paris, whose members sought to revive classical ideals. The aims of the Académie were espoused on Italian soil by Gabriello Chiabrera and Claudio Monteverdi, both of whom studied the poetry and music of the French scholars. Both were also acquainted with Andreini and her family, Chiabrera from as early as 1584 and Monteverdi, perhaps not until after the Medici wedding of 1589, from the time he entered Mantuan service in 1590 or 1591.[56]

The first evidence we have of the rapport between Chiabrera and Andreini is the report of Giovanni Vincenzo Verzellino, who in 1584 wrote about the Gelosi's performances in Savona: 'Isabella Andreini, a comedienne of supreme intelligence, with her company of ingenious nomads, came to Savona and for some days recited comedies of various sorts in the Palace of Civic Affairs, to the very great pleasure of the citizens, and particularly of Sig. Gabriello Chiabrera, who would sing of her when she feigned madness on the stage.'[57] Chiabrera's sonnet 'Nel giorno che sublime in bassi manti', probably written on this occasion, lauds the actress for her imitations of divine madness. The poem is particularly appropriate to discussion of *La pazzia d'Isabella* in that it describes Andreini's lofty ascent while in lowly garb and performing a comedy. As ever, the divine fury erupts in song:

---

[56] See Bruno, *Gabriello Chiabrera e Isabella Andreini*; and Fabbri, *Monteverdi* (trans. Carter), 22.

[57] As cited in Marotti and Romei, *La professione del teatro*, 55: 'Isabella Andreini, comica di suprema intelligenza, con la sua compagnia di pellegrini ingegni venne in Savona, e recitò per alquanti giorni comedie di varie sorti nella sala del Palazzo delle Cause Civili, con grandissimo gusto de' cittadini, e particolarmente del signor Gabriello Chiabrera, che di lei ebbe a cantare, allorquando comparve sulla scena fingendosi pazza.'

> Nel giorno che sublime in bassi manti
> Isabella imitava alto furore;
> estolta con angelici sembianti
> ebbe del senno altrui gloria maggiore;
>   Alhor saggia tra 'l suon, saggia tra i canti
> non mosse piè, che non sorgesse Amore,
> nè voce aprì, che non creasse amanti,
> nè riso fè, che non beasse un core.
>   Chi fu quel giorno a rimirar felice
> di tutt'altro quaggiù cesse il desio,
> che sua vita per sempre ebbe serena.
>   O di Scena dolcissima Sirena,
> o de' Teatri Italici Fenice,
> o tra Coturni insuperabil Clio.

(The day when, sublime in lowly cloaks, Isabella imitated high madness, and foolish with an angelic countenance, won greater glory from the wisdom of others; then, wise amid the music, wise amid the songs, she took no step that Love did not direct, nor lifted voice that did not create lovers, nor smiled that did not delight a heart. Whoever on that day watched happily, for all else of this world desire ceased, for his life was forever serene. Oh, of the stage sweetest Siren, oh, of Italian theatres the Phoenix, oh, among thespians unsurpassable Clio.)[58]

    In turn, Andreini wrote canzonettas (*canzonette morali*) on the subject of virtue for her 'Ligurian Amphion'. 'Vago di posseder l'indico argento' is prefaced by the phrase 'nothing more lasting than virtue' and its companion piece 'Faccia al gran marte risonar le 'ncudi' engenders the motto 'that virtue makes the true prince'.[59] In these, Andreini returned Chiabrera's praises by implying his own inspiration to divine madness, as well as affirming the bond between the genre of the canzonetta and concepts of virtue. Some of Andreini's *scherzi*, written in the style of Chiabrera, purposefully called *scherzi* in imitation of his and dedicated to him in the later editions of her *Rime*, include 'Io credèa che tra gli amanti', 'Ecco l'Alba ruggiadosa', and 'Movèa dolce un zefiretto', all *poesia per musica* and set to music by various composers, albeit after the Medici wedding of 1589.

    Chiabrera composed and, in 1599, published a collection of *poesia per musica* written in imitation of the odes of Pierre de Ronsard and his cultural heirs in Baïf's Académie. He distinguished these neoclassical canzonettas from others that did not bespeak the influence of the Pléiade

---

[58] I. Andreini, *Rime*, 200.
[59] 'Nessuna cosa esser più durabile della virtù' and 'Che la virtù fa il vero Principe', respectively. See ibid. 20, 23.

by calling them *scherzi*.[60] The new style would emphasize a naturalness scorning the artificiality of courtly love and requiring no scholastic mediation to be appreciated. As Chiabrera wrote,

> I believe that you should read French poetry: recall their amorous charms, those flatterings, those tendernesses, which every woman and every man can and knows how to express. And everyone, when they are expressed, understands them easily. Do you not take pleasure in seeing such *scherzi* so lovingly represented, which require no effort, nor comment, nor gloss to be understood?[61]

The naturalism of Chiabrera's *scherzi* and, in spite of their debt to Ronsard, their anti-intellectualism, make them particularly apposite for performance in commedia dell'arte plays and the pastoral settings of song contests. The Gelosi's stage works rarely received the kind of managed interpretation provided by publications like Rossi's *Descrizione* of 1589 or Federico Follino's *Compendio* of 1608, and so it behoved comedians to adopt styles of composition and performance that might easily be understood without mediation. And what better language than the language of love, which Chiabrera characterized so charmingly in the passage above, to express the artful conceits of the *innamorata*?

We do not know by name the songs Andreini performed in Florence in 1589, although any of her Chiabreresque *scherzi* are likely candidates. She may have performed them, as her predecessor Vincenza Armani was said to do, 'in the manner of a musician and poet', implying an improvisatory singing of the text to a simple harmonic accompaniment played on the lute or guitar. Andreini also wrote two encomiastic poems for Christine of Lorraine, 'Quando scendeste ad'illustrare il mondo' and 'D'amor l'aria sfavilla', for presentation at the wedding, and it may be that she sang or recited these as part of her offering. The canzona and epithalamium Andreini composed for the new Grand Duchess occupy a small book, carefully copied on gilded paper in the comedienne's own hand and bound in vellum that has been treated with a purple wash (Pl. 2.2). It exists in one copy only, housed in the Biblioteca Nazionale in Florence, and has

---

[60] Chiabrera, *Scherzi e canzonette morali*; id., *Canzonette, rime varie* (ed. Negri). The best source for discussions of the Pléiade's influence on 16th- and 17th-c. Italian poetry is still F. Neri, *Il Chiabrera e la Pléiade francese*. See also Pirrotta, 'Scelte poetiche di Monteverdi'; Cardamone, *The Canzona villanesca alla napolitana and Related Forms*; Tomlinson, *Monteverdi and the End of the Renaissance*.

[61] Chiabrera, *Canzonette, rime varie* (ed. Negri), 564, as cited in Fabbri, *Monteverdi* (trans. Carter), 73.

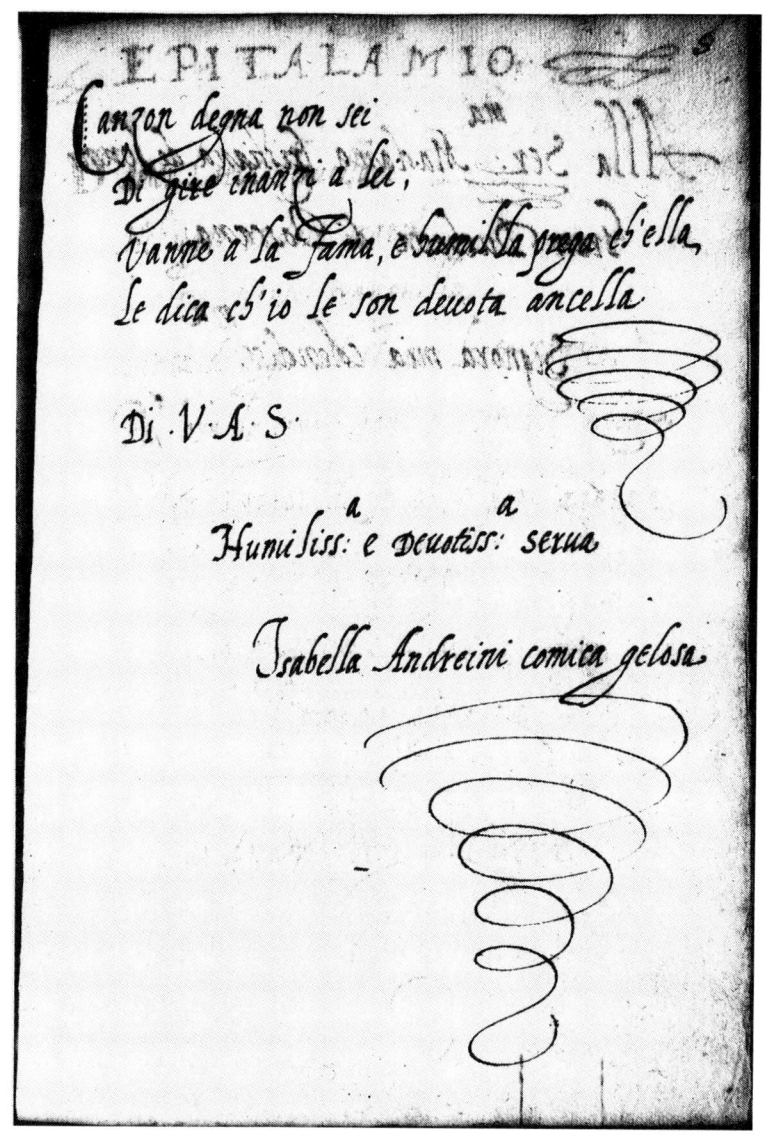

PL. 2.2. Conclusion of the canzone 'Quando scendeste ad'illustrare il Mondo' dedicated to Christine of Lorraine on the occasion of her marriage to Ferdinando de' Medici, 1589. Autograph. Florence, Biblioteca Nazionale Centrale, Magl. VII. 15

escaped notice before now. The imagery of the verses is breathtaking for its sensual femininity:

> Quando scendeste ad'illustrare il mondo
> Venere con le gratie in sen' v'accolse,
> E ne suoi veli avvolse
> Le membra pargolette,
> E con viso giocondo
> Il cinto di beltade a sè disciolse
> E à voi legollo, indi le schiere elette
> De i propitii celesti, et almi Numi
> Pieni di gioia, e festa
> Girorno à terra i lumi,
> E dissero hoggi à questa
> Regia Fanciulla à gara ogn'un di noi
> Infonda lieto tutti i pregi suoi.
>
> Ne di donna le mamme v'allattaro,
> Ma come al folgorante Giove piacque
> Le tremanti, e dolci acque
> Del famoso Hippocrene
> In latte si cangiaro
> Per darvi gli alimenti, e si compiacque
> Tanto del vostro bello il sommo bene
> Ch'ogni virtute in quell'humore ascose,
> E col latte suggeste
> Quant'ei saggio ripose
> Nell'onda, o don celeste
> A null'altra concesso, con ch'appieno
> V'hornò di vago, e casto il volto, e 'l seno. . . .

(When you descended to illuminate the world, Venus with the graces gathered you in her breast, and in her veils she wound your childlike limbs, and with merry face unbound the girdle of beauty from herself and fastened it around you, then the elect legions of the favourable, celestial, and blessed gods, filled with joy and festivity, turned their eyes to earth, and said today to this royal maid, in competition each of us instils happily all your merits. Nor did woman's breasts give you milk, but as it pleased the thunderous Jove to change the trembling and sweet waters of the famous Hippocrene to milk to give you nourishment, and was so struck by your beauty, the sum of goodness, that he hid every virtue in those humours, and with the milk you sucked as he, wise one, rested in the surf, o celestial gift, to no other conceded, with which he adorned your face and breast with loveliness and chastity.)[62]

---

[62] BNC, Magl. VII, 15. Both poems written by Andreini for Christine of Lorraine are given in their entirety below (Doc. 41).

Similarly delicate imagery infuses Andreini's *scherzi*. Several, like many of Chiabrera's, follow the double-system strophic structure associated with Ronsard's neoclassical *odes*, comprising six short lines arranged in stanzas of two equal systems. Andreini's homage to the rising sun and her lament on love betrayed offer good examples:

> Ecco l'Alba rugiadosa
> Come rosa,
> Sen di neve, piè d'argento,
> Che la chioma inannellata
> D'or fregiata
> Vezzosetta sparge al vento.
> I Ligustri, e i Gelsomini
> Da' bei crini,
> E dal petto alabastrino
> Van cadendo; e la dolce aura
> Ne ristaura
> Con l'odor grato divino.
> Febo anch' ei la chioma bionda
> Fuor de l'onda
> A gran passo ne discopre;
> E sferzando i suoi destrieri
> I pensieri
> Desta in noi de l'usate opre.
> Parte il Sonno, fugge l'ombra,
> Che disgombra
> Delio già col chiaro lume
> La caligine d'intorno:
> Ecco il giorno,
> Ond'anch'io lascio le piume.
> E'infiammar mi sento il petto
> Dal diletto,
> Che 'n me spiran le tue Muse
> Cui sequir bramo; e s'io caggio
> Nel viaggio
> Bel desir teco mi scuse.
> Ma s'avvien, ch'opra gentile
> Dal mio stile
> L'alma Clio giamai risuone;
> Si dirà si nobil vanto
> Dessi al canto
> Del Ligustico Anfione.

(Behold the dewy dawn, like a rose, breast of snow, feet of silver, who prettily scatters her curly golden hair in the wind. The lilies and the jasmines from the beautiful locks and from the alabaster breast cascade; and the sweet, gentle breeze restores us with a pleasant, divine fragrance. Phoebus too, shows us his blonde hair coming swiftly out of the waves; lashing at his steeds, he awakens in us thoughts of our usual routine. Sleep departs, the shadows flee because Delius chases away the darkness with clear light; here is the morning, so I, too, leave my bed. I feel my breast inflamed with delight, inspired by your muses whom I desire to follow; and if I fall in the path, let my good intentions excuse me. But if it should happen that beloved Clio ever makes beautiful music from my style, one will say I gave high honour to the song of the Ligurian Amphion.)[63]

'Ecco l'Alba ruggiadosa' typifies the standard patterns of Andreini's Chiabreresque canzonettas in affect, form, and sonance. Her language is delicate and descriptive, interweaving emotion with images from myth and nature. And the whole tells a simple story, from the first moments of awakening to the full blaze of sun and inspiration to compose, ending with the author's hope that her poem will be worthy of its dedicatee. The 'Ligurian Amphion' is Chiabrera, born in Liguria and who, according to Isabella's metaphor, could cause even the stones to move at the sound of his—that is, Amphion's—lyre.

The harmonious qualities achieved through Andreini's use of assonance and alliteration are equally reminiscent of Chiabrera's *poesia per musica*. In the first stanza, for example, consonant sounds play off each other within individual lines, as in 'Che la chioma inannellata' and 'Vezzosetta sparge al vento', and between lines, as in 'Come rosa' and 'Che la chioma inannellata'. Assonance, too, contributes to the poem's aurality, drawing together the first and second lines of the stanza with the persistent sounds of 'a' and 'o' vowels in 'Ecco l'Alba rugiadosa / Come rosa' and setting off the third verse with a change to the brighter sound of the 'e' vowels in 'Sen di neve, piè d'argento'. This wordplay is kept within strict bounds by the poem's metre and rhyme, which govern each stanza with a repeated metric grouping of 8 + 4 + 8 syllables per line, the verses rhyming *aabccb*.

'Io credèa che tra gli amanti' is perhaps best suited to performance in *La pazzia d'Isabella*, for its story is of love's disdain and the song's surviving sources recommend theatrical performance. Like 'Ecco l'Alba ruggiadosa', 'Io credèa che tra gli amanti' narrates a scene in imagistic, uncomplicated words that bespeak Chiabrera's inducement to read

[63] I. Andreini, *Rime*, 22–3.

French poetry for the simple, amorous turnings of its conceits. Andreini in this poem discloses an antagonism between thought and emotion by her insistence on beginning most of the strophes with 'Io credèa', 'Nè credèa', 'e stimai' or, 'non pensai'. With this trope, she also takes advantage of the implied musical setting, which will, of necessity, be the same for each stanza. Like 'Ecco l'Alba ruggiadosa', Andreini's lament comprises the double-system strophic form reminiscent of Ronsard's odes, as well as the same *aabccb* rhyme scheme.

> Io credèa, che tra gli amanti
> solo i pianti,
> sol l'angosce, sol le pene
> senza spene fosser quelle
> rie procelle
> turbatrici d'ogni bene.
>
> Io credèa, che 'nfausta sorte,
> doglia, e morte
> sostenesse un cor lontano
> da la mano, che 'l saetta,
> che l'aletta,
> per cui piange, e stride in vano.
>
> Io credèa quando sdegnose
> le amorose
> luci il vago afflitto mira,
> e sospira, fosse questa
> pena infesta
> sol cagion di sdegno, e d'ira.
>
> Io credèa, che 'n fier tormento
> il contento
> si cangiasse d'un'amante,
> che 'l sembiante amato perde,
> onde 'l verde
> fugge al fin di speme errante.
>
> E stimai, che senza esempio
> fosse l'empio
> fato (ohimè!) di quel dolente,
> che languente non ha pace,
> e si sfacene l'incendio vanamente.
>
> Ma godendo non pensai,
> che trar guai
> da due gioie un cor devesse,
> o potesse nel gioire

sì languire,
ch'a doler d'Amor s'havesse.
 Nè credèa, ch'amante amato
del suo stato
sospirasse. Hor da l'effetto
de l'affetto provo, Amore,
che 'l dolore
segue sempre il tuo diletto.
 Stringa pur l'amato collo,
che satollo
mai non sia quei che ben ama:
perche brama il bel celeste
chiuso in queste
membra, e 'n van lo cerca, e brama.
 O d'amor sorte infelice
se non lice
mai gioir. Tue cure ponno
(Fero donno!) scure e chiare,
dolci amare
torne dunque il cibo, e 'l sonno?

(I used to think, among these lovers, that there could be naught but weeping only, anguish, only hopeless pain amidst vile hurricanes, disrupters of every good. I used to think ill-omened fate, sorrow, and death a heart would undergo far distant from the hand that with an arrow pierces it, that charms it so, for which it weeps and cries out all in vain. I used to think that when the lovely, smitten one looks on those lights, scornful and amorous, and sighs, this grievous pain alone would be the only cause of wrath and of disdain. I used to think that into torment fierce the happiness would change of one who loves, but loses the beloved face, whence in the end the springtime's errant hope will flee. I judged too that unparalleled the wicked fate would be (alas!) of that woeful one who, grieving, finds no peace and is undone with burning in vain. But, rejoicing, I'd not thought that from its joys a heart would have to draw its woes, or could, in finding joy, so languish that it would have to complain of love. Nor did I think a lover who was loved would sigh about his state: now by the consequence, by the desire, O Love, I prove that sad remorse forever follows your delight. Hug tight, then, the beloved neck, for never will those have their fill who truly love; for one who yearns for loveliness celestial in earthly limbs seeks it out and yearns for it in vain. O wicked fate, if never one can righteously rejoice for love—since light and dark you cares (a savage lord) impose, both sweet and bitter too—when, then, will sleep and appetite return?)[64]

---

[64] I. Andreini, *Rime* (based on an unpublished translation by James Wyatt Cook).

This *scherzo* appears in two sources outside of Andreini's *Rime* that show it to have become a popular song, perhaps set to more than one tune, and accompanied by the Spanish guitar. The first time it appears is in Remigio Romano's first collection of 'bellissime canzonette' published in 1618.[65] Romano's massive anthology, printed in five volumes, contains a number of songs made famous by comedians' performances, including the *Lamento d'Arianna*, Giulio Caccini's *Tu c'hai le penne Amor* and *Amor ch'attendi*, the *Barzelletta di Scapino* and his *Scapinata*. These appear together with a host of compositions featuring the stage names of various comedians, such as *Deh, Florinda gratiosa* in reference to Virginia Andreini. The collection thus seems to focus, especially in volumes 2 and 5, on songs made popular in the theatre. Romano provides the full text of 'Io credèa che tra gli amanti' and instructs the performer to sing it to the tune of an unknown canzonetta, *Caro labbro vermiglietto*. The tune of *Caro labbro vermiglietto* may or may not be the same as that written out in the only other source of Andreini's *scherzo*, Eleuterio Guazzi's compendium of 'arias, madrigals and romanesca to be sung with theorbo, cembalo, guitar (chitariglia) and other instruments', published in 1622.[66] This does seem likely, however, because Guazzi's setting offers not only the tune and its lightly figured bass, but also *alfabeto* notation for Spanish guitar (see Ex. 2.2).

The formulaic structures of 'Ecco l'Alba ruggiadosa' and 'Io credèa che tra gli amanti', together with their reliance on rhetorical consonance, narrative, and their emphasis on sound and imagery, recommend a style whose main interest lies in the oral unfolding of the poem's performance rather than in its written text. As in the song contest in *Mirtilla*, the familiar and repetitive organizational framework of Andreini's Chiabreresque *scherzi* provides a strong, steady foundation against which the performer

[65] Romano, *Prima raccolta di bellissime canzonette musicali, e moderne, di autori gravissimi nella poesia, & nella musica* (1618). Romano published five volumes of *canzoni* and *canzonette* between 1618 and 1626, all with the printer Angelo Salvadori: the *Prima raccolta* cited above; *Seconda raccolta di canzonette musicali; bellissime per cantare & sonare, sopra arie moderne* (1620); *Terza raccolta di bellissime canzoni alla romanesca. Per suonare, e cantare nella chitara alla Spagnuola, con la sua intavolatura. Con altre canzonette vaghe, & belle* (1620); *Nuova raccolta di bellissime canzonette musicali, e moderne, di auttori gravissimi nella poesia, & nella musica* (1626). A detailed discussion of the publication history of the volumes and their reprints may be found in Roark Miller, 'The Composers of San Marco and Santo Stefano and the Development of Venetian Monody (to 1630)' (Ph.D. diss., University of Michigan, 1993), ch. 4.

[66] Guazzi, *Spiritosi affetti a una e due voci. Cioè arie madrigali & romanesca da cantarsi in tiorba incimbalo & chitariglia & altri istromenti con l'alfabetto per la chitara spagnola.*

Ex. 2.2. Eleuterio Guazzi, *Io credèa che tra gli amanti* (*Spiritosi affetti a una e due voci*, 1622)

might indulge the imagination, creating endless nuances and variations through rhetorical wordplay and ornamentation. Implied in this style of *poesia per musica* is a bardic performance practice, reminiscent of Amphion, or indeed of Ficino, singing celestial songs to the accompaniment of his lyre.

This may be the extent of Andreini's bow to the French style embodied in Pavoni's phrase 'canzonette pure alla francese', although use of these words demands recognition of Giulio Cesare Monteverdi's discussion of the 'canto alla francese' in reference to his brother Claudio's compositions.[67] With the publication of the *Scherzi musicali* in 1607, Giulio Cesare

---

[67] Further discussion of the *canto alla francese* and the impact of the Pléiade on Monteverdi's music may be found in Prunières, 'Monteverdi and French Music'; id., 'Monteverdi e la musica francese'; id., *La Vie et l'œuvre de Claudio Monteverdi*, translated as *Monteverdi: His Life and Work* (trans. Mackie); Schrade, *Monteverdi, Creator of Modern Music*; Gallico, 'Emblemi strumentali negli "scherzi" di Monteverdi'; Pirrotta, 'Scelte poetiche di Monteverdi'; Stevens, 'Monteverdi' in *New Grove*; Cardamone, *The Canzona villanesca alla napolitana*;

heralded the arrival in Italy of a new, French style in music that is particularly associated with settings of Chiabrera's *scherzi*. This *canto alla francese*, so wrote Giulio Cesare, was brought by Claudio when he returned from a sojourn in Flanders accompanying Vincenzo Gonzaga in the autumn of 1599—the same year that Chiabrera first published his own canzonettas. As demonstrated in the *Scherzi musicali* of 1607 (although these are not the only compositions Monteverdi wrote in the French style), the *canto alla francese* is particularly applicable to Chiabrera's style and to the ode-like form of his canzonettas.

> if the matter has to be considered in this light, my brother would have not a few arguments in his favour, in particular regarding the *canto alla francese* in this modern manner that is seen in publications of the last three or four years, now set to the words of motets, now of madrigals, now of canzonettas and of arias; who before him would have brought it back to Italy when he came from the baths of Spa, the year 1599? And who began to set it to Latin orations and familiar texts in our tongue before him? Did he not at that time compose these scherzi?[68]

Readings of this troublesome passage have identified the *canto alla francese* as that which was new in 1599, although the context of Giulio Cesare's gloss within a discussion of the *seconda prattica* suggests that it was the 'modern manner' that Monteverdi brought back with him from Spa. And Pavoni's diary of the 1589 wedding implies that while the manner may have been new at the turn of the century, the *canto alla francese* was not, for his description of Andreini's performance provides us with a much earlier reference to a practice of performing *canzonette alla francese* in Italy. His description of the mad scene and its musical episode in *La pazzia d'Isabella* pre-dates by ten years both the publication of Chiabrera's *scherzi* and Monteverdi's fateful trip to Spa. Monteverdi's compositions must, therefore, be understood either as a codification of an existing style of performance, or, as is more likely, an adaptation of compositional

---

Tomlinson, *Monteverdi and the End of the Renaissance*; Ossi, 'Claudio Monteverdi's Concertato Technique'; id., 'Claudio Monteverdi's *Ordine novo*'.

[68] Monteverdi, *Canzonette* (*Tutte le opere*, x, ed. Malipiero), preface: 'li faccio sapere che se si havesse a considerare la cosa per questo verso, haverebbe non pochi argomenti in suo favore, mio fratello, in particolare per il canto alla francese in questo modo moderno che per le stampe da tre o quattro anni in qua si va mirando, hor sotto a parole de motetti, hor de madregali, hor di canzonette, & d'arie, chi fu il primo di lui che lo riportasse in Italia di quando venne da li bagni di Spà, l'anno 1599, & che incominciò a porlo sotto ad orationi lattine & a volgari nella nostra lingua, prima di lui? non fece questi scherzi all'hora?' The translation used here is based on that of Ossi, 'Claudio Monteverdi's *Ordine novo*', 272; see also Fabbri, *Monteverdi* (trans. Carter), 71.

technique to a particular style of poetry and method of delivery. And indeed, Monteverdi's identification of the French style in his *Ottavo libro de madrigali* with a method of singing in a full voice ('cantato a voce piena, alla francese') appears to confirm this conclusion. It is the most concise definition of the term, and it may well indicate a style of singing suited to the stage. This seems to be the inference also in a letter written by Francesco Rasi in 1600, where he complains that his student Sabina will lose her ability to sing in the Italian style, adopting instead the ugly movements of the mouth and shoulders characteristic of the French style—movements that might result from singing loudly and with affective gestures.[69]

One might easily imagine Andreini in 1589 singing the narrative lines of songs like 'Io credèa che tra gli amanti' or 'Ecco l'Alba ruggiadosa' in a full voice and with affective gestures, and in so doing betraying the superiority of her models of imitation, the virtuous ordering of her mind, and the valour of her performance. The omnipresent anapests, in both poetic metre and implied musical inflection, together with the rigorous regularity of the poems' repeated strophes and half-strophes representing a hard yoke to which the singer must submit, here too, the actress might make a metaphorical display of her virtue. Variation of the melody, however, would also come into play, for Pavoni's diary highlights the variation of the mad scene, Andreini proving her valour by performing the trope 'so naturally and with so many eccentricities'.

Isabella's madness, and the comedy with it, ended in her oration on the topic of love. As with the comedienne's songs, we do not know the words Andreini used to delight and astound her Florentine audience, although several of her published monologues offer speeches on this *soggetto*, and we might imagine the actress intoning something along the lines of the already cited paragraph from 'La forza d'Amore'. Andreini's speeches about Love (as she writes in Christine of Lorraine's epithalamium, 'true Love, sainted Love') identify the god as the source of musical and poetic inspiration, achieved within a pure and undefiled sanctuary wherein 'Love holds the keys to everything enclosed by heaven and earth' ('Amor tien le chiavi di quanto chiude la Terra e 'l Cielo').[70] Andreini's metaphorical name among the members of the Accademia degli Intenti of Pavia, 'l'Accesa', reminds us of the amorous inspiration that fires her eloquence.

[69] See Fabbri, *Monteverdi* (trans. Carter), 71.
[70] I. Andreini, 'Delle lodi d'Amore', *Lettere*, fo. 120^{r-v}; ead., in Marotti and Romei, *La professione del teatro*, 192.

The opening paragraphs of 'La forza d'Amore' speak to her obligation to perform in this vein, almost as if she were speaking directly to Christine of Lorraine from the stage:

> The obligation I have to Love for having ignited me with such a noble flame and for having made me the servant of such rare beauty as yours, my most gentle Signora, is incredible no less because of the ineffability of your valour, which is so great that it alone is its own equal.
>
> Love is no less potent than wise and no less wise than good. He is truly the first among the gods, who themselves know and confess his invincible power: power that in heaven, on earth, in the sea, and in Hell is feared more than any other.[71]

In this monologue, the dynamic of love is shorn, finally, of its associations with abduction, domination, and madness. The experience of the poet, enacted in Andreini's comedy, is almost entirely omitted here in favour of its ultimate, idyllic portrayal of the harmony and concord resulting from the poet's implied dementia and its indebtedness to the valour of its audience, just as the sixth intermedio washes away the turmoil of transcendence, leaving only the harmonious Eden that celestial inspiration brings. This metaphor of divine madness, together with the sensual and pastoral themes outlined above, binds Andreini's performance of *La pazzia d'Isabella* to the other contests discussed in this chapter. The song competition rehearsed in Andreini's *Mirtilla* and its author's performance of the madwoman the following spring both conclude in a pastoral homage to Love that offers up music-making as a Neoplatonic yearning to approach the Harmony of the Spheres. And in both works, celestial harmony is embodied in the form of a canzonetta—a form that imposes a structural yoke on its singers. Moreover, Filli's and Mirtilla's pastoral contest and *La pazzia d'Isabella* together demonstrate the metaphorical significance of representations of the wind. The 'breath of inspiration ravishing a virgin soul' that Boreas brings to the rape of Oreithyia might apply as well to the figure of Zephyrus in Opico's verdant grove. And it is a credit to Andreini's artistic elegance that, for her, Zephyrus served both the Neoplatonic allegory and the practical musical requirements of the scene.

---

[71] I. Andreini, *Lettere*, 'La forza d'Amore', in Marotti and Romei, *La professione del teatro*, 171–2: 'L'obligo ch'io tengo ad Amore per avermi acceso di così nobil fiamma e per avermi fatto servo di così rara bellezza, com'è la vostra, gentilissima Signora mia, è incredibile non meno che sia indicibile il suo valore, il qual è così grande ch'è solo a se medesimo eguale.

Amor è non meno potente che savio, e non men savio che buono; ed è veramente il primo fra gl'Iddii, i quali conoscono e confessano anch'essi la sua invincibil possanza: possanza che in Cielo, in Terra, nel Mare e nell'Inferno è più d'ogn'altra temuta.'

Finally, what better description is there for the act of performing in competition than that of the Phaedran charioteer, whose horses, representing two opposing wills, are bound together by a common harness? Binding themselves by the common yoke of shared dramatic and musical genres, comediennes' submission to the emulative impulse raises both performers to the heights of celestial song.

3

Behold, now there are Amazons of Learning

IN 1601, the year the Conte de Fuentes petitioned Vincenzo Gonzaga to send Isabella Andreini and her company to Pavia to perform for the negotiators of the treaty between France and Savoy, the Duke of Mantua set out for Hungary on his third campaign against the Turks, and academic interests in Mantuan music and theatre came to a boil. The comedians left for Milan just before Easter. Vincenzo left to join the papal troops in Kanizsa in July. And Claudio Monteverdi, in the first flush of contention with Giovan Maria Artusi over the compositional tenets of the *seconda prattica*, prepared himself in the autumn of 1601 to succeed Benedetto Pallavicino as *maestro di cappella* at Vincenzo's court. His music garnered the interest of the new Accademia degli Intrepidi in Ferrara, which inaugurated its activities at the end of August with a speech by Guidubaldo Bonarelli and the ground-breaking for construction of a new theatre.[1] Andreini, riding the crest of her fame as the *prima donna innamorata* of the Duke's comedians (as her troupe had now become), in June initiated a poetic exchange with the members of the Accademia Filarmonica of Verona.[2] From November into the new year, she broadened her intellectual horizons further with an epistolary correspondence with the Belgian academician Erycius Puteanus, then living in Milan (Doc. 42).

In the last week of Advent, when Vincenzo Gonzaga returned to Mantua from the battle of Kanizsa, he recalled Andreini and her troupe—who were in Pavia as late as Christmas eve—and the Duke's comedians

---

[1] Fabbri, *Monteverdi*, 57; Newcomb, 'Alfonso Fontanelli and the Ancestry of the Seconda Pratica Madrigal', 50.

[2] Andreini exchanged encomiastic sonnets with various members of the Accademia Filarmonica, and one of her poems, 'Quel ciel, che sovra il liquefatto argenti', was read out in a meeting of the membership on 22 June 1601. The Academy responded officially, charging Cristoforo Ferrari to write a sonnet in reply. His poem, 'Mentre pien di stupor l'Adige intento', was read in the Academy's meeting of 29 June. Verona, Archivio dell'Accademia Filarmonica, Registro 41: Atti 1601–1605, fos. 54–5.

were again at the Gonzaga court by the beginning of February, where Monteverdi had remained throughout the campaign. Staying on in Mantua through Easter, the actors did not leave the city again until just after Monteverdi was made a citizen by ducal decree—an honour conferred on Francesco Andreini the summer before.[3]

Isabella Andreini's successes in 1601 culminated in two major academic achievements: she was invited to become a member of the Accademia degli Intenti of Pavia, the academy to which Puteanus belonged, and in September the publishers Girolamo Bordone and Pietromartire Locarni commemorated the event by publishing her first book of *Rime*.[4] For both Andreini and Monteverdi, whose fourth book of madrigals appeared in 1603, it had been about a decade since their last publications, and it seems momentous that both performers' unpublished works garnered such intense academic attention in 1600 and 1601—moreover, that both felt compelled after such long silence to put those works into print.[5] Andreini's and Monteverdi's mutual dedication to creating avant-garde theatre, combined with Vincenzo's enthusiasm for their experiments and his desires to ensure their permanent fealty to the Gonzaga court through conferral of citizenship, made Mantua the new Parnassus of European music and theatre, outshining the fallen splendour of the Ferrarese court and even the radiance of the Grand Duchy of Tuscany, as reflected in its lavish entertainments of 1589.

Both the intellectual foment concerning music and theatre at the Mantuan court and the treaty negotiations to which the Duke's comedians had been called were continuations of events set in motion in 1598 and 1599 during the monumental passages through Italy of Albert and Margherita of Austria. Margherita and Philip III of Spain were married by Pope Clement VIII in Ferrara in November 1598, and Albert of Austria wed the Infanta Isabella in Milan the following July. Commemoration of the new alliance between Austria and Spain took shape during Albert's

[3] Francesco Andreini, born in Pistoia, became a Mantuan citizen on 6 June 1601, and Claudio Monteverdi, Cremonese by birth, on 10 Apr. 1602; see ASMN, Notarile, notaio Forti Siniforiano, 1607, 7 June, and Fabbri, *Monteverdi* (trans. Carter), 56.

[4] For information on the founding, rules, and membership of the Accademia degli Intenti, which merged in the 17th c. with the Accademia degli Affidati, see Maylender, *Storia delle accademie d'Italia*, s.v. 'Intenti' and 'Affidati'; Spelta, *La curiosa, et dilettevole aggionta*, 170; Comi, *Ricerche storiche sull'Accademia degli Affidati*; and *Frammenti storici dell'Argo ticinese*, ed. Vidari, 154.

[5] Andreini's only previous publication was the pastoral play *Mirtilla* in 1588, and Monteverdi's third book of madrigals had appeaed in 1592.

and Margherita's passages in a variety of musical and theatrical events, including a memorable performance of Battista Guarini's *Il pastor fido* in Mantua, the construction of a new theatre in the Sforza palace in Milan, called the 'Salone Margherita', and the performance in the new theatre of Giovan Battista Visconte's *Armenia*, with intermedii by Camillo Schiafenati.[6]

The Mantuan court's involvement in these Imperial alliances with Spain was consanguine: as the son of Eleonora of Austria, Vincenzo Gonzaga was Margherita's cousin, and in this capacity he organized the celebrations for her wedding. The Imperial court's presence in Italy and the newly strengthened alliance between Austria and Spain that resulted from the two marriages engendered a large-scale realignment of European political power. In Italy, this reorganization encompassed a stronger presence of papal authority in the north due to the excommunication of Cesare d'Este and the ensuing devolution of Ferrara to papal rule. It was further characterized by the signing of the Treaty of Vervins by Henri IV and Philip II on 2 May 1598, which effectively ended Spain's nine-year intervention in France.[7] Subsequent treaties relative to the Peace of Vervins centred on control of Saluzzo, the marquisate adjacent to the Mantuan domain of Monferrato, and included the negotiations held in Tortona in 1600 between Henri IV and Carlo Emanuele of Savoy, mediated by the papal legate Pietro Aldobrandini. Here, Isabella Andreini, Pedrolino, and their colleagues performed not only for the treaty's negotiators, but for the newly-wed Maria de' Medici as well.[8] The turmoil regarding Mantua's neighbours to the west, together with the Duchy's new Roman neighbours to the east, created an exacting political situation

---

[6] Various contemporary descriptions of the entries of and festivities for Albert and Margherita were published, including the *Relatione dell'entrata*, the *Relatione de' ricevimenti*, and *La felicissima entrata*. According to Vigilio, *La insalata* (ed. Ferrari and Mozzarelli), 84–8, the Austrian assembly entered Mantua on Friday, 20 Nov. 1598, and heard the performance of *Il pastor fido* on the subsequent Sunday evening. In Milan, payments for the construction of the Salone Margherita are recorded from 2 Nov. 1598 to 29 Jan. 1599 in the ASM, Registro delle Cancellerie, s. XXII, n. 42, fos. 19^r, 37^r, 41^v, and 60^v; Margherita, however, suspended all festivities in January out of respect for Philip II's death; see *Storia di Milano*, xii. 834. Celebrations for the wedding of Albert and Isabella took place in July 1599, and a detailed account of the performance of *Armenia* may be found in Negri, *Le gratie d'amore*.

[7] For an outline of the impact of the events of 1597–1602 on Vincenzo's reign, see S. Maffei, *Gli annali di Mantova*, 920–9; an extensive, although not always reliable, history of Milan appears in the monumental *Storia di Milano*. For information on the Treaty of Vervins, see Elliott, *Europe Divided*, 339–66.

[8] Mamone, *Firenze e Parigi*, 135.

for Vincenzo Gonzaga, one which required dextrous handling of old and new allegiances. His comedians' performances on the occasions when European powers met are a testament to the importance of theatre as a tool for bringing its auditors into harmony with one another and to the trust endowed in Andreini and her colleagues to ply their craft well at delicate, stressful times.

Vincenzo Gonzaga's campaign to increase Mantua's political standing among the powers of Austria, France, and Spain at this time included a programme to bolster the perception of his court's power and prestige through its indulgence in expensive and luxurious court spectacles and its patronage of the actors and musicians who conspired to create to them. His administration of fealty through the conferral of citizenship created strong bonds of obligation between the Gonzaga and the Monteverdi and Andreini families that in turn fortified the musical and theatrical vitality of the Mantuan court. Citizenship established a mutual covenant between Vincenzo and his subjects wherein the Duke assumed responsibility for the well-being, not only of the men who were now citizens by his decree, but of their family and heirs as well, in return for the family's fidelity to his court and authority. Monteverdi on numerous occasions would take advantage of this extension of citizenship to his sons to urge Vincenzo to remember his patronymical obligations towards them. In comparison with the artistic patronage that had been exercised by Alfonso II d'Este in Ferrara, where women of the *concerto delle donne* were granted temporary positions at court with the opportunity of improving their social standing through marriage, Vincenzo's strategy of granting citizenship to the head of an artistic family created a bond that was stronger, more wide-ranging, and not as heavy a drain on the infrastructure of the court.[9]

Benefits of Mantuan citizenship included the ability to enter and leave the city without permission or taxation and the right to trade and to own property within the duchy—a privilege the Andreini family began to enjoy in June of 1607 when Francesco purchased the villa in Castelbelforte in which he died in 1624—a house he never shared with his beloved wife Isabella. Prior to 1607, the family occupied a home in the Contrada dell'Aquila, located near the Palazzo Ducale. Francesco's and Isabella's son Giovan Battista and daughter-in-law Virginia later added to the family estates two houses and arable land, also in Castelbelforte,

---

[9] For Monteverdi's appeals to Vincenzo Gonzaga on behalf of his sons, see *The Letters of Claudio Monteverdi*, trans. Stevens, 68–70, 217, 238–42, 247–8, 304–5, 311–12, 287–94. For information on Alfonso II's patronage of the *concerto delle donne*, see Newcomb, *The Madrigal at Ferrara*.

known as the Case del Mandragola. The property is impressive: the expansive foundations of the two houses still stand at the end of the road named for them, and the surrounding lands support a dairy farm.[10] Tristano Martinelli also owned property in Castelbelforte, sold to him by Virginia Andreini in January 1608, just a few months prior to her memorable performance as Arianna.[11]

Battista Guarini's *Il pastor fido* stands at the centre not only of the wedding festivities for Margherita of Austria and Phillip III of Spain but of the last literary quarrel of the sixteenth century. The debate between Guarini and his detractors concerning the author's adherence to Aristotelian poetics in turn inspired exchanges about musical composition and the representation of women that focused attention on members of Mantua's musical and theatrical elite, most notably Claudio Monteverdi and Isabella Andreini. Criticism of the pastoral tragicomedy began even before the play was published in 1590, but rose again with renewed vigour after its performance in Mantua in 1598, and especially with the publication of Faustino Summo's *Discorsi poetici* in 1600.[12] Contemporary descriptions of the performance emphasize the expense and grandeur of its spectacle. The play and its intermedi, which presented the tale of the wedding of Mercury and Philology, were 'beautiful and splendid', and the event was commemorated in a sumptuous two-volume German edition of Guarini's tragicomedy and the intermedi that accompanied it. The intermedi were filled with music and machinery, and additional musical performances were inserted between each act of *Il pastor fido* and the intermedio that followed it. The prologue, enacted by a trio of women in the guises of Venus, Hespero, and Giulia, included the performance of a madrigal sung 'in honour of Her Majesty the Queen Bride, demonstrating that heaven, by way of this Royal marriage, had procured the peace of the world'.[13] Ferrante Persia's description of the drama, however, is disappointingly vague in regard to

---

[10] ASMN, Notarile, notaio Forti Siniforiano, 1607, 7 June; notaio Dall'Oglio Arsenio, 1616, 7 Mar.; notaio Dall'Oglio Arsenio, 1616, 30 Aug.; and G. B. Andreini's letter to Ferdinando Gonzaga on 3 Aug. 1616: ASMN, Autografi, b. 10, fo. 27^{r-v}, transcribed in *Comici dell'arte: corrispondenze*, ed. Ferrone et al., 109–10. Giovan Battista's and Virginia's son Pietro Enrico inherited the Case del Mandragola in 1655; see ASMN, Notarile, notaio Bartolini Lodovico, 1655, 5 Jan.

[11] ASMN, Notarile, notaio Forti Siniforiano, 1608, 21 Jan.

[12] Weinberg, *A History of Literary Criticism*, 1093.

[13] Achille Neri, 'Gli "intermezzi" del "Pastor fido"', 407, citing Giovan Battista Grillo, *Breve trattato di quanto successe alla Maestà della Regina D. Margarita d'Austria NS dalla città di Trento fine d'Alemagna, e principio d'Italia fino alla Città di Genova* (Naples: Costantino Vitale, 1599).

the performance, naming none of the artists who participated, nor discussing any of the music in other than the most general terms.

The next evening, His Highness had *Il pastor fido*, the tragicomic pastoral by Cavalier Battista Guarini, performed in the usual theatre of the castle with the fable of the wedding of Mercury and Philology, symbolizing the wedding of His Majesty, for intermedi. The one and the others were most beautiful and splendid, as much for the great expense of the costumes as for the scenery and the great number of machines that were used in the intermedi, of which I will send Your Lordship a brief summary at the earliest opportunity. The spectators in the said theatre, apart from the families of the Queen, the Archduchess, the Archduke, and the Condestabile, one might say comprised nearly all the nobility of Italy, coming from Venice, Florence, Genoa, Verona, Brescia, and other nearby cities in order to see a performance that everywhere was experiencing such acclaim, and which was heard and seen with much satisfaction by all, and by the Queen and her mother, for whom a compendious translation in German was prepared of all that was recited and performed, which was given to them at the beginning of the work, bound in two separate volumes.[14]

Giovan Battista Grillo's account of the intermedi, the *Breve trattato di quanto successe*, similarly lacks notification of the entertainment's actors and musicians, referring to all by the names of their characters.[15] As seen in the chronicles commemorating the Medici wedding of 1589, discussed in Chapter 2, comedians' participation in court festivities is rarely documented, but the descriptions of entertainments for the nuptials celebrated in Mantua in 1598 are particularly arid.

Although documentation concerning the actors and musicians who collaborated on the November 1598 performance of *Il pastor fido* is scarce, it is tantalizing to think that both Andreini and Monteverdi may have been

---

[14] Marciana, Misc. 425.14, fo. 4ᵛ: 'La sera poi S.A. fece rappresentare nel solito suo Teatro del Castello, il Pastor Fido Tragicomedia Pastorale del Cavaliere Battista Guerino, con la favola delle nozze di Mercurio, & Filologia, significanti figuratamente quelle di S.M. per intermedij, l'una, & gl'altri bellissimi, & pomposi, sì per la molta spesa de' vestiti, come anco per l'apparato, & gran numero delle machine, che intervennero ne gl'intermedij, i quali con la prima occasione manderò a V.S. in breve sommario. Fù spettatrice in detto Teatro, oltre le famiglie della Regina, Arciduchessa, Arciduca, & Contestabile, quasi si può dire tutta la nobiltà d'Italia, concorsa da Vinegia, Firenze, Genova, Verona, Brescia, & altre Città circonvicine, per vedere rappresentatione, che portava così celebre grido per ogni parte, & che fù sentita, & veduta con molta sodisfattione da tutti, & dalla Regina, & madre ancora, alle quali si era preparata una compendiosa tradottione in lingua Alemanna di quanto fù recitato, & rappresentato, che fù loro data nel principiare dell'opera, legata in due libretti separatamente.'

[15] The text of the intermedi is given in Neri, 'Gli "intermezzi" del "Pastor fido"'.

involved. Andreini and her troupe performed for Archduke Ferdinand in Bologna during the summer, and the troupe was recalled to Mantua shortly thereafter by Vincenzo's order. The Austrian assembly, travelling via Ferrara for the nuptials, followed them in a few months' time. The comedians then appeared again at the request of Archduke Albert, at his own wedding celebrations in Milan the following July.[16] One can only speculate that Vincenzo Gonzaga recalled Andreini and her company—known favourites of the Archduke and Margherita—to Mantua in order to secure their participation in the November festivities.

Monteverdi's potential contribution to the *Il pastor fido* performance is similarly elusive. His settings of excerpts from the play bore the brunt of Artusi's denunciations of his compositional technique, which took the form of a dialogue between the fictive Austrian, 'Luca'—presumably a personification of one of the Archduke's or Margherita's courtiers—and his Italian counterpart, 'Vario' of Arezzo. And although the madrigals were unpublished when Artusi wrote his diatribe, he related that 'Luca' had heard them at the house of Antonio Goretti in Ferrara on 16 November, during the celebrations organized in conjunction with the royal wedding.[17] Whatever Andreini's and Monteverdi's contributions to the Mantuan festivities in 1598, they were both in the immediate vicinity and in the Duke's employ, and the work they produced during that time gave a startling new look to Mantuan music and theatre, the intellectual repercussions of which arrived in full force with the turn of the new century.

Both the argument between Artusi and Monteverdi over compositional techniques used to set dramatic texts to music and Andreini's epistolary exchange with Puteanus on the nature of women's intellectual creativity assumed appearances familiar to Italian artists, courtiers, and scholars, which, writ large, enunciated the broader philosophical conflict between

---

[16] Datio Spinola, a Mantuan functionary in Bologna, wrote in a letter of 9 June 1598 to excuse the comedians from immediately obeying Vincenzo's command to return to Mantua because they were under temporary obligation to the Archduke; see ASMN, Gonzaga, b. 1166, fos. 317–18. Payment made in Aug. 1599 to Pedrolino and his company, which included Isabella Andreini, 'for performances for the Infanta and Archduke Albert' is recorded in ASM, Registro delle Cancellerie, s. XXII, n. 42, fo. 232^r. An important, although rarely mentioned, source concerning *Pastor fido* is Ingegneri, *Della poesia rappresentativa*, which the author dedicated to Vincenzo Gonzaga in commemoration of the 1598 performance of Guarini's play and which mentions Andreini's *Mirtilla* in its prologue; for Ingegneri's letter of dedication to Vincenzo, see ASMN, Gonzaga, b. 1261, unnumbered pages, and for Vincenzo's response, ASMN, Gonzaga, b. 2156, fos. 327–8.

[17] Fabbri, *Monteverdi* (trans. Carter), 34–6.

humanism as an educational system and a humanistic art.[18] Puteanus and Artusi adopted the postures of well-educated scholars trained in the tradition of Guarino of Verona—the famed fifteenth-century forebear of the author of *Il pastor fido*—who codified a highly influential system of humanist education in Ferrara in the 1430s, 1440s, and 1450s. At the basis of Guarino's system stood the impassive assertion that rhetorical studies prepared the student for life within the Renaissance court. This position is echoed, in turn, in the writings of Guarino's followers, as may be seen in the works of Angelo Poliziano and in Ludovico Carbone's funeral oration for his teacher in 1460; here, the equation between eloquent speech and the nobility and virtue characteristic of 'the blameless life' is made explicit:

It was shameful how little the men of Ferrara knew of letters before the arrival of Guarino. There was no one who even understood the basic principles of grammar, who understood the propriety and impact of words, who was able to interpret the poets, let alone who was learned in the art of oratory, who professed rhetoric, who was competent to speak gravely and elegantly and dared to do so in public.... No one was considered noble, no one as leading a blameless life, unless he had followed Guarino's courses. So that in a short space of time our citizens were led out of the deepest shadows into a true and brilliant light, and all suddenly became eloquent, learned, elegant and felicitous of speech.[19]

Subscription to this belief in the relationship between rhetoric and life often generated an unyielding insistence on decorum and the rules appropriate to expressive composition, as Artusi demonstrated in his indictment of Monteverdi's 'unprecedented' and 'unnatural' uses of dissonance in the five-part madrigals heard on that fateful evening in November 1598. Artusi's humanistic training, accrued through years of repetitive exercise,

[18] The late 16th c. was rife with conflicts of this type, most pronounced in literary criticism, with the quarrels over Ariosto's *Orlando furioso*, Tasso's *Gerusalemme liberata*, and especially Guarini's *Il pastor fido* and its attendant definition of the new genre, pastoral tragicomedy. For an excellent overview of the literature on poetics, see Weinberg, *A History of Literary Criticism*. In the late 16th and early 17th cc., debates crystallized into Ciceronian and anti-Ciceronian camps, the anti-Ciceronian faction led by Puteanus' teacher, Justus Lipsius. For arguments concerning the Artusi–Monteverdi controversy, see most notably, Palisca, 'The Artusi–Monteverdi Controversy'; Carter, 'Artusi, Monteverdi, and the Poetics of Modern Music'; Cusick, 'Gendering Modern Music'; and Ossi, 'Claudio Monteverdi's *Ordine novo*'.

[19] *Ludovici Carbonis Ferrariensis . . . oratio habita in funere praestantissimi oratoris et poetae Guarini Veronensis*, in *Prosatori Latini del Quattrocento*, ed. Garin, 381–417, as cited in Grafton and Jardine, *From Humanism to the Humanities*, 34. The equation of rhetoric and successful entry into the social order is axiomatic to Renaissance humanism; in addition to Grafton and Jardine, see Grendler, *Schooling in Renaissance Italy*.

compelled him to grant priority to the rules of pure counterpoint over new, interdisciplinary ideals grounded in the representation of affect. As Artusi states in his treatise of 1600,

> Do you not know that all the arts and sciences have been brought under rules by scholars of the past and that the first elements, rules, and precepts on which they are founded have been handed down to us so that, as long as there is no deviation from them, one person shall be able to understand what another says or does? And just as, to avoid confusion, it is not permitted to every schoolmaster to change the rules bequeathed by Guarino, nor to every poet to put a long syllable in verse in place of a short one, nor to every arithmetician to corrupt the processes and proofs which are proper to that art, so it is not permitted to everyone who strings notes together to deprave and corrupt music . . .[20]

In short, he did not view music as a component of rhetorical composition, but rather as an analogue to it. Monteverdi's standing in the inner circle of Mantua's theatrical elite, however, together with librettists and performers like Alessandro Striggio, Ottavio Rinuccini, and the Andreini family, gave him rein to consider the musician's art as part of a greater whole, in which the texts of his madrigals and their dramatic impact—while they may have been allowed to detract from the integrity of his counterpoint in certain instances—strengthened the madrigals' overall rhetorical designs. In this sense, Monteverdi's music, like the early modern schoolboy's exercise in composing laments patterned on classical models of noble women *in extremis*, represents the exertion of emotional self-control through the rapid reining in of brief outbursts of excess, bringing them under the authority of the composition's prevailing rationality, which was guaranteed by the formulaic use of figures of words. That Monteverdi translated the humanist's figures of words into 'figures of music' reveals the comprehension and subtlety of his craft.[21]

As Suzanne Cusick has pointed out in reference to Monteverdi's much studied *Cruda Amarilli* and its famous dissonant canto entrance at the words 'Ahi lasso!', 'Artusi's attack . . . focuses on the errors and unnatural acts of the highest sounding part, which, because it is generated by the lower one, ought to have obeyed the latter's desire for consonant

---

[20] Translation after Strunk, *The Baroque Era* (ed. Murata), 25.

[21] For a detailed treatment of the history of schoolboys' exercises in composing and reciting noble women's laments, see Woods, 'Rape and the Pedagogical Rhetoric of Sexual Violence'; Grendler, *Schooling in Renaissance Italy*; and Grafton and Jardine, *From Humanism to the Humanities*. For a more substantive discussion of Ciceronian rhetoric as it relates to Monteverdi's *Lamento d'Arianna*, see my 'Weeping at the Water's Edge'.

harmony.'²² Drawing on the foundation of Susan McClary's 'Constructions of Gender in Monteverdi's Dramatic Music' (ch. 2 of *Feminine Endings*), Cusick focuses her own argument on the gendered aspects of the discourse, emphasizing the time-worn comparison of *serva* and *padrona*, and showing how Artusi's criticisms of the composer's skill in writing polyphony might also be read not only as attacks on Monteverdi's masculinity, but on the overall effeminacy of modern music:

> This metaphor is, however, only a tiny part of a complex fabric of explicit and implicit gender references in Artusi's several attacks on the imperfections of modern music, references that constitute an attempt to discredit modern music as unnatural, feminine, and feminizing of both its practitioners and its listeners. Read against the gender rhetoric of Artusi's work, the Monteverdi brothers' famous reply can be understood as a defense of the composer's masculinity that acknowledges and even reaffirms the femininity of music itself.²³

Artusi's was a formulaic intellectual gambit, however, based on rhetorical tropes handed down through several generations of Renaissance scholars and cannot, therefore, be read as an unmediated response to Monteverdi's music. Moreover, because of the basic perception of education as the preparation for adult life at court, Artusi figured Monteverdi's compositional technique within an allegorical context that centres more on conceptions of coming of age, the adoption of the habits of a good citizen, and the submission of the individual to social convention.²⁴ Elucidation of the pedagogical role of gendered constructions like Artusi's and their tenacity over time may be seen in a letter Guarino wrote to Isotta Nogarola, chastising her for an unchecked expression of anger and frustration:

---

²² Cusick, 'Gendering Modern Music', 18.
²³ Ibid. 3.
²⁴ Note, for example, that Cusick's Table 1, labelled 'Gendered oppositions in late-Renaissance thought', which (erroneously, I would argue) equates man with masculinity and woman with femininity, is derived solely from sources concerning the role of women in Renaissance society rather than cultural constructions of order and disorder, and solely from modern sources at that: Ginevra Conti Odorisio, *Donna e società nel Seicento* (Rome, 1979); Ian Maclean, *The Renaissance Notion of Woman* (Cambridge, 1980); Constance Jordan, *Renaissance Feminism* (Ithaca, NY, 1990); and Evelyne Berriot-Salvadore, 'Il discorso della medicina e della scienza', in Natalie Z. Davis and Arletter Farge, *Storia delle donne* (Rome, 1991). For well-documented studies of gender roles assigned to pre-pubescent boys, for example, see Rocke, *Forbidden Friendships*, and Saslow, *The Poetry of Michelangelo* and *Ganymede in the Renaissance*. For a basic study on the use of the Achillead in the humanist classroom, see Woods, 'Rape and the Pedagogical Rhetoric of Sexual Violence'.

This evening I received your letters, full of complaints and accusations, in which you render me uncertain as to whether I should feel pain for you or congratulate myself. For when I saw fit to give my attention to that outstanding intellect of yours, with its attendant embellishments of learning, I was accustomed besides to express strongly my opinion that you were manly of spirit, that nothing could happen which you would not bear with a courageous and indomitable spirit. Now, however, you show yourself so cast down, humiliated and truly womanish that I am able to perceive nothing which accords with my previous magnificent opinion of you.[25]

In addition to their uses as correctives for anger and emotional excess, Guarino's letters to Nogarola, together with Angelo Poliziano's letters to Cassandra Fedele and Puteanus' to Andreini, suggest that the concept of the heroic woman who wielded an Amazonian command of oratory, like her classical predecessors Cassandra and Penthesilea, fascinated early modern scholars. Expressions of this idolization of the eloquent woman emerged not only in humanists' letters and their advocacy of such women in their academies, but also in the widespread rise of commedia dell'arte actresses in the 1570s and in the configuration of a new kind of aristocratic performing ensemble in the 1570s and 1580s—the *concerto delle donne*. As Anthony Newcomb has shown, Ariosto, too, publicized the esteemed ideal of the heroic woman in his *Orlando furioso* and placed the image within a historical continuum; the epic begins:

> Le donne son venute in eccellenza
> di ciascun'arte ove hanno posto cura;
> e qualunque all'istorie abbia avvertenza,
> ne sente ancor la fama non oscura.
> Se 'l mondo n'è gran tempo stato senza,
> non pero sempre il mal influsso dura;
> e forse ascosi han lor debiti onori
> l'invidia o il non saper degli scrittori.

(Women have arrived at excellence in every art in which they have striven; in their chosen fields their renown is apparent to anyone who studies the history books. If the world has long remained unaware of their achievements, this sad state of affairs is only transitory; perhaps envy concealed the honors due to them, or perhaps the ignorance of historians.)[26]

---

[25] Guarino, *Epistolario di Guarino Veronese*, 3 vols., ed. R. Sabbadini (Venice, 1915–19), ii. 306–7; translation given in Grafton and Jardine, *From Humanism to the Humanities*, 52.
[26] Newcomb, 'Courtesans, Muses, or Musicians?', 90. Newcomb more accurately associates the rise of female singers in Italy, which Cusick attaches to the formation of the *concerto*

In politics as in literature, noble women's roles gained significance in early modern society as marriage became one of the primary avenues for negotiating diplomatic relations among courts. Espoused women like Margherita of Austria became permanent representatives of their paternal dynasties at their husbands' courts, assuming a diplomatic function parallel to that of official ambassadors who, paid out of the chancellery, were charged to take up residence in a foreign ruler's domain and to maintain their patron's (read, father's) interests there. Wives' ambassadorial functions, although unofficial and unpaid, were no less critical to the exercise of international diplomacy, as Maria de' Medici's often contentious relationship to her husband's and son's courts, especially in regard to French policies concerning Spain, so powerfully demonstrates.[27] The relationship of a noble wife to her father's court took effect also in matters of artistic patronage. As shown in Chapter 2, Medici support of the Andreini family extended to Mantua and to Paris when Maria and Eleonora de' Medici married and relocated their courts to those cities.

Within this context of diplomacy by marriage, when the realignment of European political forces signalled by Margherita's marriage to Philip III gave urgency to the arts of diplomacy and international communication, the perception of humanist rhetoric as the marker of adulthood and good citizenship endowed the practice of oratory and oratorical composition with phenomenal significance. Artusi took this concept one step further and applied it to musical as well as rhetorical composition. For him, the rules of conduct embodied within the compositional process contributed to a nascent nationalist sensibility, wherein the Arezzan Vario demonstrated the good and noble face of the Italian court to the foreigner Luca of Austria.

Humanist conceptions of the noble or heroic woman, however, resulted in a tension between representations of art and nature as inherently masculine or feminine traits. Artusi's arguments show evidence of a backlash against this burgeoning feminine agency in his insistence that the feminine be subsumed within a dominant masculine frame that he identified as 'natural' because he perceived it as normative. Not all scholars subscribed to such rigid constructions, however, and elsewhere, as in the

delle donne in Ferrara in the 1580s, with the earlier appearances of singing actresses, such as Vincenza Armani, in the 1560s.

[27] Maria de' Medici, good citizen of her father's court, upheld Florentine support of Spain, and in 1619 and 1620 staged two revolts against the French crown's anti-Iberian policies. See Yates, *Astraea*, 209–11.

literary quarrels about Ariosto's *Orlando furioso* and Tasso's *Gerusalemme liberata*, nature and truth are portrayed as feminine and the falsity of art as masculine. This late Renaissance tension between conceptions of nature and art as either feminine or masculine is nowhere more apparent than in early modern women's constructions of self and in the styles of theatrical performance practised by Andreini and her peers.

Men's self-fashionings, most notably recorded in Stephen Greenblatt's writings on the works of Sir Thomas More, Edmund Spenser, and others, did not usually broach the topic of art versus nature because men's authority depended on the perception of wealth, position, and even virtue, but not on their sex.[28] Andreini, however, invoked a dichotomy between art and nature in her compositions and performances that constructed a hermaphroditic persona credible within both masculine and feminine authoritative spheres.[29] Formulation of such a persona was complicated, for it relied on tortuous intellectual arguments regarding the aesthetic evaluation of poetry and art, which might be posited in either a negative or a positive light. The letter that inspired Guarino's chastisement of Nogarola speaks directly to this point:

You have treated me wretchedly, and have shown as little consideration for me as if I had never been born. For I am ridiculed throughout the city, those of my own condition deride me. I am attacked on all sides: the asses inflict their bites on me, the oxen attack me with their horns (Plautus). Even if I am most deserving of this outrage, it is unworthy of you to inflict it. What have I done to be thus despised by you, revered Guarino?[30]

The question was not one of *attaining* social authority, but of *trading* one form of authority for another, and Nogarola's letter demonstrates that the effort often outweighed the effect. As we shall see, Andreini's self-fashioning similarly gained her, in Puteanus' estimation, only the status of a Penthesilea—an impressive icon, but nothing more.

---

[28] Greenblatt, *Renaissance Self-fashioning*. An interesting feminist response to Greenblatt's study may be found in Marguerite Waller, 'The Empire's New Clothes: Refashioning the Renaissance', in Sheila Fisher and Janet E. Halley (eds.), *Seeking the Woman in Late Medieval and Renaissance Writings* (Knoxville: University of Tennessee Press, 1989), 160–83.

[29] For a thorough discussion of such hermaphroditic constructions, see Jordan, *Renaissance Feminism*, 134–247. As Susan McClary and others have noted, even women invested with social and political power re-fashioned their public images in accordance with prevailing masculine orders, and thus Elizabeth I of England was known as 'the Virgin Queen' and Catherine de' Medici as Artemisia; see McClary, *Feminine Endings*, 38 n. 13.

[30] Grafton and Jardine, *From Humanism to the Humanities*, 38.

Andreini's self-fashioning, like that of the men Greenblatt describes, was also closely tied to economics, and in this she differed from other women artists of the period. As an actress, she by necessity solicited benefaction, and so she does not fall under the same category of creative women as a Gaspara Stampa or a Laura Guidiccioni—noblewomen who wrote and published poetry but eschewed contracts and monetary remuneration. Andreini's social position more closely resembled that of musicians like Tarquinia Molza and Adriana Basile, for whom patronage was a fact of life and whose financial security depended on their artistic success.[31] This association of creativity with economics in certain respects links Andreini's self-fashioning to Artusi's mapping of economic household hierarchies onto musical composition. It also fosters a sense of awareness in the analysis of Andreini's works of stratagems pertaining to the differences between men's and women's social spaces—a compositional negotiation that is generally absent in the writings of noblewomen. In essence, Andreini engaged in creative as well as economic barter with her benefactors, whereas noblewomen like Stampa and Guidiccioni could perform similar creative roles within the circles of female court culture, with little or no regard for broaching the distance between themselves and masculine spheres of patronage.

The resulting image that Andreini upheld to the world's eye reflects a curious combination of both feminine and masculine attributes, which show the strain of pressure to publicize her various saleable talents. Indeed, her notoriety relied on the fact that she did not permanently trade her femininity for its masculine complement, but alternately exercised both forms of artistic authority, triumphing in the wit and élan that allowed her to move back and forth between them. On the one hand, authors depicted her as a childbearer, devoted wife, and Christian mother, and on the other, as a classical artist and creative authority. Nor do her writings suggest any attempt to resolve these juxtapositions or meld them into an androgynous unity; rather, they provide a comparative framework for her self-image within which masculine and feminine traits are

---

[31] Andreini often took charge of the Gelosi's financial negotiations, arranging performances and accepting payments on behalf of the troupe, as is documented in multiple sources, including ASM, Autografi, cart. 94, fasc. 3 and BNF, Généalogies d'Hozier, piece originale 59, 'Andriny'. Andreini presents a fascinating foil for female performers like the singing ladies of Ferrara, whose social and economic deficiencies were masked, as Newcomb has shown, in order to display the semblance of noble birth; see Newcomb, *The Madrigal at Ferrara*; for a more general discussion of patronage of female musicians, see also his 'Courtesans, Muses, or Musicians?'

contrasted equally. This unique polarity resonates with Andreini's profession as a commedia dell'arte actress, which invites reference to masking and unmasking and to the illusion of opposites embodied within a single image; no other actress of the time, however, including Vincenza Armani and Vittoria Piisimi, so successfully infused both life and work with this juxtaposition of humanistic virtue and the characteristics of Christian femininity.

The confrontation of Andreini's constructed self-image with contemporary humanistic culture gave birth to a variety of intellectual and artistic responses to her work that help to illustrate how she and other members of elite society integrated changing ideas about the meanings of courtliness, diplomacy, and women's roles into their preconceptions of the world and its hierarchies. These exchanges include the correspondence with Puteanus on the subject of women and rhetoric, musical settings of Andreini's lyric poems by various Italian composers, and intertextual imitations of dramatic topoi in plays concurrently within Andreini's performing repertory. In each case, the author or composer addressed the trans-gendering of Andreini's self-image in either words, actions, or music, as well as its play with ideas of truth, falsity, and art.

Puteanus contrasted masculine art and feminine nature in his letter to Andreini of 14 December 1601 (Doc. 42d).[32] He wrote in reply to the gift she had sent him—a copy of the book of poetry published that year in commemoration of her initiation in the Accademia degli Intenti, and which included a Latin encomium from Puteanus as the first poem in the volume. In the course of his epistle, Puteanus invoked the usual humanistic arguments associating masculinity with the literary and rhetorical arts, and with them traced an outline of Andreini that was overwhelmingly manly, as was Guarino's initial assessment of Nogarola. In ascribing masculine traits to a woman and to art rather than to nature, Puteanus' treatment of the masculine/feminine dichotomy contrasted with Artusi's in

---

[32] Puteanus, *Epistolarum fercula secunda* (Doc. 42d). Puteanus was a pupil of the renowned Belgian humanist Justus Lipsius at Louvain's Trilingual College. Studying history and philology, he received the Master of Arts degree in 1595, and two years later moved to Milan, where governor Juan Hernández de Velasco conferred on him a post in classical languages at the Palatine school. Puteanus wrote most of his own textbooks, and with his treatise *Modulata pallas* became known as a reformer of the science of music. He dedicated *Modulata pallas* to a student of Philippe de Monte, Gian Vincenzo Pinelli, who then invited the classicist to become his secretary in Padua, a position he accepted in 1599. In 1624, at the age of 50, Puteanus returned north to succeed Lipsius in the post of Headmaster and Director of Classical Letters at Louvain.

that Puteanus appeared to celebrate nature's undeniable femininity, whereas Artusi isolated the errant feminine outside the natural order. Puteanus' bold assertion of Andreini's artistic masculinity extended to the ridiculous end of calling her a man, but he palliated his conclusion by appealing to the predictable image of a community of Amazons and their legendary queen, Penthesilea, who was said to have been so beautiful, young, and valorous that Achilles bitterly regretted having triumphed over her in battle at the fall of Troy. He held up Andreini as a new Penthesilea who, although rhetorically masculine, possessed profound feminine beauty and strength, and, finally, he made an etymological pun on the name Andreini, alluding to the similarities between it and the Greek words *aner* and *andros*, to show that even Andreini's name betrayed her inherent manliness. On the surface, and contrary to the theories advanced by McClary and Cusick regarding the framing of women in early modern art, Puteanus here astonishingly appears to have placed masculine art within a feminine frame.

That such eloquence, that such learning should fall to the part of a woman! Where does that sex, which is mighty in writing, which sweats in public declamation, which grows old in literary studies, where does it show itself stronger than in you? Behold, now there are Amazons of learning, and they have their own Penthesilea! Shall I not call you by the name Andreina with good reason and compare you to men? It has been implanted in women by nature to be able to speak, but in you to be able to speak well, whence it arises that by correcting a feminine vice you surpass even the virtue of the male.[33]

How like the beginning of canto 37 from Ariosto's *Orlando furioso*, cited in Chapter 2, where literary studies similarly cause women to surpass the male sex. Towards the end of the letter, Puteanus compared Andreini's natural, or physical, female self with the virile traits he ascribed to her by urging the actress to increase her masculine creativity and match it to her already fecund woman's procreativity. In so doing, he established a parallelism between nature and art that equated the workings of the mind with the mysteries of the womb. In this light, thinking again of Artusi's commentaries on Monteverdi's madrigals, the theorist's parallelisms between social, economic, and gendered hierarchies are shown to pervade humanist discourse. As Puteanus writes,

[33] Puteanus, *Epistolarum fercula secunda*, 17: 'Tantam facundiam, tantas litteras . . . , ut corrigendo muliebre vitium, virilem virtutem superes' (Doc. 42d).

Nature herself and father time have given you to our age, but you will give yourself to posterity. What we admire in you, we owe to your own industry and at the same time to benign Nature, but what posterity will admire in you will redound to you alone. For which reason I exhort and beg you the more vehemently, to commend yourself no less to posterity by writing than by speaking you commend to us the kindness of Nature. We have seen the *Mirtilla* eclogue and now your *Rime*. Bring out more, so that fertile with children as you are, you may also become fertile with books.[34]

Puteanus' letter to Andreini, however, conforms to the language of a similar letter written by Angelo Poliziano to Cassandra Fedele, a congruency that demonstrates the formulaic derivation of Puteanus' praise. It is clear from the imitation that Puteanus sought not so much to describe Andreini as to locate her within a tradition of learned, inspired women—a contextualization that would in turn solidify his own position in line with the great Renaissance humanists Guarino and Poliziano and, ultimately, with the ancient Greeks whose language he appropriated for the word 'men' within his text. As Poliziano wrote in the 1490s,

What an astonishing impact it must make upon us, truly, that it was possible for such [letters] to be produced by a woman—what do I say, a woman? By a girl, rather, and a virgin. It shall therefore no longer be the exclusive privilege of antiquity to boast of their Sybils and their Muses, the Pythagoreans of their female philosophers, the Socratics of their Diotima, of Aspasia; and neither will the relics of Greece proclaim those female poets, Telesilla, Corinna, Sappho, Anyte, Erinna, Praxilla, Cleobulina and the others. Now we shall readily believe the Roman account of the daughters of Laelius and Hortensius, of Cornelia, mother of the Gracchi, as matrons of surpassing eloquence. Now we know, truly by this we know, that your sex has not after all been condemned to slowness and stupidity. . . . But truly in our age, in which few men indeed raise their head to any height in letters, you, however, stand forth as the sole girl who handles books in place of wool, a reed pen instead of vegetable dye, a quill pen instead of a needle, and who instead of daubing her skin with white lead, covers paper with ink.[35]

In an earlier letter (Doc. 42a), Puteanus had established a theoretical formulation by which he reasoned the gendering of Andreini's persona, and this construct is important, not only because it outlines the humanistic method by which a woman acquired masculine-gendered traits, but also because he oversteps the boundary between ascribing masculine

---

[34] Ibid.: 'Te nobis Natura ipsa, . . . ut liberis foecunda, libris quoque evadas' (see Doc. 42d).

[35] Translation given in Grafton and Jardine, 49.

attributes and denying female physical fact. In doing so, he turns Andreini into an *objet d'art*, and dissolves the boundary between nature and art in a manner that echoes Artusi's disregard for the feminine in reference to music. Just as Artusi characterizes the feminine as a disruptive force within the masculine compositional hierarchy of the madrigal (if we follow Cusick's interpretation), Puteanus here describes the feminine as an individualistic form of irrationality to be overcome by communal masculine rationality. In this, he follows the educational scheme that Guarino had modelled after the myth of Achilles, wherein the feminine represents the unruly expression of individual will in confrontation with the good of the state, and the masculine the adherence to social convention. Puteanus subsumes the errant excess of Andreini's femininity into his constructed image of her by way of a comparison between the Latin words *virtus* (virtue) and *vir* (man). Virtue, in terms derived from Aquinas's *Summa theologica*, proceeds from an ordering of the mind, demonstrated in acts of rational thought and scholarship, and thus Puteanus' clever but predictable and overwrought etymological game—a humanistic trademark—results in the bald statement that Andreini is, in fact, a man:

> Truly in my opinion you supply a defect of nature, Andreina, who are not only capable of male glory but in fact an equal partner in it. Nay more, abandoning your own sex, you transform yourself by the labour of virtue into a man. Now if the word virtue derives from the word man, then you are more fruitful than a man, you who, though a woman, bring forth the fruit of virtue. But if the word 'man' derives from the word 'virtue', then the reward of the better name, I mean the name of man, is due to you who perform the offices belonging to the better name. Therefore you are a man. And indeed you are called a man by name, if you look closely at the name Andreina.[36]

In spite of their author's undoubtedly good intentions, to modern readers, Puteanus' letters leave a bitter aftertaste, and I wonder if Andreini found them equally pungent. In praising the individual, he derides women as a group, stating that Andreini's birth in female form is a defect (in essence, a 'monstrous birth') to be overcome by her masculine virtue; that all women by nature chatter and babble, whereas Andreini speaks well; and that eloquence and learning are foreign to women in general, whereas the great actress proves her manhood (so to speak) through writing and rhetoric. Moreover, he likens Andreini to the legendary Penthesilea—a

---

[36] Puteanus, *Epistolarum fercula secunda*, 41: 'Nae tu mihi animo defectum Naturae..., si Andreinae nomen examinas' (Doc. 42a).

woman who, although beautiful and valorous, dies a violent death and is essentially a tragic, impotent figure.

Andreini's own forays into masking her womanhood with virile armour take a playful, wayward turn, and are not centred on humanistic definitions of *virtù*. She takes a Petrarchan route, born of the 'constructive' arts[37] rather than humanistic philosophy, and, by commending the female sex while in masculine guise, manages to sing her own praises as a woman. In this, Andreini's self-fashioning draws on contemporary court literature such as Ariosto's *Orlando furioso* and Tasso's *Gerusalemme liberata*, with their depictions of bold, valorous women like Bradamante, Marfisa, and Clorinda, whose nobility and heritage incite them to don armour and ride into battle. These are the images of femininity valued by the rulers of Renaissance courts—not for nothing were generations of Este daughters after the publication of *Orlando furioso* named Marfisa and Bradamante—and Andreini, in adapting her self-image to ideals of noble heroism rather than disobedience, reinforces her patrons' ideas of dynastic integrity and virtue by blood rather than gender.[38]

Andreini formulates her masculine persona partly by writing poetry and *poesia per musica* in what we have come to call the male voice, and she is one of only two known female poets of the Renaissance to do so, the other being Laura Terracina. What has been called the 'male voice', however, I would more accurately describe as the 'feminine ear', for the gender of these poems' protagonists is rarely indicated and arguments concerning the 'male' and 'female' voices often erroneously assume a heterosexual relationship between author and auditor that is particularly inappropriate to Renaissance poetry.[39] It also assumes that the author of a poem would be its intended performer, rather than the poem's recipient—another misstep in interpreting Renaissance verse. What *is* clear in analysing Andreini's musical lyrics and early modern verse in general is the establishment of a dyad consisting of dominant and submissive partners—just as there is a *serva* and *padrona* within the Artusi's idealized

---

[37] My use of the term 'constructive' arts is based on that in a letter from Girolamo Mei to Piero Vettori, 10 Jan. 1560; London, British Library, Add. 10268, fo. 209. See Claude Palisca, *Girolamo Mei: Letters on Ancient and Modern Music*, 45, and id., *Humanism in Italian Renaissance Musical Thought*, 333–48.

[38] For detailed discussion of the Este family in relation to Ariosto's and Tasso's works, see Ascoli, *Ariosto's Bitter Harmony*, and Quint, *Origin and Originality*.

[39] James Saslow's wonderfully rich studies of Michelangelo's art and poetry offer compelling examples of the variety of gendered interpretations available to Renaissance painting and verse; see his *The Poetry of Michelangelo* and *Ganymede in the Renaissance*.

Renaissance household, but also a *servo* and *padrone*—which are usually construed as respectively feminine and masculine. In this, she follows the fundamental humanistic scheme laid down by Guarino, in which knowledge and civic responsibility are gendered masculine. This hierarchical structure, however, cannot be taken for granted as an indication of the sex of its protagonists for, as Michael Rocke shows in his fascinating study of homosexuality and male culture in Renaissance Florence, submissive partners in sodomitic relationships are consistently gendered as feminine in court records and diaries as well as in carnival songs, even though their sex is decidedly male.[40] The feminine position, therefore, is one of submission, like Artusi's *serva*, and identified not by the presumed sex of the poem's interlocutors, but by the style of its rhetoric.

The style of Andreini's poetry varies depending on her adoption of a dominant or submissive authorial tone and on the individual construction of her lyrics—their genre, sources of imitation, subject matter, and poetic conceit. At times, her verses describe innocent, almost asexual pastoral or courtly love in a Petrarchan mode, as in the madrigals 'Ove sì tosto voli sogno?' and 'Per lo soverchio affanno', the latter of which inspired Sigismondo D'India's muse:[41]

> Ove sì tosto voli
> sogno? Deh, non partire,
> poichè dolce consoli
> l'amaro ed angoscioso mio martire.
> Se pietosa tu sol Madonna fai
> del mio lungo languire
> cortese ingannator, perchè te n' vai?
> Ben è ver, che 'l contento
> d'Amor fugge qual nube innanzi al vento.

(Where do you so suddenly fly, dream? Ah, do not depart, since sweetly you console my bitter and anguished suffering. If you alone make my Lady compassionate of my long suffering, kind deceiver, why do you go? It is certainly true that the contentment of love flees like a cloud in the wind.)

---

[40] Rocke, *Forbidden Friendships*. Interestingly, and in conformity with the Achillean model of humanist education, the partners identified as 'feminine' in homosexual relationships, as described by Rocke, were pre-adolescent boys, and homosexuality, per se, was treated as illicit only when the 'feminine' was absent—when both partners were adult men.

[41] D'India's setting survives in only four of its five parts (*Settimo libro de madrigali a cinque voci* (Rome, 1624)).

> Per lo soverchio affanno
> Gli miei spirti dolenti
> Abbandonato m'hanno;
> E i sensi, che già fur di fiamma ardenti
> Freddo ghiaccio si fanno:
> Ond'io chiudo le luci, e mi scoloro,
> E crede Amor ch'io dorma, & io pur moro.

(For excessive suffering my sorrowful spirits have abandoned me; and my senses, which formerly had burned in flame, are becoming cold ice; whence I close my eyes and I go pale, and Amor believes that I sleep, and yet I die.)[42]

Andreini's poems can convey, however, a deeper, more burning passion and more forceful delivery, as in the madrigals 'Quella bocca di rose' and 'Amorosa mia Clori':

> Quella bocca di rose
> la mia vaga Licori
> tutta ridente, e bella
> in premio al fin de' miei gravi dolori
> mi porge lieta. (ahi scaltra Pastorella)
> ecco i' la bacio, ed ella,
> che 'n bocca asconde l'amorose faci
> m'incende l'alma co' suoi dolci baci.

(That red mouth my charming Licori, all smiling and beautiful, offers me at last in reward for my great pain (ah! cunning shepherdess!). Behold, I kiss her, and she, who in her mouth hides the torches of love, sets my soul on fire with her kisses.)

> Amorosa mia Clori
> Se ti rimembra un bacio mi donasti
> Lungo questo bel Rio tra questi fiori;
> E s'io tacèa, giurasti
> Che mille ancor me ne daresti poi.
> Io 'l tacqui, e 'l taccio, e s'io no 'l fò palese
> Bella Ninfa e cortese,
> Perche non servi i giuramenti tuoi?
> Baciami, che i tuo' baci
> Fièn de la lingua mia nodi tenaci.

(My amorous Clori, if you remember the kiss you gave me alongside that beautiful brook among these flowers; and if I were silent you swore that a thousand

---

[42] I. Andreini, *Rime*, 171.

more you would give me. I was silent about it, and am silent about it, and since I do not let it be known, beautiful and kind nymph, why do you not keep your promises? Kiss me. Let your kisses be the tight knots that hold my tongue.)[43]

In both styles, Andreini engages an authoritative perspective that deconstructs or otherwise fragments the subject of the verse. In the first poem, 'Ove sì tosto voli', the lady love is nearly invisible—an apt characterization for an image that occupies only a fleeting dream, and yet typical of the dominating (heretofore 'masculine') authorial gaze. She is held on a pedestal and, like a living statue, is capable only of recognizing or remaining blind to the poet's anguish, much like Puteanus' characterization of the poem's author. In contrast, the feminized object of 'Quella bocca di rose' is more clearly in evidence, although fragmented. 'She' has a name and we are told that she is a shepherdess, but the view we have of her is only from chin to nose—a fractured image of the feminine object that marks the dominant gaze even today.[44] But few women composed poetry from such a powerful perspective. The prismatic view of Licori in Andreini's madrigal, for example, may be fruitfully compared to the more comprehensive, submissive vision of the lover in Gaspara Stampa's sonnet 'Or sopra il forte e veloce destriero':

> —Or che sopra il forte e veloce destriero—
> io dico meco—segue lepre o cerva
> il mio bel sole, or rapida caterna
> d'uccelli con falconi o con sparviero.
>   Or assal con lo spiedo il cignal fiero,
> quando animoso il suo venir osserva;
> or a l'opre di Marte, or di Minerva
> rivolge l'alto e saggio suo pensiero.
>   Or mangia, or dorme, or leva ed or ragiona,
> or vagheggia il suo colle, or con l'umana
> sua maniera trattiene ogni persona.
>   Così, signor, bench'io vi sia lontana,
> sì fattamente Amor mi punge e sprona,
> ch'ogni vostr'opra m'è presente e piana.

(I tell myself I see my lovely sun mounted upon his powerful, swift steed, chasing the hare or hart, or rapid flock of birds, with falcon or with sparrowhawk; Now with his spear he fights the savage boar, awaiting its attack with fierce disdain;

---

[43] I. Andreini, *Rime*, 185–6.
[44] A very good summary of current literature on the male gaze may be found in Walters, *Material Girls*.

again, he bends his wise and lofty thoughts to the pursuits of Mars and of Minerva. He eats now, now he sleeps, he rises, speaks, now gazes on his hill, now with humane welcoming manner he receives all guests. And so, my lord, though I am far away, love so inspires me and spurs me on that I can plainly see your every act.)[45]

The poem's 'author' might be an adoring adolescent of either sex. From the submissive subject position, however, the author not only sees the lover's every act, but also imagines him so completely that the vision includes his horse, the prey he hunts, his lands, and his guests, however equivocal those metaphors might be. By contrast, although Andreini's verse is written in a more terse, epigrammatic style than Stampa's sonnet, the dominating gaze of the madrigal, in focusing exclusively on the shepherdess's mouth, is exceedingly narrow. Taking the two poems together, whereas the submissive position is characterized by fragmentation, the dominant is shown to be comprehensive and all-encompassing. This is the same formulation posited by Artusi in reference to Monteverdi's madrigals, wherein a single, dissonant voice is construed as feminine within the overall consonance of the five-voice texture.

Further demonstrations of the differences between the dominant and submissive authorial voices look beyond the poetry's meaning to its sound—a theoretical move that brings us closer to a construction of the authorial voice in music. Stampa's soft, 'oh'- and 'ah'-laden verse, for example, with its insistent repetition of the word 'Or' at the beginnings of lines 1, 5, 7, 9, and 10 and the predominance of its sensuous 'oh' vowels in the incipit, more closely resembles the dreamy wistfulness of 'Ove sì tosto voli sogno?' (also made up primarily of 'oh' vocables) than with the greedy, staccato accents of '*k*s (as in '*Qu*ella bo*cc*a', 'E*cc*o', and 'Bo*cc*a as*c*onde'), '*t*s ('*tu*tta'), and double consonants ('bo*cc*a', 'E*cc*o', 'tu*tt*a') in 'Quella bocca di rose'.

Musical settings of Andreini's poetry offer a variety of responses to her adoption of the dominating authorial perspective, just as Monteverdi's setting of 'Cruda Amarilli' offers a response to Guarini's poem and a musical characterization of the dramatic moment within *Il pastor fido* in which it occurs. Pietro Paolo Torre's setting of 'Ove sì tosto voli sogno?' (Ex. 3.1), beyond exhibiting minor alterations in grammar and punctuation, eradicated Andreini's obvious referent to a feminized object by omitting lines 5 and 6 of the poem, which also weakens the poem's rhetorical

---

[45] Stampa, *Selected Poems* (trans. Stortoni and Lillie), 119.

Ex. 3.1. Pietro Paolo Torre, *Ove sì tosto voli sogno?* (*Primo libro delle canzonette*, 1622)

19
- ce con - so - li l'a- ma - ro ed an-go-scio - so ed an-go
23
Poi - che dol - ce con - so -
-scio - so mio mar - ti - re
27
- li l'a - ma - ro ed an-go-scio - so ed an-go-scio - so mio mar-
ed an-go-scio - so mio mar-
31
-ti re
-ti - - re Cor - te - se cor -
35
Cor - te - se
- tes' in - gan - na - tor per - chè te'n va - i

Ex. 3.1. *continued*

strength, making hash of its rhyme scheme and stanzaic structure. Nor does the poem's subject matter remain convincingly secular, once the lines 'Se pietosa tu sol Madonna fai / Del mio lungo languire' (If you alone make my Lady compassionate / of my long suffering) are excised:

> Ove sì tosto voli
> sogno[?] Deh non partire
> poiche dolce consoli
> l'amaro ed angoscioso mio martire[.]
> Cortese ingannator perchè te'n vai[?]
> Ben è ver che 'l contento
> d'Amor fugge qual nube innanzi al vento.

(Where do you so suddenly fly, dream? Ah, do not depart, since sweetly you console my bitter and anguished suffering. Kind deceiver, why do you go? It is certainly true that the contentment of love flees like a cloud in the wind.)

Torre's madrigal might speak as clearly to the anguish of lapsed faith in God or the conclusion of an ecstatic vision as it does in Andreini's version to the pangs of love. In removing the reference to a 'Madonna' who responds to feelings of desire, Torre—an organist and monk at the monastery of S. Gieronimo near Milan—turns the poem from a Petrarcan love lyric into a song of devotion in which love emanates only from the first person. In so doing, although the word 'Madonna' may well have been what drew him to the poem in the first place, he also removes from the song's construction any issues of corporeal sexuality or illicit thoughts about the lady that might arise from a setting of the entire stanza.[46] Since it is written in a simple, easily performable style, one can readily imagine Torre teaching two of S. Gieronimo's novices to sing the voice parts. The imitative entries hardly overlap (when they do, one of the voices tends to hold to a single pitch while the other moves, as at bars 10–11), and when the voices sing together, it is in a facile texture of parallel thirds over a sustained bass that is immediately satisfying to the ear. There is little dissonance, other than a few carefully controlled suspensions on 'martire', and none of the unruly, acrid entrances that caused Artusi to complain so bitterly about Monteverdi's compositional technique. Indeed, if we were to transfer Artusi's anthropomorphic characterizations to Torre's madrigal and call the two canto parts the *servi* of the controlling, dominating bass, we would find no dissention in Torre's compositional household, for here the upper voices obey the lower and the poem (to its disfigurement) submits to the rules of musical counterpoint.

The more forceful 'Quella bocca di rose', however, set to music by the Neapolitan composer Donat'Antonio Spano (Ex. 3.2), brings a different musical style to Andreini's poetry that admits no tension, as in Torre's madrigal, between the poet's forceful authorial stance and the collective, universalizing voice of its five-part polyphonic setting.[47] In this, it resembles Santi Orlandi's setting of the equally forceful 'Amorosa mia Clori', which unfortunately survives in only four of its five parts.[48] In 'Quella bocca di rose', Andreini's text is given in full, with particular musical attention lavished, in all voices, on already highly charged words like 'gravi dolori' and the 'Ahi!' of 'Ahi! scaltra pastorella'. Spano mirrors the strength of Andreini's poetic style in the full texture and contrapuntal conformity of his setting, although his musical imagination does not match Andreini's capacity for invention.

As I have argued in regard to Andreini's musical lyrics and her correspondence with Erycius Puteanus, and with reference to Michael Rocke's work on male culture in Renaissance Florence, conceptual boundaries between masculinity and femininity in rhetorical strategies are extremely thin, and are founded more on stylistic characteristics than on representation. I should therefore hesitate to argue that an independent, five-voice

---

[46] Torre, *Ove sì tosto voli*, in *Il primo libro delle canzonette, madrigali, et arie* (Venice, 1622).
[47] Spano, *Di Donat'Antonio Spano il primo libro de madrigali a cinque voci* (Naples, 1608).
[48] Orlandi, *Libro terzo de madrigali a cinque voci* (Venice, 1605).

Ex. 3.2. Donat'Antonio Spano, *Quella bocca di rose* (*Primo libro de madrigali*, 1608)

Ex. 3.2. *continued*

24
por-ge lie - ta Mi por-ge lie - ta
lie - ta Mi por-ge lie - - - - ta
Mi por-ge lie - ta
Mi por-ge lie - - ta
Mi por-ge lie - ta
28
ahi scal - tra pa - sto - rel -
ahi scal -
ahi scal - tra pa - sto -
ahi
ahi scal -
31
-la scal - tra pa-sto - rel - la Ecc'
- tra pa-sto - rel - - la Ecc' io la
-rel - la Ecc' io la ba - ci'ed
scal - tra pa-sto - rel - la
- tra pa-sto - rel - - la

Ex. 3.2. *continued*

44
M'in - cen-de l'al - ma M'in - cen-de
M'in - cen-de l'al - ma M'in - cen-de l'al -
l'al - ma M'in - cen- de l'al - ma M'in-
- cen-del'al - ma M'in - cen-de l'al - ma
M'in - cen-de l'al - ma M'in-
48
l'al - ma M'in - cen-de l'al - ma con suoi dol -
-ma M'in-cen-de l'al - ma con suoi
- cen-de l'al-ma con suoi dol - ci ba -
M'in - cen-de l'al-ma con suoi dol - ci ba -
- cen-de l'al - ma con suoi dol -
52
- ci ba - - - ci.
dol - ci ba - - - - - ci.
-ci con suoi dol-ci ba - - ci.
-ci con suoi dol - ci ba - - ci.
- ci ba - - - - ci.

imitative texture might be construed as feminine because the text reads from a feminine subject position, although Susan McClary's analysis of Monteverdi's dramatic music suggests one might do so. As she states,

> It may be possible to trace some of the musical signs for 'masculinity' or 'femininity' that are displayed in opera back into earlier genres such as the madrigal. . . . Because madrigal texts typically speak from the masculine subject position that is assumed as normative in Western culture, they are usually treated as neutral or undifferentiated with respect to gender. However, there are texts—especially those drawn from Guarini or Tasso—that are understood to be female utterances, and some musical settings of these seem subtly coded as 'feminine'.[49]

McClary is constrained to make an exception to her general statement that polyphonic textures signify a masculine subject position in identifying Monteverdi's *Io mi son giovinetta* (Book 4) and *O Mirtillo* (Book 5; *O Mirtillo*, like *Cruda Amarilli*, sets text from *Il pastor fido*) as feminine because her definitions of femininity and masculinity are based on representational veracity. Humanists' constructions of heroic women, however, like those depicted in the letters of Guarino, Poliziano, and Puteanus, show that a different premiss is at work, wherein the feminine subject position is understood as an expression of individual emotion that defines the boundaries of communal decorum by temporarily exceeding them. The fragmentary characterization of the feminine, as well as its associations with adolescence and hormonally charged narcissism and yearning, may be seen in other composers' settings of Guarini's texts as well, such as Giaches de Wert's setting of 'Tirsi morir volea' (1581). Wert's dialogue distinguishes between the feminine voice of the anonymous Nymph (as Rocke would argue, Guarini's nymph might have been a boy), Tirsi's similarly feminine-gendered voice (because adolescent and fragmented), and the omniscient role of the narrator through textural means:

> Thyrsis wished to die,
> Gazing at the eyes of his beloved,
> When she, whose ardor equalled his,
> Said, 'Alas, my love,
> Do not die yet,
> Since I long to die with thee.'
> Thyrsis curbed the desire
> Which by then had almost ended his life;
> He felt death near, yet could not die,

---

[49] McClary, *Feminine Endings*, 36.

> And while he kept his gaze
> Fixed upon those eyes divine,
> And drank from thence the nectar of love,
> His pretty Nymph, who felt Love's heralds near,
> Said with languishing and trembling looks:
> 'Die, my love, for I die.'
> At which the shepherd replied,
> 'And I, my love, die.'
> Thus the happy lovers died,
> A death so sweet and pleasant
> That in order to die again, they returned to life.

Through most of the composition, both the narrator's and Tirsi's words occupy the same musical space, in the lower four voices of the texture, while the upper three parts are reserved for the voice of the Nymph—thus depicting an overall textural fragmentation that is augmented by the increasingly brief motifs exchanged between the voices of Tirsi and the Nymph. Only at the end of the madrigal, when the lovers come together in metaphorical sexual death, do the voices of the nymph, Tirsi, and the narrator assimilate all parts of the musical texture, thereby suggesting the absorption of the 'feminine' submissive into the encompassing, and at this point sexually mature, whole (Ex. 3.3).

Just as the theatrical styles of 'Tirsi morir volea', 'Cruda Amarilli', and 'Quella bocca di rose' bring questions of sexual representation to the surface, so too does Andreini's masking of her own body take on a more empirical aspect onstage than in her poems and other writings. At times, the female members of Andreini's troupe were asked to provide private entertainment for noblewomen and ladies-in-waiting, and on these occasions Andreini might play either a female or a male character. Indeed, Ferdinando Taviani convincingly argues that one of Andreini's theatrical triumphs was the role of Aminta in Tasso's pastoral drama of that name.[50] Similarly, circumstances under which it was deemed inappropriate for the women of the troupe to appear—in Rome, for example, where women were forbidden attendance at public theatrical performance—resulted in the younger men of the troupe dressing in women's clothes to play the female roles. The homoeroticism latent in these performances, as well as their satirical employment of the suspension of disbelief when transvestite characters transvest again within the context of the play, suggests an attitude towards the characterization of masculinity and femininity in

[50] Taviani, 'Bella d'Asia', 7.

Ex. 3.3. Giaches de Wert, *Tirsi morir volea*, bars 34–51, from Wert, *Opera omnia*, xiv, ed. MacClintock

38
mo - ro. Co - sì mo - rir - no i
mo - ro. Co - sì mo - rir - no i
ch'io mo - ro. Co - sì mo - rir - no i
vi - ta, mo - ro. Co - sì mo - rir - no i
vi - ta, mo - ro. Co - sì mo - rir - no i
vi - ta, mo - ro. Co - sì mo - rir - no i
vi - ta, mo - ro. Co - sì mo - rir - no i
40
for - tu - na - ti A - man - ti. Di mor - te sì so - a - ve e
for - tu - na - ti A - man - ti. Di mor - te sì so - a - ve e
for - tu - na - ti A - man - ti. Di mor - te sì so - a - ve e
for - tu - na - ti A - man - ti. Di mor - te sì so - a - ve e
for - tu - na - ti A - man - ti. Di mor - te sì so - a - ve e
for - tu - na - ti A - man - ti. Di mor - te sì so - a - ve e
for - tu - na - ti A - man - ti. Di mor - te sì so - a - ve e

Ex. 3.3. *continued*

46
vi - ta. Che per an - co mo - rir, che
vi - ta. Che per an - co mo - rir tor -
vi - - - ta. Che per an - co mo - rir tor -
- ta. Che per an - co mo - rir, che
- co mo - rir, che per an - co mo - rir tor - na-re in vi - -
vi - - - - ta. Che per an - co mo -
vi - - ta. Che per an - co mo - rir
48
per an - co mo - rir tor - na-re in vi - ta. Che per an -
-na - re in vi - ta. Che per an - co mo -
-na - re in vi - - ta. Che per an -
per an - co mo - rir tor - na - re in vi - ta.
- ta. Che per an - co mo - rir tor - na - re in
-rir tor - na - re in vi - ta. Che per an - co mo -
tor - na - re in vi - - ta, tor -

Ex. 3.3. *continued*

Renaissance drama that is anything but rigidly constructed, although it clearly plays on the gendered hierarchies propounded by academicians like Puteanus and Artusi. Iconographic evidence of this masculine gendering may be seen in the collected portraits of Isabella Andreini, specifically in reference to her gaze. The frontispiece from the publication of her *Rime* (Pl. 3.1) shows the typical feminine gaze, with eyes averted. The other portraits, most notably that by Raffaello Sadeler and its copies (Pl. 3.2), together with the anonymous sketch derived from the *Rime* portrait (Pl. 3.3) and the engraving presumably made for an unknown French publication (Pl. 3.4) all show a direct, masculine gaze, where the figure looks directly out at the viewer. Part of Taviani's proof lies in the first poem in Andreini's first book of *Rime*, which I transcribe here in order to demonstrate the actress's conscious use of transgendering in the rhetoric of her self-fashioning. Here, Andreini adopts an unashamedly Petrarchan idiom that centres on the idea of stylistic variation and then incorporates into this framework comparisons between poetry and theatre, man and woman, art and nature:

PL. 3.1. Portrait of Isabella Andreini from the frontispiece to her *Rime* (Milan, 1601). Rome, Biblioteca e Raccolto Teatrale Burcardo

PL. 3.2. Portrait of Isabella Andreini, after the engraving by Raffaello Sadeler. Venice, Museo Correr

Amazons of Learning

Isabella Andreini

PL. 3.3. Anonymous portrait of Isabella Andreini derived from the frontispiece of her *Rime* (Milan, 1601). Venice, Museo Correr

PL. 3.4. Portrait of Isabella Andreini. Rome, Biblioteca e Raccolto Teatrale Burcardo

Amazons of Learning

> S'alcun sia mai, che i versi miei negletti
> Legga, non creda a questi finti ardori,
> Che ne le Scene imaginati amori
> Usa a trattar con non leali affetti:
>   Con bugiardi non men con finti detti
> De le Muse spiegai gli alti furori:
> Talhor piangendo i falsi miei dolori,
> Talhor cantando i falsi miei diletti;
>   E come ne' Teatri hor Donna, ed hora
> Huom fei rappresentando in vario stile
> Quanto volle insegnar Natura, et Arte.
>   Così la stella mia seguendo ancora
> Di fuggitiva età nel verde Aprile
> Vergai con vario stil ben mille carte.

(If ever anyone reads my neglected verses, do not believe in their false ardours, for loves imagined on stage I have set forth with feigned affects. With lies, no less with false words, I have portrayed the Muses' high madnesses, sometimes bewailing my fictive sorrows, sometimes singing my fictive delights. And as in the theatre I have played now a woman, now a man, in varied style, as Nature would instruct, and Art as well, thus, following once more my star of fleeting years, in green April, with varied style, I have penned a good thousand pages.)[51]

    The grammatical parallelisms in the first tercet of the sonnet outline a level of comparison that associates man with art and woman with nature, as Puteanus had done in his letters, but Andreini tells us in lines 10 and 14 that representation of gender is a style—a compositional technique—that she adopts both onstage and in her poems. Her allusions to the relationship between her published verses and dramatic performances are noteworthy, as she tells her readers that the poems open before them have their origins not in a book-lined cell or other private space where female authors are traditionally said to have sat in solitude with pen and paper, but rather on stage in the marketplace of imaginary lives enacted there.[52] The fictions she pens, therefore, self-consciously contradict the authorial stance of authors like Gaspara Stampa, whose poetry is said to have been typically autobiographical.[53] While embracing Petrarchan conceits of variation and contrast, Andreini pokes fun in this sonnet at the Neoplatonic ideal of divine madness—the representation of which

---

[51] I. Andreini, *Rime*, 1.
[52] For an elegant study of the production of women's scholarship in the early Renaissance, see King, 'Book-Lined Cells'.
[53] Stampa, *Selected Poems*, pp. ix–xxvii.

formed the cornerstone of her theatrical fame and stands as the foundation of humanistic thought concerning the perfection of nature and the Music of the Spheres. As thoughtfully explored by Gary Tomlinson in his studies of Ficino's *De vita coelitus comparanda*,[54] Renaissance humanists construct a philosophical systemization of the universe in which one might achieve transcendence to the divine through poetic inspiration from the Muses, but Andreini in this poem admits that she deceives her audiences, play-acting divine madness and reciting not cosmic truth but lies. Her parody of early modern Neoplatonists is obvious, as she defines yet another border, between pedantry and intellectual fashion. She also distances herself from the concomitancy of nature, truth, and femininity, while more firmly binding her theatrical and poetic creativity to concepts of fantasy and art.

Even when portraying a woman on stage or writing for female characters, Andreini often uses gender reversals to parody known authors or stereotypical situations and to bring the contrasts between masculine and feminine constructs to the surface. In her pastoral play *Mirtilla*, for example, she produces a proto-feminist reading of a famous scene from Torquato Tasso's *Aminta* that also parodies contemporary erotica. Tasso's version, from Act II, Scene i, lines 804–5, features the Satyr, who declares his lust for the nymph Sylvia. He plans to abduct her and, if she does not concede to his desires, says he 'will force her, will rape her who denies him love's reward'.[55] We are never shown the fulfilment of these wishes on stage, but in a later scene Sylvia relates to another shepherdess that she has narrowly escaped capture in the forest.

In *Mirtilla*, Andreini begins her satiric theatregram[56] in precisely the same manner, showing the Satyr alone on stage, declaring his lust for the nymph Fillide and asserting that, if she continues to reject him as she has in the past, he will rape her. At this point, Andreini's text diverges from Tasso's. Fillide or Filli—the part habitually played by Andreini, as was the role of Sylvia—enters the scene and is perforce abducted by the Satyr who declares his intention to tie her, naked, to an oak tree and force himself on her.

> Ah dispietata,
> or non ti goverà l'esser crudele,

---

[54] Tomlinson, *Music in Renaissance Magic* and *Metaphysical Song*.
[55] Tasso, *Aminta* (ed. Varese), 73, Act II, Scene i, ll. 804–5.
[56] The term 'theatregram' was coined by Clubb in her book *Italian Drama in Shakespeare's Time* to refer to recurring theatrical topoi.

Amazons of Learning

né l'adeguar nel corso
i più veloci venti,
di qui non partirai s'a le mie pene
non dai qualche mercede.
E quando tu non voglia a l'arso core
dar qualche refrigerio, ingrata voglio
nuda legarti a quella dura quercia,
ove con strazio finirai tua vita.

(Ah! merciless nymph, now you will not profit from being cruel, nor from taking the course of the fastest winds; from here you will not depart if you do not give some mercy to my pains. And should you not want to give some cooling relief to my parched heart, ungrateful nymph, I want to tie you, naked, to that hard oak, where with torment I will end your life.)[57]

Not only does Andreini's veiled reference to Tasso's oak make the source of her literary imitation explicit, but the idea of the Satyr ripping off her clothes alludes to another stereotype of the baser sort of comedy, which Andreini had built her reputation on thwarting. The image of a nymph tied, naked, to a tree and beaten or otherwise physically abused is also a topos that appears in erotic literature, engravings, and other prurient art forms in the late Renaissance, as may be seen in the pornographic series of engravings entitled 'Lascivie' by Agostino Carracci (1557–1602), now housed in the British Museum (see Pl. 3.5).[58]

Perilously close to having at least her bosom bared, Filli appears to warm to the Satyr's advances as she stalls for time. She promises him a kiss if he will allow her to secure his arms so they will not bruise her delicate skin. Stupidly, he agrees, and once he is bound firmly to the tree, Fillide degrades him, tearing his beard, choking him, and pinching *his* bared breast. She leaves finally, triumphant, and the Satyr is subsequently discovered in his humiliating predicament by an old goatherd, who offers him consoling words about the 'safer' satisfactions of food and wine.[59] In

---

[57] Andreini, *Mirtilla* (ed. Doglio), 85, Act III, Scene ii, ll. 1317–26.

[58] A delightful modern edition of this series of engravings, together with the sonnet collection by Pietro Aretino entitled *I modi*, may be found in *I modi: The Sixteen Pleasures*, ed. Lawner.

[59] I. Andreini, *Mirtilla* (ed. Doglio), 81–99, Act III, Scenes i–iii. Analogous scenes in Guarini's *Pastor fido* (Act I, Scene v and Act II, Scene vi) similarly show the nymph, Corisca, playing up to the Satyr's prurient overtures, but he doesn't believe her and they quarrel. Locked in a wrestler's hold, Corisca invites the Satyr to tear her head off, if he's strong enough, and she escapes as he falls hard to the ground, a worthless prosthesis in his hands. Although injured by the fall, Guarini's Satyr escapes the humiliation suffered by Andreini's.

124 *Amazons of Learning*

PL. 3.5. Satyr flogging a Nymph, engraved by Agostino Carracci, from the 'Lascivie' series. © Copyright The British Museum

the equivocal language of Renaissance theatre and erotic poetry, the old man's character and advice suggest that the Satyr exercise his lust on boys instead of women, the goatherd's words implying that children are less conniving than their female elders.[60]

In all of these demonstrations of Andreini's self-fashioning, she is shown to have invoked a fundamentally Petrarchan dualism that contrasts feminine style with its masculine counterpart, playing at the boundary of decorum and excess. This relegation of femininity and masculinity to concepts of style satirizes contemporary humanist exposition of art, nature, masculinity, and femininity, wherein nature is often accorded a dominating, masculine characterization and the feminine is sometimes seen not only as submissive, but as unnatural. For Artusi, for example, lingering traces of his scholastic music theory, wherein the Harmony of the Spheres held mastery over dissonance, invite an interpretation of consonance as both natural and masculine and dissonance as unnatural and feminine. Wert's *Tirsi morir volea* upholds this schema of the feminized object subsumed within a dominating frame, although his dialogue makes the transitional character of the feminine apparent, whereas humanistic music theory does not. Puteanus' construct, in contrast, although heavy-handed and caught up in rhetorical convention, maintains an opposing dichotomy in which Nature is feminine and art is masculine, which erupts in the seemingly ridiculous assertion that Andreini is a man. The crux of his argument, however, lies in the humanistic notion of virtue, by which Puteanus associates creativity and aesthetic value with man by way of Latin etymologies, and so Andreini, by virtue of her art, is a man.

The actress' own self-imaging is more subtle. On one hand, she provides her theatre audiences with a clear-cut feminist parody of a stereotypical scene that lands humiliation on the male animal in retribution for acting on his lust. On the other, she appropriates to herself a forceful, dominating authorial perspective that expresses sexual desire for the feminine persona and imitates the fragmentation of the female object typical of that subject position. She leaves unspoken Puteanus' correspondence between virtue and masculinity, derived from Poliziano and Guarino, although remnants of this concept lie at the foundation of any early modern association of man with art. When literary ideals equating nature and truth with aesthetic value are added to it, however, the result

---

[60] For an excellent and inspired discussion of equivocal language in Renaissance poetry, see Saslow, *The Poetry of Michelangelo*; a comprehensive listing of terms may be found in Toscan, *Le Carnaval du langage*.

is a less overtly mysogynist construct by which art strives towards truth and nature—as the Tassists argue for *Gerusalemme liberata*—and by which Andreini's representations of women are seen as divine truth, instructed, as she tells us, by Nature. But finally, to draw a tantalizing veil of uncertainty over the entire enterprise of her theatrical art, her self-fashioning, and her attendance on humanistic themes of aesthetic valuation and its gendering, Andreini tells us that her writings, like her theatrical performances, are false and not to be trusted. Like the liar who presents the listener with the impossible conundrum, 'I am a liar', so Isabella Andreini dares us to deny both her powerful, artful image and her playful, practical female nature.

4

The Politics of Description

SEVEN years after Isabella Andreini's conversations with Erycius Puteanus on the nature of love and virtue, Andreini's daughter-in-law Virginia enacted the same debate on the stage of the Sala degli Specchi in Mantua. The play was Ottavio Rinuccini's *Arianna*, set to music by Claudio Monteverdi, and the famous lament sung by Virginia Andreini revealed a woman caught between her desire for love and the suppression of that desire required by virtue:

> Lasciatemi morire,
> lasciatemi morire,
> e che volete voi,
> che mi conforte
> in così cruda sorte,
> in così gran martire?
> Lasciatemi morire.

Standing on a rocky shore, Arianna wept for her fate at the wedding of Francesco Gonzaga and Margherita of Savoy on 28 May 1608, and all the ladies of the court were said to have wept with her.[1] Indeed, whose heart could steel itself against her, given the image of the beautiful 25-year-old comedienne in the intimate salon adjacent to the private apartments of

---

[1] Follino, *Compendio*, 30. See Fabbri, *Monteverdi* (trans. Carter), 86: 'and being performed thus by men as well as by women in the art of most excellent singing, in every way, it was more than wonderful in the lament that Arianna, abandoned by Theseus, sang from atop the rock, which was performed with such affect and with such piteous modes, that no listener was found who was not enthralled and there was no lady who did not shed some small tear at her plaint' ('e venendo rappresentata sì da uomini come da donne nell'arte del cantare eccellentissime, in ogni sua parte riuscì più che mirabile nel lamento che fece Arianna sovra lo scoglio, abbandonata da Theseus, il quale fu rappresentato con tanto affetto e con sì pietosi modi, che non si trovò ascoltante alcuno che non s'intenerisse, è fu pur una Dama che non versasse qualche lagrimetta al suo pianto').

Vincenzo Gonzaga in the Palazzo Ducale, imploring them to let her die? 'What comfort', she asked, 'can I take in such harsh fate, in such cruel suffering? Let me die, let me die.'

Surely these words and this tale of betrayal and abandonment were not meant to represent either the bride's thoughts on entering matrimony or the court's hopes for the success of the alliance between the two dynasties. But embedding the story of Arianna and Teseo within celebrations anticipating Margherita's fruitfulness and Francesco's virility inextricably binds the tale to themes of marriage, heredity, dynastic expansion, and the representation of state. And although the lament's outward characteristics—Arianna's desperation and tears, her extended soliloquy, and her confinement to a rocky shore—seem at odds with these expectations of future prosperity, they are capable of conveying powerful meaning as ritualistic symbols of the spiritual, philosophical, and legal enactment of the couple's passage into adulthood and their initiation into decision-making roles as rulers of both family and, eventually, duchy.

Themes of abduction, abandonment, and sacrifice were, in fact, common to early modern European wedding celebrations, and the practice of lamenting nuptials as if they were funerary rites, routine. We have seen that the Gelosi performed tragedies since the earliest days of the company, and that comediennes were lauded for their laments. The Fedeli continued this tradition into the seventeenth century. At the 1608 festivities alone, there were four staged entertainments that featured such acts of brutality as their central themes, and which called for women's laments: the tragedy *Arianna*, *Il ballo delle ingrate*, the intermedi performed between the acts of Battista Guarini's comedy *L'idropica*, and the second ballo, *Il sacrificio d'Ifigenia*. Intellectual fashion, too, contributed to the custom of weeping at weddings when humanists like Ottavio Rinuccini invoked classical sources in modern texts. The philologist Rush Rehm has shown that the conflation of wedding and mourning rituals spins like Arianna's thread through ancient tragic drama. And as Leofranc Holford-Strevens has demonstrated, Latin rhetorical sources are similarly rife with the laments of women on the brink of matrimony.[2]

My aim here is thus to contextualize the performance of *Arianna* as one of four representations of the marriage rite offered at the 1608 festivities, and to posit potential social and ideological meanings of its famous lament for the participants in the Mantuan celebration and their guests. For

---

[2] Rehm, *Marriage to Death*; Holford-Strevens, ' "Her eyes became two spouts" '.

although the tearful ritual was a common one, and the display of humanistic erudition axiomatic to court spectacles, Margherita and Francesco would marry but once, and the hoped-for descendants of their union would rule one of the great households of northern Italy. As a symbol of that union, their wedding would offer the ruling family of Mantua its first and perhaps most important opportunity to demonstrate the majesty, the grandeur, and, in all its aspects, the potency of its future monarch's house. This bright image of the Gonzaga line was, pathetically, short-lived. When Vincenzo died in February 1612, Francesco ruled for a brief ten months before he too died, and without progeny. Francesco's brother, Cardinal Ferdinando Gonzaga, took the throne in December 1612, and by 1627 it passed to a distant branch of the family.

Federico Follino's published description of *Arianna*, together with Rinuccini's libretto and Monteverdi's score for the lament (no more survives), comprise the foundation for analysis of the event. It is therefore worth looking closely at certain apparently minor anomalies in these sources to see more clearly their relationships to conventions of the wedding ritual. Follino's narration of the entertainments' preparations, performances, and reception, for example, contains tropes that are more suggestive of guided interpretation (or, indeed, of court propaganda) than of eyewitness testimony, although there is no doubt that its author, the director of the 1608 festivities, was present when the works were staged.[3] Follino's position of responsibility, especially in the light of Vincenzo Gonzaga's forceful strategies to advance Mantua's prestige following the devolution of Ferrara, would have strongly motivated him to ensure an appropriate and appreciative response to his spectacle from potentially inattentive

[3] The sources used in the preparation of this study are Rinuccini, *L'Arianna tragedia*; Follino, *Compendio*, 29–65 (containing both Follino's description of the performance and a copy of Rinuccini's text), and Monteverdi, *Lamento d'Arianna*, in *Tutte le opere*, ed. Malipiero, xi. 159–67. Secondary literature about the lament is outlined in Cusick, ' "There was not one lady" '.

I use the term 'author' in regard to Follino with reservation, because it is clear from the text of the *Compendio* and its preface that he collected and edited other authors' works and descriptions in addition to writing his own. The relevant passage reads, 'hò poi ritrovato nel volere por mano à questa impresa, che uno de Cancellieri di S.A. si era ben diligentemente adoprato nel raccogliere quanto era passato; io perciò subito mosso dalla strettezza del tempo, mi diedi tutto à pregarlo, che volese col mezzo delle stampe dar vita ad opere tanto celebri, & maravigliose; laonde l'hò finalmente ridotto à contentarsi, ch'io rivedendo, & riformando quanto per l'impression bisognava, da me stesso le mandi in luce, ricusando lui tuttavia di volere, che sotto suo nome cosa fatta in fretta si lasci vedere in cospetto del mondo; in modo che dopò molte difficoltà, hò finalmente essequito il mio primo pensiero' (fo. [2ᵛ]).

courtiers and guests foreign to Mantuan custom. And he would have served both Duke Vincenzo's interests and his own by putting the right 'spin' on the proceedings. His explanation of the staged dramas and their meanings is therefore central to unravelling the Mantuan court's modelling or, in Stephen Greenblatt's terms, its self-fashioning at a time when its perceived strength in the West was paramount.[4] The differences between a managed description of festivities like Follino's and an observation of events like Pavoni's diary of the Medici wedding of 1589 are vast.

Suzanne Cusick has argued that the tears of Arianna and the ladies of the court were symbols of painful female submission to an oppressive patriarchal social system.[5] This would certainly be the case were the report of these tears an unmediated one. But Follino's depiction of the courtiers weeping is a recurring trope repeated for each of Andreini's performances of laments—Arianna's 'Lasciatemi morire', which occasioned the account that 'there was no lady who did not shed some small tear at her plaint' and 'Ahi troppo è duro' from *Il ballo delle ingrate*, for which 'there was no woman's heart in that theatre which did not let loose from the eyes some pitying tear'. Such tears must therefore be seen in the light of a tradition of troped responses to the performance of laments.

> Ah, it is too, ah, too hard!
> Cruel sentence and even crueler torments,
> To return to weep in the dark cavern!

The opening phrases of the laments of Arianna and the Ingrata are remarkably similar (see Ex. 4.1), for all that Monteverdi wrote of his difficulties in composing *Arianna*, while the *Il ballo delle ingrate* figures into his correspondence hardly at all. Both are written initially in an affective recitative style, and they share an opening melodic profile that may be as symbolic of the genre as the descending tetrachord that graces the bass part of the Ingrata's plaint at the repetition of the refrain and at the beginning of the second strophe. This profile comprises the statement of an arched opening motif that is immediately repeated with a chromatic inflection, peaking a third higher than its initial utterance. Quarter-, or

---

[4] Greenblatt, *Renaissance Self-fashioning*. Not for nothing did Vincenzo Gonzaga marry off his eldest son to the daughter of the Duke of Savoy when the political fate of the Marquisate of Saluzzo was so hotly contended. Francesco's marriage to Margherita of Savoy would ensure the safety of neighbouring Monferrato and place Mantua in a strong position with regard to France and Spain, who had been battling for control of the Savoyard domain for a decade.

[5] Cusick, '"There was not one lady"'.

Ex. 4.1. Monteverdi: (*a*) beginning of the *Lamento d'Arianna*, 'Lasciatemi morire', from Arianna (1608), from Tutte le opere, xi, ed. Malipiero; (*b*) Lamento dell'Ingrata, 'Ahi troppo è duro', from *Ballo delle ingrate* (1608), from *Tutte le opere*, viii, ed. Malipiero

(b)

Ex. 4.1. *continued*

sometimes eighth-note rests separate segments of the phrase. After the two opening gestures, the third segment of the phrase drops suddenly in pitch, only to build back up over five phrase segments either to or a step above the climactic pitch of the beginning. Thus, the start of the Ingrata's lament mirrors Arianna's opening cries, in musical detail as in poetic theme. Whether these similarities were the result of Monteverdi's invention or Virginia Andreini's is anyone's guess. Tim Carter has suggested, quite plausibly, that Andreini may have had more to do with the composition of Arianna's lament than the evidence of Monteverdi's publications allows.[6] Indeed, the formula of this opening gesture may be the imprint of Andreini's compositional hand.

The reception of these two works, however, together with Monteverdi's discussion of compositional process for *Arianna*, shows the laments to be fundamentally different. *Arianna* had the more enduring success, for in 1620, when Giovan Battista Andreini celebrated his *emancipazione* (coming of age as a comedian), garnering gifts of money and jewels from many of the noble houses of Europe in honour of his first twenty-five years on the stage, Vincenzo Gonzaga's contribution commemorated Virginia Andreini's performance of *Arianna*: 'From the Most Serene Signor Duke Vincenzo for the comedy of Arianna recited at court, a necklace with medallion valued at 210 scudi.'[7] In contrast, the Fedeli's other performances for the wedding of 1608 receive no mention in this document, and their participation in Ferdinando's wedding to Caterina de' Medici in 1617 is remembered in only the most general terms.

From the conclusion of their opening phrases, the two laments diverge in form and style and one can only surmise that these differences, one the embodiment of a radically new compositional style, the other of a type, contribute to the cause of *Arianna*'s more lasting success. Whereas 'Lasciatemi morire' continues in a free flow of recitative wherein the text truly governs the musical setting, 'Ahi troppo è duro' evinces a stronger musical voice that demands poetic servitude. Monteverdi's 'via naturale alla immitatione' thus stands in stark contrast to the French style of the Ingrata's lament, two of the defining features of which are structural repetition and the alternation of textures.

As examples of the types of music performed by the *prime donne innamorate* of the commedia dell'arte, the laments of Arianna and the Ingrata stand at opposite ends of a spectrum. The first, written in a style evocative of the improvisatory singing implied in Garzoni's epithet regarding Vincenza Armani, that she sang 'in the manner of a musician and poet', brings neoclassicism to life in music. The second embodies a formulaic approach to theatrical practice that easily matches the

[6] Tim Carter, 'Lamenting Ariadne?'
[7] ASMN, Notarile, notaio Pallini Giulio Cesare, 1620, 31 Jan. 'Dal Ser.mo S.r Duca Vincenzo p[er] la comedia di Arian[n]a recitata in corte una colanna con medaglia di valore di scudi n.o 210.' Ferdinando's contribution, which is substantial, is listed as follows: 'Dal Ser.mo S.r Duca Ferdinando in più volte di oro regali, et altre bonemani nelle sue nozze collana gargantilia in tutto alla somma di scudi n.o 1900.'

generation of *scenari* and set *contrasti* in the composition of plays. This is not to say that the performance styles employed for each would be inherently different, although as written artefacts the two laments certainly are. The strophic repetitions of 'Ahi troppo è duro', like those of the song contest in *Mirtilla* discussed in Chapter 2, recommend to the singer an indulgence in ornamentation that is circumscribed by the yoke of structural regularity. 'Lasciatemi morire', by contrast, contains such improvisatory outpourings within the composition itself, and can therefore shy away from cyclic patterns of repetition. Comparisons of the compositional techniques, musical and poetic forms, and performance styles embodied in the two songs will illustrate the enormous breadth of musical experience that encompassed the lament genre and which demanded of its audiences a studied, tearful response.

The lament of the Ingrata provides us with one of the finest examples of a *canzone alla francese* and is therefore related, in some degree, to Monteverdi's *Scherzi musicali* of 1607, to Isabella Andreini's performance of *canzonette alla francese* for the Medici wedding of 1589, and to her canzonette written in imitation of Gabriello Chiabrera's *scherzi* and published in 1601. Just as discussion of the *canto alla francese* in Chapter 2 was limited to vocal production and the establishment of a time frame during which the French style was said to be performed at Italian courts, I limit my discussion of it here to issues of form and specifically to those works written in the strophic form of the canzonetta. Imbedded within Rinuccini's French-styled court ballet, the Ingrata's plaint follows structural outlines very much like those dictated in the preface to Monteverdi's *Scherzi musicali* the year prior to Francesco's and Margherita's wedding:

Before beginning to sing, the Ritornello should be played two times.

The Ritornellos should be played at the end of each stanza in the upper parts by two violini da braccio, and in the bass by the chitarrone, or harpsichord, or other similar instrument.

The first Soprano, the first stanza having been sung by three voices with the two violins, can be sung solo, or at the lower octave, in the following stanzas, returning, however, in the last stanza to the same three voices and the same violins.

Where lines are drawn in place of the words, the notes that are placed above the lines are to be played, but not sung.[8]

---

[8] Monteverdi, *Scherzi*, trans. based on Ossi, 'Claudio Monteverdi's *Ordine novo*', 277: 'Prima che si cominci a cantare, si dovrà sonare due volte il Ritornello. I Ritornelli dovranno esser sonati in fine d'ogni stanza ne i Soprani da due Violini da braccio, & nel Basso dal

In addition to this explication of musical form and instrumentation, analysis of Monteverdi's compositions written in the French style has enabled scholars, most notably Claudio Gallico and Nino Pirrotta, to infer other compositional techniques of the *canto alla francese*. Gallico and Pirrotta share a belief that the French manner of Monteverdi's *scherzi* comprises in part an imitation of the *musique mesurée*, but also of the less systematic *air de cour*. From the *air de cour*, Pirrotta says, the *canto alla francese* derives a measured dignity, a prevalent quarternary rhythm, a frequent inflection of two eighth notes for one syllable of text, and perhaps also a certain intangible harmonic quality. This elusive whisper of harmony evinces itself in Monteverdi's *scherzi* in a tendency towards homophonic textures between vocal and instrumental parts.[9] His setting of Chiabrera's 'Amorosa pupilletta' illustrates each of these characteristics (see Ex. 4.2).

Isabella Andreini's *scherzi*, especially those written in honour of Chiabrera, imply a similar style and form of musical setting with their steady strophic repetitions, narrative intimacy, and ubiquitous anapaests. Giulio Santo Pietro del Negro's setting of 'Movèa dolce un zefiretto', for example, designated Neapolitan yet published in Venice the same year as Monteverdi's *Scherzi musicali*, imitates the French style recommended by the song's lyrics and shows marked similarities to Monteverdi's compositional technique as well (Ex. 4.3). I include a brief analysis of it here to demonstrate a different, yet contemporary, composer's approach to setting the formulaic stress patterns of Chiabreresque canzonettas and also to show the genre's capacity for variation in the use of instrumental passages.

Negro's *Movèa dolce un zefiretto* has the same fully texted, three-part, homophonic format of Monteverdi's *scherzi*, which emphasizes the harmonic sweetness of its setting. Its unwavering eight-syllable lines inspiring a somewhat different treatment of the anapaests that pervade the poem, the *scherzo*'s playful banter between rhythm and metre still yields a delightful buoyancy reminiscent of Chiabrera's characterization of

Chitarrone, o Clavicembalo, o altro simile instrumento. Il primo Soprano, cantata, che sia la prima stanza a tre voci con i Violini potrà esser cantato solo, o vero all'ottava bassa nelle stanze che seguono, ripigliando però l'ultima stanza con l'istesse tre voci; & i violini stessi. Dove si vedranno tirate alcune linee nella sede delle parole, quelle note che sono ad esse linee sopraposte dovranno esser sonate, ma non cantate.'

[9] Gallico, 'Emblemi strumentali negli "scherzi" di Monteverdi'; Pirrotta, 'Scelte poetiche di Monteverdi'.

EX. 4.2. Monteverdi, *Amorosa pupilletta*, from *Tutte le opere*, x, ed. Malipiero

French love poetry. This buoyancy matches the lilting play of images in Andreini's poem, conveyed by a prismatic combination of changing accents and soft, open vowels:

> Movèa dolce un zefiretto
> I suoi tepidi sospiri,
> E lasciando l'aureo letto
> Fiammeggiò per gli alti giri
> L'Alba. E 'l Mondo colorìo
> Mentre rose, e gigli aprìo.
>   Quando Ninfa Amor m'offerse
> Ch'adornò d'altr'Alba i campi.

Ex. 4.3. Giulio Santo Pietro del Negro, *Movèa dolce un zefiretto* (*Il terzo libro dell'amore canzonette, villanelle, et arie napoletano a tre voci*, 1607)

> Forse Pari in Ida scerse
> Così chiari ardenti lampi?
> Nò, che Venere si crede
> Finta alhor, che costei vede.
>   Ella ornava gli ornamenti
> Col sembiante pellegrino:
> E giovan gli elementi
> Vagheggiando il bel divino:
> E sù l'oro de i capelli
> Rideàn lieti i fior novelli. . . .

(A little zephyr sweetly moved his warm sighs and Dawn, leaving her golden bed, passed afire through the high circlings while it gave colour to the world and opened roses and lilies. When Love offered me the Nymph, who beautified the fields with another dawn, perhaps Paris on Ida chose such clear, ardent lights? No, Venus is thought a fiction now that he has seen her. She adorned that which adorned with her strange countenance; and the elements benefit, gazing fondly on divine beauty; and upon the gold of her hair fresh flowers laughed for joy.)

The texture and voicing for two canti and a basso that *Movèa dolce un zefiretto* shares with Monteverdi's *scherzi* suggests that the architecture of musical performance outlined above might also apply to Negro's composition, which carries the instruction 'for playing and singing on the chitarrone, clavicembalo, and other instruments'.[10] Its lack of a separate ritornello, however, apart from the implication that *Movèa dolce un zefiretto* was not intended for the stage, dictates either that the instrumental passages between stanzas be left out entirely or that some or all of the music that sets the text be used also for the ritornello.

Monteverdi's scenario for *Il ballo delle ingrate* instructs the performers to follow a related format that alternates between orchestral ritornello and verses of the strophic song. Beginning with a statement of the *entrata*, which encompasses sixteen bars of four-part instrumental homophony played twice, the Ingrata's lament follows with the phrase shown in Ex. 4.1(*b*). At the conclusion of the recitative-like opening, the Ingrata sings a refrain, the last line of which is repeated by a chorus of four voices. She then sings another five lines in recitative style before repeating the refrain. The lament ends with the chorus's final imitation of the last line. Monteverdi's scenario reads:

Of the ungrateful souls, their clothing will be the colour of ashes, adorned with false tears. At the end of the *ballo* they return to the Inferno in the same manner as they left it, and to the same sorrowful music. One remains on stage at the end, performing the written lament, then she enters the Inferno. As the curtain rises, a symphony will be played *ad libitum*.[11]

Although 'Ahi troppo è duro' follows a different and more complicated poetic structure than Chiabrera's *scherzi*, which modifies the archetype, Monteverdi's instructions for the performance of *canzonette alla francese* call for the adoption of a similar alternation of instrumental, solo vocal, and choral textures within the architecture of the simpler strophic form. Each *scherzo* is to begin with an initial instrumental ritornello that is played twice, like the *entrata* of the Ingrata's lament.

What follows is less overt because the choral repetitions of the refrain in 'Ahi troppo è duro' serve a double function as both choral verse and ritornello. For the *scherzi*, the ritornello is to be played and repeated after

[10] The title page of Negro's publication reads: *Il terzo libro dell'amorose canzonette, villanelle, & arie napolitane a tre voci. Da sonare, & cantare su 'l chitarrone, clavicembalo, & altri stromenti.*

[11] Monteverdi, *Ballo delle ingrate*, in *Tutte le opere*, viii (ed. Malipiero), 314: 'Delle anime ingrate, il lor vestito sarà di color ceneritio, adornato di lacrime finte; finito il ballo tornano nel Inferno, nel medesimo modo del'uscita, e al medesimo suono lamentevole, restandone una nella fine in scena, facendo il lamento che sta scritto, poi entra nel'Inferno. Al levar de la tela si farà una sinfonia a beneplacito.'

each stanza of the song, forming a kind of refrain. A chorus is to frame the entire song by singing the first and last stanzas, and a soloist may perform the remaining strophes, singing the canto part either at pitch or an octave lower. In the *ballo*, there is no allotment of an instrumental interlude between verses (bar 673) or a sinfonia at the end, and so the soloist's refrain and its foreshortened choral repetition act as the ritornello. Allowing for the necessary distinctions between a strophic song and a song comprising verses and a refrain, the principal differences in the performance of the two genres lie in the presentation of the initial text by the soloist rather than the chorus and in the vocal enunciation of the ritornello. (See Table 4.1.)

A schematic comparison of the two forms affords a clearer sense of the stylistic features of the *canzone alla francese* and, in retrospect, suggests how the performance by Andreini's mother-in-law in Florence in 1589 might have unfolded. Incorporating in some measure a repeated refrain structure, which may be enunciated either instrumentally or vocally, the *canzone alla francese* as seen here also comprises an alternation of solo vocal and choral textures, wherein the chorus repeats musical material, either as part of the refrain or in the body of a strophic repetition. Further, the song begins with an instrumental overture played twice by an ensemble of viole da braccio together with a clavicembalo and a chitarrone and ends with the final articulation of the refrain.

This analysis shows the lament of the Ingrata to be very different from Arianna's plaint, and the crux of their difference lies in the relationship of poetic text to music. Whereas *Arianna* demanded of Monteverdi the creation of a musical rhetoric, which he found difficult to conceive, the lament of the Ingrata evinces a musical style and language that he had worked out nearly a decade before, during his trip to Spa in 1599. The rhetorical aspects of Arianna's lament denied to Monteverdi the structural repetitions he wrote so beautifully into 'Ahi troppo è duro', and apart from the sporadic insertions of 'O Teseo, o Teseo mio' into the text, Rinuccini's poetry gave him little indication of large-scale points of articulation that might be served by the return of a motif or the repetition of a musical phrase. The additive repetitions of Cicero's rhetorical system, which engendered a stuttering phrase in Rinuccini's text such as 'non son, non son quell'io, non son quell'io che i feri detti sciolse', required Monteverdi to learn to imitate not the singer's words, but her passions. His setting of the line, which ignores the text repetition and sets the words 'non son' with three different inflections and three different rhythmic patterns,

TABLE 4.1. *Comparison of Monteverdi's* Lamento dell'ingrata *and his instructions for performing* scherzi

Lamento dell'ingrata			*Scherzi musicali*
five viole da braccio			two violini da braccio
clavicembalo			clavicembalo
chitarrone			chitarrone
entrata			ritornello
entrata			ritornello
			stanza 1: chorus
			ritornello
			ritornello
a	[Andreini] 'Ahi troppo, ahi troppo è duro crudel sentenza, e vie più cruda pena! tornar a lagrimar ne l'antro oscuro.'		stanza 2: soloist
R	'Aer sereno e puro, addio, per sempre, addio o cielo, o sole, addio, lucide stelle, apprendete pietà, donne e donzelle.'		ritornello
[R]	[chorus] 'Apprendete pietà, donne e donzelle.'		ritornello (abbreviated)
b	[Andreini] 'Al fumo, a' gridi, a' pianti, a sempiterno, affanno! Ahi dove son le pompe, ove gli amanti, dove sen vanno donne che sì pregiate al mundo furno?'		stanza 3: soloist
R	'Aer sereno e puro, addio, per sempre, addio o cielo, o sole, addio, lucide stelle, apprendete pietà, donne e donzelle.'		ritornello
[R]	[chorus] 'Apprendete pietà, donne e donzelle.'		ritornello (abbreviated)

demonstrates the kind of imitation of abstractions he confronted in this lament (Ex. 4.4). Herein lies the heart of the *via naturale alla immitazione*.

The fundamental conceptual difference between the laments of Arianna and the Ingrata points towards a typological opposition as well, for the Ingrata awaits no *deus ex machina* to release her from her fate, as the

Ex. 4.4. Monteverdi, *Lamento d'Arianna*, 'Non son, non son quell'io'

sympathetic Bacchus provides for Arianna. And Arianna, guilty of loving to foolish excess, reflects, like Alice in the mirror, the antithesis of the Ingrata, who is guilty of not loving at all. And yet the courtiers wept for both. They also wept, so writes Follino, for the lament of Europa in the second intermedio for *L'idropica* and for the lament of Iphigenia in *Il sacrificio d'Ifigenia*. Europa's plaint, 'Cari paterni regni', elicited tears of pity ('she singing with sweetest harmony these grieving notes, that tears of pity arose in the audience') and Iphigenia, on the verge of death by sacrifice, 'with so beautiful a lament invited the stones to weep with her'.[12]

Follino's tearful imagery invokes a studied refrain that had signified an empathetic response to the recitation of laments since Augustine, and

---

[12] The passage regarding Arianna's lament ('è fu pur una dama che non versasse qualche lagrimetta al suo pianto') is famous; the others are not as well known. The description of the lament from the *Ballo delle ingrate* reads, 'una delle Ingrate, ch'era rimasta sù 'l palco quando le altre discesero à ballare, proruppe in così lagrimosi accenti accompagnati da sospiri, e da singulti, che non fu cuor di donna così fiero in quel teatro che non versasse per gli occhi qualche lagrima pietosa. Le parole, ch'ella disse nel suo bel pianto furono le seguenti. *Ahi troppo, ahi troppo è duro . . .*' (Follino, *Compendio*, 133; see also Fabbri, *Monteverdi* (trans. Carter), 86, 88). Of Europa's lament, 'Cari paterni regni', Follino wrote 'cantando ella con dolcissima armonia queste lagrimose note, che destarono per la pietà le lagrime ne gli ascoltanti . . .' (p. 84). And finally, of Iphigenia, on the verge of sacrifice: 'l'infelice Donzella, che con sì bel lamento invitava le pietre à pianger seco . . .' (p. 146).

which testified to the emotional catharsis designated by Aristotle as the primary aim of tragic poets. Confirmation of the trope's classical antecedents appears in the preface to Marco da Gagliano's *Dafne*, where he wrote that Monteverdi brought back to life the passionate affects of music from the ancient world: 'Sig. Claudio Monteverdi, most celebrated musician, director of your highness's music, composed the arias in a manner so exquisite that one can in truth affirm that the valour of ancient music is renewed, since he visibly moved the entire theatre to tears.'[13] It is worth noting that Frangipani wrote in similar terms of the music composed by Claudio Merulo for the Gelosi's performance of his *Tragedia* in 1574. These descriptive metaphors suggest that the Mantuan ladies' purported tears may not necessarily be read as an unmediated response to the play put before them, or to its musical representation. They perhaps did not weep at all, although Gagliano suggests they did, or their tears may have been a studied reaction to an equally studied trope. For, as Anthony Grafton has written in regard to Renaissance humanism and its texts, 'reading, of course, requires more than a text and an editor; the reader must also play a part and have a stage on which to play it'.[14]

Mantuan courtiers were well versed in enacting texts as part of the reading experience, as Augustine had been before them. In the first book of his *Confessions*, Augustine described school exercises he performed as a boy, of a variety later adopted by Guarino Guarini, whose pedagogical system, mentioned in Chapter 3, originated in Ferrara and subsequently spread throughout northern Italy and into France, the Low Countries, and the Empire.[15] Augustine wrote of his tearful empathy for Dido, as he and his classmates were required to compose—and to recite—their own versions of women's laments from Virgil's *Aeneid*, using set figures of words to create speeches appropriate to each woman's social station, sex, and predicament.[16] Figures of words, like the rules of counterpoint for

---

[13] Gagliano, *Dafne* (Florence, 1608), cited in Solerti, *Gli albori*, ii. 69: 'il signor Claudio Monteverdi, musico celebratissimo, capo della musica di S.A., compose l'arie in modo sì esquisito, che si può con verità affermare che si rinnovasse il pregio dell'antica musica, perciò che visibilmente mosse tutto il teatro a lagrime.'

[14] Grafton, *Commerce with the Classics*, 15.

[15] See Grafton and Jardine, *From Humanism to the Humanities*, 1.

[16] In the context of his discussion, Augustine wrote three times of his tearful empathy for Dido (*Confessions*, i. 13): 'I wept for Dido, who surrendered her life to the sword' ('et flebam Didonem extinctam ferroque extrema secutam'); 'I learned to lament the death of Dido, who killed herself for love' ('plorare Didonem mortuam, quia se occidit ab amore'); and he describes himself as 'bewailing the fate of Dido, who died for love of Aeneas' ('flente

musical composition, are the building blocks of rhetorical invention, and students were expected to employ them, in a specific order and over the course of a single speech, as a method for ensuring the composition's craft.

Guarino advocated similar rhetorical exercises as a way of preparing his students—many of whom would be secretaries—for life at court, emphasizing the modes of expression suitable to its various members. Here it was understood that figures such as Dido and Juno (the other prominent high-born lamenting woman in the *Aeneid*) embodied the majesty and decorum appropriate to the noblewomen of the court. Still in practice a century later, the recitation of laments of goddesses and ancient queens continued to be viewed as an introduction to the rhetorical styles proper to women such as the Infanta of Savoy and the Duchess of Mantua.

The exercise of impersonating noblewomen *in extremis* defined for schoolboys the boundaries between propriety and prodigality through the expression and subsequent retraction of emotional outbursts. Although a woman's nature was seen as volatile and prone to excesses of emotion (as true in early modern literature as it had been in the ancient world), the composition's prevailing rationality was guaranteed by its formulaic structure, achieved through the use of figures of words. Allegorically, the emotional outbursts conceived within this formulaic compass might be seen as equivalent to individualistic errancy within the otherwise sound and well-organized hierarchy of the court. Laments thus taught schoolboys not only rhetoric, but decorum. Learning to lament further gave them an outlet for the emotional stress of their own adolescence and showed them how 'feminine' excesses of emotion were impulses to be tamed and brought into harmony with the self-discipline of becoming an adult male.

The rhetorical imitation of affects and its attendant effect on a play's audience is also the focus of Aristotle's discussion of tragedy in the *Poetics*: 'Tragedy is an imitation of an action that is serious, complete, and possessing magnitude; in embellished language, each kind of which is used separately in the different parts; in the mode of action and not narrated; and effecting through pity and fear [what we call] the *catharsis* of such emotions.'[17] In this passage, Aristotle identifies not only the primary

Didonis mortem, quae fiebat amando Aenean'). For a more detailed treatment of this discussion, see Woods, 'Rhetoric in the Medieval Classroom'; Grendler, *Schooling in Renaissance Italy*, 203–34; Grafton and Jardine, *From Humanism to the Humanities*, chs. 1–2.

[17] Aristotle, *The Poetics* (trans. Hutton), 50.

emotional content of tragedy, but also the central characteristics that distinguish tragedy from epic poetry. Both relate serious events of magnitude, and both are expected to present a complete plot, with beginning, middle, and end. The most commonly cited difference between the two genres is the unity of time: whereas epic carries no restriction with regard to the passage of time, events represented in tragedy are normally to conclude within a single revolution of the sun.

But Aristotle also notes in this passage two features that had an even greater impact on the representation of tragedy in Renaissance Mantua, and which bear directly on the interpretation of the performance of *Arianna* and on Rinuccini's unprecedented use of the generic label 'tragedia' in the libretto. These are that tragedy should be recited 'in embellished language' and that its poetry should be 'in the mode of action and not narrated'. Both refer to the staging of the play and to its visual and aural representation.

Rinuccini's (and Follino's) designation of *Arianna* as a tragedy made that play the first of its kind to be set to music in its entirety. (As stated in Chapter 2, Frangipani's *Tragedia* belies its title by taking the form of a set of intermedi.) Rinuccini had deliberately eschewed the appellation for *Euridice*, written for the wedding of Maria de' Medici and Henri IV in 1600. And *Arianna*, for much of the period of its preparation, was referred to by contemporary writers, including Carlo Rossi and Antonio Costantini, as a 'commedia'. Nor did the comic label disappear with time, as the passage cited above from Giovan Battista Andreini's *emancipazione* shows.[18]

Paolo Fabbri has written that 'Arianna tends only partly towards tragedy—the genre is diluted by contact with the elements of the piscatorial eclogue and with more extrinsic demands for spectacle . . .'.[19] And Tim Carter has shown that, in spite of Rinuccini's ultimate designation of *Arianna* as a tragedy, the structure of his libretto is atypical of its genre. It was probably altered, Carter argues, a number of times in the course of preparations for the performance on 28 May.[20] The lament itself may have

---

[18] ASMN, Gonzaga, b. 2712, fasc. 20, lett. 6 (Carlo Rossi, 4 Mar. 1608) and lett. 7 (Carlo Rossi, 10 Mar. 1608); a transcription of the letter dated 10 Mar., together with a transcription of Costantini's letter of 18 [recte 15] Mar., is given in Solerti, *Gli albori*, i. 94–5. For the latter, see also Besutti, 'The "Sala degli Specchi" Uncovered'. Translations of Solerti's transcriptions appear in Fabbri, *Monteverdi* (trans. Carter), 82–3.

[19] Fabbri, *Monteverdi* (trans. Carter), 96.

[20] Carter, 'Lamenting Ariadne?', 399–400.

been an insertion, formed in part by Andreini's extrapolations, and its inclusion makes Arianna's role by far the longest of any female operatic character to date. It compares favourably, however, with the role of Amarilli in Guarini's *Il pastor fido*, whose lines, albeit spoken, number 600 to Arianna's 146, and with the title role in Giovan Battista Andreini's *Lo schiavetto*, one of Virginia Andreini's showpieces, which has 432 lines. Nor does the work end in tragedy; instead it sports a *lieto fine*, the protagonist whisked off to heaven in blissful wedlock with the god of merriment and laughter: the same Bacchus who tamed tigers and whose gift of harmony and rhythm to the Florentines in 1589 symbolized the civility of the Medici court.

Rinuccini's original conception of the play's form thus does not seem to have been that of a strictly defined Aristotelian tragedy, and the generic designation may have come late in the process of composition, perhaps after the important meeting with Duchess Eleonora de' Medici on 26 February, during which she is reported by Carlo Rossi to have called the play 'very dry' ('assai sciutta'), or perhaps after Virginia Andreini was engaged to sing the leading role, on or about 9 March. In any event, Rinuccini's insertion of the lament between the two narratives of Nunzio Primo and Nunzio Secondo brings the poetic mode of the play into greater conformity with Aristotle's dictum that tragic poetry should be in the active mode rather than narrated. And inclusion of the sung lament gives the play more of what Aristotle called 'embellished language', which he identified as the inclusion of music and spectacle in performance: 'some parts of the play carried on solely in metrical speech while others again are sung'.[21] Monteverdi's musical setting of the lament in the recitational style that he later called the 'via naturale alla immitatione' seems further to reinforce this Aristotelian aesthetic of setting tragedies in 'embellished language'.[22]

Duchess Eleonora de' Medici's interest in *Arianna* and her intervention in its preparation may have derived in part from the festivities staged in honour of the wedding of her husband's cousin, Margherita of Austria, to Philip III of Spain ten years earlier, the last wedding celebrated in Mantua

---

[21] Aristotle, *The Poetics* (trans. Hutton), 50.
[22] Tomlinson has described *Arianna* as Monteverdi's 'first thorough-going realization' of the *via naturale alla immitatione* 'and its highest fulfillment', an assessment that is borne out in the composer's letters regarding his own work on the lament and his close collaboration with Rinuccini on the development of a musically sound manifestation of its poetry. See Tomlinson, 'Madrigal, Monody, and Monteverdi's "via naturale alla immitatione"'.

of a relative of the ruling family, and therefore a logical prototype for the 1608 celebrations.[23] Follino had been in charge of entertainments at court since the late 1580s, and so his recollection of the 1598 festivities would derive from his own participation in the event.[24] Monteverdi, too, whether or not he took part in the earlier wedding festivities, was certainly present, his settings of texts from *Il pastor fido* vetted at the home of Antonio Goretti in Ferrara the day after the groom's proxy and the bride took their vows in that city. When Margherita's entourage relocated to Mantua four days later, the composer presumably returned with them to the court of his employment. As noted in Chapter 3, Vincenzo Gonzaga recalled the Andreini family and their troupe from Bologna just weeks prior to the performance, and on 22 November the Gonzaga court mounted its elaborate spectacle of Guarini's *Il pastor fido*.

Composed in the 1580s and published in 1589, Guarini's pastoral tragicomedy had a tortured history, due to the play's enormous length and generic unconventionality, which kept it from being staged for over a decade after its conception. Vincenzo Gonzaga had initially asked Guarini to finish it in time for his wedding to Eleonora de' Medici in 1584. Even when complete, the work required extensive editing for every performance. Its author's deconstruction of dramatic genres, debated at length in the published quarrels between Guarini and Giason Denores, caused an upheaval in the literary world that resulted both in a polarization of theoretical positions and in an explosion of compositional energy in the pastoral genre.[25] Nor did Monteverdi escape the negative reception of *Il pastor fido*, for his settings of excerpts from Guarini's poem—themselves a deconstruction of musical convention—bore the brunt of Giovanni Maria Artusi's denunciation of his compositional authority in 1600. And

---

[23] Margherita of Austria and Philip III of Spain were married by Pope Clement VIII in Ferrara on 15 Nov. 1598. Margherita's aunt, Eleonora of Austria, was Guglielmo Gonzaga's wife and Vincenzo's mother. Due in part to the devolution of the city of Ferrara to papal authority the year prior to Margherita's marriage, the central festivities were hosted by her cousin in Mantua.

[24] For evidence of Follino's directorship of theatrical activities from 1588, see the financial records conserved in ASMN, Gonzaga, b. 402, fos. 75^r–203, 359^v, 360^v; b. 410-B, fasc. 43, fo. 24^v. As the court's chronicler, he produced, among others, the *Descrittione delle solenni cerimonie* and the *Descrittione dell'infirmità*, both published in 1587.

[25] Denores, *Poetica*; Guarini, *Il Verrato*; Denores, *Apologia*; Guarini, *Il Verato secondo*; id., *Compendio*. The most comprehensive history I have found of the early performances and contemporary reception of Guarini's tragicomedy is the introduction to Guarini, *Il pastor fido* (ed. Guglielminetti). The best overview of the theoretical debate and its primary sources is still Weinberg, *A History of Literary Criticism*, 1074–105.

who could ignore his search for yet another musical style for *Arianna*? Not even the works of Plato, he wrote, could help him create it.[26]

The composition of *Arianna* may thus have caused its authors and sponsors some concern, given the negative press from Denores and Artusi regarding innovations in compositional technique stemming from *Il pastor fido* and given Monteverdi's continued exploration of new musical languages. Clearly, the new work would either be a smashing success or a crashing disaster. Rinuccini's insistence on the label *tragedia* for *Arianna* suggests that the critical reception of Guarini's tragicomedy was as troubled as its pre-performance history, and that a firm generic designation for his own play was desired in order to foster more positive reviews. Follino, too, in describing the audience's tearful reaction to *Arianna* in terms of emotional catharsis, highlighted the play's adherence to Aristotelian rules and thus guarded against its potential detractors. In stressing the play's conformity to classical poetic theory, both authors betrayed a shared belief that *Arianna* in fact did not conform, and that in both its composition and its performance, their tragedy—and Monteverdi's and Andreini's—was perilously new.

Reports regarding Virginia Andreini's preparations for the role of Arianna suggest similar management of interpretation along humanist lines. When Antonio Costantini noted on 15 March 1608 that she had memorized the part in six days, he invoked the Ciceronian notion of a facile memory as one of the traits of a fine rhetorician and thereby ascribed to Andreini Orphic powers (all the better that the comedienne actually pulled it off). The Mantuan courtiers and their peers would have understood this from childhood studies of the *Rhetorica ad Herennium*. According to statistics taken in Venice in 1587–8—when a 28-year-old courtier listening to Andreini perform Arianna would have been 8 years old and reciting his own laments at school—the *Rhetorica ad Herennium* was by far the text most widely used to teach rhetoric in the early modern classroom.[27] Reference to it would have been as transparent to the Mantuan courtiers and their peers as Follino's depictions of courtiers weeping.

Costantini's praise, together with Follino's account of Andreini's

---

[26] Fabbri, *Monteverdi* (trans. Carter), 96. For arguments concerning the Artusi–Monteverdi controversy, see most notably, Palisca, 'The Artusi–Monteverdi Controversy'; Carter, 'Artusi, Monteverdi, and the Poetics'; Cusick, 'Gendering Modern Music'; and Ossi, 'Claudio Monteverdi's *Ordine novo*'.

[27] Grendler, *Schooling in Renaissance Italy*, 213.

affecting performance, conspired to ennoble not only the work but also the performer, a strategy that neutralized the danger of having in the title role a professional actress whose talents might otherwise be misconstrued as bawdy or rough. In spite of Andreini's renown as a tragic actress and her incontestable strength of memory, the courtiers probably did not weep, or, if they did, they wept in response to having recognized their own roles in this humanist drama. For what Follino's report shows is the existence of an interpretative agenda for the wedding's souvenir publication—an agenda founded on the rhetorical education of its audience and their knowledge of humanist tropes—which operated independently of the publication's function as description, and which places the veracity of that description in question.

The story of Arianna's betrayal was anything but new to the Mantuan and Savoyard courtiers in 1608, and it would not have required either Follino's or Rinuccini's recitation to recall its plot or characters to mind. Versions of the tale type circulated in the poems of Catullus and in Ovid's *Metamorphoses* and *Heroides*, among other sources. Interpretation of the myth, however, and elucidation of its tropes did bear repeating, if the classical text were to have meaning in a seventeenth-century environment. Follino's interpretive management led his readers to see beyond the Mantuan stage play to its Greek and Roman antecedents. As the following passage from the lament of Ariadne in the *Heroides* shows, the Cretan princess's predicament, in its classical guise, is interwoven with themes of death and mourning:[28]

> Yet try to see me now, not with your eyes but
> with your mind, as I cling to this rock
> that is drenched again and again by the waves.
> See my hair, loose like one in mourning;
> . . .
> . . . And if I die before you return,
> it will be you who carries my bones from this place.[29]

---

[28] Rose, Robertson, and Dietrich note that 'Originally Ariadne was a Minoan goddess of nature . . . Her myth centres on marriage and death, combining the sorrowful and happy aspects of the annual decay and renewal of vegetation. Each part is celebrated in her two festivals on Naxos, and both elements are preserved in the Attic Anthesteria', a Dionysian festival of wine and death; *Oxford Classical Dictionary*, 3rd edn. (Oxford, 1996), s.v. 'Ariadne'; cf. also 'Anthesteria'.

[29] Ovid, *Heroides* (trans. Innes), 94. The parallel text from Rinuccini's *Arianna* reads 'E in queste arene ancora, / cibo di fere dispietate e crude, / lascierà l'ossa ignude.'

The Politics of Description 151

This helps to account for the odd insistence of Rinuccini's Arianna that she will die abandoned on the island of Dia, even though a stalwart squad of fisherfolk stands near:

> And on these shores,
> food for the wild, merciless, and cruel beasts,
> she will leave her bare bones.

Surprisingly, such allusions to death and mourning more closely relate Ariadne's tale to weddings and to the other entertainments sponsored by the Mantuan court in 1608. Death and mourning as marriage equivalents form the basis of dramatic conflict in the tragedies of Euripides, Aeschylus, and Sophocles, and the simultaneous representations of these themes defines the focus of activity in the ballet organized by Prince Francesco Gonzaga for the conclusion of the 1608 celebrations, *Il sacrificio d'Ifigenia*. Rehm has called this kind of conflation of wedding and funerary rites 'marriage to death'.

Francesco's *balletto* has leading roles for Iphigenia, her father Agamemnon, Achilles, and Ulysses, all of whom sing. As in the performance of *Arianna*, the adaptation of Iphigenia's tale offered to the courtiers and their guests includes a *deus ex machina* that turns the imminently bleak conclusion of the plot into a *lieto fine*. The goddess Diana forestalls the protagonist's death just as the Sacerdote concludes his prayer and raises the sacrificial sword. The Sacerdote's prayer is preceded by a train of laments, beginning with that of Iphigenia, and followed in succession by those of Achilles, Agamemnon, and the Chorus. The sacrificial altar thereafter becomes a wedding altar, and Iphigenia is given in marriage to Achilles.

The ritualistic outline of the scenario consists of three parts. The first comprises Iphigenia's removal from her father's care, symbolized by Agamemnon offering his daughter for sacrifice:

> Figlia mia, cara figlia,
> chi mi concede, ohime, che per te mora?
> Perche non può 'l mio sangue
> spegner l'ira del Cielo?
> E se de l'aspra offesa
> la colpa fù sol mia,
> perche non è sol mia la pena ancora?
> Figlia mia, cara figlia,
> chi mi concede ohime, che per te mora?

(Daughter mine, dear daughter, who would allow me, alas! to die for you? Why cannot my blood dispel the ire of Heaven? And if of the sharp offence the blame was mine alone, why is not the pain also mine alone? Daughter mine, dear daughter, who would allow me, alas! to die for you?)[30]

The second phase of the ritual encompasses Iphigenia's tearful passage through a liminal state of uncertainty and fear, culminating in the lament:

> Morir dunque pur deggio?
> Padre mio, caro padre,
> e tù ancor m'abbandoni al punto estremo?
> Così condotta sono
> da le nozze à l'esequie? ò Cielo, ò stelle
> perche non posso almen prima, ch'io mora
> con le compagne mie per monti alpestri
> girmen piangendo la mia dura sorte?

(Must I die then? Father, dear father, and you would still abandon me in the end? Am I thus to be conducted from my wedding to my funeral? Oh heaven, oh stars, why may I not at least, before I die, wander with my companions among the alpine mountains, weeping my hard fate?)[31]

Finally, the third part of the scenario embodies Iphigenia's transferral to the protective custody of her husband Achilles, as implied by the participation of both men and women together in the final dance.

Securely framed within the confines of her father's authority in the first phase of the ritual and of her husband's authority in the third, the bride in the interior second phase languishes in a never-never land devoid of community and patriarchal authority. Read from a different perspective, however, her lament, although riddled with anxiety and fear and by definition indicative of emotional stress, represents no one's thoughts but her own, and thereby communicates the perspective of the individual on the ritualistic ceremony in which she is a central participant. The position of the lament at the end of this second phase, serving as the catalyst to the conclusion of the ritual, is also important, because it thus carries an implication of complicity in the process, the bride's formal agreement to enter into the marriage, and even more, her yearning for the matrimonial rite to continue.

The scenario for *Arianna* is identical to this arrangement, even though Arianna motivates her own removal from her father's care by

---

[30] Follino, *Compendio*, 144.
[31] Ibid. 145.

undermining his authority. In the classical version of the myth, the people of Athens pay tribute to the Kingdom of Crete by offering up seven women and seven men every year to the Minotaur in exchange for peace. With Arianna's help, Teseo kills the Minotaur, thus thwarting the treaty enforced by her father and ending Athenian servitude to the foreign power. Arianna's actions, therefore, subverted not only her father's authority over her, but his authority as ruler of his people. The ties to her parents severed, Arianna in Rinuccini's poem enters a liminal state of transition, symbolized in part by her embarkation and by the movement of Teseo's ship over the waves. While still at sea, in all senses of the phrase, Arianna concludes the second phase of the 'marriage to death' ritual in lament ('Let me die, let me die . . .'), at which point the *deus ex machina* descends to bring about the reversal of the plot. The third and concluding phase of the rite, in which Arianna is conducted into the care of her husband, is embodied in the first and only utterance of Bacchus, 'Joined with me in eternal serenity . . .'.

The reference to Achilles in *Il sacrificio d'Ifigenia* bolsters the interpretation of 'marriage to death' rituals like this one as rites of passage from childhood to adulthood, and it further encourages a perspective of the lamenting woman as a representation of masculine, as well as feminine, adolescence. As portrayed in Statius' epic poem the *Achilleid*, Achilles' mother Thetis, in order to keep her son from the Trojan War, dressed him in girl's clothing and hid him among the cloistered daughters of Lycomedes on the island of Scyros. Unable to suppress his adolescent sexual desires for long, Achilles rapes the girl Deidamia. Ulysses then tricks the young hero into betraying the falsity of his feminine disguise with gifts of armaments—a shining sword and shield—which Achilles finds irresistible. The King of Ithaca removes the boy's girlish attire and leads him into battle at Troy, where Achilles subsequently wins the war for the Athenian forces by besting the Trojan leader Hector before the gates of the city. He thus stands as the archetypical example of manhood and virility. David Konstan has explained the significance of Achilles' adolescent transvestism as a prelude to sexual desire and the will to procreate:

The tale of Achilles' disguise has the appearance of a myth of maturation from the status of preadolescence when a boy still dwelt among the women of the house, to adulthood, when he would be expected to manifest an interest in manly occupations such as warfare, and also in women both as objects of sexual desire and as potential bearers of his offspring. Achilles' assumption of the guise of a girl may be seen, on this interpretation, as an allegorical expression of the still equivocal sexuality of the child, at the same time that it locates the adolescent in the liminal space characteristic of rites of passage, in which normal codes of dress and comportment are typically suspended or inverted for a while.[32]

Konstan's gloss on the tale writes the myth of Achilles as an indication of the imminent birth of heirs and continuation of dynasty, the most important aspects of Margherita's and Francesco's marriage for the Duchy of Mantua and, indeed, its *raison d'être*.

Rehm has further shown how 'marriage to death' ceremonies such as that of Iphigenia and Achilles reflect not only the individual's negotiation of adolescence and sexual initiation, but also the formation of the family and household in regard to *patria*. This reading speaks to Margherita's and Francesco's dual roles both as private individuals and as icons of the Mantuan state. Marriage, Rehm explains, opens up the family to outside influences and to the inclusion of others within its protective sphere, whereas funerals represent a consolidation of the household and a closing of ranks that excludes foreigners. Both are rituals of transition: the wedding to the formation of a new household and its generation of heirs; the funeral to the contraction and withdrawal of the household through the death of one of its members. The parallelism and shared tripartite structure of the two ceremonies further reflect the common function of their enacted rites, that of framing the family and its members within the community. Both, for example, contain rituals of preparatory bathing and hair-cutting, and both include symbolic acts of veiling or enshrouding, as the bride or corpse is symbolically guided from one community to the next. Just as schoolboys' exercises in rhetoric helped to define the boundaries between courtly decorum and excess, the conflation of wedding and funeral rites helped to define the limits of kinship within the community, and of the community within the republic. Rehm's argument stresses this definition of kinship and blood relations in the depiction of 'marriage to death' rites:

---

[32] Konstan, *Broken Columns* (trans. Slavitt, 83; see also Woods, 'Rape and the Pedagogical Rhetoric'. Heller, in 'Reforming Achilles', has written of the Achilles tale-type as an 'atypical use of male transvestism' (562) and an indication of the effeminacy of pre-Metastasian opera, in that it comprises an 18th-c. 'reconstitution of operatic masculinity' (567). I disagree with both points. Given the myth's long history as a teaching text for the study of rhetoric and law, the male transvestism it depicts can hardly be described as atypical. Moreover, the composition of Metastasio's *Achille in Sciro* (set by Caldara) for the wedding of Maria Theresa and François Etienne, Duke of Lorraine (13 Feb. 1736), places the work firmly within the tradition of representing the myth of Achilles at noble weddings as a neoclassical metaphor for coming of age, sexual initiation, and childbearing.

... marriage involved reaching out beyond immediate blood-kin to incorporate an outsider and so guarantee the future of a new (or renewed) *oikos* [household]. Extending the family through nuptial ties of kinship, the *kedos* [in-law] relationships opened up new duties and opportunities in both the private and public spheres. Burial involved a counter movement, the return of a corpse (in the case of a male) from the public sphere back into the private, as the *oikos* took back the dead as one of its own.[33]

The relationship between family and state implied in the formulaic structures of wedding and funeral rituals—and by extension, the relationship between the individual and the state—resonates throughout Arianna's lament, as we read of her having left kingdom and country for Teseo:

> Turn back and look again
> at her who left country and kingdom for you,
> and of her misapprehension that she would become your queen:
>
> Are these the crowns,
> with which you adorn my brow?
> Are these the sceptres,
> these the gems and the gold . . . ?

Indeed, Arianna's first utterance in the play is not a proclamation of love for Teseo, but rather an apology that her sorrow at having left family and country disturbs him. Her words thus emphasize the cognitive dissonance between individual desire and royal responsibility:

> Sir, concede to me,
> in abandoning the land of my birth,
> at least one sigh
> to honour its remembrance.
> I know well that my sorrows give you pain,
> but as a virgin torn
> from her mother's breast,
> I cannot keep back every sigh.

Apollo's prologue to Rinuccini's *Arianna*, as reported by Follino, offered the conflation of such themes of marriage, sacrifice, and the relationship of family and individual to the state as lessons to the audience, and especially to Margherita of Savoy, whose wedding would serve as her initiation into Mantuan law and custom. And the aim of rhetoric, as defined by Giason Denores in his edition of Aristotle's *Ars rhetorica*, is

---

[33] Rehm, *Marriage to Death*, 70.

exactly this: to persuade the audience of the benefits of community, laws, and customs: 'from which Plato judged rhetoric to be a certain outgrowth of philosophy and of that most serious mode of poetry, which has as its aim to persuade its listeners of the comunal benefit of civic communities with laws, and with universal counsels concerning affairs, speech and customs'.[34] Apollo's words, invoking images of Parnassus and Olympian approval of the Mantuan marriage, thus seem also to entreat Margherita to view Arianna as a representation of herself and, as Suzanne Cusick argues, to interpret the tragedy as a warning to anyone who would follow her heart rather than submit it to royal honour and the common weal. Follino's Apollo sings from atop the same rock where Arianna later delivers her lament:

> Listen, royal bride, how
> a betrayed woman in love sighs on the solitary bank:
> perhaps it will happen that of the Argive state
> you may admire the ancient honour in new songs.

A mid-sixteenth-century reading by Giuseppe Orologgi of Giovanni dell'Anguillara's redaction of Ariadne's lament in his translation and expansion of Ovid's *Heroides* supports this interpretation. Orologgi draws particular attention to Ariadne's folly in betraying her father's household and government on the basis of a fickle promise of love: 'Let this tale of Arianna serve as a document to incautious women not to want to believe in the promises of one who appears to love them, because they run the risk of throwing themselves into the arms of ungrateful and faithless young men, for which they are left, with greatest infamy, often ruined.'[35]

But an earlier version of Rinuccini's prologue, found in the Mantuan edition of the libretto issued before Follino's account, differs from that given by Follino and does not conform to Orologgi's moralizing version of the tale type. Addressed 'Odi, Carlo immortal', rather than to the

---

[34] Denores, *Della rhetorica*, fos. 9ᵛ–10ʳ: 'dal che Platone giudicò la Rhetorica essere una certa raunanza di Philosophia, & di quella maniera di poesia più grave, che havesse per fine l'indur gli ascoltanti al beneficio commune della compagnia civile con regole, & con avvertimenti universali intorno alle cose, alle parole, & a' costumi'. Questions of the individual's relationship to the state and the benefits of communal law are also the focus of Monteverdi's later opera *L'incoronazione di Poppea*, especially as voiced in the role of Seneca.

[35] Ovid, *Le metamorfosi* (ed. Anguillara), cited in Cusick, ' "There was not one lady" ', 24: 'Sia questo caso d'Arianna per documento alle donne incaute, a non voler credere alle promesse di chi dimostra amarle, perche corrono pericolo di gettarsi nelle braccia di giovani ingrati, & infedeli, per il che ne rimangono con grandissima infamia spesso ruinate.'

The Politics of Description 157

'Sposa real', Rinuccini's stanza is not an injunction to the bride. Nor can this have been its primary meaning, given the stemmatic relationship between the libretto and Follino's *Compendio*. Both Rinuccini's and Follino's publications carried court sanction, because both were issued by the ducal printer in 1608. And although Rinuccini's libretto lacks a dedication and date other than the year given on the title page, the printer's citation shows it to have pre-dated the *Compendio* and to have only briefly postdated the death of Francesco Osanna, ducal printer since at least 1587 until the early months of 1608.[36] Thus, the text that appears in Rinuccini's libretto, 'Listen, immortal Carlo, how a betrayed lover sighs on the solitary bank', for reasons of both authorship and stemmatic priority, takes precedence over that subsequently altered in Follino's account.

'Carlo immortal' probably refers to Carlo Emmanuele, the Duke of Savoy and father of the bride, who was not present at the wedding. While Rinuccini's reference to him does not negate the significance of Follino's later substitution of 'sposa real' for 'Carlo immortal', it does demand a different interpretation of the passage, one that encompasses not only the women of the audience but also the men. When directed to the Duke of Savoy, Apollo's lines shed their high moralistic tone and read instead as a recommendation to admire the artistry of the play. As such they allude to what had become by the early seventeenth century a model of courtly and scholarly sophistication: a humanist ornamentation of a classical myth told through the artful manipulation of rhetorical gestures in both its composition and its delivery. Rather than focusing the attention of the bride's father on the near-fatal results of Arianna's wilful behaviour, this version of the prologue instead sanctions her actions and emphasizes the refinement of her manner in expressing the heightened emotions of a noblewoman in distress.

The emphasis on the rhetorical artistry of the composition and its performance conforms to the interpretation of Arianna's lament as a representation of the bride's perspective of the wedding ceremony and of her yearning that it continue, the interpretation generated above in relation to

[36] The libretto of *Arianna* printed in Mantua in 1608 'presso gli Heredi di Francesco Osanna Stampator Ducale' must have appeared before the official transfer of the press to those heirs, 'Aurelio, & Lodovico Osanna Stampatori Ducali', who printed Follino's *Compendio* (the dedication is dated 1 July 1608). After the transfer of the licence in 1608, Aurelio and Lodovico Osanna continued as ducal printers well into the next decade; in addition to Follino's *Compendio*, see evidence of their work in *La Galatea* (Mantua, 1614) and *Gli amori d'Aci* (Mantua, 1617). The 'Carlo immortal' reading is also followed in the editions of *Arianna* published in Florence and Venice that same year.

Il sacrificio d'Ifigenia and the formulaic order of 'marriage to death' rites. It also adheres to the pedagogical view derived from the texts of Augustine and Guarino Guarini that laments helped to teach schoolboys self-control over the extremes of emotion brought on by adolescence and situational stress. Those parts of the 1608 performance where Arianna exceeded the limits of courtly decorum exemplify this didactic concept by having her step beyond the boundary, only to retreat from it again. Censuring her own actions, Arianna exhibits cognizance of her errors, and then receives confirmation of the propriety of her self-correction from the chorus of fisherfolk surrounding her. Thus she sings,

> O storms, o tempests, o winds,
> drown him beneath your waves!
> Come, whales and monsters of the sea,
> and fill the depths with his limbs.
> Ah! what am I saying?
> What am I ranting?
> Miserable women, alas! What am I asking?
> O Teseo, o my Teseo,
> I am not, I am not the one,
> I am not the one who chose those fierce words:
> my distress spoke, my sorrow spoke;
> my tongue spoke, yes, but not my heart.

To which the chorus replies in affirmation of her moral choice,

> True love, worthy of the world's admiration!
> In the extremes of suffering
> you do not know how to seek revenge and do not invoke it.

Arianna's despondency, however, exceeds even this. Not only does she stand on the rocky shore sobbing, but she curses her departed lover in rage and despair and throws herself into the surf to die, only to be rescued and dragged back onto the beach by the fisherfolk whose tender comments frame her lovely lament. As an allegory of the 'marriage to death' rite, this might read as a deranged enactment of the preparatory bath, made as a last, desperate effort to continue through with the ritual. The scene, as described by Nunzio Primo, again emphasizes the conflation of wedding and funeral imagery in the play by presenting Arianna's allegorical baptism as a catalyst of death, the spirit abandoning her body.

> Already ranting, she immersed herself in the water;
> but, ready to her aid,
> a band of fisherfolk, as if sent from heaven,

drew her out of the waves and onto land.
Thus panting and tired,
cold and white as the snow,
the spirits vanished from that lovely breast.

The importance of water imagery in the 'marriage to death' rite, and its use as the medium by which to conduct the bride to her new home, is also expressed in the other representations of the ritual described by Follino. It is especially germane to the story of Europa presented in the intermedio performed after the second act of *L'idropica*.[37] Following the same tripartite structure as that described for *Arianna* and *Il sacrificio d'Ifigenia*, the Rape of Europa attaches further significance to the interrelationship between themes of abduction, marriage, and spiritual transcendence. The tale of Europa, as Follino tells it, stands as a metaphor for holy union, the girl ascending to the heavens as the bride of Jove. This is the standard reading of the Europa story that is also offered by early modern hermeticists like Giulio Camillo and Giordano Bruno. In Camillo's Theatre of Memory, the image of Europa and the bull stands at either end of the Jupiter series, symbolizing 'conversion, consent, holiness, humility, [and] religion' in the first row and 'the soul and the body, true religion, [and] Paradise' in the penultimate row.[38] In Follino's account, Europa, discovered riding on the shoulders of an evidently magnificent mechanical bull, and queenly in both costume and comportment, actually delivered her lament, 'Cari paterni regni', from amidst the waves, while the ladies of the court wept.

When superimposed on the lingering memory of the first intermedio

---

[37] Descriptions of the intermedi appear in Follino, *Compendio*, 72–99. In the classical world, purificatory water was 'used in rites of birth, marriage, and death, the dead being considered "thirsty". In the so-called "Orphic" texts . . . the soul is "parched with thirst" and wants to drink the water of Memory; in the eschatological myths of Plato and Virgil, the souls drink the water of Oblivion. Finally, water was the primal element in cosmogonic thought . . .'; see *Oxford Classical Dictionary*, s.v. 'water'.

[38] Giulio Camillo's 'Theatre of Memory', widely known throughout Italy and France in the 16th c., offers a fascinating complex of visual images that he used to house and recall to memory all the standard classical texts, including the complete works of Cicero, Homer, Virgil, and others. While standing in the theatre, Camillo was alleged to be able to recite these texts from memory. Built as a wooden structure in the 1530s, the theatre and its theory of construction are outlined in *L'idea del teatro* (Florence, 1550) and *Discorso in materia del suo teatro* (Venice, 1552). It comprised a visual representation of Ficinian philosophy on the effect of words and music on the soul, as described in the *De vita coelitus*, iii. 21, and as such provides an important source for interpreting images of music and the the harmony of the spheres in 16th- and 17th-c. theatre. For a thorough analysis of the theater of memory, see Yates, *The Art of Memory*, 129–59.

for *L'idropica*—and where else would water imagery weigh heavy with significance but surrounding a play entitled 'The Dropsical Woman'?—Europa's watery union with the bull suggests not only royal marriage, but the foundation of a new empire. And it is in this first intermedio that the scenic depiction of a rocky shore as the background for a woman's lament comes to be of central importance to the allegorical representation of dynastic continuity and imperial territory. It presents a bipartite tableau featuring the patron goddess of Mantua and the god of marriage. Manto, rising up out of the waves, sings a strophic paean to the city and its rulers as she creates an island on which Hymen, the god of marriage, will stand.[39] A cloud then appears from the heavens carrying Hymen, who dismounts to sing his praises of Margherita and Francesco: 'Coppia real, che di sua mano insieme'. The image of a renewed *patria* rising up out of the waves in support of a new marriage, although not exclusive to the 1608 festivities, is especially appropriate to Mantua, a city surrounded by water.[40] Dante's story of the creation of the city is less pleasant, but equally marine:

> A cruel virgin, as she passed this way,
> Chanced upon a strip of land unpeopled
> And untilled. Here, to shun humanity,
> She lived with many slaves and worked her arts.
> She left her soulless body in that place.
> Then, people living in that region came
> Together at that spot, protected well
> By virtue of the bog surrounding it.
> There Mantua was built above the bones
> Of Manto, with no further augury.[41]

The juxtaposition of water and land carries an additional meaning as the locus of conception and childbirth. This may be seen in two depictions by the sixteenth-century Mantuan court artist Giulio Romano. The first is an oil painting representing the birth of Apollo and Diana. Here, the

---

[39] Follino, *Compendio*, 75: 'si videro gorgogliar quell'onde nel mezo e spuntar da esse la testa d'una donna, che sorgendo à poco à poco, à gli habiti, & all'insegne mostrava d'esser Manto figlia di Tiresia, fondatrice di Mantova . . .'.

[40] Mantua is bounded by three lakes, Lago superiore, Lago inferiore, and Lago di mezzo, which served in the 16th c. to protect the city, to provide river access to Ferrara and Venice and to sustain the Duchy's cash crop of rice. The lakes also bred insects and disease, however, and the city was often visited by epidemics and plague.

[41] Dante Alighieri, *Inferno*, trans. Elio Zappulla (New York, 1998), 183.

midwife stands in a stream as she receives the infants from their mother Latona, who lies on the shore of Delos.[42] The second is a fresco, probably by Girolamo da Pontremoli to designs by Romano, which decorates the Grotta of the Palazzo del Tè and which appears in the 1627 inventory of Gonzaga artworks. It shows the goddess Cybele standing in a river bed, a likeness of the city atop her head, performing the duties of midwife to a woman in labour.[43]

Nor is the image of bearing babies at the water's edge forgotten in relationship to tales of Arianna's betrayal. In Ovid's *Heroides*, she claims that her lover, too, had issued from the rocky shore:

> Aegeus cannot be your father; Aethra,
> daughter of Pittheus, cannot be
> your mother, for I am sure that you were born
> from a union of rocks and the sea.[44]

Looking, then, to the symbolic content of Arianna's lament and its representational significance as a 'marriage to death' rite and as a coming-of-age ritual for the noble children of Mantua and Savoy, we may begin to find there themes of growth, change, independence, and parental responsibility. Fearful, even terrifying changes for the adolescent confronting them, they are simultaneously exciting and filled with hope and anticipation. Its setting at the rocky shore predisposing the audience to themes of childbirth, dynastic continuity, and empire, Arianna's plaint gave the courtiers cause to reflect on the vitality and continued good health of the prince's ancestral line. As an allegorical re-creation of the journey from the Savoyard court to the Duchy of Mantua, the story of *Arianna* both welcomed Margherita into her new household and initiated her into its laws and customs. And in its definition of the Gonzaga bloodline and family, told through the interwoven enactment of wedding and funeral rites, the myth further instructed Margherita and Francesco in their new roles as representatives of the Mantuan state.

Follino's, Rinuccini's, Monteverdi's, and Andreini's versions of the tale

---

[42] Giulio Romano and assistant, *Birth of Apollo and Diana*, in Frederick Hartt, *Giulio Romano* (New Haven, 1958), cat. no. 459.

[43] Assistant [probably Girolamo da Pontremoli], from designs by Giulio Romano, Loggia della Grotta, Palazzo del Tè, *Birth*, in Hartt, *Giulio Romano*, cat. no. 274. This fresco, together with a 17th-c. salt cellar decorated with the figures of Cybele and Neptune, which was commissioned as a wedding gift, as discussed in Zorach, 'Gallia Fertilis and Antique Cybele'.

[44] Ovid, *Heroides* (trans. Innes), 94.

of Arianna focused on events within the circle of the Mantuan court and its collective memory as they struggled to create and to promote an entertainment that could not afford to be mistaken for anything but a representation of the nobility and grandeur of its patron's house. Grounding their efforts in the recent history of music spectacles at the Mantuan court, and especially in recollections of the performance and reception of *Il pastor fido*, they guided their audience's reactions to the play with reference to humanist scholarship and to studied rhetorical practices.

For Rinuccini and Monteverdi, this meant constructing a music drama that impressed its audience with its allusions to ancient modes of portraying Greek gods, goddesses, kings, and queens, a drama that impressed through representation in music written in the *via naturale alla immitatione*, through poetry written in an active mode, and including a lament that would elicit childhood memories of lessons in rhetorical majesty and decorum. The mediation of audience response to Rinuccini's, Monteverdi's, and Andreini's artistry was Follino's responsibility, as he followed up the performance with a 'description' of its reception that emphasized the same goals: conformity to Aristotelian philosophy and rhetorical skill. Whatever really happened in Mantua on 28 May 1608, Rinuccini, Monteverdi, Andreini, and Follino ensured that memory of the event would be sweet, its imagery understood, and its majesty undenied. If the ladies of the court wept at Andreini's performance of Arianna's lament, then we too—as foreigners to Mantua and, like Margherita's father, unable to have attended the performance—might shed an appreciative tear for the imagined sound of her weeping at the water's edge.

5

Epilogue

LITTLE more than a year before Virginia Andreini lamented Arianna's fate in the tiny hall adjacent to Vincenzo Gonzaga's apartments in the Palazzo Ducale in Mantua, her husband Giovan Battista stood in the rooms formerly occupied by Vincenzo's sister Margherita to witness Orfeo's laments for the death of Euridice. 'I had the good fortune in Florence and in Mantua', he wrote in the preface of his 'commedietta musicale' *La Ferinda*, 'as a spectator of works recited and musical, to see *Orfeo*, *Arianna*, *Silla*, *Dafne*, *Cerere*, and *Psiche*, truly most marvellous things, not only for the excellence of those fortunate swans who gloriously sang them, but for the rarity of the melodious musicians who harmoniously and angelically realized them.'[1]

Published in Paris in 1622, the preface to *La Ferinda* situated Andreini in a distinguished line of librettists whose plays comprise the early history of music drama and characterize the lofty enunciation of Phaedran poetry. He named his sources of inspiration and imitation, offering them up to the readers of his musical comedy as evidence of the honour and valour of his creation. He commemorated, too, the Medici's long-standing patronage of his family, looking back to the time when Maria de' Medici, her uncle Ferdinando and sister Eleonora blessed Isabella and Francesco Andreini and their children with their wealth and good will. With the deaths of Ferdinando in 1609 and of Eleonora in 1611, Maria was the only one of the Medici triumvirate left, and Giovan Battista made several extended journeys with his company to her court, where he lavished on her performances and publications of his plays. In 1622 alone, following

---

[1] G. B. Andreini, *La Ferinda* (Paris, 1622), dedication to the readers, as cited in Picot, *Gli ultimi anni*, 8: 'Alhor che per mia felice fortuna in Fiorenza et in Mantova spettator d'opere recitative e musicali, vidi l'*Orfeo*, l'*Arianna*, la *Silla*, la *Dafne*, la *Cerere* e la *Psiche*, cose in vero meravigliosissime, non solo per l'eccellenza de' fortunati cigni che le cantàrono gloriose, come per la rarità de' musici canòri che armoniose et angeliche le resero.'

soon after the death of Cosimo II de' Medici, he printed six in Paris: *La campanazza, La centaura, La Ferinda, Amor nello specchio, La sultana,* and *Li duo Leli simili.*

In Mantua in 1607, however, Giovan Battista stood in the midst of that magnificent time when Gonzaga patronage, as well as Medici, formed the tidal wave on which the Andreinis' fame crested and when he was a privileged auditor of the inspiring new *Orfeo*. Alessandro Striggio's and Claudio Monteverdi's collaboration on *Orfeo* had been an experimental undertaking, offered by prince Francesco Gonzaga to a small audience of *conoscenti* from the Accademia degli Invaghiti on 24 February. Performed by an ensemble of men, including the Florentine castrato Giovan Gualberto Magli in the role of Proserpina and a little priest who sang the role of Euridice, *Orfeo* was a great success, and Vincenzo Gonzaga so enjoyed its first performance that he requested it be repeated on 1 March. Pre-printed libretti were distributed to the spectators on each occasion.[2] At the time, Andreini had been an adopted citizen of Mantua for over six years and he lived near enough to the Palazzo Ducale to walk home after the performance. *Orfeo*, together with *Arianna* and *Dafne*, inspired the comedian to write his own libretti for musical setting and to include more and more music-making in his spoken plays.

Six years after the performance of *Orfeo* in Mantua, Andreini and the librettist Striggio—who wrote not only *Orfeo* but also *Il sacrificio d'Ifigenia* for the wedding of Francesco Gonzaga and Margherita of Savoy in 1608—were both working in Milan. Andreini was on tour with his wife Virginia and the Fedeli, and Striggio was the newly appointed ducal secretary and ambassador of Mantua.[3] Although Andreini had admired Striggio's work as a playwright for some years, the two never collaborated on a libretto. In Milan, however, the comedians maintained their correspondence with the Gonzaga court via Striggio's offices and when, in the autumn of 1612, Andreini published his comedy *Lo schiavetto* with the Milanese printer Pandolfo Malatesta, he wrote a perfunctory dedication to Count Ercole Pepoli on 26 September, which was replaced by the printer within two weeks with a dedication to the Mantuan dramatist. Laura Falavolti, the editor of the modern edition of *Lo schiavetto*, has speculated

---

[2] See Fabbri, *Monteverdi* (trans. Carter), 63–5; and Whenham, 'A Masterpiece for a Court', in *The Operas of Monteverdi* (ed. John), 20–3.

[3] Tristano Martinelli refers to Alessandro Striggio as 'ambasiator nostro qui in Milano' in the postscript of a letter to Ferdinando Gonzaga in Rome dated 15 Aug. 1612. ASMN, Autografi, b. 10, fos. 162^r–163^r.

that the play's extreme popularity caused its first printing to be exhausted immediately, necessitating a second print run almost before the ink on the first was dry.[4]

Lo schiavetto recounts the story of a young noblewoman, Florinda, who disguises herself as a black male slave in order to follow her lover. It was only the second of Andreini's comedies to be published and it was conceived in the earliest years of the Fedeli's existence, perhaps even before the troupe became known as the Duke's Comedians, a title they inherited from the Gelosi. As such, it represents the mode of performance practised by the Fedeli at the end of Vincenzo Gonzaga's reign, which was at the same time the end of the golden era of the commedia dell'arte described by the printer Malatesta in his dedication and by Angelo Ingegneri in his treatise on theatrical practice. Both Andreini and Malatesta emphasize that the comedy was composed in performance, and in so doing they highlight the idea that, while Andreini's name appears on the title page, the contents of the play are in fact a collaborative effort, representing the ideas and talents of all the members of his troupe. By the time the comedian finally put pen to paper in the composition (or perhaps more accurately, the inscription) of *Lo schiavetto*, Virginia Andreini had been performing its title role for some years. Her imprint on the character of the slave may be seen in the witty banter of nearly every scene and especially in the music of the lament in Act IV. Malatesta's dedication to Striggio makes clear both the integrity of the play as a work born of composition and performance, and its history as an unpublished work in progress:

From those years, when beautiful Italy began to enjoy a tranquil peace, almost as a restorative to the hardship of such continuous wars, the most valiant persons began to rediscover the ancient forgotten practice of performing comedies. Of these, however, few were capable of knowing how to show themselves as both composer and performer. The one, content in the study and glory of invention, held others responsible for the performance. In comparing the one to the other, there is no doubt who would benefit the public more, in that, if perfect actors were not given to our age, few people would notice the composed works. Now, if anyone deserves fame from being able to perform and to compose, it is none other than the comedian Giovan Battista Andreini, called Lelio, who with no less imagination than erudition, causes us to see him perfectly, witty and handsome, fecund and wise, reciting and writing. . . .

Of the many works that the same Andreini has composed, lauded in every quarter, he has added this other most delightful comedy, entitled *Lo schiavetto*,

[4] Andreini, *Lo schiavetto* (ed. Falavolti), 55.

which has been heard first in diverse cities to grateful applause, and therefore he is pleased to put it into print.[5]

Malatesta, although perhaps prone to hyperbole, does not overestimate the number of the young Andreini's printed works. The comedian had previously published, in addition to the comedy *La turca* (another play in which Virginia Andreini appears in exotic disguise until the last act), the tragedy *La Florinda* (a particularly musical composition, which provided the comedienne with her stage name), and the sacred dramas *La divina visione* and *La Maddalena*.[6] Andreini mentioned others of his sacred works, too, in the preface to the good readers of *Lo schiavetto*—*La Tecla* and *L'Adamo*—which evidently circulated in manuscript or as *scenari*, for these were not actually put into print until some time later—*L'Adamo* in 1613 and *La Tecla* in 1623. In what would become an *idée fixe* for Andreini throughout his career, the comedian indicated to the readers of *Lo schiavetto* that he brought these works to publication, not only to leave some evidence of his art behind him when he died, but in order to uphold the honour of his family by proving the truth of the Gelosi's motto. 'These comedians', he wrote, 'who tied and untied the knots of such fables, were people who were intent on knowing the art of composition and in under-

---

[5] Andreini, *Lo schiavetto* (ed. Falavolti), 57–8: 'All'illustrissimo signor il Signor Conte Alessandro Striggio, Conte di Corticelle, Consiglier di Stato e Ambasciatore del Serenissimo Duca di Mantova in Milano.

Da quegli anni, che la bella Italia cominciò pur a godere una tranquilla pace, quasi a ristoro de' travagli di tante continuate guerre, cominciarono valentissimi personaggi a ritrovare l'antico tralasciato uso del rappresentar comedie. Di queste, nondimeno, pochi si sono potuti conoscere, che se ne dimostrassero insieme i compositori e rappresentanti; contenti gli uni dello studio e gloria della invenzione, si addossarono gli altri il carico del recitare. Per l'eccellenza di questi e di quegli, fattosi dubbio di chi più meritasse a pubblico giovamento; ché, se perfetti dicitori non ci avesse dati il nostro secolo, a notizia di picciol numero di persone sarebbero l'opere de' componenti. Ora, se alcuno acquista fama di riuscita nel rappresentare e nel comporre, altresì questi è il comico Giovan Battista Andreini detto Lelio, il quale, non meno per scelta favella che dottrina, ci se fa veder compiutamente faceto e leggiadro, facondo e saggio, pronunciando e scrivendo. Né perciò vi è chi no'l giudichi con dignità fatto capo de' comici della compagnia, ch'il Serenissimo duca di Mantova ha eletto nella sua corte. . . .

Alle molte opere, che l'istesso Andreini ha composte, in ogni parte lodate, avendo aggiunto quest'altra dilettevolissima comedia, con titolo dello *Schiavetto*, che nel farla sentire prima in diverse città è stata con ogni applauso gradita, è poscia egli compiaciuto che ne fossero anco le stampe adorne'.

[6] Andreini wrote two works entitled *La Maddalena*; this first is a poem written in ottava rima, and the second, often called *La Maddalena lasciva e penitente* to distinguish it from the first, is a sacred drama published in 1617.

standing, more than any other man might, that which perpetuates virtue and honour.'[7]

Lo schiavetto's homage to Medici patronage may be seen, not only in its use of Tuscan dialect and word spellings, but in the six musical numbers called for in its libretto. The *canzone a ballo* in Act I, Scene ii, 'Sono i capegli della manza mia', not only evinces Florentine style, it is in fact pilfered from a previously performed Florentine entertainment. Sung by the Tuscan innkeeper Succiola, a *serva* who instigates much of the music-making and dancing in the play, the *canzone a ballo* is taken, with only minor variations, from the finale of Michelangelo Buonarotti's rustic comedy *Tancia*, published in the same year as *Lo schiavetto* and performed the previous year at the Granducal court for Cosimo II de' Medici:

> Sono i capegli della manza mia,
> morbidi com'un lino scotolato;
> e 'l suo viso pulito par che sia
> di rose spicciolato pieno un prato,
> il suo petto è di marmo una mascìa,
> dov'Amor s'acovachia e sta apiattato[;]
> sue parole garbate mi sollucherano,
> gli occhi suoi mi succiellano e mi bucherano.

(My beloved's hair is as soft as boiled linen; and her clean face is like a field full of roses, and her breast is a marble mound where Love lingers and hides; her polite words send me into raptures, her eyes pacify and pierce me.)[8]

How different is the comic style of music and poetry sung by a *serva* like Succiola from the impassioned, noble arias of an Arianna or an Ingrata! The use of music as entertainment for the characters onstage rather than as an expression of one character's emotions (which is, as often as not, as meaningful for the drama's spectators as it is incomprehensible to the other characters in the play), marks the distinction between Phaedran songs of divine madness and plain old tunes. Succiola's songs, lacking significance in regard either to the drama's plot development or to her

---

[7] Andreini, *Lo schiavetto* (ed. Falavolti), 59: 'che que' comici, che tali favole annodarono e disciolsero, furono gente, che s'affaticarono in conoscer l'arte del comporre, e in sapere quanto più dell'altr'uomo quello sia, che la virtù, che l'onore, seguita.'

[8] Ibid. 75. Variations from the original song include the substitution of the word 'manza' for 'Tancia' and 'succiellano' for 'suchiellano'. The first removes the song's association with Buonarotti's comedy, the second makes a play on words with the character name Succiola. 'Mascìa' is Tuscan for 'mascerìa', a showy pile of rock.

character's personal predicament, are thereby incapable of transcending the stage to represent anything else. Whereas Arianna's lament had metaphorical significance for the marriage-to-death ritual in which it was encased, 'Sono i capegli della manza mia' is devoid of allegory and, through humour and the clumsy use of double entendre, creates a separation between drama and spectator that is absent in the Lamento d'Arianna, Monteverdi's supreme example of *musica rappresentativa*.

The songs and instrumental dances that appear in the final scene of Act III of *Lo schiavetto* are designed to show off the musical talents of Succiola, Schiavetto, and the chorus of instrumentalists who are outfitted as shepherds. All are performed as entertainment for the characters in the play, and it is important to note that Florinda, maintaining her disguise as Schiavetto, does not sing. It is rather her mask—the slave—who plays and dances in this scene and who studiously avoids the one avenue by which Florinda might become known—her outpouring of celestial song. The scene begins with a rustic *villan di Spagna*, a country dance performed by the instrumentalists. Shortly after, Schiavetto plays a *calata*—a rapid dance usually played by one or two lutes—to which Succiola sings a hendecasyllabic quatrain 'Un tordo cotto con la saivia, e l'olio' that is reminiscent of Burchiello's nonsensical Tuscan verse and utterly typical of commedia dell'arte texts, with its attention to foodstuffs and their double meanings.

> Un tordo cotto con la saivia, e l'olio
> val più che con il sal cento lupini;
> o come d'Arno i dolci pesciolini
> vaglion più che del Po que' gran storioni.

(A thrush cooked with sage and oil is worth more than a hundred lupines with salt; just as the freshwater fish of the Arno are worth more than the great sturgeons of the Po.)[9]

Little is known about the *calata* or *ballo di calata*, although the known examples of the dance are all Florentine in origin. One was performed in the Tuscan capitol on 1 March 1615 as part of the *Ballo di donne turche* by Santino Comesari,[10] and another on 17 May 1618,[11] both in the presence of

---

[9] Andreini, *Lo schiavetto* (ed. Falavolti), 137.

[10] Solerti, *Musica, ballo e drammatica*, 97: 'Il Balletto, composto da Santino Comesari ballerino di Firenze, fu meraviglioso perchè con medesimo suono ballarono quattro sorte di balli, cioè calata, corrente, canari e galliarde.'

[11] Ibid. 133: 'Et adì 17 maggio . . . doppo S.A. con la Ser.ma Arciduchessa andò su ad alto nella sala detta delle Commedie dove era all'ordine per recitare una comedina pastorale

the Archduchess of Austria. The *calata* is paired with a *galliarda*, as it was in 1615, in the carnival festivities on 31 January 1620 at the end of an evening of music performed by the *maestro di cappella* from Pisa and an unnamed woman he brought with him.[12] These examples suggest that the *calata* was a typically Florentine dance form, or perhaps a wonderfully exotic genre—a Turkish delight—favoured by Florentines. The *ballo di calata* played by Virginia Andreini in *Lo schiavetto* also serves as a reminder of her notoriety as a virtuosa of the guitar and lute. Indeed, her husband's comedies are filled with moments that highlight her talents as an instrumentalist. Giovan Battista goes so far in his *Due commedie in commedia*, published in 1623, as to make her a *maestra* of the Spanish guitar.

After the *ballo di calata*, the lowbrow Succiola performs a *sfessania*, a frenetic dance made famous by the drawings of Jacques Callot, which, from the transitive verb 'sfessare', indicates a form that is intended to exhaust the dancer. Following this, she sings the ottava 'Io son donne quel Nencio pescatore', accompanied by the chorus of shepherds. Like Succiola's first song, this one is reminiscent of a popular Tuscan verse sung in Buonarotti's *Tancia*—in this case, a song from the third intermedio. After it, the money-grubbing false nobleman Nottola, who is also cross-eyed and hunchbacked, tells the hotelier that she has sung and danced beautifully—including the bergamasca she danced with Rondone and Schiavetto—and then he leaves, commanding the instrumentalists to follow him as far as the garden, thereby bringing Act III to a close.

The final musical number called for within the text of the comedy is an aria sung by Schiavetto in the penultimate scene of Act IV. Here, the song is introduced as a bit of his/her 'mercanzia', which has already received much attention in Florence:

Schiavetto. Signori, silenzio, ch'io voglio darvi un poco della mia mercanzia.
Rondone. Oh? Signori, della sua mercanzia n'ha pur data tanto a Fiorenza, così ne dia in questa città, che si faremo ricchi.

recitata da' fillioli del sig. re Lione de' Merli, fiorentino, et da altri giovanetti fiorentini, il quale era un sogetto che Amore, non volendo più stare in corte, si ritirò nella Arcadia ad abitare fra le ninfe et pastori, il quale travalliò molto quei pastori et quelle ninfe. Et alla fine fecero un ballo di calata et piacque assai per essere ben recitata, et durò detta comedia per ispazio di un'ora.'

[12] Ibid. 152: 'la sera si fece musica dal maestro di cappella di Pisa et da una donna condotta da Pisa et doppo fu ballato la calata et galliarda da tre ragazzi vestiti da mattacini, scolari di Iacopino dell'Armaiuolo.'

Nottola. Eh? Sarò ben uomo io di pigliarne tanta quanto tutti i fiorentini.
Schiavetto. Sì? Orsù io comincio.
(*Schiavetto.* Sirs, silence, for I want to give you a bit of my merchandise.
Rondone. Oh? Sirs, he has given much of his merchandise to Florence, thus to give it in this city will make us rich.
Nottola. Eh? I would be a good man to take as much as all the Florentines.
Schiavetto. Yes? All right then, I'll begin.)

What follows are the first two strophes of Giulio Caccini's aria *Tu c'hai le penne Amore* from *Le nuove musiche et nuova maniera di scriverle* (see Pl. 5.1). This is the first time Andreini sings in the comedy, and her song betrays her to the drama's spectators as the *prima donna innamorata incognita*. The other characters in the scene, in contrast to the audience, do not recognize the representational nature of Andreini's music, and so they suspect nothing in regard to her disguise. This split between the audience's awareness and that of the characters onstage is vital to the interpretation of Andreini's canzonetta, for she is perceived at once as a woman and a man, one singing because he is commanded to do so, the other for the hopelessness of her plight. The instructions to the performers of the Venetian edition of *Lo schiavetto*, published in 1620 (Giovan Battista blithely left out all references to musical instruments in the first two editions of the text after promising in his preface to provide them[13]), dictate a 'chitarra alla Spagnola, o leuto per Schiavetto' in this scene, thus indicating that Virginia Andreini performed the song to her own accompaniment on the Spanish guitar or lute. This is a nearly omnipresent direction in Giovan Battista Andreini's early comedies, which often signals the role Virginia would have performed.

Caccini's musical setting of *Tu c'hai le penne Amore* was not printed until two years after the publication of its lyrics in *Lo schiavetto*. Its appearance in Virginia Andreini's repertory opens up new realms of interpret-

---

[13] 'Per li rappresentanti o vaghi di rappresentazioni, nemici dell'ozio, e amici de' passatempi virtuosi.

Se, per aventura, a questo *Schiavetto* si concedesse tanta di libertà che dal ceppo si sciogliesse al teatro, si potrebbe agevolare il modo di rappresentarlo con quel che si legge al fine della presente operetta, ove, a ciascuna delle scene e de gli atti, si veggono descritti gli ordigni, stormenti o le cose necessarie a rappresentarlo.

L'istesso si può veder nella *Turca* comedia dell'autor medesimo, stampata in Casale, ove il signor Fulvio Gambaloita, cavaliero virtuosissimo, pensò di farla rappresentare con sontuoso apparecchio, alla presenza del Serenissimo principe, ora duca di Mantova, e fu impedito dalla morte del Serenissimo Vincenzo, padre glorioso dell'Altezza Sua.'

PL. 5.1. Giulio Caccini, *Tu c'hai le penne Amore*, from *Le nuove musiche et nuova maniera di scriverle* (1614)

ation regarding the aria's pre-publication history, as well as its performance practice and the authorship of its music and lyrics. If Giovan Battista Andreini and Malatesta are to be believed when they write that *Lo schiavetto* was performed in many cities and for quite some time prior to its own publication, then Caccini's aria must also be seen to have a substantive performance history that pre-dates not only his publication of the music but Andreini's printing of the play. Since the composition of *Lo schiavetto* has been shown to be a collaborative effort born of the Fedeli's performances, it may similarly be true that Caccini's aria is the result of a collaboration that included its singer, Virginia Andreini.

By implication, similar questions may be asked of the other arias in Caccini's collection, and especially of *Amor ch'attendi*, which appears with *Tu c'hai le penne Amore* in Remigio Romano's anthology of canzonettas and contrafacta published in 1618. In the first volume of his *Raccolta di bellissime canzonette*, Romano prints the *scherzo Mentre vivo lontano* with the instruction that it be sung 'to the tune of Tu c'hai le penne Amore' ('Dilettevole canzone sopra l'aria, che comincia *Tu c'hai le pene Amore*'). He unfortunately does not supply the tune, the title of the *scherzo* evidently being sufficient for his readers to remember it, and so one can only surmise that it is identical with Caccini's aria. In the same vein, Romano declined to provide music for the popular tune *Ahi serpentella*, which he assigned to the text of Caccini's canzonetta *Amor ch'attendi*. Whether Caccini's setting of *Amor ch'attendi* in 1614 incorporated either the melody or harmonic outline of the anonymous *Ahi serpentella* is a matter of conjecture, and the relationship of either song to Vincenzo Pellegrini's *Canzona detta la Serpentina*, published in his *Canzoni de intavolatura d'organo fatte alla francese* in Venice in 1599, is similarly vague. For what it is worth, Caccini's aria does seem to offer a dim reminiscence of the earlier canzone, especially in regard to its sections in triple metre.[14]

The identification of *Tu c'hai le penne Amore* as a popular tune—so well known that Romano did not even inscribe *alfabeto* notation in order to recall its harmony or melody to mind—testifies to the popularity of Virginia Andreini's performances of the song in *Lo schiavetto* and to its longevity in the theatrical repertory. It appears in Romano's collection alongside a number of other arias that were either sung by commedia dell'arte players or refer to their character names. Moreover, as discussed

---

[14] A modern edition of Pellegrini's composition may be found in the anthology of Allan Atlas's text *Renaissance Music*.

in Chapter 2, Isabella Andreini's *scherzo* 'Io credèa che tra gli amanti', the text of which was first published in 1601, also appears in Romano's collection, accompanied by an intabulation for Spanish guitar. Although it is not known how long the aria *Tu c'hai le penne Amore* or *Lo schiavetto* were in the Fedeli's performing repertory before they were published, the time span represented by comedians' songs in Romano's anthology makes it reasonable to infer that Virginia Andreini's performances of this aria may have been among the reasons why Vincenzo Gonzaga suggested she sing the title role in Monteverdi's *Arianna* in Mantua in 1608.[15] At the very least, the juxtaposition in Andreini's repertory of *Tu c'hai le penne Amore*, the *Lamento d'Arianna*, and the *Lamento dell'Ingrata* provides us after the fact with a very real sense of the comedienne's vocal capabilities, if not her style or technique.

Giulio Caccini's acquaintance with the Andreini family was long-standing by 1612, when *Lo schiavetto* finally was published, although it is not known when he might have met Giovan Battista or Virginia. He performed, as did Isabella Andreini and the Gelosi, for the Medici wedding of 1589, and he, Isabella, and her husband Francesco met again in Paris in 1603, when both the Gelosi and Caccini were summoned by Maria de' Medici to perform for her court. The Roman singer's encounters with Giovan Battista and Virginia are more difficult to detail, in part because the younger Andreini and his wife did not perform for the Florentine festivities in honour of Maria de' Medici's wedding to Henri IV in 1600, when Caccini's *Il rapimento di Cefalo* was unveiled, nor did they accompany Giovan Battista's parents on their last tour of France. Moreover, Caccini was dismissed from Florentine service two years before Giovan Battista began his career as a comedian, and so it is unlikely that they had any substantive encounter before 1593.[16] In all probability, they met in Florence at about the time of one of the performances of Ottavio Rinuccini's and Jacopo Peri's *La Dafne*: during carnival in 1598, 1599, or 1600, or in October 1604.[17] Later on, but still prior to the publication of *Lo schiavetto*, Giulio's younger daughter Settimia Caccini almost certainly

---

[15] See the letter from Antonio Costantini to Carlo Rossi dated 18 Mar. 1608, as cited in Fabbri, *Monteverdi* (trans. Carter), 83.

[16] The outlines of Caccini's biography given here are based on Brown, 'The Geography of Florentine Monody', Hitchcock's introduction to his edition of Caccini, *Le nuove musiche e nuova maniera di scriverle*, and Hanning's entry 'Giulio Caccini' in *New Grove Dictionary* online.

[17] ASF, Mediceo, Guardaroba MS 3; Palisca, *Studies in the History*, 399–401.

knew Giovan Battista and Virginia Andreini in Mantua, especially after her marriage in 1609 to Alessandro Ghivizzani, who composed, together with Claudio Monteverdi, Muzio Effrem, and Salomone Rossi, the music for Giovan Battista Andreini's *La Maddalena lasciva e penitente*, published in 1617.

In detailing the potential moments of interaction between Caccini and Giovan Battista and Virginia Andreini, my point is not simply to indicate when Caccini's song might have entered Virginia's repertory, but also when the text of the aria might have come to the composer's attention. For the presence of 'Tu c'hai le penne Amore' in *Lo schiavetto*, especially because its appearance there pre-dates Caccini's publication of the aria, offers the possibility that either Giovan Battista or Virginia Andreini might be the author of the song's lyrics, which have been tentatively attributed to Ottavio Rinuccini, based on their inclusion in the Codex Palatino 249.[18] It may also be possible that Rinuccini, if he is the author of 'Tu c'hai le penne Amore', wrote the canzonetta specifically for Virginia Andreini and for performance in the Fedeli's comedy. It would not be the first time the Florentine poet composed with Virginia in mind.

The text of *Tu c'hai le penne Amore* reflects quite accurately the secret, besieged motivations of the heroine in *Lo schiavetto* and the true nature of her character. Because of this and because of its cultivated style, the aria falls within the category of Phaedran, or celestial, song, in contrast to those performed by the *serva* Succiola. And the canzonetta's relationship to the plot development of *Lo schiavetto* suggests that the text was composed by either the play's author or its heroine. As mentioned before, Schiavetto is the *prima donna innamorata* in disguise, and so she sings a love song—one that identifies her as Florentine and tells her lovelorn story, although the other characters on stage do not recognize it as such. Schiavetto's disguise casts an interesting, bifurcated light on the gendered aspects of the song's delivery and the object of the singer's passion that mirrors the conflicting perception of Andreini at this point as both Florinda and the male slave. As Wiley Hitchcock translates the first two strophes in his edition of Caccini's publication:

> Tu c'hai le penne Amore
> e sai spiegarle a volo,
> deh muovi ratto un volo
> fin là dov'è 'l mio core.

[18] Caccini, *Le nuove musiche e nuova maniera* (ed. Hitchcock), p. xxi.

> e se non sai la via,
> co' miei sospir t'invia.
>
> Va pur ch'il troverrai
> tra 'l velo e 'l bianco seno,
> o tra 'l dolce sereno
> de' luminosi rai,
> o tra bei nodi d'oro
> del mio dolce tesoro.

(You, Love, who have wings and know how to spread them in flight, ah! fly quickly where my heart is; and if you do not know the way, follow my sighs.

Go: you will find it in the veiled white breast of my dear treasure, or in the sweetness of her bright glances, or in her golden locks.)

The first stanza reflects on Florinda's inability to escape from the confines of her disguise (a standard metaphor for love that either cannot be expressed or falls on deaf ears); the second strophe wills Cupid to make her love known. The possessive pronouns in this second stanza, while they assist in the idiomatic translation of the verse, are perhaps more accurately conveyed as definite articles, which deny an explicit assignation of gender. The distinction is seemingly minor, given the rather obvious reference to the beloved's white breast, but significant to the dramatic situation, as is the delay in revealing the lover's gender until the beginning of the fourth stanza (see below), because the singer is a woman dressed as a man, whom Andreini describes in his preface as a woman who has forgotten that she is a woman: 'Schiavetto, in the end the woman Florinda, one may see as a maiden who, being in love, does not know how to moderate her affections, and thus makes her womanhood of no importance; and in order to remember her lover, she forgets herself and forgets her virginal flower, her family, and subjects herself to a thousand risks to her honour and her life.'[19]

Although the text of *Tu c'hai le penne Amore* clearly refers to the beloved as 'her', as in the penultimate strophe, where the lover is seen as a 'man of stone'—a strategy that allows the characters onstage to hear the song as sung by a man—the poem as a whole is written from a feminine subject position that encompasses the entire landscape of Florence and the nymphs and shepherds who commune there. This subject position echoes

---

[19] G. B. Andreini, *Lo schiavetto* (ed. Falavolti), 60: 'Da Schiavetto, nel fine Florinda donna, pur vedrassi come giovine che, innamorata, non sa essere moderatrice de gli affetti suoi, pone ironcale l'esser donna; e, per ricordarsi dell'amante, di sé stessa si scorda, si scorda il fior virginale, i parenti, e si supponga a mille rischi e d'onore e di vita.'

the falsity of Schiavetto's disguise. Indeed, in the final strophes, the singer confesses that she is attempting to mask her grief and does not want it to be known. She asks Love to relate how she laments the lover's absence (like Arianna, she stands weeping at the water's edge) and to describe in detail the activities of other women in which she does not join because of her sorrow. The portrait of the followers of Diana in the eighth stanza is particularly telling: if the song's protagonist were a man, would Diana's huntresses welcome him into their games?

stanzas 3–11:

> Vanne lusinga, e prega
> perchè dal bel soggiorno
> faccia il mio cor ritorno,
> e se 'l venir pur niega,
> rivolto al nostro sole,
> digli cotai parole:
>
> Quel tuo fedele amante,
> tra lieta amica gente,
> vive mesto e dolente,
> e col tristo sembiante
> d'ogni allegrezza spento
> tura l'altrui contento.
>
> Dì che fra 'l canto e 'l riso
> spargo sospir di foco,
> che fra 'l diletto e 'l gioco
> non mai sereno il viso,
> che d'alma e di cor privo
> stommi fra morto e vivo.
>
> S'entro alle tepide onde
> d'Arno, fra lauri e faggi
> fuggon gli estivi raggi,
> io, su l'ombrose sponde
> o 'n su l'ardente arena,
> resto carco di pena.
>
> Se dal sassoso fondo
> il crin stillante e molle
> Orcheno, il capo e i stolle
> di preda il sen fecondo
> ove ognun un correr' miro
> a pena un guardo io giro.
>
> Mentre per piagge e colli
> seguon fugaci fiere

>   le cacciatrici fiere;
>   lass'io con gli occhi molli
>   hor del cesto, hor del resco
>   l'onda piangendo accresco.
>   Non degli augei volanti
>   miro le prede e i voli
>   sol perchè mi consoli
>   versar sospiri e pianti—
>   ma dì ch'io non vorrei
>   far noti i dolor' miei.
>   Amor cortese impetra
>   ch'a me torni il cor mio
>   o ch'ella il mandi, ond'io
>   più non sembri huom di pietra
>   nè più con tristo aspetto
>   turi l'altrui diletto.
>   Ma se per mia ventura
>   del suo tornar dubbiosa
>   mandarlo a me non osa,
>   Amor prometti e giura,
>   che suo fu sempre, e sia
>   il core a l'alma mia.

(Go lure her, and beg that from its sweet sojourn she allow my heart to return. And if she refuses to let it come back, tell her this: 'Your faithful lover lives sorrowful and grieving among others who are happy, and with sad and joyless mien disturbs their happiness.' Say that amid song and laughter I scatter burning sighs; that among pleasures and pastimes never is my visage serene; that, deprived of heart and soul, I am at the point of death. Whereas sunbeams play on the warm waves of the Arno, flitting among laurels and beeches, I remain grief-laden on the shady banks or the burning sand. If Orcheno emerges from the rocky bottom, hair dripping wet, shirt full of booty, and everyone else rushes to look, I have hardly a glance. While over hill and dale proud huntresses follow fleeting wild beasts, I remain weeping, and from my head the wave of tears increases. I watch not the flying prey swooping down from the heights; that my only consolation is to pour forth sighs and plaints. But say also that I do not wish my grief to be known. Kind Love, beseech her to give back my heart, so that I no longer seem a man of stone nor disturb others' pleasure with sad mien. But if by unhappy chance she dares not give it back, o Love, swear to her that my heart was, and still is, hers.)[20]

---

[20] Translation based on that in Caccini, *Le nuove musiche e nuova maniera* (ed. Hitchcock), pp. xx–xxi.

Conflicting indications of gender and delays in identifying the gender of the singer or the beloved are common to the canzonetta repertory, just as transvestism—both male and female—is a commonplace of commedia dell'arte performance. Virginia Andreini's performances almost always include moments, if not hours, of transvestism during which she sings, and her mother-in-law Isabella celebrated her own ability to act the parts of both men and women in the sonnet 'S'alcun sia mai, che i versi miei negletti', discussed in Chapter 3. Several of Isabella Andreini's most often set *scherzi* delay identification of the beloved's gender until quite late in the poem, and these may serve as foils for my interpretation of 'Tu c'hai le penne Amore'. Her most famous canzonetta, 'Deh girate luci amate', studiously avoids references to gender altogether. And 'Care gioie che le noie', which was variously set to music by Domenico Brunetti, Antonio Cifra, Giovanni Ghizzolo, Nicolò Rubini, and Claudio Saracini, maintains its gender neutrality until the very last verse, when the singer admits, 'But I am delirious: I realize that Aurora does not take away beautiful nymphs. Ah, let us hope that Jove doesn't assume a new shape and take this one from me'—an ambiguous reference to the singer's gender, at best, and one that, at any rate, contradicts that of the author.

It is odd that when put onstage, a style of poetry designed to relate in the simplest terms the pleasures and pains of love offers up such hesitation and disavowal in the representation of gender. One would think that, above all others, the *scherzo* repertory would unblushingly portray the most feminine of women and the most masculine of men, but instead it is characterized by an enforced denial of the singer's gender that results in false starts and misdirection. The resulting poetic ambiguity asks for a musical setting that similarly hesitates to declare its its own masculine or feminine style. The best composers of the genre write dispassionate music that leaves implications of sex or gender unstated. Claudio Saracini is one such composer, whose setting of *Care gioie che le noie* (Ex. 5.1) also evokes a Florentine style that is particularly germane to juxtapose with Caccini's *Tu c'hai le penne Amore*.

Saracini's *Care gioie che le noie*, from his *Seconde musiche* of 1620, to be 'sung and played on the chiatarrone, arpicordo and other instruments', carries Andreini's delicately crafted poem aloft on a nonchalant Tuscan breeze. The Sienese nobleman had no need of gainful employment as a composer or otherwise, and he spent most of his life in Florence as a courtier in the Grand Duke's entourage. A less skilful setting of *Care gioie che le noie*—one that attempted to paint words in music or strove to

Ex. 5.1. Claudio Saracini, *Care gioie che le noie* (*Seconde musiche*, 1620)

redouble Andreini's astonishing sexual imagery—would crush the poem's intimate vocality and nimble wordplay:

> Care gioie,
> che le noie
> de' sospir mandate in bando
> quel diletto,
> c'hò nel petto
> scopran gli occhi sfavillando.
>   Hor non finge,
> hor non pinge
> con sua squadra falsa e vaga
> sogno vano
> quella mano,
> che sì dolce il sen m'impiaga.
>   Bell'avorio
> pur mi glorio,
> che per mille dardi e faci,
> che m'aventi,
> hor consenti,

> ch'io ti porga mille baci.
>   Fresche rose
> ove pose
> d'Ilba il miel cortese Amore
> pur delibo
> grato cibo
> premio altier del mio dolore.
>   Parolette
> vezzosette
> per cui già beàr mi sento
> pur v'ascolto,
> nè m'è tolto
> da l'Aurora il mio contento.
>   Frena, frena
> lingua piena
> di piacer la tua dolcezza:
> sai l'Aurora
> s'innamora,
> ed è scaltra à' furti avezza.
>   Ma vaneggio
> me n'aveggio
> belle ninfe ella non toglie.
> Ah pur Giove
> non ritrove
> forma nova, e me ne spoglie.

(Dear joys that banish the suffering of sighs, that pleasure I have in my breast those scintillating eyes reveal. Now that vain dream with its false and fair company doesn't feign, doesn't advance that hand which so sweetly wounds my breast. Lovely ivory, I am proud that for the thousand darts and fires you cast at me you now allow me to give you a thousand kisses. Fresh roses where kind Love placed the honey of Ilba, now I taste the desired food, proud reward for my suffering. Dear little words for which I already feel blessed, now I hear you: nor does Aurora take my contentment from me. Stop, stop your sweetness, tongue filled with pleasure: you know that Aurora falls in love and she is clever, skilled at thefts. But I am delirious: I realize that she does not take away beautiful nymphs. Ah, let's hope that Jove doesn't assume a new form and take this one from me.)

Andreini's poem is remarkable for its tactile imagery, the force of which, combined with the fractured view of the nymph's mouth, teeth, and tongue, betrays a masculine authorial voice. The sensuality of the verse is similar to that of 'Deh girate luci amate', which also lovingly dwells on metaphors for the beloved's lips and teeth. Although it never reveals the gender of the lover or the beloved in so many words, 'Deh girate luci amate', like 'Care gioie che le noie', invokes a masculine subject position through the strength of its metaphors, its deconstruction of the beloved's aspect, and its indulgence in a consonant-laden language. As the following transcription of stanza 5 shows, varying combinations of the consonants *p*, *r*, and *t* elicit an active pronunciation that engages the singer's lips and tongue as much as it dotes on those of the poem's object:

> Se v'aprite,
> se scoprite
> belle rose amate, e care
> vostre perle,
> a vederle
> riderà la Terra, e 'l Mare.

(If you open, if you disclose, beautiful roses beloved and dear, your pearls, upon seeing them the Earth and the Sea will smile.)

The combination in the canzonetta repertory of setting a visual scene and narrating a story over the course of a number of stanzas makes this type of song especially well suited to dramatic performance. The various canzonettas discussed in this book, from the song contest in Isabella Andreini's *Mirtilla* to her performance of 'canzonette pure alla francese' at the Medici wedding of 1589 and Virginia Andreini's performances of the lament of the Ingrata and *Tu c'hai le penne Amore*, testify to the genre's inherently dramatic function. Indeed, without the added features of a dense dramatic moment from which the canzonetta offers some relief and of the spectator's task of interpreting the song's text in relation to the singer's costume and character development, many canzonettas run the risk of banality, as the musician repeats musical material over and over again.

As may be seen in *Tu c'hai le penne Amore*, the song's text provides the audience with the secret behind Schiavetto's disguise and a foreshadowing of the ultimate disclosure of her true identity. The musical moment when Schiavetto sings Caccini's aria takes place a full nine scenes before she reveals her identity as La Florinda to her lover Orazio. Among the audience, however, if it had not been surmised before when she played the lute with a virtuosic hand, Florinda's identity is clear from the moment she begins to sing. Music is used in *Lo schiavetto* as a code by which characters may communicate with the play's spectators independently of their interactions with the other characters on stage, just as the music of the spheres speaks to the gods while mortal ears are deaf to it. For the audience, Schiavetto's musical performance offers an alternative version of reality that conflicts with what their eyes perceive in her blackface and slave's clothing. And this musical reality transcends not only the visual aspect of the stage, but the theatre itself, for the name Florinda has meaning outside *Lo schiavetto* as the pseudonym of Virginia Andreini, the name of her character in numerous plays, the name with which she signs letters to her various patrons and by which she is commonly known (see Pl. 5.2).[21]

Identification of the canzonetta as an inherently dramatic song—if not sung exclusively in the theatre then derived from theatrical practice—casts a new light on the publication history of the genre and on the composers who wrote in it. As noted in Chapter 3, the printing of canzonettas flourished rapidly and brilliantly in the 1580s, a date that corresponds precisely with the major turning point in Italian theatre outlined in Chapter 1. It is not possible to overestimate the significance of events that cluster around the year 1581, that great watershed in theatrical practice, when the Teatro Tron and the Teatro Michiel opened in Venice, when Pedrolino and the *canario* skyrocketed in popularity, when the great neoclassical theatres designed by Scamozzi and Palladio began to be built, when the theatre-loving Vincenzo Gonzaga came of age and began his lifelong project of making Mantua the centre of theatrical practice in western Europe and when the 17-year-old Isabella Andreini came to lead the Gelosi with such elan that the company eventually disintegrated without her.

Into this historical moment enters the canzonetta with its light, supple inflections and its tender descriptions of the intimacies of love. Claudio Monteverdi, rather than cautiously exercising a compositional technique in which he felt naive and unsure,[22] with his book of *Canzonette a tre voci* of 1584 made an astute judgement of the contemporary vogue for theatrical music and wrote an unpretentious collection of songs that are flawlessly adapted to that vein. His understanding of the canzonetta as a dramatic genre continued through his French-styled *scherzi* of 1607, the lament of

---

[21] Giovan Battista's and Virginia's letter to Vincenzo Gonzaga on 16 Nov. 1611 [ASMN, Gonzaga, b. 1170] is remarkable for its use of his real name and her pseudonym: 'obligatissimo servitore et suddito Giovan Battista et Florinda Andreini'; others written by Virginia alone are often signed 'Florinda comica' [ASF, Mediceo, f. 5143, fos. 410^{r-v} and 424^{r-v}]. Correspondence regarding Andreini's last-minute replacement of Caterina Martinelli in Monteverdi's *Arianna* in 1608 consistently refers to the actress as Florinda.

[22] Fabbri's judgement of Monteverdi's production of the collection is that 'while entering the field of secular music, Monteverdi again proceeded with caution, choosing the none too demanding genre of the three-voice canzonetta'. Fabbri, *Monteverdi* (trans. Carter), 15.

Epilogue 183

PL. 5.2. Dionisio Minaggio, *The Feather Book*, 'Florinda'. Blacker-Wood Library of Biology, McGill University

the Ingrata in 1608, and his realization of *dramma per musica* in *Orfeo*, where its use as a formal archetype provides the structure for the first two acts of the opera, up to the climactic entrance of the Messaggera. As noted by Massimo Ossi in 1992, 'most important, throughout *Orfeo* the deployment of canzonetta-style sections is not an abstract element superimposed on the work's dramatic progress, but serves to further the development of the plot'[23]—like the *scenari* used by *comici dell'arte* to formulate the structure of their plays. While contrapuntally less intricate than his five-voice madrigals, Monteverdi's canzonettas betray their difficulty in the offhanded simplicity of their manner, all the more taxing because the style brooks no whiff of compositional effort. Caccini's conception of the style, embodied in the term *sprezzatura*, is as appropriate to Monteverdi's canzonettas of the 1580s and to *Orfeo* as it is to *Tu c'hai le penne Amore* or to Saracini's setting of *Care gioie che le noie*.

The vignettes and analyses discussed in this book bring to the surface a wide variety of themes encompassing commedia dell'arte performance, theatrical representation, women's roles in humanistic thought, the use of music in the theatre, and ideas of music's meaning. Four concepts seem to me to have the most comprehensive significance. Over all, the musical and theatrical performances described in this book define a genre of human communication that gives voice to those whose voices are otherwise silent. At times as innocently conveyed as the depiction of a woman in drag, the mirror that comedians held up to their audiences at other times reveals a reflection of Renaissance society that is hard and unforgiving. Once a Schiavetto or an Isabella Andreini singing 'Io credèa che tra gli amanti' assumes her costume, she is only able to break through her masculine disguise, to express the woman's emotions she donned that armour to serve, in song. Similarly, the nymphs Filli and Mirtilla singing in contest overflow with expressions of love for the shepherd whose own love for another deafens him to their voices. Unable to be heard, the excess of their thwarted emotions finally bursts forth in a transcendent stream. More darkly, the adolescent bride in Monteverdi's *Arianna*, entering into adulthood through matrimony, is mute under her father's care and speaks through the voice of her husband when married. In the brief interstices between the two, her song overcomes the frame surrounding it to achieve a celestial song that is born of anguish and fear.

[23] Ossi, 'Monteverdi's *Ordine novo*', 282.

Epilogue

The notion of divine madness and its manifestations pervades this book because it idolizes the submissive and the errant—ideas associated primarily with the adolescent and feminine. Made apparent in Isabella Andreini's performance of the mad scene at the Medici wedding of 1589 and enunciated in the descriptions of her divine fury that occupy the poems of Chiabrera and Marino, the embattled emotions of the madwoman may be seen also in the laments sung by Virginia Andreini at the Gonzaga wedding of 1608, where Arianna's abduction resulted, as had Isabella's, in a nasty surprise that dislodged the errant adolescent from her childish, selfish thoughts. The typological similarities between *La pazzia d'Isabella* and the *Lamento d'Arianna* unfortunately mark the wedding ritual as essentially one of abduction and rape that, in its early stages, is engineered by the female protagonist, but which ultimately results in her forced submission to it. It is perhaps crude to draw a comparison between the Phaedran charioteer's horses (one dominant and willing, the other that must be beaten, bleeding, into submission) and the protagonists in the wedding ritual, but the outpouring of musical and poetic expression at the climax of the marriage-to-death rite prevents avoidance of this ugly association.

The tension inherent in Phaedran song between the charioteer's horses spins off additional meaning in commedia dell'arte performance with the practice of comediennes singing in competition. While I emphasized in Chapter 2 the distinctions between performing 'in concorrenza' and Howard Brown's emulative impulse in the composition of imitative polyphony, the two practices are based on a common philosophical foundation that the creation of music—whether in composition or in performance—arises from conflict, almost as if the spark of creativity must leap out from a point of friction. And perhaps this, too, is what happens within the marriage-to-death rite, as the bride discovers the friction of individual human interaction within the confines of marriage and her responsibilities to family and state.

Discussion of theatrical structure touches on issues of framing and the feminine- and masculine-gendered frames of comedians' plays. In some instances circumscribing a woman's lament, as in the *Lamento d'Arianna*, musical-theatrical frames can also take on a much broader aspect, demarcating entire plays by way of the prologue and *licenza*. In analysing the larger form of frame, which in comedians' performances is often gendered feminine, as demonstrated by the prologues sung by Vittoria Piisimi and discussed in Chapter 1, smaller, more closely circumscribed frames come into greater focus. The nymphs in Isabella Andreini's *Mirtilla* re-enacting in microcosm the song contest between the Muses and Pierides, which is judicated by the Hamadryads, the pastoral characterization of their contest's frame, and its association with social responsibility and living in harmony are shown to take precedence over any masculine gendering that might attach to its shepherd. Social harmony and the assumption of the responsibilities of an adult are further explored in the contextualization of Arianna's lament, where issues of adolescent education and its methods come into play as determinants of the frame.

Comedians' approaches to structural frames and their methods for composing in performance and for memorizing and improvising material for the stage engenders a wide-ranging premiss for theatrical performances of all kinds that concerns structural yokes. Discussed in one sense in Chapter 2 as the harness binding the Phaedran charioteer's horses together, this theme takes on additional meaning as the generic structure for comediennes' contests (like the song contest in *Mirtilla*), as the form governing the newly popular strophic poetry and music of the canzonetta, and as the rhetorical formula, the figures of words, that govern the recitative-like style of the lament of Arianna. When seen in this context, the light-hearted, essentially amorous subject matter of the canzonetta, with its uncomplicated compositional style, can be seen to embody a loftier ideal that enunciates in music the image of the Phaedran charioteer. Deceptively simple to analyse in traditional methods that highlight imitative procedures and modal complexity, the canzonetta embodies a philosophy of art that emphasizes the nobility of simplicity and unmediated avenues of discourse between performer and spectator, between author and God. This new way of conceiving of the harmony of the spheres as an essentially hermeneutic phenomenon dispels, finally, the humanist pedantry that characterizes the arguments of men like Artusi and Puteanus and instead engenders a more refined, rhetorically based conception of music as a representative art that encompasses the speech of women and typifies the new century and the emergence of opera.

Chronology

Unless otherwise noted, citations of rulers named, crowned, or elected derive from Adriano Cappelli, *Cronologia, cronografia e calendario perpetuo*, 7th edn. (Milan, 1998). Citations of secondary sources are given in short form; full citations may be found in the bibliography.

According to Angelo Martini, *Manuale di metrologia ossia misure, pesi e monete in uso attualmente e anticamente presso tutti i popoli* (Rome, 1976), 353, the monetary unit in use in Mantua in 1588 and throughout the period in question was the 'Lira di 20 Soldi di 12 Denari', which would yield 12 denari to the soldo and 20 soldi to the lira. In 1579 the scudo [d'argento] and ducatone were both valued at 6 lire imperiali, which in turn equalled 8.52 lire correnti. Thus, 1 scudo [S.] = 1 ducatone [D.] = 6 lire imperiali [L. imp.]; 1 L. imp = 1.42 L. correnti; 1 L. corrente = 20 soldi [s.]; 1 soldo = 12 denari [d.]. In this index, lire or L. are understood to be lire correnti, unless otherwise indicated.

1544

unknown   Birth of Francesco Andreini in Pistoia to Antonio Andreini [ASMN, Gonzaga, Registro Necrologico 30, 1624 agosto 21]

1549

30 July   Birth of Ferdinando de' Medici to Eleonora di Toledo and Cosimo de' Medici

1550

22 Feb.   Guglielmo Gonzaga named Duke of Mantua
24 Feb.   Ottavio Farnese named Duke of Parma
6 Mar.   Albrecht IV named Duke of Bavaria

1552

27 Sept.   Birth of Flaminio Scala in Rome [ASV, Notarile testamenti, Beacian Fabrizio, b. 56, no. 236]

1557

7 Apr.   Birth of Tristano Martinelli in Mantua [ASMN, Registri necrologici, vol. 33]

1559

18 Sept.	François II (Valois-Angoulême) crowned King of France; Caterina de' Medici regent
3 Oct.	Death of Ercole II d'Este
26 Nov.	Alfonso II d'Este named Duke of Ferrara, Modena, Reggio, and Rovigo

1560

17 Feb.	Wedding of Lucrezia de' Medici and Alfonso II d'Este in Ferrara [Solerti, *Ferrara e la corte estense*, p. xxiv]
5 Dec.	Death of François II, King of France; Caterina de Medici and Antoine de Bourbon regents

1561

26 Feb.	Luigi d'Este made cardinal
21 Apr.	Death of Lucrezia de' Medici, Duchess of Ferrara
26 Apr.	Entry of Eleonor of Austria into Mantua [Vigilio, *La insalata*, 39]
Apr./May	Wedding of Guglielmo Gonzaga, Duke of Mantua, and Eleonor of Austria in Mantua
May	Luzzasco Luzzaschi enters the service of the Estense court in Ferrara [Solerti, *Ferrara e la corte estense*, p. lxi]
25 May	Charles IX (Valois-Angoulême) crowned King of France; Catherine de Médicis and Antoine de Bourbon regents

1562

unknown	Birth of Isabella Canali [later Andreini] in Padua
12 Jan.	Birth of Carlo Emanuele of Savoy
24 Jan.	Prohibition against masquerading in the guise of a priest or a nun in Milan [ASM, Atti del governo, Spettacoli pubblici, parte antica, cart. 12, fasc. 1]
21 Sept.	Birth of Vincenzo Gonzaga in Mantua [Vigilio, *La insalata*, 41]
Oct.	Birth of Cesare d'Este
24 Nov.	Maximilian II crowned King of Germany
20 Dec.	Death of Cardinal Giovanni de' Medici

1563

2 Jan.	Ferdinando de' Medici named cardinal
Mar.	Gonzalo Fernández de Cordova named Governor of Milan
7 Apr.	Baptism of Vincenzo Gonzaga in Mantua

1564

unknown	Birth of Vincenzo Giustiniani

Chronology

8 Feb.	Death of Michelangelo Buonarotti in Rome
16 Feb.	Ash Wednesday
2 Apr.	Easter
25 July	Maximilian II, Emperor and King of Germany and Hungary, named Archduke of Austria

1565

7 Mar.	Ash Wednesday
22 Apr.	Easter
13 May	Birth of Giovanni de' Medici
26 Nov.	Barbara of Austria and Giovanna of Austria depart Mantua [Solerti, *Ferrara e la corte estense*, p. xxiv]
3 Dec.	Entry of Barbara of Austria into Ferrara [Solerti, *Ferrara e la corte estense*, p. xxv]
5 Dec. (Wed.)	Wedding of Barbara of Austria and Alfonso II d'Este, Duke of Ferrara, in Ferrara [Solerti, *Ferrara e la corte estense*, p. xxv]
16 Dec.	Entry of Giovanna of Austria into Florence [Gaeta Bertelà and Petrioli Tofani, *Feste e apparati medicei*, 15]
18 Dec.	Wedding of Giovanna of Austria and Francesco Maria de' Medici in Florence [Gaeta Bertelà and Petrioli Tofani, *Feste e apparati medicei*, 19]
26 Dec. (Wed.)	Performance of *La cofanaria* by Francesco d'Ambra in Florence, with intermedi by Giovan Battista Cini in honour of the wedding of Giovanna of Austria and Francesco Maria de' Medici. Music for the 1st, 2nd, and 5th intermedi by Alessandro Striggio; music for the 3rd, 4th, and 6th intermedi by Francesco Corteccia; Giorgio Vasari architect. [Grazzini, *Descrizione degl'intermedii rappresentati colla commedia*]

1566

2 Feb. (Sat.)	Performance of *Il canto de sogni* in Florence [*Descrizione del canto de sogni*]
21 Feb. (Thu.)	Performance of *La genealogia degli dei de' gentili* in Florence [Baldini, *Discorso sopra la mascherata*]
26 Feb.	Performance of the *Mascherata delle bufole* in Florence [Gaeta Bertelà and Petrioli Tofani, *Feste e apparati medicei*, 19]
27 Feb.	Ash Wednesday
10 Mar.	Performance of the *Annunciazione* in Florence [Gaeta Bertelà and Petrioli Tofani, *Feste e apparati medicei*, 19]
14 Apr.	Easter
28 Dec.	Death of Margherita Paleologa, Duchess of Mantua

1567

12 Feb.	Ash Wednesday
28 Feb.	Baptism of Eleonora de' Medici in Florence; Giorgio Vasari signs his *Descrizione dell'apparato fatto nel tempio di S. Giovanni di Fiorenza per la battesimo*
30 Mar.	Easter
15 Apr.	Request of a licence by Leone de' Sommi to open a hall in Mantua for performing comedies, open to any who pay the price of admission, for a period of ten years, with a provision for de' Sommi to pay alms from the proceeds to the poor at the Misericordia [Taviani and Schino, *Il segreto*, 194–5]
11 May (Sun.)	Luigi Rogna, Mantua, to Pietro Martire Cornacchia, [unspecified]: [Guglielmo Gonzaga] today heard a comedy by the Gratiani, performed in the *scena* of the castle [ASMN, Gonzaga, b. 2577, fo. 23ʳ]
18 May (Sun.)	Luigi Rogna, Mantua, to Pietro Martire Cornacchia, [unspecified]: yesterday the Gratiani performed a comedy in the palace of Cesare [Gonzaga, Prince of Guastalla] [D'Ancona, 'Il teatro mantovano', pt. 2, p. 9]
June	Luigi Rogna, Mantua, to Pietro Martire Cornacchia, [unspecified]: last Sunday Flaminia's company [Accesi] performed a comedy in Mantua [D'Ancona, 'Il teatro mantovano', pt. 2, p. 11; D'Ancona, *Origini del teatro*, ii. 447–9]
June	Orlando di Lasso visits Ferrara from the court of Bavaria [Solerti, *Ferrara e la corte estense*, p. lix]
1 July (Tue.)	Luigi Rogna, Mantua, to [Pietro Martire Cornacchia, unspecified]: today two comedies were performed in Mantua at the same time: one by Flaminia, Angela, and Pantalone in the usual place, and the other in the house of Lanzino in the neighbourhood of Purgo [near S. Andrea] by Vincenza [Armani]. Both comedies had a good audience, but Flaminia's was nobler; she performed a tragicomic version of the tragedy of Dido [D'Ancona, 'Il teatro mantovano', pt. 2, pp. 12–13] (Doc. 1)
6 July (Sun.)	Luigi Rogna, Mantua, to [Pietro Martire Cornacchia, unspecified]: the other day, Flaminia was commended for her laments in a tragedy, based on Ariosto [*Orlando furioso*, canto 37] performed by her troupe; Vincenza was praised for her music-making, even though the subject of her tragedy didn't come out as well as the other. Then yesterday Vincenza played the part of Cupid in the intermedi, and Flaminia appeared well in other ways [D'Ancona, 'Il teatro mantovano', pt. 2, pp. 14–15] (Doc. 2)
9 July	Antonio Ceruto, Mantua, to [not stated]: his friends in Mantua

	argue about which they like better, Flaminia or Vincenza [ASMN, Gonzaga, b. 2578, fo. 38ᵛ]
10 July	Antonio Ceruto, Mantua, to [not stated]: the comedians are losing audience [D'Ancona, 'Il teatro mantovano', pt. 2, p. 16]
11 July (Fri.)	Luigi Rogna, Mantua, to [Pietro Martire Cornacchia, unspecified]: Cesare [Gonzaga] returned from Guastalla for the baptism of the son of Massimiliano Gonzaga, and arranged for a comedy yesterday by Flaminia, a pastoral on the story of Jupiter and Io, in honour of the baptism [D'Ancona, 'Il teatro mantovano', pt. 2, p. 16]
15 July	Luigi Rogna, Mantua, to [Pietro Martire Cornacchia, unspecified]; Vincenza's company has gone to Ferrara [D'Ancona, 'Il teatro mantovano', pt. 2, p. 17]
17 July	Luigi Rogna, Mantua, to Pietro Martire Cornacchia, [unspecified]: the comedies go on and the Dominican brothers go in order to do their work for the inquisition [ASMN, Gonzaga, b. 2577, fo. 218ʳ⁻ᵛ]
25 July	Antonio Ceruto, Mantua, to [not stated]: all Mantua is in terror of the inquisitors and the only amusement is Flaminia and her comedies. [ASMN, Gonzaga, b. 2578, fos. 45ʳ⁻ᵛ, 46ᵛ–47ʳ]
3 Aug.	Luigi Rogna, Mantua, to [Pietro Martire Cornacchia, unspecified]: they are preparing a comedy by Flaminia's company to be performed in the Palazzo della Ragione [D'Ancona, 'Il teatro mantovano', pt. 2, p. 17]
3 Sept. (Wed.)	Luigi Rogna, Mantua, to [Pietro Martire Cornacchia, unspecified]: a comedy was performed today, in which Gratiano was especially good [D'Ancona, 'Il teatro mantovano', pt. 2, p. 17]
4 Nov.	Death of Doge Girolamo Priuli
26 Nov.	Pietro Loredan elected Doge of Venice

1568

10 Jan.	Ordinance prohibiting masquerading in religious garb or carrying weapons while masquerading in Milan [ASM, Registri delle Cancellerie, s. XXI, no. 7, fos. 107ᵛ–108ʳ]
2 Feb.	Luigi Rogna, Mantua, to the Castellano of Mantua, Casale Monferrato: they are working on the *scena* for the *barriera*, which will take place the night of carnival [2 Mar.], and for the comedy, which will be performed on Fat Thursday [D'Ancona, 'Il teatro mantovano', pt. 2, pp. 17–18]
13 Feb.	Luigi Rogna, Mantua, to [Pietro Martire Cornacchia, unspecified]: the Jews are preparing a comedy [D'Ancona, 'Il teatro mantovano', pt. 2, p. 18]
20 Feb.	Teodoro Sangiorgio, Mantua, to Guglielmo Gonzaga, Mantua: the

	comedy for the night of carnival is ready [D'Ancona, 'Il teatro mantovano', pt. 2, p. 18]
22 Feb.	Wedding of Renée of Lorraine and Wilhelm V of Bavaria in Trausnitz [Leuchtmann, *Orlando di Lasso*, 147]
26 Feb.	Fat Thursday
28 Feb.	Baptism of Eleonora de' Medici, daughter of Giovanna of Austria and Francesco Maria de' Medici, in Florence [Vasari, *Descrizione dell'apparato*]; performance of the comedy *I fabii* by Lotto del Mazzo in Florence in honour of the baptism [*I fabii comedia di Lotto del Mazza*]
3 Mar.	Ash Wednesday
8 Mar.	Performance by Orlando di Lasso, Giovan Battista Scolari, Massimo Troiano, Don Carlo Livizzano, Giorgio Dori, and the Marchesa di Malaspina of a *commedia all'improvviso* in Trausnitz in honour of the wedding of Renée of Lorraine and Wilhelm V of Bavaria [Leuchtmann, *Orlando di Lasso*, 147]
12 Mar. (Fri.)	Bernardo Canigiani, Ferrara, to [unknown, Florence]: Don Francesco last Tuesday celebrated the octave of carnival with a comedy at Schifanoia, which lasted five hours [Solerti, *Ferrara e la corte estense*, p. lxxxvi]
18 Apr.	Easter
26 Apr.	Baldassare de Preti, Mantua, to the Castellano of Mantua, Casale Monferrato: Guglielmo Gonzaga arranged comedies by two companies, Pantalone's and Ganaza's [Alberto Ganassa's], and he wanted the best players to unite into one company, among whom were Vincenza and Flaminia [D'Ancona, 'Il teatro mantovano', pt. 2, p. 18]
29 May	Birth of Virginia de' Medici to Camilla Martelli and Cosimo de' Medici

1569

23 Feb.	Ash Wednesday
25 Mar.	The Duke of Albuquerque [Gabriel de la Cueva], Milan, to Marcello Rincio, [Milan]: cites various abuses occurring in comedies performed in the city and relays the decision of the *Consiglio Segreto* that comedies not be performed on feast days, that all comedies be previewed by Rincio, and that they not contain perversions of good habits and the common good. Officers designated to carry out these ordinances are the Capitano di Giustitia and the Podestà [ASM, Autografi, cart. 94, fasc. 44]
10 Apr.	Easter
25 Apr.	Massimo Troiano dedicates his *Discorsi* to Christine of Lorraine

	[Troiano, *Die Münchner Fürstenhochzeit von 1568*, ed. Leuchtmann, 11–13]
27 Apr.	Entry of Archduke Carlo of Austria into Florence [*Raccolto delle feste fatte*]
1 May (Sun.)	Performance in Florence of the comedy *La vedova* by Giambattista Cini, with intermedi by an unknown author, in honour of Archduke Carlo of Austria. Music for the intermedi by Alessandro Striggio; architect Bernardo Buontalenti [(Passignani), *Descrittione dell'intermedii fatti nel felicissimo palazzo del Gran Duca Cosimo*]
5 May	Performance of *La mascherata delle bufole* in Florence [*Descrittione della mascherata delle bufole*]
11 Sept.	Death of Vincenza Armani by poisoning [Valerini, *Oratione*, preface; Marotti and Romei, *La professione del teatro*, 28]

1570

19 Jan.	Wedding of Lucrezia d'Este and Francesco Maria della Rovere, Prince of Urbino
8 Feb.	Ash Wednesday
26 Mar.	Easter
3 May	Death of Doge Pietro Loredan
10 May	The Duke of Albuquerque [Gabriel de la Cueva], Milan, to Giovanni Arcimboldo, Marcello Rincio, and Oratio Archinto, Milan: repeats his concerns of 25 Mar. 1569, repeats the ordinances established then by the *Consiglio Segreto*, and orders that all comedies be previewed by at least two of the letter's recipients [ASM, Autografi, cart. 94, fasc. 44]
11 May	Alvise Mocenigo elected Doge of Venice
17 Nov.	Earthquakes begin in Ferrara and continue through 1572 [Solerti, *Ferrara e la corte estense*, pp. xcvii–xcviii]
22 Dec.	Borso Trotti, Paris, to [a Florentine court functionary, Florence]: a company of Italian comedians are in Paris, who are truly bestial; the king likes them, however, and pays them 45 scudi per week [Solerti and Lanza, 'Il teatro ferrarese', 163]

1571

28 Feb.	Ash Wednesday
15 Mar.	Luzzasco Luzzaschi dedicates his *Primo libro de' madrigali à 5 voci* to Lucrezia d'Este della Rovere
4 Mar. (Sun.)	Lord Buckhurst, Paris, to Queen Elizabeth, [London]: he dined at the Hôtel de Nevers with the Duke of Nevers and the king, and a company of Italians performed a comedy [Baschet, *Les Comédiens italiens*, 15–16]

15 Apr.	Easter
1 May (Tues.)	Performance by the Gelosi, 'Comédiens du Roy', of a comedy for the baptism of Charles Henri de Clermont. Attended by the king, M d'Anjou, and M d'Alençon, the Queen Mother, the Queen, the Cardinal of Lorraine, the Duke de Guise, M du Maine, the Dukes of Vaudemont, Mercoeur, and d'Aumale, the Marquis d'Elbeuf, all the gentlemen of the king's court, the ambassadors of Spain, England, and Poland, the king's sister, the ladies of Lorraine, Mme de Montpensier and Mme de Guise [Baschet, *Les Comédiens italiens*, 17–18]
30 July	Giacomo Grana, Belriguardo, to Luigi d'Este, Paris: the Bendidio sisters made music for the Duchess of Ferrara at Belriguardo [ASMO, Cancelleria ducale, Particolari, Grana]
12 Aug. (Sun.)	Giacomo Grana, Belriguardo, to Luigi d'Este, Paris: there was a *ballo* at which Lucretia Machiavella danced and after which the Bendidio sisters sang [ASMO, Cancelleria ducale, Particolari, Grana]
13 Aug. (Mon.)	Bernardo Canigiani, Belriguardo, to Cosimo de' Medici, Florence: there was a *ballo* on Wednesday [8 Aug.], at which Lucrezia Machiavella and Isabella Bendidio sang to the accompaniment of Luzzasco Luzzaschi on the gravicembalo [ASF, Mediceo, f. 2892]
21 Aug.	Alonso Pimentel, with the counsellors of the Consiglio Segreto, named Governor of Milan
15 Sept.	Ordinance prohibiting the performance of comedies in Paris, public and private [Paris, Archives nationales, Registres du Parlement, Conseil. X, no. 1633, fo. 261]
mid-Sept.	Álvaro de Sande named Governor of Milan
15 Oct.	Ordinance prohibiting the performance of comedies in Paris, specifically those by Alberto Ganassa and his Italian troupe, in public and in private [Paris, Archives nationales, Registres du Parlement, Conseil. X, no. 1633, fo. 321]
29 Dec.	Receipt for payment to the Italian comedians in Lyons of 26 l. 11 s. 1 d. [Lyons, Archives hospitalières, Registre des recteurs-trésoriers de l'aumône générale, receptes no. 28, fo. 9]

1572

20 Feb.	Ash Wednesday
6 Apr.	Easter
7 Apr.	Luis de Zúñiga y Requesens named Governor of Milan
1 May	Death of Pope Pius V
21 May	Request of a licence for the Gelosi to perform in Milan, which is granted [ASM, Autografi, cart. 94, fasc. 42]

25 May	Ugo Boncompagni (Gregorio XIII) elected Pope
13 June	Request of a licence by Fortunio, *maestro di comedie*, to perform comedies in Milan with his company; licence denied [ASM, Autografi, cart. 94, fasc. 43]
18 June	The Commendatore Maggiore, Milan, to the Governor of Milan, Milan: nine ordinances regarding the performance of comedies in Milan [ASM, Autografi, cart. 94, fasc. 42]
5 Aug.	Giovan Paolo de' Medici, Montalta, to [not stated], Mantua: Vincenza and her company are performing in Montalta, but he is sick of the comedies [D'Ancona, 'Il teatro mantovano', pt. 2, p. 22]
18 Sept.	Death of Barbara of Austria, Duchess of Ferrara [Solerti, *Ferrara e la corte estense*, p. xxviii]
13 Oct.	Licence granted to the Gelosi to perform in Genoa throughout Nov. [D'Ancona, 'Il teatro mantovano', pt. 3, pp. 318–19]

1573

4 Feb.	Ash Wednesday
13 Mar.	Performance by the Gelosi for Alfonso II d'Este and the Countess of Sala, Barbara Sanseverino, at Belvedere [Romei, *I discorsi*, ed. Shalvi]
22 Mar.	Easter
1 May	Request of a licence for the Intronati to perform comedies in Milan; granted on 8 May [ASM, Autografi, cart. 94, fasc. 43]
9 May	Henri of Valois elected King of Poland
10 May	Ordinances for the State of Milan decree that comedians may not dress in ecclesiastical robes of any kind; that they may not speak of the Sacred Word or of anything pertaining to religion, or use words from the sacrament; that they may not induce simple listeners to superstition or recite incantations; that they may not speak or act in a lascivious manner (such as having women dress as men); that the comedies' amorous subjects must be honest; that comedians may not name God in their comedies; that they may not speak in any way that would be injurious to anyone; and that all comedies must be previewed by the delegates of the state [ASM, Autografi, cart. 94, fasc. 44]
13 June	Request of a licence for Fortunio, *maestro di comedie*, to perform in Milan [ASM, Autografi, cart. 94, fasc. 43]
16–24 July	First performance of *L'Aminta* at Belriguardo by the company of Zan Battista Boschetti [Pittorru, *Torquato Tasso*, 103–4]
1 Sept.	Antonio de Guzmán y Zúñiga, Marchese d'Ayamonte, named Governor of Milan

27 Nov.	Request of a licence for Milanese youths to perform comedies in Milan, granted on 5 Dec. [ASM, Autografi, cart 94, fasc. 43]

1574

1568 × 1574	Report of comedians at the Imperial court lists a 'Flaminio' [Flaminio Scala], a 'Julo Comediante' [Giulio Pasquati da Padova], a 'Francischo ysabella Camediannte' [Francesco and Isabella Andreini], and an 'Antonio Soldino Florentino' [Pandolfi, *La commedia dell'arte*, ii. 250; i, 297; cfr. 22 June 1576]
Feb.	Henri of Valois crowned King of Poland
12 Feb.	Rinaldo Petignoni, Venice, to Guglielmo Gonzaga, Mantua: writes on behalf of the Gelosi that they will not come to Mantua this carnival to perform, tells the Duke of a misunderstanding between the company and Agosto Trissino, and asks the Duke to intercede and protect them from Trissino's anger [D'Ancona, 'Il teatro mantovano', pt. 2, pp. 24–5]
24 Feb.	Ash Wednesday
11 Apr.	Easter
21 Apr.	Death of Cosimo de' Medici; Francesco Maria de' Medici named Grand Duke of Tuscany
30 May	Death of Charles IX, King of France; succeeded by Henri III (Valois-Angoulême), Duke of Anjou and King of Poland
8 June	Request of a licence for the Confidenti to perform comedies in Milan, under the same regulations as last year; granted 13 June [ASM, Autografi, cart. 94, fasc. 43; ASM, Registri delle Cancellerie, s. XXI, n. 10, fo. 10^v]
26 June (Sat.)	Performance of a mascherata by Cesare Negri in Milan in honour of Don Juan of Austria [Negri, *Le gratie d'amore*, 9]
6 July	Licence granted to the Gelosi to perform comedies in Milan [ASM, Registri delle Cancellerie, serie XXI, n. 10, f. 34^r]
7 July	Alvise Bonrizzo, Pontieba, to the Senate, Venice: Sig. Abbate [Beltrame] has recommended for the king's entertainment in Venice the comedians who were there in the winter [ASV, Dispacci al Senato, Francia, f. 5; Nolhac and Solerti, *Il viaggio*, 230; cfr. 12 Feb. 1574]
[10 July]	The College of the Senate, Venice, to [Ottaviano Maggi], Milan: they understand the Gelosi, with the woman Vittoria, are in Milan, and request that the Gelosi be sent to Venice with all speed [ASV, Collegio IV, f. 50; Nolhac and Solerti, *Il viaggio*, 231]
13 July	Ottaviano Maggi, Milan, to Aloisio Mocenigo, Venice: the Gelosi have requested permission of Don Juan of Austria to leave Milan, which has been granted; the company should therefore be in Venice

	in three days [ASV, Senato III, Secreta, Lettere del Residente a Milano; Nolhac and Solerti, *Il viaggio*, 231]
13 July	Ottaviano Maggi, Milan, to Aloisio Mocenigo, Venice: the Gelosi have requested a letter stating that they are in service to Mocenigo and may therefore not be obliged to stop to perform in Mantua [ASV, Senato III, Secreta, Lettere del Residente a Milano; Nolhac and Solerti, *Il viaggio*, 232]
16 July (Fri.)	Teodoro San Giorgio, Mantua, to [Guglielmo Gonzaga, Mantua]: he has received from Ferrara the music to be performed in the *cappella* in Mantua for the visit of Henri III [ASMN, Gonzaga, b. 2592]
[17 July]	Account of the funds spent by the Ca' Foscari for the entry of Henri III; records the presence of 30 comedians, 50 musicians, and 40 who played tambourines and trumpets [Venice, Museo Civico 3281 (Cicognini 2982), IV, no. 53]
18 July (Sun.)	Passage in the anonymous MS 'Entrata d'Enrico III in Venetia' states that the comedians [Gelosi] performed a comedy for the king and Alfonso II d'Este at the residence of the Duke of Ferrara [Paris, BNF, ital. 1494, fo. 49]
21 July (Wed.)	Performance of a pastoral comedy in Ferrara at a banquet for Henri III [*Le feste et trionfi*, fo. 15ᵛ; Nolhac and Solerti, *Il viaggio*, 292]
24 July (Sat.)	Performance in Ferrara by the Gelosi of *Tragedia* by Cornelio Frangipani, with music by Claudio Merulo, in honour of Henri III. 'Tutti li recitanti hanno cantato in suavissimi concenti, quando soli, quando accompagnati, e infin il coro di Mercurio era di sonatori, che avevano quanti vari istrumenti che si sonarono giamai. Li trombetti introducevano li Dei in scena, la qual era istituita con la macchina tragica, ma non si è potuto ordinar per il gran tumulto di persone che quivi era. Non si è potuto imitare l'antichità nelle composizioni musicali, avendole fatte il S. Claudio Merulo, che a tal grado non devono giamai esser giunti li antichi . . .' [Nolhac and Solerti, *Il viaggio*, 133–4; Frangipani, *Tragedia*, 2nd edn.]
31 July (Sat.)	Performance by the Gelosi of a pastoral in Venice in the hall of the Palazzo Giustinian [Dorron, *Discours des choses mémorables*; Nolhac and Solerti, *Il viaggio*, 144]
2 Aug. (Mon.)	Entry of Henri III into Mantua [Virgilio, *La insalata*, 44; *Entrata del Christianiss. Re Henrico III . . . nella città di Mantova*; Vigenère, *La Sumptueuse et Magnifique Entrée*]
3 Aug.	Banquet in Mantua in honour of Henri III [Vigilio, *La insalata*, 44]
6 Aug.	Departure of the Marchese d'Ayamonte and his court from Milan for Cremona and then to Polezzo to greet Henri III of France, the

	Duke of Savoy, the Duke of Ferrara, the Duke of Anvers, and the Prior of France [Negri, *Le gratie d'amore*, 11]
8 Aug.	Entry of Henri III into Cremona [Negri, *Le gratie d'amore*, 11]
9 Aug.	Entry of Henri III into Fontanella [Negri, *Le gratie d'amore*, 11]
10 Aug.	Entry of Henri III into Monza [Negri, *Le gratie d'amore*, 11]
11 Aug.	Performance by Giovan Stefano Faruffino, a student of Cesare Negri's, of a *ballo* in Monza for Henri III. Henri III lodges in Mazenta, where another of Negri's students, Giulio Cesare Lampugnano, and Martino da Asso also dance for him [Negri, *Le gratie d'amore*, 11–12]
12 Aug.	Entry of Henri III into Vercelli; departure of the Marchese d'Ayamonte for Milan [Negri, *Le gratie d'amore*, 12]
28 Sept.	Death of Guidobaldo II della Rovere; Francesco Maria II della Rovere named Duke of Urbino

1575

1575–7	Plague ravages northern Italy
	Vincenzo Giustiniani writes in his *Discorso sopra la musica de' suoi tempi* that, in 1575 or shortly thereafter, a new way of singing began, much different from the previous style, mainly in the style of singing with a solo voice over instrumental accompaniment, as in the practice of Giulio Cesare Brancaccio [Giustiniani, *Discorso*, trans. MacClintock]
23 Jan.	Guglielmo Gonzaga, Duke of Mantua, invested with the Duchy of Monferrato [Vigilio, *La insalata*, 46]
15 Feb.	Henri III (Valois-Angoulême), Duke of Anjou and King of Poland, crowned King of France
16 Feb.	Ash Wednesday
3 Apr.	Easter
1 June	Request of a licence by the Gelosi to perform in Milan for an unspecified period; granted 3 June, accompanied by a confirmation of the ordinances dated 18 June 1572 and a testimony by Giovanni Arcimboldi and Marcello Rincio dated 28 May that the Gelosi's comedies conform to the ordinances [ASM, Autografi, cart. 94, fasc. 42; cfr. 18 June 1572] (Doc. 5)
16 June	Death of Renée of France
15 July	Henri III, King of France, deposed as King of Poland
27 Oct.	Rudolph II crowned King of Germany
3 Dec.	Ercole Cortile, Florence, to [not stated], Ferrara: a performance of a comedy in Florence by Vittoria [Piisimi] and company [ASMO, Cancelleria ducale, *Dispacci da Firenze*; Solerti and Lanza, 'Il teatro ferrarese', 160]

| 20 Dec. | Ercole Cortile, Florence, to [not stated], Ferrara: a performance of a comedy in the house of Isabella Orsini in Florence [ASMO, Cancelleria ducale, Dispacci da Firenze; Solerti and Lanza, 'Il teatro ferrarese', 160] |

1576

24 Jan.	Bernardo Canigiani, Ferrara, to [Belisario Vinta], Florence: Leonora Sanvitale Sanseverino, Giulio Thiene, and the Countess of Sala are expected in Ferrara in two day's time [Solerti, *Ferrara e la corte estense*, p. cxiii]
6 Feb. (Mon.)	Bernardo Canigiani, Ferrara, to the Grand Duke, [Florence]: the wedding [of Bradamante d'Este and Bevilacqua] will be on Thursday [9 Feb.], and the other newlyweds [Leonora Sanvitale and Giulio Thiene] will be there on Friday [ASF, Mediceo, f. 2895, fo. 8^r]
9 Feb. (Thurs.)	Wedding of Bradamante d'Este and Ercole Bevilacqua in Ferrara [ASF, Mediceo, f. 2895, fo. 8^r]
9 Feb.	Birth of Giovan Battista Andreini, firstborn son of Isabella and Francesco Andreini, in Florence; godparents are Cavaliere Cornelio Lanci and Marietta di Lorenzo de' Fiesoli [Florence, Archivio dell'Opera del Duomo, Registro dei battezzati maschi dal 1571 al 1577 dalla lettera A alla lettera G, lett. G, fo. 172^v]
13 Feb. (Mon.)	Bernardo Canigiani, Ferrara, to Belisario Vinta, Florence: the Gelosi are in Ferrara for the wedding, but the woman and the better characters have gone on to Venice, much satisfied with Florence, but afraid of Ferrara, where they are not paid well [ASF, Mediceo, f. 2895, fo. 7^{r-v}]
17 Feb. (Fri.)	Bernardo Canigiani, Ferrara, to the Grand Duke, Florence: the Duke has recalled the Gelosi with the sound of money, and they expect the rest of the troupe—Vittoria [Piisimi] and Orazio [de' Nobili]—from Venice. Their stage is set up under the loggia of the cortile [ASF, Mediceo, f. 2895, fo. 11^{r-v}]
7 Mar.	Ash Wednesday
13 Mar. (Tues.)	Bernardo Canigiani, Ferrara, to [not stated]: a banquet put on yesterday by Alfonso II d'Este for Barbara Sanseverino at Belvedere, at which the Gelosi performed a tragedy [Solerti, *Ferrara e la corte estense*, p. cxvi]
2 Apr.	Plague strikes Mantua [Vigilio, *La insalata*, 50]
22 Apr.	Easter
18 May	Ordinance of the *Consiglio Segreto* in Milan records that Doctor Francesco d'Arona has died and names Doctor Diego de la Piazza as his successor as superintendent of 'comedianti, cerretani, canta in banco, bagatelleri herbolari, et altri, che vendono historie, cose

	d'ogli, unguenti, et altre simili cose medicinali ne le strade publiche, et piazze di questa città di Milano, così in terra, come in banco' [ASM, Atti del governo, Spettacoli pubblici, parte antica, cart. 12. fasc. 1; ASM, Registri delle Cancellerie, s. XXI, no. 10, fos. 301^v–302^r]
25 May	Henri III, Paris, to Monsieur Du Ferrier, [Venice]: invites the Gelosi to perform at the French court [Pandolfi, *La commedia dell'arte*, ii. 329; Baschet, *Les Comédiens italiens*, 63]
6 June	Deaths in Mantua due to the plague: 113 [Vigilio, *La insalata*, 50]
22 June	M. Du Ferrier, Venice, to Henri III, Paris: has spoken to the Gelosi's Magnifico regarding the king's invitation, who has said that he will be returning to the Imperial court [Baschet, *Les Comédiens italiens*, 63–4]
24 June	Deaths in Mantua due to the plague: 99 [Vigilio, *La insalata*, 50–1]
9 July	Death of Eleonora of Toledo, Grand Duchess of Tuscany, in Florence [Gaeta Bertelà and Petrioli Tofani, *Le feste e apparati medicei*, 201]
16 July	Death of Isabella de' Medici, Duchess of Bracciano [Gaeta Bertelà and Petrioli Tofani, *Le feste e apparati medicei*, 201]
28 July	Fr[ances]co Cap[po]ni, Pisa, to Cosimo de' Medici, Florence: requests permission, on behalf of the Compagnia di Pedrolino [Giovanni Pellesini], for the company to spend the greater part of the winter in Florence, and then to travel on to Pisa, Lucca, and back to Pisa again [ASF, Mediceo, f. 687, fo. 135^r]
29 July	Deaths in Mantua due to the plague: 135 [Vigilio, *La insalata*, 51]
24 Aug.	Deaths in Mantua due to the plague: 98 [Vigilio, *La insalata*, 51]
2 Sept.	Ordinance for the State of Milan, declaring to the Capitano di Giustitia, to the Podestà, and to all other officials of the state that comedians who want to perform in that city are required to obtain permission from Dr Diego de la Piazza, and to submit their comedies to preview by Dr Marcello Rincio [ASM, Registri delle Cancellerie, s. XXI, no. 10, fo. 338^{r-v}]
7 Oct.	Giacomo Grana, [Ferrara], to Luigi d'Este, Paris: Lucrezia Machiavella sang divinely for the Duchess of Urbino the other night [ASMO, Cancelleria ducale, Particolari, Grana]
11 Oct.	Deaths in Mantua due to the plague: 61 [Vigilio, *La insalata*, 52]
12 Oct.	Death of Maximilian II; Rudolph II, Emperor and King of Germany and Hungary, succeeds
21 Oct.	Deaths in Mantua due to the plague: 36 [Vigilio, *La insalata*, 52]
6 Nov.	Lodovico de' Bianchi, Florence, to Ferdinando de' Medici,

Florence: pays reverence in language typical of the Dottor Graziano character [ASF, Mediceo, f. 717, fo. 352]

13 Dec.   Deaths in Mantua due to the plague: 99 [Vigilio, *La insalata*, 52]

1577

17 Jan.   Quarantine lifted in Mantua; commerce between Mantua and Verona re-established [Vigilio, *La insalata*, 53]

23 Jan.   Sinolfo Saracini, Blois, to [Ferdinando de' Medici], Florence: the Gelosi have been taken hostage by the Huguenots [Baschet, *Les Comédiens italiens*, 71]

25 Jan.   Deaths in Mantua due to the plague: 42 [Vigilio, *La insalata*, 54]

25 Jan.   Quarantine re-established in Verona; commerce between Mantua and Verona prohibited [Vigilio, *La insalata*, 54]

27 Jan.   Ferrante Guisoni, Blois, to [Guglielmo Gonzaga], Mantua: the Gelosi arrived in Blois the day before yesterday and that very evening performed a comedy for the king and his court [Baschet, *Les Comédiens italiens*, 72]

Feb.   Deaths in Mantua due to the plague: 3 [Vigilio, *La insalata*, 54]

20 Feb.   Ash Wednesday

28 Feb.   Entry in the *Mémoires de M. le Duc de Nevers* record that the Gelosi performed a pastoral for the king [Baschet, *Les Comédiens italiens*, 73]

Mar.   Deaths in Mantua due to the plague: 13 [Vigilio, *La insalata*, 55]

11 Mar.   Bernardo Canigiani, Ferrara, to [unknown, Florence]: encloses a list of interlocutors for a comedy performed by the Estense courtiers, in which Tasso is given as the inventor and actor of the prologue, Ercolino Tassoni the *innamorato*, Barbara Sanseverino the *innamorata*, Alfonso II d'Este the *tedesco*, Cornelio Bentivoglio the innkeeper, Anna Bendidio the Franceschina, Il Pignino the Pantalone, Leonora Sanvitale the Graziano, Don Alfonso the Francatrippa, Giulio Thiene the bravo Il Mosca, Isabella Bentivoglio the mother of the *innamorata*, and Lucrezia Bentivoglio the mother's servant [Solerti, *Ferrara e la corte estense*, p. cxxii]

Apr.   Deaths in Mantua due to the plague: 9 [Vigilio, *La insalata*, 55]

7 Apr.   Easter

May   Deaths in Mantua due to the plague: 2 [Vigilio, *La insalata*, 56]

18 May   Entry in the *Histoire manuscrite du théâtre en France* records that the Gelosi have established residence in Paris after having obtained a licence from the Confrères de la Passion to perform. They begin performing on 19 May in the Salle de Bourbon [Paris, BNF, Manuscrits, f. fr. 9230, fo. 215]

20 May	Birth of Filippo de' Medici to Giovanna of Austria and Francesco Maria de' Medici, Grand Duchess and Grand Duke of Tuscany [Gaeta Bertelà and Petrioli Tofani, *Le feste e apparati medicei*, 201]
June	Deaths in Mantua due to the plague: 2 [Vigilio, *La insalata*, 56]
4 June	Death of Doge Alvise Mocenigo
11 June	Sebastiano Venier elected Doge of Venice
[Aug.]	Francesco Patrizi dedicates his *L'amorosa filosofia* to Tarquinia Molza
29 Sept.	Baptism of Filippo de' Medici in Florence [Gaeta Bertelà and Petrioli Tofani, *Le feste e apparati medicei*, 202]
14 Dec.	Bernardo Canigiani, Ferrara, to Belisario Vinta, Florence: Giulio Cesare Brancaccio, Lucrezia Bendidio, and Vittoria Bentivoglio sang in the rooms of the Duchess of Urbino [ASF, Mediceo, f. 2895]

1578

9 Jan.	Antonio Serguidi, Florence, to Francesco Maria de' Medici, Florence: requests a licence for the Gelosi to perform in Florence and states that, since the Gelosi are currently in Lombardy, it will not be possible to make an account of their belongings [ASF, Dogana di Firenze, f. 218, suppl. 147]
8 Feb. (Sat.)	Bernardo Canigiani, Ferrara, to Belisario Vinta, Florence: the Uniti performed their comedy yesterday in the room [*camera*] of the Duchess of Urbino [ASF, Mediceo, f. 2896, lett. 35]
12 Feb.	Ash Wednesday
22 Feb. (Sat.)	Bernardo Canigiani, Ferrara, to the Grand Duke: Monday evening there was a comedy that lasted 7 hours and wasn't very good [ASF, Mediceo, f. 2896]
3 Mar.	Death of Doge Sebastiano Venier
11 Mar.	Nicolò da Ponte elected Doge of Venice
30 Mar.	Easter
10 Apr.	Death of Giovanna of Austria, Grand Duchess of Tuscany [Gaeta Bertelà and Petrioli Tofani, *Le feste e apparati medicei*, 202]

1579

9 Jan.	Bernardo Canigiani, Ferrara, to [unknown]: Alfonso II has arranged with the Gelosi, who have gone to Venice, that they will return to Ferrara in 15 or 20 days, to stay for the rest of carnival [Solerti and Lanza, 'Il teatro ferrarese', 171]
2 Feb.	Performance of a *commedia di Zanni* in Ferrara in honour of the

	wedding of Margherita Gonzaga and Alfonso II d'Este, attended by Archdukes Ferdinand and Maximilian of Austria [Solerti and Lanza, 'Il teatro ferrarese', 171]
4 Feb.	Leonardo Conosciuti, Ferrara, to Luigi d'Este, Paris: on Thursday, the Duchess of Urbino, the Bendidio sisters, the Scandiano ladies, and Bradamante d'Este secluded themselves in the rooms of the Duchess of Urbino and sang beautifully [ASMO, Cancelleria ducale, Particolari, Conosciuti]
22 Feb. (Sun.)	Aurelio Zibramonte, Mantua, to Giorgio Carretto, Vienna: they are expecting the arrival of Alfonso II d'Este today, and Margherita Gonzaga will make her entry into Ferrara on 26 Feb. [Solerti, *Ferrara e la corte estense*, pp. xxviii–xxix]
27 Feb. (Fri.)	Wedding of Margherita Gonzaga and Alfonso II d'Este, Duke of Ferrara, in Ferrara [Vigilio, *La insalata*, 57]
4 Mar.	Ash Wednesday
19 Apr.	Easter
5 May	Decree of Guglielmo Gonzaga, Mantua, states that the Gelosi—Simone [Basilea], Orazio [de' Nobili], Adriano [Valerini], Gabrielle [Panzanini], and Domenico and Pirro, zanni—who are lodged at the Osteria run by the Signori Bissoni, are to be evicted from the city [ASMN, Gonzaga, b. 2208]
13 June	Licence for the Gelosi to perform in Milan for one month from the day they begin performing. ASM, Registri delle Cancellerie, serie XXI, n. 12, fo. 168^r]
4 Aug.	Request of a one-month renewal by the Gelosi of the licence to perform in Milan (refers to a prior prolongation of the licence, dated 23 July 1579) [ASM, Registri delle Cancellerie, serie XXI, n. 12, fo. 196^r]
12 Oct.	Coronation of Bianca Cappello in Florence in the council hall of the Palazzo Vecchio [Gaeta Bertelà and Petrioli Tofani, *Le feste e apparati medicei*, 202]
Oct.	Performance of the *Maschere d'Amazzoni* by Ottavio Rinuccini in Florence in honour of the wedding of Bianca Capello and Francesco Maria de' Medici [Solerti, *Gli albori*, ii. 1–4]
24 Oct.	Death of Albrecht IV; Wilhelm V named Duke of Bavaria
15 Nov. (Sun.)	Bernardo Canigiani, Ferrara, to [not stated]: describes a splendid banquet given by Cornelio Bentivoglio, attended by Alfonso II and Margherita Gonzaga, Marfisa and Bradamante d'Este, the Countess of Scandiano, etc., at which the Gelosi performed a comedy [Solerti, *Ferrara e la corte estense*, p. lxxvii]
30 Dec.	Licence granted by the Council of Ten for performances of comedies in Venice during carnival, provided they conclude before the

fourth hour of night and are recited with honesty and modesty [Mancini et al., *I teatri di Venezia*, i, p. xxvi]

1580

16 Feb. Decree of the Duke of Mantua that everyone except *religiosi* may, from the 23rd hour until an hour following the conclusion of the comedy this evening, masquerade, according to the dictates of the already proclaimed *grido* [ASMN, Gonzaga, b. 2040–1, fasc. 23, fo. 21ʳ]

17 Feb. Ash Wednesday

14 Mar. Decree of the Duke of Mantua that Filippo Angelone will govern the licensing of 'tutti li comici mercenari, zaratani et cant' in banchi' for the Duchy of Mantua [D'Ancona, 'Il teatro mantovano', pt. 2, p. 34] (Doc. 7)

[21] Mar. Oratio Urbani, Ferrara, to Francesco Maria de' Medici, Florence: Alfonso II returned yesterday evening from Belriguardo and, remembering a performance he had heard in Mantua, asked the Duchess to send for Laura Peverara [ASF, Mediceo, f. 2899]

3 Apr. Easter

18 Apr. (Mon.) A Mantuan court functionary, Ferrara, to Guglielmo Gonzaga, Mantua: a comedy was performed recently in the rooms [*alle stanza*] of the Duchess [Margherita Gonzaga] [ASMN, Gonzaga, b. 2209]

19 Apr. (Tues.) Teodoro San Giorgio, Ferrara, to Guglielmo Gonzaga, Mantua: Duke Alfonso heard a comedy yesterday at the house of Marfisa d'Este, and tonight another will be performed in the Duchess's rooms [ASMN, Gonzaga, b. 1255]

20 Apr. (Wed.) Leonardo Conosciuti, Ferrara, to Luigi d'Este, [Padua]: a comedy was performed Monday night by Pedrolino in the room [*salotto*] of Duchess Margherita Gonzaga, to which many women of the city were invited [Solerti, *Ferrara e la corte estense*, p. xc]

27 Apr. Guglielmo Gonzaga, Mantua, to Cardinal d'Este, [Padua]: Vittoria [Piisimi] and her company wish to perform in Padua [D'Ancona, 'Il teatro mantovano', pt. 2, pp. 34–5]

30 Apr. Request of a licence by the Gelosi to perform in Milan; granted on 2 May for two months [ASM, Autografi, cart. 94, fasc. 42; ASM, Registri delle Cancellerie, serie XXI, no. 12, fo. 246ᵛ]

4 May Leonardo Conosciuti, Ferrara, to Luigi d'Este, Paris: a 'damisella' [Laura Peverara] who sings and plays beautifully has arrived from Mantua [ASMO, Cancelleria ducale, Particolari, Conosciuti]

4 May Margherita Gonzaga, Ferrara, to Vincenzo Gonzaga, Mantua: has received Vincenzo's letter via Sig. Peveraro, and will never, as

	Vincenzo instructs, fail to recommend Laura Peverara [ASMN, Gonzaga, b. 1214]
30 May	Guglielmo Gonzaga, Mantua, to the Podestà of Verona: the Confidenti, who are currently in Mantua, wish to perform in Verona [D'Ancona, 'Il teatro mantovano', pt. 2, p. 34]
22 June	Agostino Trissino, [Venice], to Marcello Donati, [Belriguardo]: Vittoria came to him after Vincenzo Gonzaga's departure, saying that Vincenzo had told certain members of her company that they had to join another company and asking Trissino to intercede with Vincenzo on her behalf [D'Ancona, 'Il teatro mantovano', pt. 2, p. 35]
22 June	Marcello Donati, Belriguardo, to Aurelio Zibramonte, Mantua: he did not send a letter by the boy who was sent yesterday to make the comedians come because he had written to Vittoria in the presence of others who are not to be trusted [ASMN, Gonzaga, b. 1255]
July	Sancho de Guevara y Padilla named Governor of Milan
4 July	Lanfranco Turino, Ferrara, to [a Ferrarese court functionary, Ferrara]: the Chancellor Cav. Pigante had commanded him to go see and judge the new comedians, which he did. The woman had good presence and sang to the lute very pleasingly, and two youths danced [*saltare*] honestly. They lack a Pantalone and an *innamorato*, with which the company expects to improve. One of the comedians told him in confidence that many of them are obligated to remain in Mantua to serve the prince [Vincenzo Gonzaga], which they do mainly out of respect for the woman. Having left Mantua without Vincenzo's permission, they are now trying to make enough money for most, if not all, of them to return [ASMO, Archivio per materie, Comici]
9 July	Giulio Cesare Brancaccio, Rome, to Alfonso II d'Este: two things disgrace him: (1) that Alfonso has ignored his first book, which he sent some time ago, and (2) that he was badly treated at Belriguardo, especially now that he has put in order some not displeasing *arie* of sonnets and *canzone villanesche* [ASMO, Archivio per materie, Letterati, b. 11]
20 July	Renewal of the Gelosi's licence in Milan for one month [ASM, Registri delle Cancellerie, serie XXI, no. 13, fo. 17^v; cfr. 30 Apr. 1580]
8 Aug.	Luca Marenzio dedicates his *Primo libro dei madrigali à 5* to Luigi d'Este
20 Aug.	Request by the Gelosi to be permitted to continue performing comedies in Milan in the wake of Justice Monforte's prohibition [ASM, Autografi, cart. 94, fasc. 42]
20 Aug.	Renewal of the Gelosi's licence to perform in Milan through Sept.

	[ASM, Registri delle Cancellerie, s. XXI, n. 13, fo. 17^v; cfr. 20 July 1580]
27 Aug.	Vincenzo Gonzaga, Gonzaga, to Cardinal Luigi d'Este, [Ferrara]: Vittoria [Piisimi] and her company would like permission to perform in Padua [ASMO, Archivio per materie, Comici, fasc. 20]
30 Aug.	Carlo Emanuele becomes Duke of Savoy
17 Oct.	Drusiano Martinelli, Florence, to [Vincenzo Gonzaga, Mantua]: he and his wife Angelica would have liked to join the company of Pedrolino [Giovanni Pellesini], as Vincenzo had requested, but the Pedrolini already include Vittoria [Piissimi], and Martinelli has a good company. Martinelli's troupe would like to come to Mantua for carnival, since the Gelosi and the Confidenti will be in Venice, but if he does not hear from Vincenzo in a month's time, they will depart for Naples [ASMN, Gonzaga, Autografi, b. 10, fo. 130^r]
28 Oct. (Fri.)	The Provost of Ferrara, Ferrara, to Cardinal d'Este, [unknown]: a comedy was performed yesterday in the room [*camera*] of Margherita Gonzaga by Vittoria [Piisimi] and her company [ASMO, Cancelleria ducale, Particolari; Solerti and Lanza, 'Il teatro ferrarese', 174]
31 Oct.	Orazio Urbani, Ferrara, to Francesco Maria de' Medici, Florence: Giulio Cesare Brancaccio will present himself for service to the Grand Duke within a few days [ASF, Mediceo, f. 2899]
2 Nov.	The Legate of Bologna, Ferrara, to [not stated]: he thoroughly enjoyed a performance by Vittoria [Piisimi], and highly recommends her [ASMO, Cancelleria ducale, Minute di lettere a Rettori esteri]
8 Nov.	Battista Guarini, Ferrara, to Alfonso II d'Este, [unspecified]: sends a *canzonetta ariosa*, which he hopes will be set to music for the *concerto delle dame* [Campori, *Lettere*, 190–1]
20 Nov. (Sun.)	Federico Miroglio, Ferrara, to Alfonso II d'Este, Comacchio: yesterday evening Laura Peverara and Anna Guarini sang for the Duchess of Urbino and [Margherita] Gonzaga, and Eleonora de' Medici had last rites [Campori and Solerti, *Luigi, Lucrezia e Leonora d'Este*, 132]
3 Dec.	A Mantuan court functionary, Revere, to Leone Ebreo, [Mantua]: Vincenzo Gonzaga has commanded Leone Ebreo to prepare a comedy for his wedding [ASMN, Gonzaga, b. 2210]
20 Dec.	Aldo Manuzio dedicates the first edition of Tasso's *Aminta* to Don Ferrando Gonzaga
25 Dec.	Aug.o Trissino, [Venice], to [not stated]: Filippo Angeloni has written to him, saying that Vittoria and her company wish to come to Mantua during carnival for the wedding of Margherita Farnese

	and Vincenzo Gonzaga [D'Ancona, 'Il teatro mantovano', pt. 2, p. 38]
26 Dec.	Orazio Urbani, Ferrara, to Francesco Maria de' Medici, [Florence]: on the 21st there was an earthquake and Giulio Cesare Brancaccio has arrived in Ferrara [ASF, Mediceo, f. 2899]

1581

[not stated]	Alessandro Farnese named governor of the Netherlands
	State Ordinances for Bologna decree that, for the year 1581, because of the building of a new monastery for the nuns of Corpus Domini, comedians who perform in the Sala del Podestà are to pay the monastery a tax of L. 100 per week, and the box office [Mastri de Ponti] is to pay L. 20 per week. Beginning in 1582, the comedians are to pay only L. 15 per week [ASB, Demaniale 220/2127, 339–40, par. 107; 902–3] (Doc. 8)
4 Jan.	Vittoria Piissimi, Venice, to Alfonso II d'Este, Ferrara: begs the Duke's pardon, says that she cannot serve him this carnival, and asks that she and Pedrolino may remain in his good graces [ASMO, Archivio per materie, Comici; cfr. 5 Mar. 1581]
4 Jan.	Ettore Tron, Venice, to Alfonso II d'Este, Ferrara: has hired the Comici Confidenti to perform in Venice at great expense and Vittoria [Piisimi] tells him that Alfonso has recalled Pedrolino [Giovanni Pellesini] to his service; informs Alfonso that Pedrolino is otherwise obligated and asks that he be allowed to remain in Venice with the rest of the company [ASMO, Archivio per materie, Comici] (Doc. 6)
carnival	The Teatro Michiel opens in Venice [ASV, Dieci Savi sopra le Decime, Condizion Dorsoduro, b. 172, no. 1376; Mancini et al., *I teatri del Veneto*, iv. 94]
carnival	The Teatro Tron [Teatro San Cassan] opens in Venice with performances by the Confidenti. Mancini et al., *I teatri del Veneto*, iv. 148]
18 Jan.	Recapiti of the Monasterio Corpus Domini in Bologna: payment of the tax on the Gelosi for a week's performances ending on this date: L. 100 [ASB, Assunteria di Munizione, Recapiti, b. 3, fasc. 18]
26 Jan.	Ettore Tron, Venice, to Alfonso II d'Este, Ferrara: thanks Alfonso for allowing the comedians to remain in Venice [ASMO, Archivio per materie, Comici]
27 Jan.	Recapiti of the Monasterio Corpus Domini in Bologna: payment of the tax on the Gelosi for a week's performances: L. 100 [ASB, Assunteria di Munizione, Recapiti, b. 3, fasc. 18]
4 Feb.	Recapiti of the Monasterio Corpus Domini in Bologna: payment of

208   Chronology

	the tax on the Gelosi for a week's performances: L. 100 [ASB, Assunteria di Munizione, Recapiti, b. 3, fasc. 18]
4 Feb. (Sat.)	[Francesco] Borsato, [Mantua], to [unknown]: some youths performed a beautiful pastoral with very good music and intermedi yesterday in his house, for the recreation of Mons. d'Osmo [ASMN, Gonzaga, b. 2615]
8 Feb.	Ash Wednesday
8 Feb.	Giovanni Pellini and Gabriel Beato, Bologna, to Guglielmo Gonzaga, Mantua: Antonio [Ricio] has returned to Bologna [ASMN, Gonzaga, b. 1161]
11 Feb.	Recapiti of the Monasterio Corpus Domini in Bologna: payment of the tax on the Gelosi for a week's performances: L. 100 [ASB, Assunteria di Munizione, Recapiti, b. 3, fasc. 18]
13 Feb. (Mon.)	Orazio Urbani, Ferrara, to Francesco Maria de' Medici, Florence: they are having some residual carnival activities in Ferrara, and tomorrow a comedy is planned for which there is a beautiful set; the *musica secreta* is also performing, including Laura Peverara and Giulio Cesare Brancaccio [ASF, Mediceo, f. 2900]
18 Feb.	Recapiti of the Monasterio Corpus Domini in Bologna: payment of the tax on the Gelosi for a week's performances: L. 100 [ASB, Assunteria di Munizione, Recapiti, b. 3, fasc. 18]
19 Feb.	Death of Leonora d'Este in Ferrara
23 Feb.	Recapiti of the Monasterio Corpus Domini in Bologna: payment of the tax on the Gelosi for a week's performances: L. 100 [ASB, Assunteria di Munizione, Recapiti, b. 3, fasc. 18]
28 Feb.	Recapiti of the Monasterio Corpus Domini in Bologna: payment of the tax on the Gelosi for a week's performances: L. 100 [ASB, Assunteria di Munizione, Recapiti, b. 3, fasc. 18]
2 Mar.	Wedding of Margherita Farnese and Vincenzo Gonzaga in Parma
5 Mar.	Vittoria Piissimi, Venice, to Alfonso II d'Este, Ferrara: begs Alfonso's pardon for not having been able to serve him during carnival and asks that she and Pedrolino be reinstated to his good graces [ASMO, Archivio per materie, Comici; cfr. 4 Jan. 1581]
5 Mar.	Fourth Sunday in Lent
26 Mar.	Easter
28 Mar.	Cesare Cavriani, Parma, to Guglielmo Gonzaga, Mantua: Margherita Farnese had a party last night; she will take the medicine, if not this evening, tomorrow morning, and she undertakes to purge herself willingly [ASMN, Gonzaga, b. 201, fo. 39^{r-v}]
29 Mar.	Cesare Cavriani, Parma, to Guglielmo Gonzaga, Mantua: Margherita Farnese last evening took five mouthfuls of cassia, which have had no effect [ASMN, Gonzaga, b. 201, fo. 40^{r-v}]

31 Mar.	Cesare Cavriani, Parma, to Guglielmo Gonzaga, Mantua: Margherita Farnese is following doctor's orders and took a dancing lesson from Isachino da Mantova [ASMN, Gonzaga, b. 201, fo. 41^{r-v}]
5 Apr.	Cesare Cavriani, Parma, to Guglielmo Gonzaga, Mantua: Margherita Farnese is dining and dancing today at the fountain [ASMN, Gonzaga, b. 201, fo. 49^{r-v}]
19 Apr.	Cesare Cavriani, Parma, to Guglielmo Gonzaga, [Mantua]: Margherita Farnese was very lively today, and she is happy that the day of her entry into Mantua draws near [ASMN, Gonzaga, b. 201, fo. 53^{r-v}]
20 Apr.	Cesare Cavriani, Mantua, to Guglielmo Gonzaga, Mantua: Margherita Farnese is pleased that the time to enter Mantua is near, and she passes time by singing, accompanied by Cavriani on the flute [ASMN, Gonzaga, b. 201, fo. 61^{r-v}]
22 Apr.	Vittoria Piissimi, Bologna, to [Guglielmo Gonzaga, Mantua]: she received a letter from Orazio Cavalli, written in Guglielmo's name, but it arrived late and so she sends the present letter to assure him of her ardent desire to serve him [ASMN, Gonzaga, b. 1161, fos. 332^r–333^v]
25 Apr.	[Jacopo] d'Osmo, Bologna, to Guglielmo Gonzaga, Mantua: the comedians are coming to Mantua [ASMN, Gonzaga, b. 1161, fos. 266^r–267^v]
26 Apr.	Cesare Cavriani, Parma, to Guglielmo Gonzaga, Mantua: Margherita Farnese is overwhelmed with joy that she is coming to Mantua [ASMN, Gonzaga, b. 201, fo. 68^{r-v}]
30 Apr.	Entry of Margherita Farnese into Mantua [Vigilio, *La insalata*, 58]
15 May	Orazio Urbani, Ferrara, to Francesco Maria de' Medici, Florence: the *concerto delle dame* had given a performance before Vincenzo Gonzaga, whose response was 'Gran cosa son le Donne, in effetto io vorrei essere innanzi un Asino che una Donna'; Vincenzo then rose to go to the *Commedia di Zanni*, which had intermedi with music [ASF, Mediceo, f. 2900]
23 May	Cardinal Cesi, Bologna, to [Jacopo] d'Osmo, Ferrara: has received d'Osmo's two letters from 20 May and 21 May, and, in response to the first, he would not fail to reserve space [*luoco*] for the comedians [Confidenti], as he had promised [ASMN, Gonzaga, b. 1161, fos. 356^r–357^v]
27 May	Cardinal Cesi, Bologna, to Guglielmo Gonzaga, Mantua: as he wrote to Sig. d'Osmo, he did not fail to reserve the space in Bologna for the Confidenti [ASMN, Gonzaga, b. 1161, fos. 358^r–359^v]
5 July	[not stated], Saileto, to Marcello [Donato, Mantua]: [Vincenzo

6 July	Gonzaga] has secluded himself in Saileto and he sent for the Gelosi [ASMN, Gonzaga, Minute della Cancelleria, b. 2212]
6 July	[not stated], Genza, to Cesare Cavriani, [Mantua]: [Vincenzo Gonzaga] sent for the Gelosi yesterday evening [ASMN, Gonzaga, Minute della Cancelleria, b. 2212]
6 July	Daniele Cincinnati, Porto, to Guglielmo Gonzaga, Mantua: while Margherita Farnese is pleased that the Duke sought to entertain her, she is not pleased that he licensed the Gelosi to come to her because she has no desire to hear comedies [ASMN, Gonzaga, b. 2615, fasc. 31]
8 July	[Vincenzo Gonzaga], Genza, to Marcello [Donato, Mantua]: the Gelosi cannot come at the moment [ASMN, Gonzaga, *Minute della Cancelleria*, b. 2212]
9 July	Vincenzo Gonzaga, Genza, to Marcello [Donato, Mantua]: under no conditions is the Princess to travel in such bad rainy weather [ASMN, Gonzaga, Minute della Cancelleria, b. 2212]
26 July	Licence granted to the Gelosi to perform in Milan for three months from the day they begin [ASM, Autografi, cart. 94, fasc. 42; ASM, Registri delle Cancellerie, serie XXI, no. 13, fos. 213^r–214^r]
20 Aug.	Battista Guarini, [Ferrara], to Alfonso II d'Este, [Belriguardo]: sends the canzonetta Alfonso requested ['Mentre vaga angioletta'], which is to be set to music [by Claudio Monteverdi] for the *concerto delle dame* [ASMO, Archivio per materia, Letterati, b. 29]
25 Sept.	Ordinance of the Council of Ten, prohibiting the performance of comedies in Venice [Mancini et al., *I teatri di Venezia*, pp. xxvi–xxvii]
7 Oct.	Paolo Moro, Venice, to [Giulio] Strozzi, Mantua: the Council of Ten has decreed that there will be no more comedies performed in Venice [ASMN, Gonzaga, b. 1512]
10 Oct.	Antonio Serguidi, Florence, to Ferdinando de' Medici, Florence: requests a waiver for the Confidenti of the laws regarding certain props and items of clothing that are prohibited; they further request the release from prison of one of the women of the troupe who was arrested for wearing silver-coloured veils [ASF, Dogana di Firenze, serie antica, f. 219, suppl. 116]
25 Oct.	Luca Marenzio dedicates his *Secondo libro de' madrigali à 5 voci* to Lucrezia d'Este, the Duchess of Urbino
6 Nov.	Orazio Urbani, Ferrara, to [Francesco Maria de' Medici, Florence]: for the entry of Archduke Maximilian of Austria, some think a pastoral by Guarini should be performed, but there is not enough time [Solerti and Lanza, 'Il teatro ferrarese', 178]
18 Nov.	Recapiti of the Monasterio Corpus Domini in Bologna: payment of

	the tax on those who go to see the comedies performed above the Sala del Podestà for one week: L. 20 [ASB, Assunteria di Munizione, Recapiti, b. 3, fasc. 18]
25 Nov.	Recapiti of the Monasterio Corpus Domini in Bologna: payment of the tax on the Gelosi for two weeks' performances, beginning on 11 Nov.: L. 200 [ASB, Assunteria di Munizione, Recapiti, b. 3, fasc. 18]
2 Dec.	Recapiti of the Monasterio Corpus Domini in Bologna: payment of the tax on the Gelosi for a week's performances: L. 100 [ASB, Assunteria di Munizione, Recapiti, b. 3, fasc. 18]
11 Dec.	Recapiti of the Monasterio Corpus Domini in Bologna: payment of the tax on the Gelosi for a week's performances: L. 100 [ASB, Assunteria di Munizione, Recapiti, b. 3, fasc. 18]
18 Dec.	Recapiti of the Monasterio Corpus Domini in Bologna: payment of the tax on the Gelosi for a week's performances: L. 100 [ASB, Assunteria di Munizione, Recapiti, b. 3, fasc. 18]
23 Dec.	Recapiti of the Monasterio Corpus Domini in Bologna: payment of the tax on the Gelosi for a week's performances: L. 100 [ASB, Assunteria di Munizione, Recapiti, b. 3, fasc. 18]
29 Dec.	Recapiti of the Monasterio Corpus Domini in Bologna: payment of the tax on the Gelosi for a week's performances: L. 100 [ASB, Assunteria di Munizione, Recapiti, b. 3, fasc. 18]

1582

9 Jan.	Recapiti of the Monasterio Corpus Domini in Bologna: payment of the tax on the Gelosi for a week's performances: L. 100 [ASB, Assunteria di Munizione, Recapiti, b. 3, fasc. 18]
12 Jan. (Fri.)	Cesare Cavriani, Ferrara, to Aurelio Zibramonte, Mantua: describes the entry of Margherita Farnese and Vincenzo Gonzaga in Ferrara; there was a *comedia di Zanni*, to which the court went in masquerade, and afterwards a dance that lasted until the fifth hour of night [ASMN, Gonzaga, b. 201, fos. 74ʳ–75ᵛ]
15 Jan.	Recapiti of the Monasterio Corpus Domini in Bologna: payment of the tax on the Gelosi for a week's performances: L. 100 [ASB, Assunteria di Munizione, Recapiti, b. 3, fasc. 18]
20 Jan.	Danielle Cincinnati, Ferrara, to Aurelio Zibramonte, Mantua: Margherita Farnese goes in costume to parties, to comedies, and throughout the city [ASMN, Gonzaga, b. 1256]
24 Jan.	Recapiti of the Monasterio Corpus Domini in Bologna: payment of the tax on the Gelosi for a week's performances: L. 100 [ASB, Assunteria di Munizione, Recapiti, b. 3, fasc. 18]
27 Jan.	Recapiti of the Monasterio Corpus Domini in Bologna: payment of

	the tax on the Gelosi for a week's performances: L. 100 [ASB, Assunteria di Munizione, Recapiti, b. 3, fasc. 18]
6 Feb.	Battista Guarini, Ferrara, to Guglielmo Gonzaga, Mantua: sends the words to a *ballo*, as per the Duke's orders [ASMN, Gonzaga, b. 1256]
28 Feb.	Ash Wednesday
1 Mar.	Luzzasco Luzzaschi dedicates his *Terzo libro de' madrigali à 5 voci* to Margherita Gonzaga, the Duchess of Ferrara
7 Mar.	Doctor Alberini, Mantua, to [Alfonso II], Ferrara: a performance of a comedy with noteworthy intermedi was performed on the day of carnival [27 Feb.] by the *ebrei* [Solerti, *Ferrara e la corte estense*, p. lxxxiii]
28 Mar.	Leonardo Conosciuti, [unspecified], to Luigi d'Este, [Paris]: Laura Peverara will marry Count Annibale Turco [ASMO, Particolari, Conosciuti]
9 Apr.	Ferrarese ambassador's report from Rome: the Mons. di Savigni accompanied the Duke [of Mantua] and all his family to Montagnola, where they heard comedies performed by 'Vittoria famosa' [Piissimi] [ASMO, Cancelleria ducale, Avvisi e notizie dall'estero, b. 127]
15 Apr.	Easter
30 Apr.	Wedding by proxy of Anna Caterina Gonzaga and Ferdinand of Bavaria in Mantua [Vigilio, *La insalata*, 58]
4 May	Departure of Anna Caterina Gonzaga from Mantua for Innsbruck in the company of Archduke Ferdinand of Austria, her mother Eleonora, and her brother Vincenzo Gonzaga [Vigilio, *La insalata*, 58; ASMN, Gonzaga, b. 388]
4 May	Departure of Margherita Farnese from Mantua for Parma, accompanied by her brother Ranuccio Farnese [Vigilio, *La insalata*, 58]
18 June (Mon.)	Ferrarese ambassador's report from Rome: Don Alfonso [uncle of Alfonso II d'Este] gave a banquet in the house of Donna Marfisa [d'Este], which included a comedy by Vittoria [Piissimi] in the presence of the Duke and guests from Mantua, including the Duke of Mantua and the Signori Arigoni [ASMO, Cancelleria ducale, Avvisi e notizie dall'estero, b. 127]
28 June (Thurs.)	Ferrarese ambassador's report from Rome: the Gelosi performed a ridiculous comedy for the Duke of Mantua, in which all the characters were hunchbacks [ASMO, Cancelleria ducale, Avvisi e notizie dall'estero, b. 127]
6 July	Confidenti, Bologna, to Guglielmo Gonzaga, Mantua: the Confidenti are ready to come to Mantua [Pandolfi, *La commedia dell'arte*, ii. 324]

21 July	Marcello Donati, Ferrara, to Aurelio Zibramonte, Mantua: he has written another letter and sent it with the comedians who will depart either today or tomorrow [ASMN, Gonzaga, b. 1256]
13 Aug.	Giorgio Fintler, Ferrara, to [Guglielmo Gonzaga, Mantua]: the comedians performed 5 or 6 comedies at Belriguardo and have been paid 30 scudi [ASMN, Gonzaga, Autografi, b. 10, fo. 224]
21 Nov.	Cesare Cavriani, Parma, to Theodoro Sangiorgio, Revere, and to Marcello Donati, Mantua: Margherita Farnese asked him to compose a melody [*il canto*] for a stanza of *ottava rima* by Ariosto ['Mi parea sù una lieta et verde riva'], which he encloses [ASMN, Gonzaga, b. 201, fo. 224^{r-v}]
17 Dec.	Annulment by the Council of Ten of the ordinance prohibiting the performance of comedies in Venice dated 25 Sept. 1581 [Mancini et al., *I teatri di Venezia*, p. xxvii; cfr. 25 Sept. 1581]
29 Dec.	Giovan Battista Concini, Florence, to Ferdinando de' Medici, Florence: relays the request by the Gelosi for permission to depart Florence for Venice [ASF, Dogana di Firenze, serie antica, f. 219, suppl. 355]
29 Dec.	Federico Cozzi, Ferrara, to Luigi d'Este, [unknown]: Laura Peverara's father has returned to Mantua saying that Vincenzo Gonzaga does not want to grant the licence for her marriage to Annibale Turco [ASMO, Particolari, Cozzi]

1583

1 Jan.	Birth of Virginia Ramponi [*Comici dell'Arte: Corrispondenze*, i. 78]
5 Jan.	Proposal in the Council of Ten to license comedians to perform in Venice for periods of 15 days; voted down [Mancini et al., *I teatri di Venezia*, p. xxvii]
14 Jan.	Proposal in the Council of Ten to license comedians to perform in Venice for periods of 15 days; voted down [Mancini et al., *I teatri di Venezia*, p. xxvii]
15 Jan. (Sat.)	[not stated], Rome, to Marcello Donati, Mantua: Cardinal Borromeo left Rome last Thursday to go to Loreto, and from there to Ferrara, Mantua, and Parma in order to end the marriage of Vincenzo Gonzaga [and Margherita Farnese] [ASMN, Gonzaga, b. 202, fo. 10^{r-v}]
15 Jan.	Angelica Albirigi [Alberghini], Bologna, to Vincenzo Gonzaga, Ferrara: requests exclusive rights for her company to perform in Mantua this carnival [ASMN, Gonzaga, b. 1162]
31 Jan.	Orazio Urbani, Ferrara, to Francesco Maria de' Medici, Florence: Giovanni Antinori and Giovanni de' Bardi and the other Florentines have arrived in Ferrara [ASF, Mediceo, f. 2900]

7 Feb.	Marcello Donati, Mantua, to [not stated]: the Duke has asked him to report on relations between Margherita Farnese and Vincenzo Gonzaga; in his opinion, the princess is incurable of the impediment regarding the consummation of their marriage and of her incapacity to give birth without risk to her life. Further asks that he be excused to Cardinal Borromeo because Guglielmo Gonzaga sends him to Ferrara [ASMN, Gonzaga, b. 202, fo. 66^{r-v}]
12 Feb.	Giulio Caccini, Ferrara, to Francesco Maria de' Medici, Florence: he has arrived in Ferrara and every evening they hear the *concerto delle dame* [ASF, Mediceo, f. 759, fos. 371–5]
14 Feb.	Orazio Urbani, Ferrara, to Francesco Maria de' Medici, Florence: the Florentines [Antinori, Bardi et al.] will depart today for Florence [ASF, Mediceo, f. 2901]
23 Feb.	Ash Wednesday
21 Mar.	Carlos de Aragón, Duke of Terranova, named Governor of Milan
10 Apr.	Easter
13 Apr.	Francesco Andreini, Ferrara, to Vincenzo Gonzaga, Mantua: has received, by the musician Antonio [Ricio], Vincenzo's offer for Francesco and Isabella Andreini to form a new company under Vincenzo's patronage. He responds that he and Isabella are under obligation to the Gelosi, and to Alvise Michiel, patron of the hall [*stanza*] in Venice, and therefore cannot accept Vincenzo's offer [ASMN, Gonzaga, b. 1256] (Doc. 9)
14 Apr.	Lodovico Agostini, Ferrara, to Guglielmo Gonzaga, Mantua: Antonio [Ricio] is visiting the Ferrarese court and is completely satisfied with the music of the *concerto delle dame* [Cavicchi, 'Lettere di musicisti ferraresi', 196]
25 Apr.	Tarquinia Molza enters employment at the Este court [ASMO, Archivio per materia, Letterati, b. 35; cfr. 11 July 1583]
4 May	Giovan Battista Guerrieri, Mantua, to Vincenzo Gonzaga, Mantua: Bernardino Pino's comedy, *Gli ingiusti sdegni*, is being prepared by Leone de' Sommi, Pietro Canal, and Giaches de Wert [ASMN, Gonzaga, b. 2624]
11 July	Account books of the Ferrarese court indicate payment to Tarquinia Molza at a rate of 160 gold scudi per year plus residence for her and her family [ASMO, Archivio per materia, Letterati, b. 35]
1 Aug.	Orazio Urbani, Ferrara, to [Francesco Maria de' Medici, Florence]: the arrival of the Duke de Joyeuse in Ferrara has caused Giulio Cesare Brancaccio to leave Estense service [Solerti, *Ferrara e la corte estense*, p. lxii]
13 Sept.	Fabio Mirti named governor of Bologna [Pasquali and Ferretti, 'Cronotassi']

23 Sept.	Decree of the entrance of Margherita Farnese Gonzaga in the Monasterio Monalium S. Pauli in Parma [ASMN, Gonzaga, b. 202, fos. 380^r–384^v]
28 Sept.	Camillo Gatico, Parma, to Theodoro Sangiorgo, [unspecified]: Margherita Farnese Gonzaga renounced her dowry and took the veil this morning [ASMN, Gonzaga, b. 202, fos. 395^r–396^v]

1584

3 Jan.	Federico Miroglio, Ferrara, to Marcello Donati, Mantua: he goes sometimes to see the comedy, but the comedians are not very good [ASMN, Gonzaga, b. 1257, fos. 7^r–8^v]
8 Jan.	Battista Guarini, Padua, to [unknown], [Mantua]: the Muses have abandoned him, and he doubts that he will return to their good graces because *Il pastor fido* still lacks its fifth part [*membro*] [ASMN, Gonzaga, b. 1514]
15 Feb.	Ash Wednesday
1 Apr.	Easter
3 Apr.	Giovanni Pellesini [Pedrolino], Ferrara, to Vincenzo Gonzaga, Mantua: Pedrolino's company and the Uniti have formed a new troupe and he requests a licence to perform in Mantua. They have not come already because Filippo Angeloni musico has told them not to. The comedians named are Pedrolino, Bertolino, Magnifico, Gratiano, Lutio, Capitan Cardone, Flaminio, Battista da Treviso, Franceschina, Giulia Brolo, Isabella, Giovanni Donato, Grillo [ASMN, Gonzaga, b. 1257, fos. 2^r–3^v] (Doc. 10)
4 Apr.	Margherita Gonzaga, Ferrara, to Vincenzo Gonzaga, Mantua: supports the request of Pedrolino and the Uniti to come to Mantua [D'Ancona, 'Il teatro mantovano', pt. 2, pp. 45–6]
4 Apr.	Vincenzo Gonzaga, Mantua, to Battista Guarini, [Padua]: asks Guarini to send him what is finished of the text of *Il pastor fido* because he wants it performed at his wedding to Eleonora de' Medici [D'Ancona, 'Il teatro mantovano', pt. 4, p. 52]
5 Apr.	Luigi Olivo, Mantua, to a Mantuan ducal secretary: Vincenzo Gonzaga's marriage [negotiations] were concluded yesterday [ASMN, Gonzaga, b. 2625]
7 Apr.	Battista Guarini, Padua, to Vincenzo Gonzaga, [Mantua]: *Il pastor fido* will not be finished at any time this year; sends *L'idropica* instead. He recommends comedies and pastorals, because these are the kinds of plays that may be adorned with intermedi with machines to give pleasure to those who do not understand, follow, or like the comic arts [ASMN, Gonzaga, b. 1514] (Doc. 11)

17 Apr.	Entry of Vincenzo Gonzaga into Florence [Gaeta Bertelà and Petrioli Tofani, *Le feste e apparati medicei*, 203]
18 Apr.	Ceremony of the gift of the golden rose to Eleonora de' Medici in Florence [Gaeta Bertelà and Petrioli Tofani, *Le feste e apparati medicei*, 203]
18 Apr. (Wed.)	Performance by Vittoria and other famous musicians at a *ballo* in Florence that lasted until the fifth hour of night [Fortuna, *Le nozze di Eleonora de Medici con Vincenzo Gonaga*]
22 Apr.	Performance of the *Mascherata delle bufole* in Florence in honour of the wedding of Eleonora de' Medici and Vincenzo Gonzaga [Gaeta Bertelà and Petrioli Tofani, *Le feste e apparati medicei*, 204]
29 Apr.	Wedding of Eleonora de' Medici and Vincenzo Gonzaga in the church of Santa Barbara in Mantua [ASMN, Gonzaga, b. 168, fos. 1^r–72^v; Vigilio, *La insalata*, 59–60]
1 May	Performance of Bernardino Pino, *Gli ingiusti sdegni* in Mantua [cfr. 2 May 1584]
2 May	Belisario Vinta, Mantua, to Francesco Maria de' Medici, Florence: *Gli ingiusti sdegni* was well performed yesterday by the Università degli ebrei [ASF, Mediceo, f. 6354, fo. 421^{r-v}]
10 May	Agosto Trissino, Revere, to [not stated]: Guglielmo Gonzaga has heard of a company of comedians performing in Mantua without a licence, which is forbidden [D'Ancona, 'Il teatro mantovano', pt. 2, p. 47]
13 May	Guidobono Guidoboni, Gazo, to [Guglielmo Gonzaga, Mantua]: the comedians in Mantua do, in fact, have a licence to perform [D'Ancona, 'Il teatro mantovano', pt. 2, p. 47]
28 May	Orazio Urbani, Ferrara, to Francesco Maria de' Medici, Florence: Giovanni de' Bardi has arrived in Ferrara [ASF, Mediceo, f. 2901]
13 July	Alessandro Striggio, Mantua, to Francesco Maria de' Medici, Florence: he has been invited to go to Ferrara for 15 days to hear the *concerto delle dame*, but cannot go because he has been sick in bed for the last 20 days [ASF, Mediceo, f. 768]
23 June	Girolamo Buoncompagni, Bologna, to Vincenzo Gonzaga, Mantua: the Uniti have always favourably impressed him and he recommends them to be licensed to perform [ASMN, Gonzaga, b. 1162, fos. 377^r–378^v]
20 July	Vincenzo Gonzaga, Mantua, to [Aurelio] Pomponazzi, Milan: asks to have Lodovico [de' Bianchi] Gratiano sent to Mantua to perform with Diana's company [D'Ancona, 'Il teatro mantovano', pt. 2, p. 47]
24 July	Eleonora de' Medici, Marmirolo, to Francesco Maria de' Medici,

	[Florence]: she is passing the time with comedies [ASF, Mediceo principato, f. 2939]
26 July	Girolamo Belli dedicates his *Primo libro de' madrigali à 5 voci* to Margherita Gonzaga
27 July	[Aurelio] Pomponazzi, Milan, to Vincenzo Gonzaga, Mantua: he has spoken with Lodovico [de' Bianchi] Gratiano, who wants Giulio [Pasquati] da Padova [Pantalone] to perform with him [D'Ancona, 'Il teatro mantovano', pt. 2, p. 48]
28 July	Alessandro Striggio, Ferrara, to Francesco Maria de' Medici, Florence: he has been in Ferrara for 6 days and hopes to return to Mantua in another 8 or 10 days; he has heard the *concerto delle dame*, and sent a madrigal 15 days ago and is sending a dialogue now [ASF, Mediceo, f. 768]
1 Sept.	Cristofano Malvezzi, Florence, to Eleonora de' Medici, Mantua: writes to express his faithful servitude, since Eleonora has sent for Zazzerino [Jacopo Peri] to come to Mantua [ASMN, Gonzaga, b. 1113, fos. 524ʳ–525ᵛ]
19 Sept.	Pedrolino [Giovanni Pellesini] and the Uniti, Mantua, to [Guglielmo Gonzaga], Mantua: asks that the Duke write on behalf of the Uniti to request that their costumes be ushered through the Dogana of Florence without the company having to pay tax on them [ASMN, Gonzaga, b. 2627]
8 Oct.	Giovan Battista Castagna named legate of Bologna [Pasquali and Ferretti, 'Cronotassi']
31 Oct.	Giovan Battista Concini, Florence, to Ferdinando de' Medici, Florence: asks that Pedrolino [Giovanni Pellesini] and the Uniti be excused from paying the Dogana tax on the clothing they used to perform pastorals, tragedies, and intermedi [ASF, Dogana di Firenze, serie antica, f. 220, suppl. 317]
31 Oct.	Claudio Monteverdi dedicates his *Canzonette a tre voci* to Pietro Ambrosini
4 Dec.	Hercole Zirolani, Castel[nuo]vo di Carfagnana, to Giovan Battista Laderchi, Ferrara, responding to a letter of 27 Nov.: he has found three youths and a man of the quality to be able to perform in Tasso's [*sic*: Guarini's] pastoral [*Il pastor fido*]. The youths, 16 or 17 years old, are ready to come to Ferrara; they have not recited before, but would be good in the role of the Nymph. The man, who has recited before, is on a par with Baldassare Mentessi [ASMO, Archivio per materie, Comici]
5 Dec.	Ferrante Estense Tassone, Modena, to Giovan Battista Laderchi, [Ferrara]: he does not find in Modena youths of the age and quality that Laderchi has requested for the tragicomedy, nor does he find a

	man of an age to suit this purpose [ASMO, Archivio per materie, Comici]
11 Dec.	Battista Guarini, Ferrara, to Ferrante Gonzaga, Mantua: he will gladly stage *Il pastor fido* in Mantua at carnival and asks if Ferrante knows of a boy of 16 or 17 years who could play the Nymph [Ronchini, *Lettere d'uomini illustri*, 650]
31 Dec.	Angelo Ingegneri dedicates his *Danza di Venere* (Vicenza: Stamperia Nova) to Camilla Lupi

1585

12 Jan.	Gabrielle Calzoni, Venice, to Guglielmo Gonzaga, Mantua: the nuns of the city scandalously have been receiving visitors at all hours and introducing into their monasteries *mascarate*, musicians for dancing and for singing, parties, and games; the Council of Ten has decreed that no one, including family, be allowed to see or speak to the nuns without licence; the nuns say they want to return to their fathers' homes [ASMN, Gonzaga, b. 1515]
6 Feb.	Pirro Malvezzi, Bologna, to Vincenzo Gonzaga, Mantua: yesterday the printer published the description of the wedding festivities of Sig. Periteo, and sends a copy [ASMN, Gonzaga, b. 1162, fos. 516^r–517^v]
18 Feb.	Account books of the Mantuan court record payment for a big key, a false beard, and a nose for Lione ebreo, on commission of Signor Arrigo [ASMN, Gonzaga, b. 401, fo. 419^r]
19 Feb.	Ercole Rosa, Ferrara, to Vincenzo Gonzaga, Mantua: the comedians were coming to Mantua, but a messenger arrived saying that the Archduchess would arrive in Ferrara on Thursday, and so Alfonso II has detained them [ASMN, Gonzaga, b. 1257, fos. 597^r–598^v]
21 Feb.	Licence granted to the Gelosi to perform in Milan during the entire carnival season [ASM, Registri delle Cancellerie, serie XXI, no. 18, fo. 100^r]
26 Feb.	Vincenzo Gonzaga, [Mantua], to [Alfonso II], Ferrara: his sister the Archduchess is coming and asks that the comedians to be sent to Mantua [ASMN, Gonzaga, b. 2955, fo. 166^{r-v}]
6 Mar.	Ash Wednesday
21 Apr.	Easter
1 May	Felice Peretti (Sixtus V) elected Pope
4 May	Licence granted to the Uniti to perform in Mantua from today and for the whole time they remain in the city. Licence signed by Carlo Luzzara, Collaterale of Mantua Generale, and notarized by Christoforo Acquanegra [ASMN, Gonzaga, b. 2632, fo. 218 bis]
11 May	Agostino Trissino, Revere, to [not stated], Mantua: the Duke

	understands that there are comedians in Mantua who are reciting without a licence, but does not know if perhaps Vincenzo gave them leave. In any case, they are not to recite in Mantua without a licence [ASMN, Gonzaga, b. 2632, fo. 237 bis]
13 May	Guidobono [Guidoboni], Gazo, to [not stated], Mantua: Guglielmo Gonzaga has ordered the comedians to be granted a licence to perform in Mantua [ASMN, Gonzaga, b. 2632, fo. 247 bis]
14 May	Guidobono [Guidoboni], near Verona, to [not stated], Mantua: the comedians are blameless in the business regarding their licence, and the Collaterale's behaviour in granting a licence without consulting the Duke was irregular. The comedians are nevertheless to leave the city because the Duke does not want any troupe performing at this time [ASMN, Gonzaga, b. 1515]
15 May	Antonio Maria Salviati named legate of Bologna [Pasquali and Ferretti, 'Cronotassi']
13 July	Festivities in Mantua in honour of the Japanese prince and ambassadors [Vigilio, *La insalata*, 62–3]
20 July	Annibale Romei, Ferrara, to Alfonso II d'Este, [Ferrara]: sends a copy of his newly published *Discorsi*, dedicated to Lucrezia d'Este, the Duchess of Urbino [ASMO, Cancelleria ducale, Letterati]
22 July	Anteo Cizzuolo, Mantua, to [unspecified], Mantua: Vincenzo Gonzaga is preparing to depart for Marmirolo with a company of comedians, saying that he hopes to find Don Ferrando Gonzaga there [ASMN, Gonzaga, b. 2630, fo. 486^r]
30 July	Death of Doge Nicolò da Ponte
10 Aug.	Vincenzo Gonzaga, Rovere, to Annibale Romei, [Mantua]: he has read Romei's book with much pleasure, as the work of a gentleman and friend, and it is filled with wisdom and beauty; thanks him for the gift [ASMN, Gonzaga, b. 2955]
13 Aug.	Battista Guarini, Ferrara, to Alfonso II d'Este, Ferrara: he has arrived in Ferrara to effect his daughter Anna's wedding [Campori, *Lettere*, 192]
18 Aug.	Pasquale Cicogno elected Doge of Venice
2 Sept.	Pirro Malvezzi, Bologna, to Vincenzo Gonzaga, Mantua: of the three comedians for whom Vincenzo has comanded Malvezzi to write a play [*che io facessi opera*], two—Marc'Antonio Galbiati and Giacomo Ponsini—departed before Vincenzo's letter arrived, and the third, Giovan Paolo [Fabbri], says that this must have been the work of some enemy of the company. Malvezzi asks Vincenzo how he would like him to proceed [ASMN, Gonzaga, b. 1162, fos. 692^r–693^v] (Doc. 12)
2 Sept.	Luigi Oliva, Mantua, to a Mantuan court functionary: there was a

(Mon.)	comedy today, and afterwards, the Duke departed in a boat as far as the Fornace di Porto, on his way to Marmiruolo [ASMN, Gonzaga, b. 2631]
7 Oct. (Mon.)	Luigi Oliva, Mantua, to a Mantuan court functionary: Vincenzo Gonzaga had a comedy performed today in the castle [ASMN, Gonzaga, b. 2631]
30 Oct.	Passport granted to Hercole Marliani, secretary of the Mantuan court, for travel outside Milan with two horses [ASM, Registri delle Cancellerie, s. XXI, no. 19, fos. 85^v–86^r]
16 Dec.	Lodovico de' Bianchi, Bologna, to Vincenzo Gonzaga, Mantua, signing himself Dottor Graziano comico geloso: the company is in Bologna, ready to depart for Mantua; he does not want to perform with Delia [Camilla Rocca Nobili], and because of her, the company has refrained from asking Adriano [Valerini] and Silvia [Roncagli] to join them—parts needed for performing the intermedi and other things. [ASMN, Gonzaga, b. 1162, fos. 743^r–744^v] (Doc. 13)

1586

	Publication of Tasso's dialogue *La Molza overo de l'amore*
[not stated]	De Nores dedicates his *Discorso intorno à que' principii* to Galeazzo Riario
1 Jan.	The Gelosi, Bologna, to Vincenzo Gonzaga, Mantua: the Gelosi have been awaiting the arrival of the licence to perform in Mantua, but it has not come; they therefore renew their request [ASMN, Gonzaga, b. 1163]
7 Jan.	Federico Cattaneo, Goito, to Vincenzo Gonzaga, Mantua: Guglielmo Gonzaga has conceded a licence to the Gelosi to perform in Mantua [ASMN, Gonzaga, b. 2635, fo. 783^r]
14 Jan.	Pirro Malvezzi, Bologna, to Vincenzo Gonzaga, Mantua: supports the Gelosi's request of a licence to perform in Mantua [ASMN, Gonzaga, b. 1163]
6 Feb.	Wedding of Virginia de' Medici and Don Cesare d'Este in Florence
9 Feb.	Camillo Albizi, Ferrara, to Vincenzo Gonzaga, Mantua: Don Cesare made his entrance into Florence last Monday; the wedding was last Thursday, but the comedy was postponed because Cardinal de' Medici had not yet arrived from Rome; instead, Antonio Salviati and Girolamo de' Rossi put together a *quintana* [ASMN, Gonzaga, b. 1257, fos. 236^r–237^v]
16 Feb.	Bastiano de' Rossi dedicates his *Descrizione del magnificentiss[imo] apparato* to Don Alfonso d'Este
16 Feb.	Performance in Florence of the comedy *L'amico fido* by Giovanni

(Sun.)	de' Bardi, with intermedi by Bardi, in honour of the wedding of Virginia de' Medici and Don Cesare d'Este. Music for the 1st, 2nd, and 5th intermedi by Alessandro Striggio; 3rd and 4th intermedi by Cristoforo Malvezzi; 6th intermedio by Bardi; Bernardo Buontalenti architect [Gaeta Bertelà and Petrioli Tofani, *Le feste e apparati medicei*, 56–61]
19 Feb.	Ash Wednesday
20 Feb. (Thurs.)	Performance by the Gelosi in Rome of the comedy *L'amor costante* by Alessandro Piccolomini at the house of Orazio Ruccellai [D'Ancona, 'Il teatro mantovano', pt. 3, p. 320]
23 Feb.	Camillo Albizi, Ferrara, to Vincenzo Gonzaga, Mantua: he will not report on the festivities in Florence because surely someone has already done so or they have sent the published description of the *apparato* [ASMN, Gonzaga, b. 1257, fos. 242^r–243^v]
26 Feb.	Vincenzo Gonzaga, Mantua, to Alfonso II d'Este, [Ferrara]: he is expecting his sister the Archduchess and asks Alfonso to send him the comedians to entertain her [ASMN, Gonzaga, b. 2955, fo. 166^{r-v}]
3 Mar.	Battista Guarini, Ferrara, to Giovanni de' Bardi, Florence: sends his congratulations that Bardi had his works performed by the comediennes; the Ferraresi who saw the performance have said it was very beautiful [Guarini, *Lettere* (Venice, 1593), 80–1]
6 Apr.	Easter
7 May	Birth of Francesco to Eleonora de' Medici and Vincenzo Gonzaga [Vigilio, *La insalata*, 63–5]
15 May	Baptism of Francesco Gonzaga in Mantua
31 May	Licence granted to the Gelosi to perform in Milan 'per tutto S. Michele pross[imo]' [ASM, Registri delle Cancellerie, serie XXI, no. 19, fo. 158^r; cfr. 29 Sept. 1586]
13 July	Release of Torquato Tasso from the prison of S. Anna
22 Aug.	Enrico Gaetani named legate of Bologna [Pasquali and Ferretti, 'Cronotassi']
post-Aug.	Giaches de Wert dedicates his *Ottavo libro de' madrigali à 5 voci* to Alfonso II d'Este
4 Sept.	Licence granted to the Uniti to perform comedies above the Sala del Podestà in Bologna [ASB, Legato, Expeditiones no. 98, fos. 63^v–64^r]
18 Sept.	Alessandro Farnese named Duke of Parma
29 Sept.	Feast day of San Michele
8 Oct.	Lionardo Salviati, Florence, to Battista Guarini, Ferrara: sends corrections and annotations to *Il pastor fido* [Weinberg, *A History of Literary Criticism*, 1074]
30 Dec.	Death of Luigi d'Este

1587

[1587–1600] Account books of the Mantuan court list Lavinia [Andreini] 'figlia della Comediante' under the Guardarobba, to be paid: for one mouth, two measures of bread, one and a half measures of veal, one and a half measures of fish, one measure of salt. In the same salary role, Giaches de Wert is listed as *maestro di cappella*, with Benedetto Pallavicino and Filippo Angeloni as *cantori*; Salomone Rossi and his sister Madama Europa are listed under *spese straordinari* [ASMN, Gonzaga, b. 395, fos. 154–61]

[not stated] Giovan Battista Licino, [Bergamo], dedicates his *Rime di diversi celebri poeti* to Carlo and Giorgio Spinoli

14 Jan. Isabella Andreini, Florence, to Eleonora de' Medici, Mantua: thanks Eleonora for taking Andreini's daughter Lavinia into service. She sends the letter by Claudio francese [ASMN, Gonzaga, Autografi, b. 10, fos. 50–1] (Doc. 14)

14 Jan. Isabella Andreini, Florence, to [Vincenzo Gonzaga], Mantua: thanks Vincenzo for taking Andreini's daughter Lavinia into service. She sends the letter by Claudio francese [ASMN, Gonzaga, Autografi, b. 10, fos. 52–3]

11 Feb. Ash Wednesday

29 Mar. Easter

5 Apr. Isabella Andreini, Florence, to Eleonora de' Medici, Mantua: thanks Eleonora again for taking Lavinia into service and informs her that the Grand Duke and Duchess of Tuscany have accepted Lavinia's younger sister into service. She sends the letter by Claudio francese. [ASMN, Gonzaga, Autografi, b. 10, fos. 54–5] (Doc. 15)

20 Apr. Annibale Coma dedicates, from Mantua, his *Quarto libro de' madrigali à 5 voci* to Alfonso II d'Este

1 May Guglielmo Gonzaga, Goito, to Francesco Maria de' Medici, [Florence]: reassures the Grand Duke that Alessandro Striggio is well loved at the Mantuan court, and that Guglielmo will not hesitate to favour him [ASF, Mediceo, f. 2940]

12 May Baptism of Philip Emanuel, firstborn son of the Infanta Catherina of Spain and Carlo Emanuele, the Duke of Savoy, in Turin [Scalini, *Breve discorso*]

11 July Lodovico de' Bianchi, Venice, to Ferdinando de' Medici, Florence: sends the Grand Duke 'un pocho de la mia sciencia', which may have been excerpts from his *Le cento e quindici conclusioni in ottava rima del plusquam perfetto Dottor Gratiano Partesana da Francolino comico Geloso* (Florence, 1587) [D'Ancona, 'Il teatro mantovano', pt. 2, p. 10]

29 July Licence granted to the Uniti to perform comedies in Milan for an

	unspecified period [ASM, Registro delle Cancellerie, serie XXI, no. 20, fo. 142^v]
14 Aug.	Death of Guglielmo Gonzaga at Goito [Vigilio, *La insalata*, 67–70]
17–18 Sept.	Funeral for Guglielmo Gonzaga in the church of Santa Barbara in Mantua [Vigilio, *La insalata*, 70–2]
22 Sept.	Vincenzo Gonzaga named Duke of Mantua and Monferrato [Vigilio, *La insalata*, 72–4]
19 Oct.	Deaths of Francesco Maria de' Medici and Bianca Capello; Ferdinando de' Medici named Grand Duke of Tuscany
26 Oct.	Alessandro Peretti di Montalto named legate of Bologna [Pasquali and Ferretti, 'Cronotassi']
10 Dec.	Anselmo Dandini named governor of Bologna [Pasquali and Ferretti, 'Cronotassi']

1588

[unknown]	Birth of Francesco Gabrielli
carnival	Licence granted to Francesco Amadini to *montar in banco* in the piazza in Bologna to sell his wares, but without playing instruments or singing [ASB, Legato, Expeditiones, no. 103, fo. 12^v]
21 Jan.	Cosimo Cicognini, Ferrara, to Belisario Vinta, Florence: Vincenzo Gonzaga entered Ferrara yesterday by the Porta a gli Angeli [ASF, Mediceo, f. 2904]
29 Jan.	Licence granted to Antonio Porcellino to open a perfume stand at the Porta Romana in Milan for the present carnival season [ASM, Registri delle Cancellerie, s. XXI, no. 21, fo. 81^r]
Feb.	Entry of Vincenzo Gonzaga into Milan
24 Feb.	Isabella Andreini, Verona, dedicates her *Mirtilla pastorale* to Lavinia della Rovere, the Marchesa del Vasto (Doc. 16)
2 Mar.	Ash Wednesday
17 Apr.	Easter
26 Apr.	Sebastiano dalle Donne, Verona, dedicates a reprinting of Isabella Andreini's *Mirtilla pastorale* to Lodovica Pellegrina, Cavaliera
28 Apr.	Battista Guarini dedicates his *Il verrato* to Iacopo Contarini and Francesco Vendramini [Weinberg, *A History of Literary Criticism*, 1131]
May	Vincenzo Scamozzi proposes plans for the Teatro di Sabionetta to Duke Vespasiano Gonzaga [Paolucci and Maffezzoli, *Sabbionetta, il teatro all'antica*, 7]
17 June	Vincenzo Gonzaga, Mantua, to Don Cesare d'Este, [Modena]: requests that Don Cesare grant a licence to the Accesi to perform in Modena and Reggio [ASMN, Gonzaga, b. 2956, fo. 78^{r-v}]
17 June	Vincenzo Gonzaga, Mantua, to the Governor of Milan, Milan:

	requests the return of the Gelosi to Mantua [Pandolfi, *La commedia dell'arte*, ii. 329]
26 June (Sun.)	Ottavio Lambartesco, Mantua, to [Vincenzo Gonzaga, Mantua]: the *ebrei* have agreed to perform a comedy or pastoral for the Duke's birthday [21 Sept.], but they are waiting for Leone de' Sommi, who should arrive on Monday, to finalize the arrangement [ASMN, Gonzaga, b. 2642, fo. 168^r]
1 July	Ottavio Lambartesco, Mantua, to [Vincenzo Gonzaga, Mantua]: Leone de' Sommi has yet to appear, but Il Massaro and the other *ebrei* have asked Lambartesco to forward the enclosed document to the Duke. The enclosed document, identifying the *ebrei* as 'l'università degli hebrei', requests that the Duke call for Leone de' Sommi, who is in Piemonte, and that the Duke choose the play he would like performed so that the actors may learn their parts. It further says that 22 Sept. is one of the most solemn of Jewish holidays, as is the 23rd, and that the 24th is Saturday, so they cannot perform then; therefore, it would be best to wait until that Sunday [25 Sept.] to have the play [ASMN, Gonzaga, b. 2642, fos. 170^r–171^v] (Doc. 17)
15 Aug.	Note of consignment written by Michele Tedesco on behalf of the Università degli Ebrei of Mantua listing various costumes given to Giulio Spagnolo of the Gelosi by command of the duke as related by Filippo Angeloni [ACIM, filza 3, doc. 1/170]
1 Sept.	Account books of Federico Cattaneo for the Mantuan court list Duc. 100, equalling L. 605, paid to the comedians, into the hands of Filippo [Angeloni] and Lucio [Fedele] [ASMN, Gonzaga, b. 410-B, fasc. 45, fo. 7^r]
17 Sept.	Account books of Federico Cattaneo for the Mantuan court list Duc. 80, equalling L. 484, paid to the comedians, into the hands of Adriano [Valerini] and Giulio [Pasquati] [ASMN, Gonzaga, b. 410-B, fasc. 45, fo. 7^r]
20 Sept.	Camillo Borghese named governor of Bologna [Pasquali and Ferretti, 'Cronotassi']
6 Oct.	Anselmo Dandini named governor of Bologna [Pasquali and Ferretti, 'Cronotassi']
6 Oct.	Licence granted to Giovanni Gabrielli to perform comedies in Bologna in the hall above the Pescarie [ASB, *Legato, Expeditiones*, no. 105, fo. 59^v]
19 Oct.	Camillo Borghese named governor of Bologna [Pasquali and Ferretti, 'Cronotassi']
[27] Oct.	Account books of Federico Cattaneo for the Mantuan court list Duc. 122, equalling L. [imp.] 738 s. 2, paid to the comedians. Duc. 8 per day from 15 Aug. until the end of the month, plus costs for 6

	Sept. and 14 Oct. at Duc. 5, plus payment for performing five times in the rooms of Vincenzo Gonzaga and for coming now and then to the palace: Duc. 402, from which they had 100 in hand, another 80, and 100 from the magistracy, leaving Duc. 122 [ASMN, Gonzaga, b. 410-B, fasc. 45, fo. 7^v]
6 Nov.	Account books of Federico Cattaneo for the Mantuan court list Duc. 51, equalling L. [imp.] 308 s. 11 paid to the comedians for 28 Oct. to 6 Nov. [ASMN, Gonzaga, b. 410-B, fasc. 45, fo. 8^r]
6 Dec.	Vincenzo Gonzaga, Mantua, to the Marchesa di Soragna, [unspecified]: requests the services of a castrato named Cesarino to sing in the intermedi for a comedy [ASMN, Gonzaga, b. 2956, fos. 146^v–147^r]
24 Dec.	Account books of Federico Cattaneo for the Gonzaga court list L. 468 paid to Giulio spagnolo to close the account with the comedians [ASMN, Gonzaga, b. 410-B, fasc. 45, fo. 130^r]

1589

6 Jan.	Deaths of Caterina de' Medici, Queen of France, and Henri, Duke of Guise [S. A. Maffei, *Gli annali di Mantova*, bk. 11, p. 919]
20 Jan.	Orazio della Rena, Ferrara, to Belisario Vinta, Florence: Giovanni de' Bardi, Jacopo Corsi, and Ottavio Rinuccini arrived yesterday in Ferrara [ASF, Mediceo, f. 2906]
29 Jan.	Alfonso Fontanelli, Ferrara, to Ridolfo Arlotti, [unspecified]: preparations for performing a comedy by Orazio Ariosto this carnival in the Sala Grande in Ferrara [Bibl. Estense, Ms. ital. 699]
9 Feb.	Orazio della Rena, Ferrara, to Belisario Vinta, Florence: Giovanni de' Bardi, Jacopo Corsi, and Ottavio Rinuccini have gone to Mesola and then on to Comacchio [ASF, Mediceo, f. 2906]
16 Feb.	Orazio della Rena, Ferrara, to Belisario Vinta, Florence: Giovanni de' Bardi, Jacopo Corsi, and Ottavio Rinuccini have returned to Ferrara from Casetta [ASF, Mediceo, f. 2906]
19 Feb.	Ash Wednesday
19 Feb.	Licence granted to Giuseppe Scarpetta and his company by Cardinal Montalto to perform comedies in Bologna [ASB, Legato, Expeditiones no. 106, fo. 99^v]
2 Apr.	Easter
24 Apr.	Entry of Christine of Lorraine into Pisa [*Descrizione delle pompe e feste*]
30 Apr. (Sun.)	Entry of Christine of Lorraine into Florence [Pavoni, *Entrata della sereniss[i]ma Gran Duchessa sposa*]
2 May (Tues.)	Performance of the 'gran commedia' *La pellegrina* by Girolamo Bargagli, with intermedi, in Florence. Project for the intermedi by

	Giovanni de' Bardi; texts by Ottavio Rinuccini and Laura Guidiccioni Lucchesini; music for the 1st, 4th, and 5th intermedi and part of the 6th intermedio by Cristoforo Malvezzi; for the 2nd and 3rd intermedi by Luca Marenzio; for part of the 6th intermedio by Emilio de' Cavalieri; architect Bernardo Buontalenti [Gualterotti, *Descrizione del regale apparato*; Rossi, *Descrizione dell'apparato e degl'intermedi*]
6 May (Sat.)	Performance by Vittoria Piisimi and the Gelosi of the comedy *La cingana*, with Bardi's intermedi, in Florence [Pavoni, *Diario* (BAV Rossiana 6980); Gaeta Bertelà and Petrioli Tofani, *Le feste e apparati medicei*, 205]
May 13 (Sat.)	Performance by Isabella Andreini and the Gelosi of the comedy *La pazzia d'Isabella*, with Bardi's intermedi, in Florence [Pavoni, *Diario* (BAV Rossiana 6980); Gaeta Bertelà and Petrioli Tofani, *Le feste e apparati medicei*, 205]
15 May (Mon.)	Second performance of *La pellegrina*, with Bardi's intermedi, in Florence [Pavoni, *Diario* (BAV Rossiana 6980)]
4 June	Raffaello Gualterotti dedicates his *Descrizione del regale apparato* to Ferdinando de' Medici, the Grand Duke of Tuscany
10 June	Giuseppe Pavoni, Bologna, dedicates his *Diario* to Giasone and Pompeo de' Vizani [BAV Rossiana 6980]
2 Aug.	Assassination of Henri III (Valois-Angoulême), King of France; succeeded by Henri IV (Bourbon), King of Navarre and Duke of Vendôme
6 Sept.	Lodovico de' Bianchi, Milan, to Ferdinando de' Medici, Florence: renews his request to come to Florence to perform [ASF, Mediceo, f. 808, fo. 369]
8 Oct.	Francesco Biffoli, Florence, to Ferdinando de' Medici, Florence: reminds Ferdinando that in 1587 he had waived the Dogana's fee for Vittoria Piisimi and her troupe in years past and asks if it should be waived again. The annotation by Giovan Battista Concini indicates that the troupe should pay one scudo per day in alms to the friars of Giovanni de Dios in the Borgo Ognissanti. Further annotation indicates that payment due was extended to 14 Dec. 1598 [ASF, Dogana di Firenze, serie antica, f. 221, suppl. 276]
20 Oct.	Request by Vittoria Piisimi and her company that they be excused from paying tax to the Dogana for their costumes; permission granted for used articles [ASF, Dogana di Firenze, serie antica, f. 221, suppl. 261]
21 Oct.	Lodovico de' Bianchi, Pistoia, to Ferdinando de' Medici, Florence: reminds Ferdinando of his promise to provide Bianchi with meat from the first hunt at Poggio [ASF, Mediceo, f. 809, fo. 579]

12 Dec.	Payment made to the Gelosi, in Mantua, by the president of the Mantuan magistrate: S.100 [D'Ancona, *Origini del teatro italiano*, ii. 495]

1590

Reprinting of Isabella Andreini, *Mirtilla* (Ferrara, Vittorio Baldini).

Battista Guarini dedicates his *Il pastor fido* to Carlo Emanuele, the Duke of Savoy, in honour of his marriage to Catherine of Austria

4 Jan.	Vincenzo Gonzaga, Mantua, to the Cardinal of Verona: orders Primocerio Cattaneo to perform the baptism of Vincenzo's third child next Sunday [7 Jan.] [ASMN, Gonzaga, b. 2956, fo. 33^v]
carnival	The Teatro di Sabbionetta opens [Paolucci and Maffezzoli, *Sabbionetta: il teatro all'antica*, 41–2]
7 Jan.	Vincenzo Gonzaga, Mantua, to Count Honorio Scotto, [Verona]: the Accesi have been performing comedies in Mantua for some months; asks that Scotto and the Rectors of his city provide a licence for them to perform in Verona for the carnival season [ASMN, Gonzaga, b. 2956, fo. 34^r]
24 Jan.	Ulisse Bentivoglio, Bologna, to Marcello Donati, Mantua: the story of an imbroglio concerning the comedian Andreazzo Graziano, who refuses to go to Rome with Diana Ponti's company in the service of Cardinal Montalto [ASMN, Gonzaga, b. 1164, fos. 348^r–349^v]
2 Feb.	Ulisse Bentivoglio, Bologna, to Marcello Donati, Mantua: Andreazzo has disappeared [ASMN, Gonzaga, b. 1164, fos. 356^r–357^v]
8 Feb.	Federico Miroglio, Ferrara, to Marcello Donati, Mantua: responds to Donato's letter of 24 Jan. recommending the Accesi, saying that the Giudice di 12 Savi has sent away another company of comedians who had been performing in Ferrara in order to accommodate the Accesi [ASMN, Gonzaga, b. 1259]
15 Feb.	Denores dedicates his *Apologia contra l'auttor del Verato* to Iacomo Contarini and Francesco Vendramini [Weinberg, *A History of Literary Criticism*, 1124]
7 Mar.	Ash Wednesday
7 Apr.	[Cesare] Cavriani, Mantua, to Luigi Olivo, Milan: he has sent Filippo Angeloni to escort the comedians from Milan to Mantua [D'Ancona, 'Il teatro mantovano', pt. 3, p. 321]
22 Apr.	Easter
12 May	Birth of Cosimo II, firstborn son of Christine of Lorraine and Ferdinando de' Medici

12 May (Sat.)	Licence granted to Claudio Baratti and his company to perform comedies in the *stanza sopra le pescherie* in Bologna. They begin performing on 14 May [ASB, Legato, Expeditiones no. 107, fo. 54^r]
7 June	Giovan Battista Laderchi, Ferrara, to the Governor of Modena: the Duke has agreed to license the comedians of the Duke of Sabbioneta, among them the *zanne* called Frittellino [Pier Maria Cecchini], to perform in Ferrara during the current season [ASMO, Archivio per materie, Comici]
15 Sept.	Giovan Battista Castagna (Urban VII) elected Pope [see Isabella Andreini's poem written for the occasion, 'Quando i tuoi chiari, e gloriosi honori']
26 Sept.	Ordinance regarding public performances in Milan names Dr Diomede Amici the superintendent of public performances in Milan, succeeding Dr Giuseppe Melfi, who has died [ASM, Registri delle Cancellerie, s. XXI, n. 23, fos. 112^v–113^r]
15 Oct.	Request of a licence for the Gelosi to continue performing in Milan for four months. Comedians listed are Vittoria Piisimi, Nora fiorentina, Aurelia romana, Lutio Fedeli, his son Flaminio, Oratio de Nobili, his wife Vittoria, Giuseppe Scarpetta, Giovan Battista Trombetti, Carlo Vegi, Bernardino Lombardi, Giulio Vigianti, Emilio Baldovini, Girolamo Salimbeni, and eleven servants [ASM, Registri delle Cancellerie, s. XXI, n. 23, fo. 119^{r-v}]
3 Nov.	Pirro Visconte Borromeo, Milan, to Ferdinando de' Medici, Florence: requests permission for the Gelosi, who are in Milan, to postpone coming to Florence for about two months [ASF, Mediceo del Principato, f. 812, fos. 497^r, 516^v]
8 Dec.	Niccolò Sfondrati (Gregorio XIV) elected Pope
10 Dec.	Records of the Ufficio delle Bollete in Mantua note that Leandro de Pilastro, together with Cesare Galassi, Guido Nolffi, Concordia Barbarigga, and a boy have entered the city and are lodged at the Osteria de' Tre Rè [ASMN, Gonzaga, b. 3090, fo. 80^r]
25 Dec.	Death of Taddea Guarini [Guarini, *Il pastor fido*, ed. Guglielminetti, 39]

1591

2 Jan.	Records of the Ufficio delle Bollete in Mantua note the entry of Lutio Fedele, Aurelia Sorgga, and a servant into the city, to be lodged by Camillo Sarnis [ASMN, Gonzaga, b. 3090, fo. 103^r]
7 Jan.	Eleonora de' Medici, Mantua, to Sig. Cav[riani], Florence: requests a licence on behalf of Isabella and her company to perform in the usual room in Florence [ASF, Mediceo del Principato, f. 2941]

30 Jan.	Paolo Sfondrati named legate of Bologna [Pasquali and Ferretti, 'Cronotassi']
1 Feb.	Eleonora de' Medici, Mantua, to Ferdinando de' Medici, Florence: relays the request of Adriano Valerini to remove his daughter from the Monastero Cintia so that she may marry [ASF, Mediceo, b. 2941]
6 Feb.	Records of the Ufficio delle Bollete in Mantua note the entry of Gabriele Canovaro, Pier Maria Cecchini, and Giovan Battista Austoni into the city, to be lodged at the Osteria Fontana [ASMN, Gonzaga, b. 3090, fo. 140^r]
21 Feb.	Ash Wednesday
4 Mar.	Records of the Ufficio delle Bollete in Mantua note the entry of Francesco Pilastro, Pietro Antonio Mamei, Antonio Nani, Guido Rocca, Pavia di Polini, Paolo Gazamini, Andrea di Laghi, Concordia Barbarigha, and a servant into the city, to be lodged at the Osteria Capello [ASMN, Gonzaga, b. 3090, fo. 170^r]
19 Jan.	Account books of the Mantuan court list payments received by Ottaviano Cavriani [ASMN, Gonzaga, b. 402, fos. 78^r–148^v]
7 Mar.	From Vincenzo Gonzaga for carnival entertainments totalling L. 22482 s. 13 d. 6. Summary of payment made for the *apparato* for the *barriera* and the comedy totals L. 13245 s. 16 d. 8. Payment to the comedians was Duc. 106.5, equalling L. 639. Various payments in Cavriani's name are made by Federico Follino and Bastiano de' Rossi [ASMN, Gonzaga, b. 402, fos. 78^r–148^v]
19 Mar.	Vincenzo Gonzaga, Mantua, to Count Bevilacqua, Verona: the Uniti would like to come to Verona to perform and asks Bevilacqua to support their request to the Podestà [Pandolfi, *La commedia dell'arte*, ii. 331]
22 Mar.	Records of the Ufficio delle Bollete in Mantua note the entry of Giovan Paolo Fabbri into the city, to be lodged at the Osteria Fontana [ASMN, Gonzaga, b. 3090, fo. 189^r]
23 Mar.	Count Bevilacqua, Verona, to Vincenzo Gonzaga, Mantua: responds that the Rectors of Verona will not grant the Uniti a licence [Pandolfi, *La commedia dell'arte*, ii. 331]
29 Mar.	Eleonora de' Medici, Mantua, to [Cesare] Cavriani, Florence: again requests a licence for Isabella and her company to perform in the usual room in Florence [ASF, Mediceo, f. 2941]
14 Apr.	Easter
19 May	Licence granted to the Uniti to perform comedies in Mantua [ASMN, Gonzaga, b. 2956, fo. 151^v]
27 May	The Rectors of Verona, Verona, to Vincenzo Gonzaga, Mantua: promises to grant the comedians a licence soon [Pandolfi, *La commedia dell'arte*, ii. 331]

Aug.	Account books of the Mantuan court list permission for Fortunio [Rinaldo Petignoni] to use three horses for 13 days for the trip to Innsbruck, one for the use of *maestro* Claudio [francese], the others for two Jews [ASMN, Gonzaga, b. 402, fo. 58]
21 Aug.	Account books of the Mantuan court list payment to Claudio Francese on his return from Innsbruck: L. 3 s. 10 [ASMN, Gonzaga, b. 402, fos. 48^r, 58^r]
20 Sept.	Scipione Ammirato, Florence, to Vincenzo Gonzaga, Mantua: mentions that he has long been a servant of the father and brothers of Christine of Lorraine and is now her servant, and declines Vincenzo's offer of employment [ASMN, Gonzaga, b. 1119, fos. 130^r, 135^v]
27 Sept.	Isabella Andreini, Bologna, to Belisario Vinta, Florence: the Duchess of Mantua has told Andreini of the Grand Duke's wishes to have her company perform in Florence; Andreini thus requests a licence for the usual time and the usual hall [*salone*] [ASF, Mediceo, f. 829, fo. 277^{r-v}] (Doc. 18)
2 Oct.	Birth of Margherita to Eleonora de' Medici and Vincenzo Gonzaga [Vigilio, *La Insalata*, 76]
3 Nov.	Giovanni Antonio Facchinetti (Innocenzo IX) elected Pope
10 Nov.	Birth of Eleonora to Christine of Lorraine and Ferdinando de' Medici
18 Nov.	Mutio Manfredi, Nancy, to Leone de' Sommi, Mantua: it has been a month since he sent his *poema boschereccio scenico* to Vincenzo Gonzaga, and if Vincenzo wants it staged, Manfredi is hoping de' Sommi will agree to be the *corago* [D'Ancona, 'Il teatro mantovano', pt. 4, pp. 68–9]
19 Nov.	Mutio Manfredi, Nancy, to Isacchino *ebreo, maestro di ballare,* Mantua: in the pastoral that he sent Vincenzo, the chorus's four *canzonette* are to be sung and danced without mistakes; gives instructions for each [D'Ancona, 'Il teatro mantovano', pt. 4, p. 69]
20 Nov.	Mutio Manfredi, Nancy, to Giaches de Wert, Mantua: gives instructions for how to set the chorus's four *canzonette* to music; asks that each *canzonetta* follow its affect, and that the choruses be varied, sometimes singing all together, sometimes in two parts, corresponding to the stanzas and the reprises, and always danced [D'Ancona, 'Il teatro mantovano', pt. 4, pp. 69–70]
23 Nov.	Battista Guarini, Padova, to Annibale Chieppio, Mantua: he will come to Mantua, hopefully in Dec., bringing *Il pastor fido* [D'Ancona, *Origini del teatro*, ii. 541]
24 Nov.	Guidobono Guidoboni, Florence, to Annibale Chieppio, Mantua:

	the Duke has commanded him to prepare for the comedy or pastoral that will come from Battista Guarini, regarding the staging, costumes, and other props, with the guidance of the Marchesa di Grana [ASMN, Gonzaga, b. 1119, fos. 164^r–165^v]
22 Dec.	Death of Cardinal Gian Vincenzo Gonzaga
23 Dec.	Records of the Ufficio delle Bollete in Mantua note the entry into the city of Giovan Paolo Fabbri, Jacomo Bragha, and a boy, to lodge at the Osteria Fontana [ASMN, Gonzaga, b. 3090, fo. 450^r]
26 Dec.	Annibale Chieppio, Mantua, to [Guidobono] Guidoboni, Rome: the performance of Guarini's *Il pastor fido* has been postponed [D'Ancona, *Origini del teatro*, ii. 547]
28 Dec.	Records of the Ufficio delle Bollete in Mantua note the entry into the city of Leandro Pilastro, his wife Emilia, and a servant, to lodge at the Osteria Bissone, and the entry of Girolamo Salimbeni and two servants, to lodge at the Osteria Fontana [ASMN, Gonzaga, b. 3090, fo. 455^r]

1592

6 Jan.	Wedding of Leonora d'Este and Carlo Gesualdo in Ferrara [Faustini, *Dalle historie ferraresi*, 90 ff.]
6 Feb.	Records of the Ufficio delle Bollete in Mantua note the entry into the city of Francesco Scapino, to lodge at the Osteria Angelo [ASMN, Gonzaga, b. 3090, fo. 498^r]
9 Feb.	Ippolito Aldobrandini (Clemente VIII) elected Pope
12 Feb.	Ash Wednesday
1 Mar.	Giulio Cesare Croce dedicates his *La libraria* to Cardinal Giorgio Radivil
2 Mar.	Guidobono Guidoboni, Ferrara, to Annibale Chieppio, Mantua: writes to Sig. Petrozanni that the Duke has released Abramo Sullamo from service with a security of 1,000 scudi [ASMN, Gonzaga, b. 1259]
29 Mar.	Easter
22 Apr. (Wed.)	Entry in the 'Memorie di Giovanni del Maestro': the Gelosi have arrived in Florence at the request of the Grand Duke to entertain for the baptism. The company, numbering 13, stay in Florence until 17 May, and are paid 6 scudi per day, which payment is made to Francesco Andreini. The company was licensed on 19 Apr. at the recommendation of Emilio de' Cavalieri and sent 150 scudi for transportation from Siena [ASF, Filze strozziane, serie I, fasc. 27, fos. 2^r, 6^r]
23 Apr. (Thurs.)	Annibale Chieppio, Florence, to Guidobono Guidoboni, Mantua: Vincenzo Gonzaga arranged a performance of a comedy in the

	palace, but with 'comici ordinarii', and the baptism is slated for next Sunday [ASMN, Gonzaga, b. 1119, fos. 272ʳ–273ᵛ]
25 Apr. (Sat.)	Bartolomeo Prosperi, Florence, to [unknown], Ferrara: the Medici court has been passing time with comedies performed by Isabella [Andreini] and her troupe [Solerti, *Albori*, i. 54]
26 Apr. (Sun.)	Baptism of Cosimo II de' Medici in Florence [ASF, Filze strozziane, serie I, fasc. 27, fos. 2ʳ, 6ʳ]
26 Apr.	Annibale Chieppio, Florence, to Guidobono Guidoboni, Mantua: on Wednesday and Thursday [22 and 23 Apr.], a comedy was performed by *comici publici* in the Palazzo Pitti, and yesterday there was a party, with *balli alla francese*. At the baptism this morning, the most beautiful music was heard, made by singers who were arranged in groups of 5 singers and 5 instrumentalists in the 18 windows that encircle the church, and that all told, the musicians numbered 180 with 2 *maestri di cappella* who beat time with ornamented bastoni [ASMN, Gonzaga, b. 1119, fos. 285ʳ–288ᵛ]
27 Apr. (Mon.)	Baptism of Eleonora de' Medici in Florence [ASF, Filze strozziane, serie I, fasc. 27, fos. 2ʳ, 6ʳ]
28 Apr. (Tues.)	Annibal Chieppio, Florence, to Guidobono Guidoboni, Mantua: the baptism of the princess took place yesterday, in the same church and with the same music as the baptism on Sunday [ASMN, Gonzaga, b. 1119, fos. 293ʳ–294ᵛ]
30 Apr. (Thurs.)	Annibale Chieppio, Florence, to Guidobono Guidoboni, Mantua: Vincenzo Gonzaga is passing the time with comedies and lively dances, and this evening a 'donna' of the Grand Duchess sang beautifully in Spanish and Tuscan accompanying herself on guitar in the Duchess's room [ASMN, Gonzaga, b. 1119, fos. 295ʳ–296ᵛ]
5 May	Lelio Arrivabeni, Florence, to Guidobono Guidoboni, Mantua: the festivities continue with parties, comedies, and jousts, and the negotiations for the marriage of the 'Duchino' Sforza and the sister of Don Virginio de' Medici are coming to a conclusion; he sends greetings from Battista Guarini [ASMN, Gonzaga, b. 1119, fos. 510ʳ–511ᵛ]
9 May	Annibale Chieppio, Florence, to Guidobono Guidoboni, Mantua: the marriage negotiations for the Duchino Sforza are concluded, and Cardinal Sforza departed yesterday to go to the bride; Vincenzo Gonzaga's entertainments are the usual dances, comedies, parties, and music, and Battista Guarini is included in the festivities [ASMN, Gonzaga, b. 1119, fos. 323ʳ–324ᵛ]
15 May	Baldassare Castiglione, Mantua, to a ducal secretary, Mantua: lists the actors who are to perform *Il pastor fido*: all are male, and all amateurs [D'Ancona, *Origini del teatro*, ii. 550–2]

15 May	Battista Guarini, Mantua, to Vincenzo Gonzaga, Mantua: requests that *Il pastor fido* be postponed for a season [D'Ancona, *Origini del teatro*, ii. 557–9]
27 May	Claudio Merulo dedicates his *Canzoni d'intavolatura d'organo . . . libro primo* to Ranuccio Farnese
10 June	Drusiano Martinelli, Florence, to [Vincenzo Gonzaga, Mantua]: he is making a lot of money at the Tuscan court, but he would prefer to return to his natural patron in Mantua ['l'Altezza sua, p[er] esser mio sig.re et patron naturale']; to that end, he asks Vincenzo to devise some legitimate excuse in order to not lose the good graces of the Grand Duke [ASMN, Gonzaga, Autografi, b. 10, fo. 135^{r-v}]
27 June	Claudio Monteverdi dedicates his *Terzo libro de madrigali a cinque voci* to Vincenzo Gonzaga [Fabbri, *Monteverdi* (trans. Carter), 27]
10 July	Vincenzo Gonzaga arrives in Milan and lodges with Pirro Visconte; Visconte arranges an entertainment in which the 9-year-old daughter of Rinaldo Tettone dances, makes music, and sings, whereby Visconte, at Vincenzo's recommendation, sends for two women to raise the girl and train her; Cesare Negri is called to be her dancing master [Negri, *Le gratie d'amore*, 12]
2 Oct.	Michele della Rocca, Ferrara, to Belisario Vinta, Florence: Lelio Ghirlenzoni and Giulio Caccini have arrived in Ferrara [ASF, Mediceo, f. 2906]
11 Oct.	Giulio Caccini, Ferrara, to Ferdinando de' Medici, Florence: he arrived in Ferrara last week and was immediately invited to hear the *concerto delle dame*; he has taught some arias to the women, who like his manner of singing [ASF, Mediceo, f. 835, fo. 497; Durante and Martellotti, *Cronistoria del concerto*]
11 Oct.	[Cesare] Cavriani, Mantua, to the Uniti, [Mantua]: gives permission for the Uniti to depart Mantua for Florence, and for Margherita Pauli to go with them [ASMN, Gonzaga, b. 2234]
31 Oct.	Emilio de' Cavalieri, Florence, to Luzzasco Luzzaschi, Ferrara: Giulio Caccini has come to see him [ASMO, Archivio per materia, Musica e Musicisti, b. 1/A]
4 Nov.	Alessandro Peretti di Montalto named legate of Bologna [Pasquali and Ferretti, 'Cronotassi']
3 Dec.	Death of Alessandro Farnese. Ranuccio Farnese named Duke of Parma. Pietro Ernesto, Count of Mansfeld, named governor of the Netherlands
4 Dec.	Juan Fernández de Velasco, Duke of Frias, named Governor of Milan
12 Dec.	Payment made to the Gelosi by Vincenzo Gonzaga, via the

	President of the Magistrate in Mantua: 100 scudi [Pandolfi, *La commedia dell'arte*, ii. 329]
26 Dec.	Account books of the Mantuan court list payment made to Filippo Angelone cantore to cover expenses for going from Mantua to Florence and back to conduct the comedians to Mantua: L. 225 [ASMN, Gonzaga, b. 402, fo. 295^r]

1593

[unknown]	Publication of Guarini's *Il Verato secondo*, dedicated to Vincenzo Gonzaga, Duke of Mantua [Weinberg, *A History of Literary Criticism*, 1131]
27 Jan.	Bernardo Buontalenti, Florence, to Vincenzo Gonzaga, [Mantua]: sends the designs for an instrument he has made that raises water [*alzare l'acqua*] [ASMN, Gonzaga, b. 1120, fos. 84^r–85^v]
Feb.	Account books of the Mantuan court list payments made for the comedy totalling L. 996 s. 13 [ASMN, Gonzaga, b. 402, fos. 306^v, 359^r–360^v]
3 Mar.	Ash Wednesday
15 Mar.	Receipt signed by Drusiano Martinelli for a payment of 43 scudi from Ottaviano Cavriani, which completes payment for services during Jan. [ASMN, Gonzaga, b. 402, fo. 382^r]
20 Mar.	Aurelio Pomponazzi, Venice, to [not stated], Mantua: Arlecchino's brother [Drusiano Martinelli] came to him with a request to procure him an introduction to the Imperial ambassador in Constantinople, which Pomponazzi did [ASMN, Gonzaga, b. 1525, fo. 47^r]
27 Mar.	Giusto Giusti, Verona, to [not stated], Mantua: the comedienne Aurelia would like to join the company of Vittoria [Piisimi], with hopes of advancing herself in the profession [ASMN, Gonzaga, b. 1525, fo. 406^r]
18 Apr.	Easter
19 Mar.–23 Apr.	Account books of the Mantuan court list payment for 4 trombones, 5 violins, 3 tambourines, an unspecified number of piffari and bombarderi, and a Turkish slave, employed by Vincenzo Gonzaga during travel from Mantua to Casale Monferrato and back: L. 988 [ASMN, Gonzaga, b. 402, fo. 404]
28 Apr.	Account books of the Mantuan court list receipt of payment to the comedian Leandro of 1 ducatone and 2 philippine half-scudi worth s. 23 d. 10 each, for sending two letters; one to Ferrara, and the other to Reggio to ask the comedians to serve the Duke [ASMN, Gonzaga, b. 402, fo. 457^v]
30 Apr.	Licence granted to the Desiosi to perform above the Sala del Podestà in Bologna [ASB, Legato, Expeditiones no. 112, fo. 43^{r-v}]

4 July	Minutes of the Cancelleria in Mantua request the list of expenditures made by Filippo Angeloni in going to Florence to get the Uniti [ASMN, *Schede Davari*, b. 14, fo. 185]
6 Oct.	Guidobono Guidoboni, Maderno, to a Mantuan cardinal: the courier Giulio arrived yesterday, and the Duke read his dispatches while watching the comedy, but did not order any responses [ASMN, Gonzaga, b. 1525, fo. 562^r]
8 Oct.	Emilio de' Cavalieri, Florence, to [not stated]: Vittoria will be in Rome soon, and the Duke of Nevers is anxiously waiting to hear her [ASF, Mediceo, f. 3622, fos. 32^r–33^r]
12 Oct.	Piriteo Malvezzi, Bologna, to Vincenzo Gonzaga, Mantua: asks the Duke to permit a friend of a friend, Donna Anna d'Arbisso spagnola, to run a lottery in Mantua for 4,000 scudi [ASMN, Gonzaga, b. 1165, fos. 236^r–237^v]
20 Oct.	Ottavio Bandini, Bologna, to Vincenzo Gonzaga, Mantua: both the Desiosi and Gelosi have requested licences to perform in Bologna and, because the Duke on a similar occasion favoured the Gelosi over the Desiosi, Bandini assumes that the same will hold true this time and informs the Duke that he is granting a licence to the Gelosi [ASMN, Gonzaga, b. 1165, fos. 240^r–241^v]
14 Nov.	Licence granted to Vittoria Piissimi and her company to perform comedies, tragicomedies, tragedies, pastorals, and other virtuous entertainments in the Sala del Podestà in Bologna. The licence stipulates that the comedies may not be performed until after the public lessons at the Studio have finished. Marginal note indicates that they began performing on 14 Nov. [ASB, Legato, Expeditiones, no. 114, fo. 32^v] (Doc. 19)
19 Nov.	Emilio de' Cavalieri, Rome, to Marcello Accolti, Florence: Vittoria has arrived at the house of Virginio Orsini [ASF, Mediceo, f. 3622, fos. 65^v–66^r]
15 Dec.	Ottavio Bandini, Bologna, to Vincenzo Gonzaga, Mantua: writes of the unexpected death of the Marchese del Vasto [ASMN, Gonzaga, b. 1165, fos. 258^r–259^v]

1594

[not stated]	Isabella Andreini dedicates her sonnet 'O d'Adria chiari, e generosi figli' to Silvan Capello and Nicolò Donato, Rectors of Brescia [Manzuoli, *Rime, e prose di diversi auttori*, 135]
	Reprinting of Isabella Andreini, *La Mirtilla* (Bergamo, Comin Ventura)
15 Jan.	Domenico Bruni meets Francesco Andreini and the Gelosi in

	Bologna [Bruni, *Fatiche comiche*, introduction, in Marotti and Romei, *La professione del teatro*, 346]
18 Jan.	Emilio de' Cavalieri, Rome, to Marcello Accolti, Florence: describes a performance by Vittoria yesterday in the room of Messer Filippo, where she sang a Benedictus, although everyone wanted to hear *spagnole* and *galanterie*. Sig. Filippo had a priest dance a *canario* and a *pedrolino*, and Vittoria said he dances stupendously. Messer Filippo gave Vittoria a slap and made her promise to return [ASF, Mediceo, f. 3622, fo. 112^{r-v}]
30 Jan.	Ernst of Austria named governor of the Netherlands
21 Feb.	Wedding of Leonora d'Este and Carlo Gesualdo [Solerti, *Ferrara e la corte estense*, p. xxxix]
23 Feb.	Ash Wednesday
27 Feb.	Henri IV (Bourbon), King of Navarre and Duke of Vendôme, consecrated as King of France
26 Mar.	Comici Uniti, [unspecified], to [Ferdinando de' Medici], Florence: requests a licence for the Uniti to perform comedies in Florence from 1 Nov. until the first day of Lent, in the usual hall [*stanza*] and with the same rooms and risers [*palchetti*], so they have only to pay rent. Signed Vittoria, Ardelia, Leandro, Fortunio, Petrolino, Arlecchino, Francatrippe già dei Gelosi, un Magnifico, Gratiano, Capitano Cardone, Franceschina, Piombino. Annotation to the request: the Proveditore of the Dogana [Francesco Biffoli] would like to know if Isabella Andreini intends to join this company [ASF, Dogana di Firenze, f. 223, supplica no. 318 (II)]
30 Mar.	Francesco Biffoli, Florence, to Ferdinando de' Medici, Florence: Vittoria [Piissimi] will not be able to perform with Petrolino's troupe [Uniti] and, because the Grand Duke asked that Isabella Andreini be asked to substitute, Biffoli has gone around to talk with her personally. Andreini has said that she is unable to commit herself to the Uniti because she is under obligation to her own company. Licence granted on 31 Mar. 1594. [ASF, Dogana di Firenze, serie antica, f. 223, suppl. 318 (I) (Doc. 20)
2 Apr.	Contract for the Uniti to perform in Florence from 1 Nov. until the end of the first day of Lent 1594. Signing for the Uniti are Capitano Cardone [Valentino Cortesei] and Piombino [Girolamo Salimbeni] [ASF, Dogana di Firenze, f. 223, supplica no. 318 (III)]
5 Apr.	Account books of the Mantuan court record receipt of payment of D. 28, equalling L. 168, made to the instrumentalists who played seven nights and seven days for parties for the baptism [of Vincenzo II] at a rate of pay of D. 2 per party and D. 2 per day. [ASMN, Gonzaga, b. 402, fo. 1037^r]

Chronology

10 Apr.	Easter
14 Apr.	Licence granted to Isabella Andreini *comica gelosa* and her troupe to perform comedies, tragicomedies, tragedies, pastorals, and other virtuous entertainments above the Sala del Podestà in Bologna. An annotation to the licence indicates that they began performing on 3 May [ASB, Legato, Expeditiones, no. 114, fo. 71^v] (Doc. 21)
1 May	Entry of the Duke of Nevers in Mantua [*Breve descritione della barriera*]
14 May	Birth of Francesco to Christine of Lorraine and Ferdinando de' Medici
13 June	Account books of the Mantuan court record a note from Carlo Caffini to an unknown superior, stating that the Duke commands the recipient of the note to pay the comedians D. 25 for two comedies that they performed and no others [ASMN, Gonzaga, b. 402, fo. 851^r]
[20] June	Account books of the Mantuan court record receipt of payment of D. 25, s. 6.12, equalling L. 165, made to the comedians for service from 1 June to 20 June [ASMN, Gonzaga, b. 402, fo. 848^{r-v}]
10 July	Licence granted to Giovanni Gabrielli to perform comedies in Bologna, *montar in banco* [ASB, Legato, Expeditiones, no. 114, fo. 95^v]
23 July	Licence granted to the comedian Fortunato and company to *montar in banco* in the piazza in Bologna in order to sell their wares [ASB, Legato, Expeditiones no. 114, fo. 101^v]
28 June	Wedding of Ippolita d'Este and Federico Pico da Mirandola [Solerti, *Ferrara e la corte estense*, p. xxxix]
5 Aug.	Death of Archduchess Eleonora Gonzaga of Austria at Porto [Vigilio, *La insalata*, 80–1]
13 Oct.	Performance of a comedy with intermedi in Milan in honour of the wedding of the Count of Harò. The intermedi, on the subject of Phaethon, were performed by Vittoria Piisimi (who sang), Tristano Martinelli, Pedrolino [Giovanni Pellesini], Leandro [Francesco Pilastro], and others [D'Ancona, 'Il teatro mantovano', pt. 3, pp. 332–4] (Doc. 22)
29 Oct.	Licence granted to the Comici Uniti to perform comedies, tragicomedies, tragedies, pastorals, and other virtuous entertainments above the Sala del Podestà in Bologna. Annotation to the licence: the Uniti began to perform on 29 Oct. [ASB, Legato, Expeditiones no. 115, fo. 24^v]
8 Dec.	Girolamo Salimbeni, Florence, to [Giovanni de' Medici, Florence]: responds to a letter by Alessandro Barberino about having a door in

	the Teatro di Baldracca walled up [ASF, Mediceo, f. 853, fo. 636^{r-v}; Evangelista, 'Il teatro dei comici dell'arte', 78–9]
19 Dec.	Valeriano Cattaneo, Mantua, to Margherita Gonzaga, Ferrara: sends her four *canzonette* by Claudio Monteverdi, saying that they are similar to the ones he sent to Don Bassano [Cassola] [ASMO, Cancelleria ducale, Particolari, Cattaneo]

1595

	Pietro Paolo Andreini enters the Vallombrosian order [Sala, *Dizionario storico biografico*, i. 22]
	Giovan Battista Andreini begins practising the comic arts [ASMN, *Notarile*, notaio Pallini Giulio Cesare, 1620, 31 Jan.]
	Tomaso Garzoni publishes his *Piazza universale*
8 Feb.	Ash Wednesday
21 Feb.	Pedro Enríquez de Acevedo, the Count of Fuentes, named Governor of the Netherlands
11 Mar.	Pedro de Padilla named Governor of Milan
17 Mar.	Request of a licence by Diana [Ponti] and the Desiosi to perform comedies in Milan [ASM, Autografi, cart. 94, fasc. 43]
26 Mar.	Easter
2 Apr.	Death of Doge Pasquale Cicogna
10 Apr.	Licence granted to Diana [Ponti] and the Desiosi to perform in Milan, provided they do not perform on feast days or Fridays, do not wear religious costumes, and do not recite dishonest words [ASM, Autografi, cart. 94, fasc. 43]
18 Apr.	Request of a licence by the Uniti, with the recommendation of the Mantuan ambassador, to perform in Milan during the summer; granted on 7 June, under the same conditions as those granted to Diana Desiosa [ASM, Autografi, cart. 94, fasc. 43]
26 Apr.	Marino Grimani elected Doge of Venice
30 Apr.	Licence granted to Leandro Pilastro and Girolamo Salimbeni and company to perform comedies, tragicomedies, tragedies, pastorals, and other virtuous entertainments above the Sala del Podestà in Bologna. The comedians began performing on 15 May [ASB, Legato, Expeditiones, no. 115, fo. 63^r]
2 June	Francesco Pilastro, Bologna, to Vincenzo Gonzaga, Mantua: sends some burlesque compositions written by a friend who is in Bologna en route to Hungary [ASMN, Gonzaga, b. 1165, fos. 436^r–437^v]
16 June	Licence granted to Francesco Andreini and the Uniti to return to Bologna to perform comedies, tragicomedies, tragedies, pastorals, and other virtuous entertainments above the Sala del Podestà from the eve of the feast of S. Petronio [3 Oct.] through carnival. The

	comedians began performing on 14 Sept. [ASB, Legato, Expeditiones, no. 115, fo. 73ᵛ] (Doc. 23)
5 July	Mantuan troops, under the leadership of Carlo Rossi, depart for Hungary to battle the Turks for the first time; included in Vincenzo Gonzaga's entourage were Claudio Monteverdi and five musicians [Vigilio, *La insalata*, 81–2; ASMN, Gonzaga, b. 388, fos. 358ʳ–389ᵛ]
31 July	Departure of Vincenzo Gonzaga from Mantua for Hungary [Vigilio, *La insalata*, 81–2]
3 Oct.	Giovanni de' Bardi, Florence, to Alfonso II d'Este, Ferrara: Francesco Rasi is on his way to Ferrara, carrying some music of Bardi's [ASMO, Archivio per materia, Musica e Musicisti, b. 1/A]
4 Oct.	Feast day of S. Petronio
15 Oct.	Licence granted to the Gelosi to perform for four months in Milan. The comedians named are Vittoria Piisimi, Nora fiorentina, Aurelia romana, Lutio Fedeli, Flaminio Fedeli, Oratio de' Nobili, Vittoria de' Nobili, Giuseppe Scarpetta, Giovan Battista Trombetti, Carlo Vegi, Bernardino Lombardi, Giulio Vigianti, Emilio Baldovini, Girolamo Salimbeni, Dolfino, Il Bologna, Cupido, and their servants [ASM, Registri delle Cancellerie, serie XXI, no. 23, fos. 119ᵛ–120ʳ]
23 Oct.	Death of Lodovico Gonzaga, Duke of Nevers [S. A. Maffei, *Gli annali di Mantova*, bk. 12, 926]
27 Oct.	Performance of a *commedia de' zanni* in the Pitti theatre in Florence [ASF, Guardaroba medicea, MS 3]
28 Oct.	Baptism of Francesco de' Medici in Florence; godparent is Cardinal Montalto [ASF, Guardaroba medicea, MS 3]
29 Oct.	Performance of *Il gioco della cieca* by Battista Guarini in Florence in honour of the baptism of Francesco de' Medici; poetry adapted by Laura Guidiccioni Lucchesini; music by Emilio de' Cavalieri [ASF, Guardaroba medicea, MS 3]
29 Oct.	Return of Vincenzo Gonzaga to Mantua from Strigonia [Vigilio, *La insalata*, 82]
Nov.	Juan Fernández de Velasco named Governor of Milan
18 Nov.	Licence granted to the Confidenti to perform comedies, tragicomedies, tragedies, pastorals, and other virtuous entertainments above the Sala del Podestà in Bologna. The comedians began performing on 19 Nov. [ASB, Legato, Expeditiones, no. 117, fos. 19ᵛ–20ʳ]

1596

6 Jan.	Vincenzo Gonzaga, Mantua, to Margherita Gonzaga, [Ferrara]: he has heard some comedies performed by the Desiosi with much

	pleasure, and so asks if they might remain in Mantua for carnival [ASMN, Gonzaga, b. 2242]
6 Jan.	Vincenzo Gonzaga, Mantua, to Cesare d'Este [Ferrara]: repeats his request that the Desiosi be permitted to remain in Mantua for carnival [ASMN, Gonzaga, b. 2242]
27 Jan.	Licence granted to Diana Ponti and the Desiosi to perform comedies and other scenic works above the Sala del Podestà in Bologna. The comedians began performing on 12 Feb. [ASB, Legato, Expeditiones, no. 117, fo. 36^v]
15 Feb.	The Desiosi, Bologna, to Ottaviano Cavriani, Mantua: sends a thank you present for the use of some benches [*palchetti*], and offers as a return address the comedian Giuseppe Scarpetta in the via della Mascarela [ASMN, Gonzaga, b. 1165, fos. 524^r–525^v]
28 Feb.	Ash Wednesday
11 Mar.	Tristano Martinelli, Milan, to Ferdinando de' Medici, Florence: requests an account with the Monte di Pietà in Florence [ASF, Mediceo, f. 878, fo. 154^v]
19 Mar.	Birth of Carlo to Christine of Lorraine and Ferdinando de' Medici
14 Apr.	Easter
30 Apr.	Licence granted to Giovanni Gabrielli to perform comedies in the hall above the Pescarie in Bologna [ASB, Legato, Expeditiones, no. 117, fo. 58^r]
1 June	Ferrante Estense Tassoni, Modena, to Cesare d'Este, [Ferrara]: he has granted a licence to the comedians that Cesare wrote him about so they may perform in Modena, and also to Gasparo Villi, and he will not neglect Pietro Paolo Campana [ASMO, Archivio per materie, Comici]
25 Nov.	Alessandro Striggio the younger [Sandrino] posthumously dedicates his father's *Quarto libro de' madrigali à 5 voci* to Alfonso II d'Este
27 Nov.	Isabella Andreini, Bologna, to Vincenzo Gonzaga, Mantua: asks forgiveness for a perceived offence [ASMN, Gonzaga, b. 1165, fos. 623^{r-v}] (Doc. 24)

1597

[unspecified]	Pedrolino, [Modena], to [not stated]: Jacomo Braga has told the Uniti that he would like to serve [ASMO, Archivio per Materie, Comici]
[unspecified]	Pedrolino, Jacomo Braga, and the Uniti, [Modena], to [not stated]: ask the recipient to write a letter to the Conte de Fuentes, requesting a licence for the Uniti to perform in Milan, as soon as they have finished serving in Modena [ASMO, Archivio per materie, Comici]

1 Feb.	Lavinia Andreini enters her novitiate at the monastery of the Madri della Cantelma in Mantua [ASMN, Notarile, notaio Battaleoli Cristoforo, 1627, 26 July]
19 Feb.	Ash Wednesday
28 Mar.	Death of Alfonso II d'Este [Vigilio, *La insalata*, 82–3]
6 Apr.	Easter
19 Apr.	Licence granted to the Desiosi to perform in Bologna [ASB, Legato, Expeditiones, no. 118, fo. 57^r]
7 May	Eleonora de' Medici, Mantua, to Belisario Vinta, Florence: Diana [Ponti] has asked her to intercede with the Grand Duke regarding the *scena* of the last three months of the year [ASF, Mediceo, f. 2942]
12 June	Birth of Filippo to Ferdinando de' Medici and Christine of Lorraine
29 July	Departure of Vincenzo Gonzaga from Mantua for Hungary on his second campaign against the Turks [Vigilio, *La insalata*, 83; ASMN, Gonzaga, b. 388, fos. 394^r–417^v]
29 Oct.	Cesare d'Este, Marceese di Montecchio, named Duke of Ferrara, Modena, Reggio, Carpi, and Rovigo
26 Nov.	Return of Vincenzo Gonzaga to Mantua from Hungary [Vigilio, *La insalata*, 83]
20 Dec.	Departure of Margherita Gonzaga from Ferrara to take up residence in Mantua [M. A. Guarini, *Compendio historico*, i. 317]
29 Dec.	Isabella Andreini, Florence, to Virginio Orsini, [Rome]: asks Orsini to intercede with certain signori for the return of a lottery wheel and record book [Rome, Archivio Capitolino, fondo Orsini, b. 108 (3), no. 754] (Doc. 25)

1598

Reprinting of Isabella Andreini, *La Mirtilla* (Venice, Marc'Antonio Bonibelli)

Wilhelm V abdicates the Duchy of Bavaria; Maximilian named Duke

13 Jan.	Articles of Capitulation signed by Don Cesare d'Este and Clement VIII for the devolution of Ferrara to the papal states. Articles confirmed on 19 Jan. [*Capitolationi fatte tra N. S. Papa Clemente ottavo et il S. D. Cesare da Este*]
14 Jan.	Excommunication of Cesare d'Este by Clement VIII [Vigilio, *La insalata*, 83]
21 Jan.	Performance of a *pastorella in musica* [*La Dafne*] by Ottavio Rinuccini and Jacopo Peri at the home of Jacopo Corsi in Florence [ASF, Guardaroba medicea, MS 3]

28 Jan.	Departure of Cesare d'Este from Ferrara to take up residence in Modena
29 Jan.	Entry of Cardinal Pietro Aldobrandini into Ferrara
4 Feb.	Ash Wednesday
12 Feb.	Death of Lucrezia d'Este
28 Feb.	Hercole Bellone, Milan, to Vincenzo Gonzaga, Mantua: Philip III has given Milan 'un million e meggio d'oro' for the war against Ferrara, and Don Blaseo d'Aragona departed yesterday for Genoa to find Prince Doria to tell him about the recent negotiations [ASMN, Gonzaga, b. 1721]
22 Mar.	Easter
2 May (Sat.)	Treaty of Peace signed in Vervins
3 May	Ercole Trotti has his servant Giacomo murder his wife Anna Guarini [BAV, Ottob. lat. 2774 (*Historia di Ferrara sino all'anno 1600*), folio between fos. 214 and 215]
6 May	Albert of Austria and Isabella of Spain named Governors of the Netherlands
8 May (Fri.)	Clement VIII enters and takes possession of Ferrara [Vigilio, *La insalata*, 83–4]
9 June	Datio Spinola, Bologna, to Vincenzo Gonzaga, Mantua: the comedians he has recalled to Mantua cannot come right away because they are obliged to serve the Archduke Ferdinand of Austria, who arrived in Bologna today and expressed a desire to hear one of the comediennes tomorrow [ASMN, Gonzaga, b. 1166, fos. 317^r–318^v] (Doc. 26)
13 June	Hercole Bellone, Milan, to Aurelio Pomponazzi, Mantua: he seeks to confirm the report of the Pope's entrance into Ferrara [ASMN, Gonzaga, b. 1721]
24 June	Francesco Ongarino, Mantua, to the Mantuan ambassador, Venice: Guarino's pastoral [*Il pastor fido*] was to have been performed today, but some of the machinery broke and so they've postponed the performance [D'Ancona, *Origini del teatro*, ii. 565]
1 July	Hercole Bellone, Milan, to Vincenzo Gonzaga, Mantua: the Condestabile this week has published the banns of marriage of the Prince of Spain and the daughter of Archduke Charles of Austria. The Condestabile has written to Don Guglielmo San Clemente, who will accompany the bride to Trent, where His Excellency will meet her and accompany her to Genoa, or perhaps Spain. To this end, His Excellency requests a list of all the Mantuan titled nobles, province by province [ASMN, Gonzaga, b. 1721]
15 July	Giulio Cesare Stella, Ferrara, to Vincenzo Gonzaga, Mantua: mentions having been to Mantua to see *Il pastor fido*, and says that he has

	invited Cardinal [Pietro] Aldobrandini on Vincenzo's behalf to come see such a noble and gracious spectacle; Aldobrandini has a great desire to see it [ASMN, Gonzaga, b. 1261]
1 Aug.	Annibale Chieppio, Mantua, to Giulio Contarini, Venice: writes to fulfil his promise to tell Contarini when the next performance of *Il pastor fido* would be, and to say that it will occur next Sunday [9 Aug.] in honour of the arrival of the Condestabile [Juan Fernández de Velasco] [D'Ancona, *Origini del teatro*, ii. 565]
8 Aug.	Angelo Ingegneri, Ferrara, dedicates his *Della poesia rappresentativa* to Cesare d'Este
22 Aug.	Archduke Albert and Archduchess Isabella named sovereigns of the Netherlands
6 Sept.	Performance of Battista Guarini, *Il pastor fido* in Mantua [ASMN, Gonzaga, b. 2674]
13 Sept.	Death of King Philip II of Spain; Philip III crowned King of Spain, Portugal, and Sicily
13 Sept.	Angelo Ingegneri, Ferrara, to Vincenzo Gonzaga, Mantua: sends a copy of his *Della poesia rappresentativa e del modo di rappresentare le favole sceniche* to Vincenzo, explaining that he had meant to prescribe theatrical practices elsewhere than in Mantua, where the excellence and splendour of its theatre is already well known [ASMN, Gonzaga, b. 1261]
14 Sept.	Archduke Albert leaves Brussels [Allen, *Philip III*, 19–20]
18 Sept.	Vincenzo Gonzaga, Quignentoli, to Angelo Ingegneri, [Ferrara]: thanks Ingegneri for his treatise, saying that it will truly instruct those in the future of our theatrical practices [ASMN, Gonzaga, b. 2156, fos. 327^r–328^v]
20 Sept.	Don Blaseo d'Aragona, Milan, to Vincenzo Gonzaga, [Mantua]: the engineer Tolomeo has come to look at the set and machinery for the intermedi for the comedy Vincenzo is arranging, and relays a request from the Condestabile for the services of Vincenzo's engineer [Viani] [ASMN, Gonzaga, b. 1722]
4 Oct.	Hercole Bellone, Milan, to Vincenzo Gonzaga, [Mantua]: the Queen [Margherita of Austria] left Graz on the 23rd, and the Archduke is going from Trent to Mantua and eventually to Milan by the via dei Grisoni together with the Queen, who intends to stop in Mantua before going to Ferrara. Plans for the comedy in Milan have been suspended [ASMN, Gonzaga, b. 1721]
5 Oct.	Vincenzo Gonzaga, Mantua, to Fabio Gonzaga, Casale Monferrato: notifies Fabio that the Queen should arrive in Mantua around 18 Oct., and that the Mantuan lieges should be ready from 12 Oct. to accompany her to Ferrara. Further: in Mantua they dress in black

	for the death of the Catholic king [Philip II] [ASMN, Gonzaga, b. 2156, fos. 331^r–332^v]
7 Oct.	Pietro Aldobrandini, Ferrara, to Vincenzo Gonzaga, Mantua: sends notice of the arrival of the new Queen of Spain and says he will give 'the freshest and most secure news' to Vincenzo's agent Cremasco [ASMN, Gonzaga, b. 1261]
14 Oct.	Lodovico Cremasco, Ferrara, to Vincenzo Gonzaga, Mantua: the Cardinal San Giorgio [Cinzio Aldobrandini] left yesterday for Padua [ASMN, Gonzaga, b. 1261]
15 Oct.	Lodovico Cremasco, Ferrara, to Vincenzo Gonzaga, [Mantua]: last night he spoke with the Duke of Sessa, who informed him that the Archduke had not been in Graz, but instead departed from Brussels on 1 Sept.; he went via Spira to Trent, where he met the Queen on the 25th. Together, they are going to Verona, Mantua, and Ferrara, and from there to Milan via the Pò and stopping at Cremona [ASMN, Gonzaga, b. 1261]
Nov.	Records of payments for the building of the new theatre in the palace, called the Salone Margherita in honour of Margherita of Austria [ASM, Registro delle Cancellerie s. XXII, no. 42, fos. 19, 37, 41, 60]
12 Nov. (Thurs.)	Entry of Margherita of Austria into Isola, outside Ferrara [*La felicissima entrata della serenissima Regina di Spagna*]
13 Nov. (Fri.)	Entry of Margherita of Austria into Ferrara [*La felicissima entrata della serenissima Regina di Spagna*]
13 Nov.	Giulio Strozzi, Ferrara, to Annibale Chieppio, Mantua: notifies him that a Jesuit priest has been commissioned to make a German summary of all the acts of *Il pastor fido*, together with its intermedi, so the Queen and the archduchess can follow the action and understand what is being said [ASMN, Gonzaga, b. 1261]
15 Nov. (Sun.)	Wedding by proxy of Margherita of Austria and Philip III of Spain, by the hand of Archduke Albert of Austria; wedding by proxy of Archduke Albert of Austria and the Infanta Isabella of Spain, by the hand of the Spanish ambassador [*La felicissima entrata della serenissima Regina di Spagna*]
16 Nov. (Mon.)	Margherita of Austria hears a concert by the nuns of S. Vito in Ferrara; in the evening, a Latin play, *Giudit et Oloferne*, is performed by the Jesuit fathers [*La felicissima entrata della serenissima Regina di Spagna*]
16 Nov. (Mon.)	Performance of madrigals by Claudio Monteverdi at the home of Antonio Goretti in Ferrara [Artusi, *L'Artusi*, fo. 39^r]
17 Nov.	Girolamo Giglioli, Ferrara, to Cesare d'Este [?Modena]: Livia d'Arco, Laura Peverara, [Ippolito] Fiorini, and Luzzasco Luzzaschi

	made music for Margherita of Austria [ASMO, Carteggio degli ambasciatori, Roma, Giglioli, b. 118]
17 Nov.	Giulio Cesare foresto, Ferrara, to Vincenzo Gonzaga, Mantua: Pietro Aldobrandini will accompany the Queen to Milan, and this evening they will entertain her in Ferrara with a play [*rappresentazione*] [ASMN, Gonzaga, b. 1261]
19 Nov. (Thur.)	Entry of Margherita of Austria into Revere [Persia, *Relatione de' ricevimenti fatti in Mantova*, fo. 2ᵛ]
20 Nov. (Fri.)	Entry of Margherita of Austria into Mantua [Vigilio, *La insalata*, 85–9: Persia, *Relatione de' ricevimenti fatti in Mantova*, fo. 2ᵛ]
22 Nov. (Sun.)	Performance of *Il pastor fido* in Mantua, in the 'usual theatre' of the Castello. Mass was sung in the church of Santa Barbara in the morning, followed by the baptism of Eleonora Anna Maria Gonzaga (for whom Margherita and Archduke Albert of Austria stood as godparents), and then the performance of *Il pastor fido* in the evening, together with intermedi on the story of the marriage of Mercury and Philology [Vigilio, *La insalata*, 89; Persia, *Relatione de' ricevimenti fatti in Mantova*, c. 4ᵛ]
24 Nov.	Departure of Margherita of Austria from Mantua for Milan [Vigilio, *La insalata*, 85–9]
25 Nov.	Ferrante Persia dedicates his *Relatione de' ricevimenti fatti in Mantova* to Annibale Iberti
26 Nov.	Departure of Clement VIII from Ferrara for Rome
30 Nov.	Entry of Margherita of Austria into Milan by the Porta Romana at about the 22nd hour, accompanied by her mother, the Archduchess Maria of Bavaria, Archduke Albert of Austria, papal legate Pietro Aldobrandini, Juan Fernández de Velasco the Governor of Milan, the Duke and Duchess of Candia, the Duke of Humala, M. de Barlamonte the Prince of Orange, the Count of Agamonte, and the Duchess of Frias, all dressed in brown to mourn the death of Philip II of Spain [Negri, *Le gratie d'amore*, 12–13; *Entrata reale fatta in Milano dalla serenissima regina D. Margarita d'Austria*]
2 Dec.	Hercole Bellone, Milan, to Vincenzo Gonzaga, [Mantua]: the Queen entered Milan on the day of S. Andrea [30 Nov.], together with Cardinal Aldobrandini, the Archduchess, and Archduke Albert; yesterday a comedy was performed in private for the Queen by Spanish actors, and after the comedy, one of the tapestries in the antechamber caught fire; further: the Duke of Modena is lodged, incognito, in the house of his agent [ASMN, Gonzaga, b. 1721]
4 Dec.	Account books of the state of Milan record payment to Antonio de Vigliega, *maestro di far comedie*, for comedies performed in the

	palace: D. 100 [ASM, Registro delle Cancellerie, s. XXII, no. 42, fo. 60ᵛ]
9 Dec.	Hercole Bellone, Milan, to Vincenzo Gonzaga, [Mantua]: a third fire broke out in the palace where the Queen is lodged, this time in the apartments of Archduke Albert, which are above the Cancelleria del Maestrato and its archive. Mentions that every night comedies are performed by Spaniards in the palace [ASMN, Gonzaga, b. 1721]
17 Dec.	Scipione Vargnano, Verona, dedicates Isabella Andreini's *Mirtilla* to Melchior Grande
19 Dec.	Luzzascho Luzzaschi, Ferrara, to Vincenzo Gonzaga, Mantua: sends Vincenzo a dozen songs for one, two, and three sopranos, as he had promised the last time Vincenzo was in Ferrara [ASMN, Gonzaga, b. 1261]

1599

	Reprinting of Isabella Andreini, *La Mirtilla* (Verona, Francesco Dalle Donne and Scipione Vargnano)
	Wedding of Livia di Ippolito della Rovere and Duke Francesco Maria II della Rovere of Urbino
5 Jan.	Performance of a *pastorella in musica* by Emilio de' Cavalieri in the Salone delle Statue in Florence [ASF, Guardaroba medicea, MS 3; Solerti, *Musica, ballo e drammatica*, 19–22]
6 Jan.	Performance of a *commedia de' ẓanni* in the Salone delle Statue in Florence [ASF, Guardaroba medicea, MS 3; Settimani, *Diario*, vi. 101, as transcribed by A. Solerti, *Gli albori*, ii. 17–18]
8 Jan.	Birth of Lorenzo to Christine of Lorraine and Ferdinando de' Medici
21 Jan.	Performance of *La Dafne* by Ottavio Rinuccini and Jacopo Peri in Florence in the Salone delle Statue [ASF, Mediceo, Guardaroba, MS 3]
22 Jan.	Philip III and the Infanta Isabella depart Madrid for Valencia to meet Margherita of Austria and Archduke Albert [Allen, *Philip III*, 21]
3 Feb.	Departure of Margherita of Austria from Milan for Spain by the Porta Ticinese, accompanied by her mother and Archduke Albert of Austria [Negri, *Le gratie d'amore*, 14]
4 Feb.	Philip III and the Infanta Isabella arrive in Valencia [Allen, *Philip III*, 21]
24 Feb.	Ash Wednesday
28 Mar.	Francesco Sanchez, Ferrara, to Vincenzo Gonzaga, Mantua: both the Confidenti and the Accesi are in Ferrara, but the Pope will not

Chronology

	tolerate this kind of continuous recreation for very long [ASMN, Gonzaga, b. 1261]
11 Apr.	Easter
18 Apr.	The anonymous author of the *Relatione dell'arrivo in Spagna della serenissima regina d'Austria* concludes his chronicle
29 Apr.	Tristano Martinelli succeeds Filippo Angelone as the purveyor of licences to comedians in Mantua, and he arranges that his children will inherit the position upon his death [ASMN, Decreti, vol. 52, fos. 144^v–145^r]
8 May	Tristano Martinelli, Bologna, to Ferdinando de' Medici, Florence: writes about a scheme introduced to him by Pier Maria Cecchini, which is a secret way to make thousands of scudi without aggravating anyone [ASF, Mediceo, f. 891, fo. 90^r]
19 May	Nicolò Belloni, Milan, to Vincenzo Gonzaga, Mantua: asks, on behalf of Don Blasco d'Aragon and the Condestabile, that the architect [Viani] who served in Mantua for the comedy be granted a licence to come to Milan to work on a pastoral in honour of the entry of Archduke [Albert] and the Infanta [Isabella] [D'Ancona, *Origini del teatro*, ii. 572]
26 May	The Vicario, Milan, to [Vincenzo Gonzaga, Mantua]: a performance of a pastoral [*L'Arminia*] has been proposed, but they do not find in Milan a man with enough experience to work the machinery for the intermedi, and so asks that Antonio Maria Viani [Vianino] be sent [D'Ancona, 'Il teatro mantovano', pt. 4, p. 82]
11 June	Alessandro Guarini, Mantua, to Vincenzo Gonzaga, Mantua: sends a new prologue for *Il pastor fido* [D'Ancona, *Origini del teatro*, ii. 574–5 n.]
13 June (Sun.)	Lavinia Andreini [suor Fulvia] takes final vows at the monastery of the Madri della Cantelma in Mantua [ASMN, Notarile, notaio Battaleoli Cristoforo, 1627, 26 July]
5 July (Mon.)	Entry of the Infanta Isabella of Spain and Archduke Albert of Austria into Milan by the Porta Ticinese [Negri, *Le gratie d'amore*, 14]
9 July (Fri.)	Nicolò Belloni, Milan, to Vincenzo Gonzaga, Mantua: the Archduke and Infanta made their entrance into Milan last Monday and yesterday had an audience with the ambassadors of Savoy, Mantua, and Urbino [D'Ancona, *Origini del teatro*, ii. 573]
13 July (Tues.)	Nicolò Belloni, Milan, to Eleonora de' Medici, Mantua: there was a party last Sunday in the Palazzo; there will be a mascherata next Sunday; the Monday following will be the comedy [19 July]; and the Archduke and Infanta will leave that Wednesday [D'Ancona, 'Il teatro mantovano', pt. 4, pp. 82–3]

16 July (Fri.)	Entry of the papal legate, Cardinal Diatristano, into Milan [Negri, *Le gratie d'amore*, 14]
17 July (Sat.)	Nicolò Belloni, Milan, to Eleonora de' Medici, Mantua: the comedy will be performed on Monday and the Archduke and Infanta will depart on Thursday [D'Ancona, *Origini del teatro*, ii. 573]
18 July (Sun.)	Performance of a triumph in the theatre of the Palazzo Ducale in Milan, during which there is a *ballo* and Pietro Antonio, the Duke of Parma's musician, plays the theorbo and sings verses in praise of the Infanta and Archduke of Austria [Negri, *Le gratie d'amore*, 15–16]
21 July (Wed.)	Performance of [*L'Arminia*] by Giovan Battista Visconte in the Palazzo Ducale in Milan; intermedi by Camillo Schiafenati; architect, Antonio Maria Vianini [cfr. 30 July 1599, 18 Aug. 1599]
24 July (Sat.)	Nicolò Belloni, Milan, to Aurelio Pomponazzi, [Mantua]: he is not sending a description of the comedy performed last Wednesday night because the printed description is very different from reality, and so they have decided to reprint it in a more accurate version, which Belloni will send with the next courier [D'Ancona, 'Il teatro mantovano', pt. 4, p. 83]
30 July	The Vicario, Milan, to [Eleonora Gonzaga, Mantua]: the pastoral [*L'Arminia*] could not be performed until the day before the Infanta's departure, and so Vianini will be delayed in returning to Mantua [D'Ancona, 'Il teatro mantovano', pt. 4, p. 83]
7 Aug.	[not stated] to Vincenzo Gonzaga, Mantua: Vianini returned from Milan, where he made S. 500: S. 200 from the city and S. 300 from the Infanta. The description of the intermedi and apparati has not yet been republished [D'Ancona, *Origini del teatro*, ii. 574]
18 Aug.	Account books of the Chancellery, Milan, record payment of Duc. 150 to Pedrolino [Giovanni Pellesini] and his company for comedies performed before the Infanta [Isabella] and Archduke Albert of Austria [ASM, Registro delle Cancellerie, serie XXII, no. 42, fo. 232^r]
16 Sept.	Licence granted to the Confidenti to perform comedies and other 'opere sceniche' above the Sala del Podestà in Bologna [ASB, Legato, Expeditiones, no. 121, fo. 43^v]
15 Oct.	Vincenzo Gonzaga returns to Mantua from about four months in Spa [Vigilio, *La insalata*, 91]
31 Oct.	Margherita Gonzaga d'Este founds the monastic house of Santa Orsola in Mantua in the contrada delle Borre [Vigilio, *La insalata*, 92]
11 Dec.	Entry of Carlo Emanuele, the Duke of Savoy, in Milan [Cesare Negri, *Le gratie d'amore*, 35]

21 Dec.	Henri IV, Paris, to Tristano Martinelli, [Mantua]: requests the service of Martinelli and his company of comedians [Accesi] at the French court [ASF, Mediceo, f. 896, fo. 300ʳ]

1600

Tristano Martinelli dedicates his *Compositions de rhétorique* to King Henri IV of France
Pietro Aldobrandini named legate of Bologna
Publication of Ottavio Rinuccini, *La Dafne*
Wedding of Maria Anna of Bavaria and Ferdinand II, Habsburg Emperor

2 Jan.	Departure of Carlo Emanuele, the Duke of Savoy, from Milan [Negri, *Le gratie d'amore*, 35]
16 Feb.	Ash Wednesday
27 Feb.	Treaty signed in Paris in the name of Clement VIII, relative to the Treaty of the Peace of Vervins, dated 2 May 1598, to settle the diverse disputes between the King of France and the Duke of Savoy regarding the Marquisate of Saluzzo [ASMN, Gonzaga, b. 45]
18 Mar.	Tristano Martinelli, Mantua, to Belisario Vinta, Florence: Martinelli and his company of comedians are going to France in the service of the king; the Grand Duke already has a copy of Henri IV's letter requesting Martinelli's services, and so all should be well [ASF, Mediceo, f. 896, fo. 299ʳ]
2 Apr.	Easter
15 Apr.	Report of a 'festa in castello' in Rome, during which Isabella Andreini recited *La paẓẓia d'Isabella* in the cortile del maschio [BAV, Urb. lat. 1068, fo. 249B]
7 May	Wedding of Margherita Aldobrandini [niece of Clement VIII] and Ranuccio Farnese, Duke of Parma
19 May	Departure of Maria de' Medici from Florence for Marseilles; Ottavio Rinuccini and 14 musicians are listed in her entourage, but no comedians [ASF, Filze strozziane, serie I, fasc. 27, c. 31ʳ]
17 June	Departure of Eleonora de' Medici from Mantua for Florence to attend the wedding of Maria de' Medici and King Henri IV of France [Vigilio, *La insalata*, 99]
4 Oct.	Entry of papal legate Cardinal Pietro Aldobrandini into Florence [Gaeta Bertelà and Petrioli Tofani, *Le feste e apparati medicei*, 208]
4 Oct.	Ottavio Rinuccini dedicates his *L'Euridice* to Maria de' Medici
5 Oct.	Wedding of Maria de' Medici and Henri IV of France in Florence [Gaeta Bertelà and Petrioli Tofani, *Le feste e apparati medicei*, 208]
6 Oct.	Performance of the comedy *L'Euridice* by Ottavio Rinuccini in the rooms [*stanẓa*] of Emilio [de' Cavalieri] in the Pitti Palace in

	Florence, sponsored by Don Giovanni de' Medici and Sig. Michele Cacini [ASF, Filze strozziane, serie I, fasc. 27, fos. 38ᵛ, 42ʳ]
9 Oct.	Performance of a 'gran commedia' [the tragicomedy *L'amicizia costante* by Vincenzo Panciatichi] in the hall [*salone*] of the Magistrati in Florence, attended by Christine of Lorraine, Vincenzo Gonzaga, and the French ambassadors M. LeGrande and M. de Sillery [ASF, Filze strozziane, serie I, fasc. 27, fo. 42ʳ]
9 Oct.	Performance of *Il rapimento di Cefalo* by Gabriello Chiabrera, with intermedi, in the teatro degli Uffizi in Florence; intermedi by Don Giovanni de' Medici; music by Giulio Caccini [Florence, BNC, Palatino 251; Gaeta Bertelà and Petrioli Tofani, *Le feste e apparati medicei*, 208]
16 Oct.	Pedro Enríquez de Azevedo, Conte de Fuentes, named Governor of Milan
17 Nov.	Eleonora de' Medici, Savona, to Vincenzo Gonzaga, [Mantua]: her return from Marseilles has in two days come as far as Savona, and she intends to rest in Savona for a day [ASMN, Gonzaga, b. 2157]
20 Nov.	Giovan Maria Artusi dedicates his *L'Artusi, overo Delle imperfettioni della moderna musica* to Cardinal Pompeo Arigoni
20 Nov.	Michelangelo Buonarotti dedicates his *Descrizione delle felicissime nozze* to Maria de' Medici
25 Nov.	Fabrizio Caroso dedicates his *La nobiltà di dame* to Ranuccio Farnese and Margherita Aldobrandini in honour of their wedding [Caroso, *Courtly Dance*, 70–3]
19 Dec.	Eleonora de' Medici returns to Mantua from Florence [Vigilio, *La insalata*, 102]
20 Dec.	Giulio Caccini dedicates his *L'Euridice* to Giovanni de' Bardi [Solerti, *Musica, ballo e drammatica*, 25]

1601

	Publication of Erycius Puteanus, *Erycii Puteani epistolarum promulsis*
	Pietro Mattei reports that the Gelosi performed in the presence of the King and Queen of France at the beginning of the year [Mattei, *Historia di Francia*, 227]
4 Jan.	Death of Laura Peverara in Ferrara. She is buried in the church of the Gesuiti [BAV, Barb. lat. 4948 ([Merenda], *Historia della città di Ferrara*), 196, 202]
17 Jan.	Chapters of Peace negotiated in Lyons between the deputies of the King of France and those of the Duke of Savoy, relative to the Treaty of Peace signed in Vervins on 2 May 1598 regarding disputes

	over the Marquisate of Saluzzo and other places [ASMN, Gonzaga, b. 45]
2 Mar.	Hercole Bellone, Milan, to Vincenzo Gonzaga, Mantua: the Conte de Fuentes intends to petition the Duke for his comedians; relays his own support of the Count's request [ASMN, Gonzaga, b. 1725] (Doc. 27)
7 Mar.	Ash Wednesday
7 Mar.	Vincenzo Gonzaga, Mantua, to Nicolò Belloni, Milan: as soon as he had received Belloni's letter, he informed the comedians of the Conte de Fuentes' request; says the comedians left today, expecting to arrive by the following Friday [ASMN, Gonzaga, b. 2157; cfr. 2 Mar. 1601]
11 Mar.	Hercole Bellone, Milan, to Vincenzo Gonzaga, [Mantua]: last evening there was a party at the house of Don Giorgio Manrique, where the Conte de Fuentes asked him to support his request to Vincenzo for the comedians; the count agrees to pay all the comedians' travel expenses, round trip, beginning with the enclosed D. 20 [ASMN, Gonzaga, b. 1725]
12 Mar.	Hercole Bellone, Milan, to Vincenzo Gonzaga, Mantua: reports progress of the treaty negotiations in Pavia; lists the terms named by the Duke of Savoy, the Legate [Cardinal Pietro Aldobrandini], and the Conte de Fuentes for the establishment of peace [ASMN, Gonzaga, b. 1725]
12 Mar.	Hercole Bellone, Milan, to Vincenzo Gonzaga, Mantua: the comedians sent from Mantua arrived last Saturday [10 Mar.] at dinner-time; he had Captain Cardone perform immediately, and he sent word immediately to Pavia to announce their arrival to the Conte de Fuentes [ASMN, Gonzaga, b. 1725] (Doc. 28)
14 Mar.	Hercole Bellone, Milan, to Vincenzo Gonzaga, Mantua: writes on behalf of the Conte de Fuentes to express gratitude for Vincenzo's having sent the comedians [ASMN, Gonzaga, b. 1725]
21 Mar.	Hercole Bellone, Milan, to Vincenzo Gonzaga, Mantua: reports the progress of the treaty negotiations in Pavia [ASMN, Gonzaga, b. 1725]
4 Apr.	Record of payment to Ferrante Cignardi for the 17 musicians of the Milanese *cappella* for 5 months' work: S. 494 s. 60 [ASM, Registri delle Cancellerie, s. XXII, no. 44, fo. 131^v]
22 Apr.	Easter
2 June	Renewed request of a licence for Isabella Andreini, Pedrolino [Giovanni Pellesini], and their company to perform comedies 'in the usual room of the palace' in Milan, 'having been called from Mantua to Milan, and from Milan to Pavia, for the conclave of

	Cardinal Aldobrandini and the Duke of Savoy'; licence granted 12 June [ASM, Autografi, cart. 95, fasc. 19bis] (Doc. 29)
6 June (Wed.)	Francesco Andreini decreed a citizen of Mantua by Vincenzo Gonzaga [ASMN, Notarile, notaio Forti Siniforiano, 1607 June 7]
20 June	Decree of the Conte de Fuentes: comedians, charlatans, herbalists, and those who *montar in banco* must pay a fee to the monastery of the 'virgini spagnoli' for public performances in Milan [ASM, Registri delle Cancellerie, s. XXI, no. 25, fos. 32^v–33^r]
20 June	Licence for the Comici Uniti to perform publicly and privately in Milan [ASM, Registri delle Cancellerie, s. XXI, n. 25, fos. 33^v–34^r] (Doc. 30)
22 June	Entry in the Atti of the Accademia Filarmonica of Verona: Adriano Grandi read to the members of the Academy Isabella Andreini's encomiastic sonnet 'Quel ciel, che sovra il liquefatto Argento', and Cristoforo Ferrari was charged with writing a response [Verona, Archivio dell'Accademia Filarmonica, Registro 41: Atti 1601–1605, fos. 54–5]
29 June	Entry in the Atti of the Accademia Filarmonica of Verona records the sonnet Cristoforo Ferrari wrote in response to Andreini, 'Mentre pien di stupor l'Adige intento'; makes note of the members' surety that Andreini—a member of the Accademia degli Intenti—will publish Ferrari's sonnet in her *Rime* [Verona, Archivio dell'Accademia Filarmonica, Registro 41: Atti 1601–1605, fos. 55–6]
15 July	Lelio Bellone, Milan, to Vincenzo Gonzaga, Mantua: reports progress of the treaty negotiations in Pavia; the Duke of Savoy has sent for the Uniti [ASMN, Gonzaga, b. 1725] (Doc. 31)
15 July	Departure of Vincenzo Gonzaga from Mantua for Croatia to join papal forces on his third campaign against the Turks [Vigilio, *La insalata*, 104–6; Fabbri, *Monteverdi* (trans. Carter), 52 (Fabbri gives the date as 18 July)]
23 July	Departure of Duchess Margherita Gonzaga of Ferrara, with her court, from Ferrara to Casale Monferrato [Vigilio, *La insalata*, 107]
26 Aug.	Guidubaldo Bonarelli gives inaugural address of the Accademia degli Intrepidi in Ferrara [Fabbri, *Monteverdi* (trans. Carter), 57]
27 Aug.	Baptism of Francesco, firstborn son of Claudia Cattaneo and Claudio Monteverdi in Mantua [Fabbri, *Monteverdi* (trans. Carter), 52]
7 Sept.	Lelio Bellone, Milan, to Vincenzo Gonzaga, Mantua: reports of a banquet given in the castle by Sig. Castellano, Conte Don Diego Pimentelli, and other Spanish cavaliers, which was followed by a beautiful comedy and then a *commedia di ballini* [ASMN, Gonzaga, b. 1726]

22 Sept.	Isabella Andreini, Milan, dedicates her *Rime* to Cardinal S. Giorgio, Cinzio Aldobrandini (Doc. 32)
Oct.	Luzzasco Luzzaschi dedicates his *Madrigali per cantare et sonare a uno, e doi, e tre soprani fatti per la musica del già Ser[enissi]mo Duca Alfonso d'Este* to Pietro Aldobrandini
12 Oct.	Isabella Andreini, [Pavia], to the Podestà of Pavia, Milan: requests permission for the third time to perform publicly in Pavia [ASM, Autografi, cart. 94, fasc. 3] (Doc. 33)
20 Oct.	Marie de Boussu, Paris, to the Duke of Mantua, Mantua: Piermaria Cecchini and his company are in Paris [ASMN, Gonzaga, b. 665]
9 Nov.	Erycius Puteanus, Milan, to Isabella Andreini, Pavia: describes Andreini's masculine virtue [*Erycii Puteani epistolarum fercula secunda*, 41] (Doc. 42a)
14 Nov.	Isabella Andreini, Pavia, to Erycius Puteanus, [Milan]: thanks Puteanus for his brief letter [Reulens, *Erycius Puteanus et Isabelle Andreini*, 24–5] (Doc. 42b)
19 Nov.	Isabella Andreini, Pavia, to Erycius Puteanus, [Milan]: thanks Puteanus for his letters and encomiastic poem for publication in Andreini's *Rime* [Reulens, *Erycius Puteanus et Isabelle Andreini*, 25–6] (Doc. 42c)
26 Nov.	Benedetto Pallavicino dies in Mantua [Fabbri, *Monteverdi* (trans. Carter), 52]
28 Nov.	Claudio Monteverdi, Mantua, to Vincenzo Gonzaga, Kanizsa. Claims position of *maestro di cappella* [ASMN, Gonzaga, b. 6, fos. 77–8; Fabbri, *Monteverdi* (trans. Carter), 52; *The Letters of Claudio Monteverdi*, trans. Stevens, 27–30]
28 Nov.	Federico Follino, Mantua, to [not stated]: describes a plan for five *intermedi* entitled *L'assedio di Canissa*, which he wants to stage in conjunction with a comedy performed by the *ebrei* [Faccioli, *Mantova: Le lettere*, 579]
14 Dec.	Erycius Puteanus, Milan, to Isabella Andreini, Pavia: effusively praises Andreini's *Rime* [*Erycii Puteani epistolarum fercula secunda*, 17–19] (Doc. 42d)
18 Dec.	Erycius Puteanus, Milan, to Isabella Andreini, Pavia: refers to letters received from Andreini; excuses his tardy response [Reulens, *Erycius Puteanus et Isabelle Andreini*, 33–4] (Doc. 42e)
19 Dec.	Return of Vincenzo Gonzaga to Mantua from Croatia [Vigilio, *La insalata*, 109]
24 Dec.	Isabella Andreini, Pavia, to Erycius Puteanus, [Milan]: apologizes for not writing; reports the arrival of the Mantuan envoy who has come to escort them back to Mantua [Reulens, *Erycius Puteanus et Isabelle Andreini*, 26] (Doc. 42f)

28 Dec.	Marsilio Torelli, Milan, to Vincenzo Gonzaga, Mantua: the comedians will be late in returning to Mantua because they were waylaid by bandits [ASMN, Gonzaga, b. 1725]

1602

Publication of Isabella Andreini, *Lettere* (Venice, Sebastiano Combi)

Publication of Isabella Andreini, *Myrtille bergere* (Paris, M. Guillemot)

Reprinting of Isabella Andreini, *Mirtilla* (Venice, Lutio Spinola)

4 Feb.	Isabella Andreini, Mantua, to Erycius Puteanus, [Milan]: assures him that she will write more letters [Reulens, *Erycius Puteanus et Isabelle Andreini*, 26–7] (Doc. 42g)
6 Feb.	[Vincenzo Gonzaga, Mantua], to the Conte de Fuentes, [Milan]: the company of Isabella, which is serving in Mantua during carnival, requests permission to perform in the usual room at court in Milan at the customary time [ASMN, Gonzaga, b. 2255]
13 Feb.	Erycius Puteanus, Milan, to Isabella Andreini, Mantua: discourses on love, praise, and virtue [ASM, Autografi, fo. 151ʳ; *Erycii Puteani epistolarum fercula secunda*, 90–1] (Doc. 42h)
14 Feb.	Fat Thursday
15 Feb. (Fri.)	Fortunato Cardi, Mantua, to [not stated]: yesterday, Fat Thursday, in the usual place at court, there was a beautiful barriera, and Monday a comedy with intermedi will be performed, which will be repeated the first day of Lent. [Faccioli, *Mantova: Le lettere*, 579]
20 Feb.	Ash Wednesday
6 Mar.	Isabella Andreini, Mantua, to Erycius Puteanus, [Milan]: effusively thanks him for his recent response [Reulens, *Erycius Puteanus et Isabelle Andreini*, 27–8]
1 Apr.	Isabella Andreini, Mantua, to Erycius Puteanus, [Milan]: expresses distress at his ill health [Reulens, *Erycius Puteanus et Isabelle Andreini*, 28–9] (Doc. 42i)
7 Apr.	Easter
10 Apr. (Wed.)	Claudio Monteverdi decreed a citizen of Mantua by Vincenzo Gonzaga [Fabbri, *Monteverdi* (trans. Carter), 56; *The Letters of Claudio Monteverdi*, trans. Stevens, 29]
21 Apr.	Lelio Bellone, Milan, to [Vincenzo Gonzaga, Mantua]: the same performance space had been promised to two companies of comedians, and the Podestà intends to concede the space to Isabella [Andreini] [ASMN, Gonzaga, b. 1726]
28 Apr.	Lelio Bellone, Milan, to Annibale Chieppio, [Mantua]: Flaminio Scala has arrived [ASMN, Gonzaga, b. 1726]

7 May (Tues.)	Carlo Magni, Mantua, to [not stated]: Archduke Maximilian and the Prince [Francesco Gonzaga] are going to Poggio Reale and are taking the comedians with them. Tomorrow, they will perform a comedy in the court, Sunday a *quintanata* in the piazza S. Pietro, and Monday the *barriera* [Faccioli, *Mantova: Le lettere*, 579–80]
29 May	Lelio Bellone, Milan, to [Vincenzo Gonzaga, Mantua]: the dispute about the room in the palace has been resolved by having Frittellino's company and Isabella's company perform on alternating days [ASMN, Gonzaga, b. 1726]
8 June	Second departure of Vincenzo Gonzaga from Mantua for Spa. A comedy is performed in the palace at Porto at his farewell [Vigilio, *La insalata*, 119–20]
18 June	Isabella Andreini, Brescia, to Erycius Puteanus, [Milan]: breaks the 'long and unpleasant silence' between them; asks for a recommendation to Raffaello Sadeler to engrave Andreini's portrait; her *Rime* will be reprinted as soon as she arrives in Milan [Reulens, *Erycius Puteanus et Isabelle Andreini*, 29] (Doc. 42j)
17 July	Return of Vincenzo Gonzaga to Mantua from Spa [Vigilio, *La insalata*, 122–3]
27 July	Lelio Bellone, Milan, to [Vincenzo Gonzaga, Mantua]: Giovanni de' Medici arrived in Milan late this evening [ASMN, Gonzaga, b. 1726]
1 Aug.	Cesare Negri dedicates his *Le gratie d'amore* to Philip III of Spain
14 Aug. (Wed.)	Lelio Bellone, Milan, to [Vincenzo Gonzaga, Mantua]: there was a comedy the day before yesterday [ASMN, Gonzaga, b. 1726]
14 Aug.	Isabella Andreini, Turin, to Erycius Puteanus, [Milan]: excuses her tardiness in not greeting Puteanus on her arrival [Reulens, *Erycius Puteanus et Isabelle Andreini*, 29–30] (Doc. 42k)
14 Aug.	Licence granted to the Confidenti to perform comedies above the Sala del Podestà in Bologna, paying the usual alms [ASB, Legato, Expeditiones, no. 124, fo. 133^r]
20 Aug.	Vincenzo Gonzaga decrees that Jews in Mantua will wear an orange cord on their hats to distinguish them from Christians [Vigilio, *La insalata*, 125]
9 Sept.	Flaminia Cecchini, Milan, to [Vincenzo Gonzaga, Mantua]: her husband has threatened her with a violent death and asks Vincenzo for a secret licence or letter of conduct so that she may return to Mantua where he can protect her [ASMN, Gonzaga, b. 1726]
25 Nov. (Mon.)	Performance of a comedy in Florence in the Casino of S. Marco, with 80 musicians and actors [ASF, Guardaroba medicea, MS 2]
26 Nov. (Tues.)	Performance of a *commedia di Zanni* in the corridor of the Uffizi in Florence [Gaeta Bertelà and Petrioli Tofani, *Le feste e apparati medicei*, 209]

1 Dec. (Sun.)	Performance of a comedy in the Casino of S. Marco in Florence with 65 musicians and actors [ASF, Guardaroba medicea, MS 2]
2 Dec. (Mon.)	Performance of a *commedia di Zanni* in the corridor of the Uffizi in Florence [Gaeta Bertelà and Petrioli Tofani, *Le feste e apparati medicei*, 209]
5 Dec. (Thurs.)	Performance of *La favola d'Orfeo* by Giulio Caccini 'e le sue donne', together with other musicians, in the Pitti theatre in Florence [ASF, Guardaroba medicea, MS 2]
15 Dec.	Erycius Puteanus, Milan, to Isabella Andreini, Pavia: recommends a young man to study with Andreini [*Eryci Puteani epistolarum fercula secunda*, 117] (Doc. 42l)
18 Dec.	Antonio Maria Spelta, Pavia, signs the dedication to his *La curiosa, et dilettevole aggionta del Sig. Ant. Maria Spelta, cittadino pavese, all'historia sua* (Pavia: Pietro Bartoli, 1602)

1603

Reprinting of Isabella Andreini, *Rime* (Paris, C. de Monstr'oeil)
Publication of Giovan Maria Artusi, *Seconda parte dell'Artusi*
Publication of Erycius Puteanus, *Erycii Puteani epistolarum fercula secunda*

13 Jan.	Tristano Martinelli completes payment to Silvio Paganini for a villa in Castelbelforte [ASMN, Gonzaga, notaio Gaiardi Antonio, 1603 Jan. 13]
12 Feb.	Ash Wednesday
20 Feb.	Baptism of Leonora Camilla Monteverdi in Mantua [Fabbri, *Monteverdi* (trans. Carter), 56]
1 Mar.	Claudio Monteverdi dedicates his *Il quarto libro de madrigali a cinque voci* to the Academici Intrepidi of Ferrara
16 Mar.	Tristano Martinelli writes his last will and testament [ASMN, Gonzaga, notaio Forti Siniforiano, 1603 Mar. 16]
20 Mar.	Isabella Andreini, Paris, dedicates her *Rime d'Isabella Andreini . . . seconda parte* to Sebastiano Zametti (Doc. 34)
30 Mar.	Easter
13 Apr.	Henri IV, Fontainebleau, to M. de Villeroy, [Paris]: asks Villeroy to give permission to Isabella and her company to return to Italy, and to facilitate their travel [Henri IV, *Correspondance générale*, vii. 176; Baschet, *Les Comédiens italiens*, 145]
[Apr.]	Maria de' Medici, [Paris], to Eleonora de' Medici, Mantua: informs her sister that Isabella Andreini is returning to Italy and relates her complete contentment with the actress [Paris, BNF, Fonds des 500 Colbert, Registres du cabinet de la Reine Marie de Médicis, MS 86, fo. 166; Baschet, *Les Comédiens italiens*, 145]

[Apr.]	Maria de' Medici, [Paris], to Ferdinando de' Medici, Florence: informs her uncle that Isabella Andreini is returning to Italy and recommends that she receive every good grace [Paris, BNF, Fonds des 500 Colbert, Registres du cabinet de la Reine Marie de Médicis, MS 86, fo. 166; Baschet, *Les Comédiens italiens*, 145]
17 May	Tristano Martinelli rewrites his last will and testament [ASMN, Gonzaga, notaio Forti Siniforiano, 1604 May 17]
25 June	Performance of a comedy in Florence in the casino of Don Antonio [ASF, Guardaroba medicea, MS 2]
1 July	Chapters of confederation between the Republic of Venice and the three Swiss cantons [ASMN, Gonzaga, b. 45]
26 Aug.	Isabella Andreini, Paris, to Belisario Vinta, Florence: writes under orders from Maria de' Medici to again request access to her funds in the Monte di Pietà in Florence; she has received no word on this matter since the letter written by Sig. Cioli last 14 Mar. [ASF, Mediceo, f. 917, fos. 777^{r-v}, 791^{r-v}] (Doc. 35)
8 Oct.	Payment to Isabella Andreini, Giovan Paolo Pellesini, Giovan Paolo Fabbri, and Giovan Maria Antonazoni by Henri IV: 1500 livres tournois [BNF, Généalogies d'Hozier, pièce originale 59, 'Andriny']
21 Oct.	Margherita Gonzaga enters the convent of S. Orsola in Mantua, which she had founded
7 Dec.	Isabella Andreini, Paris, to Belisario Vinta, Florence: his letter dated 8 Nov. arrived in Paris on the day of S. Catherine [25 Nov.], while she was in Fontainebleau for 36 days, entertaining either one or the other of their majesties and earning D. 200 per month. When they returned to Paris, she immediately showed Vinta's letter to Maria de' Medici, who was pleased, as was Henri IV [ASF, Mediceo, f. 920, fos. 513^{r-v}, 555^{r-v}] (Doc. 36)

1604

3 Mar.	Ash Wednesday
22 Mar.	Isabella Andreini dedicates a reprinting of her *Rime* to Cinzio Aldobrandini (Milan, Girolamo Bordone and Pietromartire Locarni)
4 Apr.	Giovan Battista Gondi, Paris, to the Duke of Mantua, Mantua: Girolamo Gondi has died [ASMN, Gonzaga, b. 665]
18 Apr.	Easter
23 Apr.	Entry of Archduke Maximilian of Austria into Florence [Gaeta Bertelà and Petrioli Tofani, *Le feste e apparati medicei*, 210]
4 May	Death of Claudio Merulo in Parma, where he had been the organist at the Chiesa della Steccata, under the patronage of the Farnese, since 1586 [Balestrieri, *Feste e spettacoli alla corte dei Farnese*, 22]

10 May	Baptism of Massimiliano Giacomo Monteverdi in Mantua [Fabbri, *Monteverdi* (trans. Carter), 56]
28 May	Licence granted to Giovan Battista Andreini and the Fedeli and Confidenti to perform comedies in Bologna, beginning on the day of S. Petronio [4 Oct.] and continuing through the winter. The comedians are to pay one scudo per day in alms to the impoverished of the city. [ASB, Legato, Expeditiones, n. 126, fo. 29^r; cfr. 4 Oct. 1604]
4 June	Birth of Claudia to Christine of Lorraine and Ferdinando de' Medici
10 June	Death of Isabella Andreini, buried in the church of St Croix in Lyons
24 Aug.	Alessandro Senesi, Bologna, to Belisario Vinta, Florence: he has heard from Francesco Gonzaga's barber that the negotiations for the marriage with Savoy are concluded [ASF, Mediceo, f. 4043]
Aug. 28	Alessandro Senesi, Bologna, to Belisario Vinta, Florence: the comedian Frittellino, who has come from Casale Monferrato, says the marriage [negotiations] with Savoy are concluded, and that he has orders to return there soon to perform the comedies in Turin [ASF, Mediceo, f. 4043]
29 Aug.	Alessandro Senesi, Bologna, to Belisario Vinta, Florence: Vincenzo Gonzaga has returned to Mantua following the marriage negotiations with Savoy [ASF, Mediceo, f. 4043]
23 Oct.	Entry of the Duke of Parma into Florence [Gaeta Bertelà and Petrioli Tofani, *Le feste e apparati medicei*, 210]
26 Oct.	Performance of Ottavio Rinuccini's *La Dafne* in Florence in the Palazzo Pitti [*La Dafne d'Ottavio Rinuccini*]

1605

	Publication of Isabella Andreini, *Rime ... parte seconda* (Milan, Girolamo Bordone and Pietromartire Locarni)
	Reprinting of Isabella Andreini, *Rime* (Milan, Girolamo Bordone and Pietromartire Locarni)
	Reprinting of Isabella Andreini, *Rime* (Paris, C. de Monstr'oeil)
	Reprinting of Isabella Andreini, *La Mirtilla* (Milan, Girolamo Bordone and Pietromartire Locarni)
23 Feb.	Ash Wednesday
10 Apr.	Easter
10 Apr.	Alessandro de' Medici (Leone XI) elected Pope
29 May	Camillo Borghese (Paolo V) elected Pope
15 Oct.	Giovan Paolo Agucchia, Turin, to Vincenzo Gonzaga, [Mantua]:

Chronology

	Giovan Battista and Virginia Andreini are joining the company of the Duke of Mantua [ASMN, Gonzaga, b. 734]
25 Dec.	Death of Doge Marino Grimani

1606

[unspecified]	Fulvia Andreini listed among the Madri della Cantelma in Mantua [ASMN, Corporazioni religiose soppresse, vol. 273]
carnival	Performance of the *balletto Dario e Alessandro* by Ferdinando Gonzaga; music by Ferdinando Gonzaga [Solerti, *Gli albori*, i. 68]
10 Jan.	Leonardo Donà elected Doge of Venice
8 Feb.	Ash Wednesday
26 Mar.	Easter
18 May	Tristano Martinelli writes codicils to his last will and testament [ASMN, Notarile, notaio Forti Siniforiano, 1606 May 18]
20 June	Giovan Battista Andreini, Milan, signs the dedication to the readers of *Lo sfortunato poeta*
1 July	Giovan Battista Andreini, Milan, dedicates *Il pianto d'Apollo, rime funebre in morte d'Isabella Andreini* to Eleonora Gonzaga, Duchess of Mantua (Doc. 37)
23 July	Giovan Battista Andreini, Milan, dedicates his *La Florinda* to Pietro Enríquez de Azevedo, the Count of Fuentes
3 Oct.	Licence granted to Florinda comica [Virginia Ramponi Andreini] to run a lottery in Milan for three months beginning 1 Nov., for the sum of L. imp. 8,000
21 Oct.	Annibale Chieppio, Mantova, to Vincenzo Gonzaga, Mantova: Giovan Battista Andreini and Virginia Ramponi Andreini are in Mantua [ASMN, Gonzaga, b. 2704, fasc. 1, lett. 64]
30 Dec.	Hercole Udine, Venice, to Francesco IV Gonzaga, [Mantua]: his negotiations to free Domenico Andreini are proceeding with difficulty [ASMN, Gonzaga, b. 1538]
	Wedding of Margherita Gonzaga and Henri of Lorraine [*Comici dell'arte: corrispondenze*, i. 96]

1607

	Francesco Andreini dedicates his *Le bravure del Capitano Spavento* (Venice, Vincenzo Somasco) to Amedeo of Savoy
	Reprinting of Isabella Andreini, *Lettere* (Venice, Marc'Antonio Zaltieri)
4 Jan.	Carlo Rossi, Mantua, to [Vincenzo Gonzaga, Casale Monferrato]: Giovan Battista Andreini is in Mantua [ASMN, Gonzaga, b. 2709, fasc. 5, lett. 1]
23 Feb.	Francesco Gonzaga, Mantua, to Ferdinando Gonzaga, Pisa: he is

(Fri.)	satisfied with Giovan Gualberto Magli's singing for the *favola* [*Orfeo*] [Solerti, *Gli albori*, i. 68–9]
23 Feb.	Carlo Magni, Mantua, to Giovanni Magno, Rome: the comedy was performed yesterday in the usual theatre and with the customary magnificence; tomorrow evening there will be a performance [of *Orfeo*] in the room of the apartment that the Duchess of Ferrara enjoyed, for which all the interlocutors will speak in music [Solerti, *Gli albori*, i. 69]
24 Feb. (Sat.)	Performance of *Orfeo* by Alessandro Striggio in the Palazzo Ducale in Mantua; music by Claudio Monteverdi
28 Feb.	Ash Wednesday
14 Mar.	Isabella [*sic*: Francesco] Andreini dedicates the *Lettere d'Isabella Andreini* (Venice, Marc'Antonio Zaltieri) to Carlo Emanuele, the Duke of Savoy. Poems lamenting Andreini's death appear in the front matter
15 Apr.	Easter
7 June	Francesco Andreini buys a villa at Castelbelforte from Veronica Toresana de Bugatis de Bellinis [ASMN, Notarile, Forti Siniforiano, 1607 June 7]
9 June	Francesco Andreini writes his last will and testament [ASMN, Notarile, Forti Siniforiano, 1607 June 9]
10 Sept.	Death of Luzzasco Luzzaschi, buried in the church of S. Domenico [S. Paolo] in Ferrara
23 Oct.	Ottavio Rinuccini arrives in Mantua [Fabbri, *Monteverdi* (trans. Carter), 78]
24 Dec.	Ferdinando Gonzaga made cardinal

1608

	Publication of Francesco Andreini, *Les Bravachieries du Capitaine Spavente*, ed. Jacques de Fonteny (Paris, Le Clerc)
27 Feb.	Carlo Rossi, Mantua, to Vincenzo Gonzaga: describes the meeting the previous day with Eleonora de' Medici, Ottavio Rinuccini, Claudio Monteverdi, Antonio Maria Viani, and Federico Follino [ASMN, Gonzaga, b. 2712, fasc. 20, lett. 3]
7 Mar.	Death of Caterina Martinelli [Fabbri, *Monteverdi* (trans. Carter), 82]
10 Mar.	Carlo Rossi, Mantua, to Vincenzo Gonzaga: the performance of *Arianna* is in confusion because a replacement for Caterina Martinelli has not yet been found [ASMN, Gonzaga, b. 2712, fasc. 20, lett. 7]
14 Mar.	Carlo Rossi, Mantua, to Vincenzo Gonzaga: Virginia Andreini has been hired to sing Arianna [ASMN, Gonzaga, b. 2712, fasc. 20, lett. 8]

18 Mar.	Antonio Costantini, Mantua, to [not stated]: Vincenzo Gonzaga has suggested La Florinda to replace Caterina Martinelli in *Arianna* [Fabbri, *Monteverdi* (trans. Carter), 83]
24 May	Margherita of Savoy arrives in Mantua [Follino, *Compendio*, 7–19]
28 May	Performance by Virginia Andreini of *Arianna* by Ottavio Rinuccini and Claudio Monteverdi in the Sala degli Specchi in the Palazzo Ducale in Mantua [ASMN, Gonzaga, b. 2712, fasc. 4, lett. 7]
29 May	Estense ambassador, Mantua, to [not stated]: describes the performances of *Arianna* and the *Il ballo delle ingrate*, writing that the actress who sang Arianna was the best of everyone [Fabbri, *Monteverdi* (trans. Carter), 92]
2 June	Performance by the Fedeli of *L'idropica* by Battista Guarini; intermedi by Gabriello Chiabrera; sets by Antonio Maria Viani [Follino, *Compendio*, 72–99]
4 June	Performance of the *Il ballo delle ingrate* by Ottavio Rinuccini in the sala delle commedie in the Palazzo Ducale in Mantua [Follino, *Compendio*, 124–34]
5 June	Performance of the *Il ballo d'Ifigenia* by Alessandro Striggio in the sala delle commedie in the Palazzo Ducale in Mantua [Follino, *Compendio*, 142–9]
1 July	Federico Follino, Mantua, dedicates his *Compendio* to Margherita Gonzaga
20 Oct.	Marco da Gagliano, Florence, dedicates his *Dafne* to Vincenzo Gonzaga

1609

Reprinting of Francesco Andreini, *Le bravure del Capitano Spavento* (Venice, Vincenzo Somasco)

7 Feb.	Death of Ferdinando de' Medici

1610

Reprinting of Isabella Andreini, *Lettere* (Venice, Marco'Antonio Zaltieri)

1611

Death of Eleonora de' Medici
Publication of Francesco Andreini, *L'ingannata Proserpina* (Venice, Giacomo Antonio Somasco)
Publication of Francesco Andreini, *L'altere≠a di Narciso* (Venice, Giacomo Antonio Somasco)
Publication of Flaminio Scala, *Il teatro delle favole rappresentative* (Venice, Giovan Battista Pulciani); preface by Francesco Andreini

	Publication of Giovan Battista Andreini, *La turca* (Casale, Pantaleone Goffi)
29 Apr.	Virginia Andreini performs *Il rapimento di Proserpina* by Ercole Marliani and Giulio Cesare Monteverdi in Casale [*Breve descrittione delle feste*]

1612

	Publication of Francesco Andreini, *Ragionamenti fantastici* (Venice, Giacomo Antonio Somasco)
	Reprinting of Isabella Andreini, *Lettere* (Venice, Sebastiano Combi)
18 Feb.	Death of Vincenzo Gonzaga
26 Sept.	Giovan Battista Andreini dedicates his *Lo schiavetto* (Milan, Pandolfo Malatesta) to Count Ercole Pepoli
6 Oct.	Pandolfo Malatesta dedicates Giovan Battista Andreini's *Lo schiavetto* to Alessandro Striggio
22 Dec.	Death of Francesco Gonzaga

1614

25 Nov.	Vincenzo Somasco, Venice, dedicates Francesco Andreini's *Nuova aggiunta alle Bravure del Capitano Spavento* to Gregorio de' Monti

1615

Wedding of Ferdinando Gonzaga and Camilla Faa

1616

Reprinting of Isabella Andreini, *La Mirtilla* (Venice, D. Imberti)

1617

	Wedding of Ferdinando Gonzaga and Caterina de' Medici
	Publication of Isabella Andreini, *Fragmenti di alcune scritture*, edited by Francesco Andreini and Flaminio Scala (Venice, Giovan Battista Combi)
	Reprinting of Isabella Andreini, *Lettere* (Venice, Sebastiano Combi)
12 Dec.	Francesco Andreini, Mantua, dedicates his *La seconda parte delle Bravure del Capitano Spavento* (Venice, Vincenzo Somasco) to Giovanni de' Medici

1620

Reprinting of Isabella Andreini, *Fragmenti di alcune scritture* (Venice, Giovan Battista Combi)

1621

Publication of Isabella Andreini, *Lettere . . . e Fragmenti di alcune scritture* (Turin, Giovan Domenico Turino)

1623

25 Apr. Domenico Bruni dedicates his *Fatiche comiche* (Paris, Nicolò Callemont) to Don Cesare di Vandome (Doc. 39)

1624

1 June Francesco Andreini, under the pseudonym Evangelista Deuchino, dedicates the definitive edition of his *Le bravure del Capitano Spavento* (Venice, Giacomo Antonio Somasco) to Altobello Bon

21 Aug. Death of Francesco Andreini in Mantua [ASMN, Gonzaga, *Registro Necrologico* 30, 1624 agosto 21]

Documents

Unless otherwise indicated, spellings and abbreviations are left as they appear in the source. Letters indicated by tilde or crossbar are given in brackets.

1. ASMN, Gonzaga, b. 2577. Luigi Rogna, Mantua, to Pietro Martire Cornacchia, Mantua, 1 July 1567
2. ASMN, Gonzaga, b. 2577, fos. 177^v–179^r. Luigi Rogna, Mantua, to Pietro Martire Cornacchia, Mantua, 6 July 1567
3. Tomaso Porcacchi, *Le attioni d'Arrigo terzo Re di Francia e di Polonia* (Venice: Giorgio Angelieri, 1574)
4. Cornelio Frangipani, *Tragedia* (Venice: Domenico Farri, 1574)
5. ASM, Autografi, cart. 94, fasc. 42. Giovanni Arcimboldi and Marcello Rincio, Milan, to the Governor of Milan, 28 May 1575
6. ASMN, Decreti, libro 49, fo. 70^v, 14 March 1580
7. ASMO, Archivio per Materie, Comici. Ettore Tron, [Venice], to Alfonso II d'Este, [Ferrara], 4 January 1581
8. ASB, Demaniale 220/2127. Memoriale di notizie attinenti all'Archivio delle RR MM del Corpus Domini (Milan, 1700)
9. ASMN, Gonzaga, b. 1256. Francesco Andreini, Ferrara, to Vincenzo Gonzaga, Mantua, 13 April 1583
10. ASMN, Gonzaga, b. 1257, fos. 2^r–3^v. The Comici Uniti, Ferrara, to Vincenzo Gonzaga, Mantua, 3 April 1584
11. ASMN, Gonzaga, b. 1514. Battista Guarini, Padua, to Vincenzo Gonzaga, [Mantua], 7 April 1584
12. ASMN, Gonzaga, b. 1162, fos. 692^r–693^v. Pirro Malvezzi, Bologna, to Vincenzo Gonzaga, Mantua, 2 September 1585
13. ASMN, Gonzaga, b. 1162, fos. 743^r–744^v. Lodovico de' Bianchi, Bologna, to Vincenzo Gonzaga, Mantua, 16 December 1585
14. ASMN, Gonzaga, Autografi, b. 10. Isabella Andreini, Florence, to Eleonora de' Medici, Mantua, 14 January 1587
15. ASMN, Gonzaga, Autografi, b. 10. Isabella Andreini, Florence, to Eleonora de' Medici, Mantua, 5 April 1587
16. Isabella Andreini, *Mirtilla* (Verona: Girolamo Discepolo, 1588), Dedication, 24 February 1588
17. ASMN, Gonzaga, b. 2642, fos. 170^r–171^v. Ottavio Lambardesco, Mantua, to Marcello Donati, Florence, 1 July 1588
18. ASF, Mediceo, f. 829. Isabella Andreini, Bologna, to Belisario Vinta, Florence, 27 September 1591

19. ASB, Legato, Expeditiones, no. 114, fo. 32^v, 14 November 1593
20. ASF, Dogana di Firenze, serie antica, f. 223, supp. 318. Francesco Biffoli, Florence, to Ferdinando de' Medici, Florence, 30 March 1594
21. ASB, Legato, Expeditiones, no. 114, fo. 71^v, 14 April 1594
22. Gentile Pagani, *Del teatro in Milano avanti il 1598*, as cited in Alessandro D'Ancona, 'Il teatro mantovano', iii. 333–4, 13 October 1594
23. ASB, Legato, Expeditiones, no. 115, fo. 73^v, 16 June 1595
24. ASMN, Gonzaga, b. 1165, fo. 623^{r-v}. Isabella Andreini, Bologna, to Vincenzo Gonzaga, Mantua, 27 November 1596
25. Rome, Archivio Capitolino, fondo Orsini, b. 108 (3), no. 754. Isabella Andreini, Florence, to Virginio Orsini, [Rome], 29 December 1597
26. ASMN, Gonzaga, b. 1166, fos. 317^r–318^v. Datio Spinola, Bologna, to Vincenzo Gonzaga, Mantua, 9 June 1598
27. ASMN, Gonzaga, b. 1725. Ercole Bellone, Milan, to Vincenzo Gonzaga, Mantua, 2 March 1601
28. ASMN, Gonzaga, b. 1725. Ercole Bellone, Milan, to Vincenzo Gonzaga, Mantua, 12 March 1601
29. ASMN, Autografi, cart. 95, fasc. 19bis, 2 June 1601
30. ASM, Registri delle Cancellerie, s. XXI, no. 25, 20 June 1601
31. ASMN, Gonzaga, b. 1725. Lelio Bellone, Milan, to Vincenzo Gonzaga, Mantua, 15 July 1601
32. Isabella Andreini, *Rime* (Milan: Girolamo Bordone & Pietromartire Locarni, 1601), Dedication, 22 September 1601
33. ASM, Autografi, cart. 94, fasc. 3. Memoriale d'Isabella Andreini, 12 October 1601
34. Isabella Andreini, *Rime [parte seconda]* (Paris: Claudio de Monstr'oeil, 1603), Dedication, 20 March 1603
35. ASF, Mediceo, f. 917, fos. 777^{r-v}, 791^v. Isabella Andreini, Paris, to Belisario Vinta, Florence, 26 August 1603
36. ASF, Mediceo, f. 920, fos. 513^r, 555^v. Isabella Andreini, Paris, to Belisario Vinta, Florence, 7 December 1603
37. Giovan Battista Andreini, *Pianto d'Apollo* (Milan: Girolamo Bordoni & Pietromartire Locarni, 1606), Dedication, 1 July 1606
38. Isabella Andreini, *Lettere* [ed. Francesco Andreini] (Venice: Sebastiano Combi, 1612), Dedication, 14 March 1607
39. Domenico Bruni, *Fatiche comiche* (Paris: Nicolò Callemont, 1623), Prologo in laude della musica
40. Comparison of Isabella Andreini, *Mirtilla*, Act III, scene v, lines 1721–97 with Virgil, *Eclogues*, Eclogue 3, lines 55–111
41. Isabella Andreini, poems for Christine of Lorraine: 'Quando scendeste ad'illustrare il mondo' and 'D'amor l'aria sfavilla'
42. Correspondence between Isabella Andreini and Erycius Puteanus

1. ASMN, Gonzaga, b. 2577 [cfr. D'Ancona, 'Il teatro mantovano', pt. 2, pp. 12–13]
 1 July 1567. Luigi Rogna, Mantua, to Pietro Martire Cornacchia, Mantua

Hoggi si sono fatte due comedie a concorrenza: una nel luogo solito, per la sig.ra Flaminia et Pantalone, che si sono accompagnati colla sig.ra Angela, quella che salta così bene; l'altra dal Purgo, in casa del Lanzino, per quella sig.ra Vincenza, che ama il sig. Federigo da Gazuolo. L'una et l'altra Compagnia ha avuto udienza grande et concorso di persone: ma la Flaminia più nobiltà, et ha fatto la tragedia di Didone mutata in Tragicomedia, che è riuscita assai bene. Gli altri, per quel che si dice, sono riusciti assai goffi. Andranno seguitando costoro a concorrenza, et con un certo non so che d'invidia, sforzandosi a fare di aver maggior concorso, a guisa dei Letori, che nelle città de' studi si industriano di aver più numero di scolari.

2. ASMN, Gonzaga, b. 2577, fos. 177^v–179^r
 6 July 1567. Luigi Rogna, Mantua, to Pietro Martire Cornacchia, Mantua

Non hieri l'altro la Flaminia era comendata per certi lamenti che fece in una tragedia che recitorno dalla sua banda, cavata da quella novella dell'Ariosto, che tratta di quel Marganorre, al figliuolo sposo del quale, la sposa, ch'era la Flaminia, sopra il corpo del primo suo sposo, poco dianzi amazzato in scena, per vendetta diede a bere il veleno dopo haverne bevuto anch'essa, onde l'uno et l'altro morì sopra quel corpo, et il padre, che perciò voleva uccidere tutte le donne, fu dalle donne lapidato et morto. La Vincenza, all'incontro, era lodata per la musica, per la vaghezza degli habiti et per altro, benchè il soggetto della sua tragedia non fosse e non riuscisse così bello. Heri poi, a concorrenza e per intermedii, in quella della Vincenza si fece comparire Cupido, che liberò Clori, nimpha già convertita in albero. Si vidde Giove che con una folgore d'alto ruinò la torre d'un gigante, il quale havea imprigionati alcuni pastori; si fece un sacrificio: Cadmo seminò i denti, vidde a nascer et a combatter quelli huomini armati: hebbe visibilmente le risposte da Febo, et poi da Pallade armata, et in fine cominciò a edificar la città. La Flaminia poi, oltre l'havere apparato benissimo quel luogo de corami dorati, et haver trovati abiti bellissimi da nimpha, et fatto venire a Mantova quelle selve, monti, prati, fiumi et fonti d'Arcadia, per intermedi della Favola introdusse Satiri, et poi certi maghi, et fece alcune moresche, a tal che hora altro non si fa nè d'altro si parla, che di costoro. Chi lauda la gratia d'una, chi estolle l'ingegno dell'altra: et così si passa il tempo a Mantova.

3. Tomaso Porcacchi, *Le attioni d'Arrigo terzo Re di Francia e di Polonia* (Venice: Giorgio Angelieri, 1574)

La quale schiera, sapete quanto suole esser rara nel recitar tragedie, comedie et altri componimenti scenici, essendovi Simon Bolognese rarissimo in rappresentar la persona d'un facchino Bergamasco ma piu raro nell'argutie et nell'incentioni spiritose, che si dilettano et s'insegnano. Giulio Pasquati sa incontrafar quello che domandano 'Il Magnifico' nella qual rappresentatione sto in dubio qual sia maggiore in lui o la gratia o l'acutezza de' caprici spiegati a tempo et sententiosamente. Evvi anche Rinaldo che vale infinitamente nell'accomodar novi argomenti et in sapergli ridurre alla scena trajica e comica con habiti con fogge e con rappresentationi nobili. Cosi vi potrei discorrer di tutti a un per uno et massimamente della donna che è unica.... Questi comici Gelosi dunque rappresentarono al Re una molto grata et gratiosa trajicomedia, della qual senti mirabil piacere; et ho inteso che gli recitarono anche la domenica sera ch'ei fu venuto una comedia; di che il Re mostrò d'allegrarsi molto.

4. Cornelio Frangipani, *Tragedia* (Venice: Domenico Farri, 1574)

Questa mia Tragedia fu recitata con quella maniera, che si ha più ridotto alla forma de gli antichi: tutti li recitanti hanno cantato in suavissimi concenti, quando soli, quando accompagnati, e infin il coro di Mercurio era di sonatori, che avevano quanti vari istrumenti che si sonarono giamai. Li trombetti introducevano li Dei in scena, la qual era istituita con la macchina tragica, ma non si è potuto ordinar per il gran tumulto di persone che quivi era. Non si è potuto imitare l'antichità nelle composizioni musicali, avendole fatte il S. Claudio Merulo, che a tal grado non devono giamai esser giunti li antichi come a quel del Monsignor Gioseffo Zarlino, il qual è stato occupato nelle musiche che hanno incontrato il Re nel Bucintoro, che sono state alcuni miei versi latini, e della Chiesa di S. Marco, & è stato ordinatore di quelle che continuamente si sono fatte ad instanzia di sua Maestà.

5. ASM, Autografi, cart. 94, fasc. 42

All Ill.mo et Ecc.mo S.r el S.r Marchese d'Aiamonte governatore del stato [di Mila]no p[er] sua M.ta Cath.ca et [*cut off with the sealing tape*] oss.mo—
[*different hand*] al primo di Giugno 75
Si concede à beneplacito di sua Ecc.a, con che si osservino i capitoli inclusi.
Guls:o
die iii Giugno 1575

Ill.mo et Ex.mo Principe
Sopra il memoriale datto a V. Ecc.a dalli comici gelosi quali domandano licenza di puoter' recitare comedie in questa città de Milano; V. Ecc.a ha decretato che noi debbiamo veder le comedie et dir' il parere n'ro; Per tanto s'espone a v'ra Ecc.a che gia cinqui anni passati sie sempre dato licenza a comedianti de recitare comedie in questa città, et anchora questo anno passato per v'ra ecc.a Però per prohibire alcune coruttelle et inconvenienti seguiti per lo adietro in le comedie con tutta v'ra diligenza havemo compilato alcuni ordini quali se havessero da obser-

vare d'essi comedianti nel recitare le loro comedie quali ordini gli sono stati inthimati di nostro ordine ogn'anno nel principio del suo recitare de quali se ne manda copia inclusa, a V. ecc.a Et in bona parte si contengono nella l'ra a voi scritta dall'Ill.mo et Ecc.mo S.r comendator Maggior' sotto il di 18 giugno 1572; Per tanto dicemo, a V. Ecc.a che per dar' tratenimento alli piu otiosi che in peggio no[n] spendono il tempo, si puo dar licenza a detti comedianti come ancora noi ne havemo hauto parere per il detto rispetto da Theologi con far' che osservino gli inclusi ordini, ancora questi doi se cosi, V. Ecc.a comandara.

P.a che questi essi comedianti no[n] possino recitare comedie in giorno di festa comandata, ne di vigilia de tal festa comandata, ne in septa feria.

2.o che per levar' alcuni inconvenienti quali seguono mentre si recita la comedia che niuno oltra li comedianti o, vero quelli che sono al servitio della comedia possi andare overo dimorare sopra il palco ch'essi comedianti ne dentro delle cortine, ne fuori sotto le penne medeme ad essi comedianti contenute nelli inclusi ordini da esser applicate come in essi, Comandando anchora questo ultimo capitolo specialmente con la auctorità de v'ra Ecc.a accio sia piu intieramente osservato, et perche v. Ecc.a ne comanda che vediamo prima le comedie gli dicemo che le sogliamo vedere de giorno in giorno inanzi si recitava et signarle conforme a la vostra deputatione, Pero nel tutto se remetiamo all'Infalibile iudicio di V.Ecc.a alla qual humilmente se Racomandiamo Da mil[a]no alli 28 magio 1575

D. V. Ecc.a
Humilissimi servitori
Gio. Arcimboldi
M. Marcello Rincio

P.a ch'essi comedianti, et ciascuno di loro nelle sue comedie no[n] puossino usar' in alcuno modo vestiti pertinenti a sacerdoti, o, altre persone sacre ne paramenti di chiesa di sorte alcuna, ne meno alchuna sorte de vesti che habbi simiglianza alle sopradette

2.o no[n] possino parlar' in modo alchuno della sacra scritura, et sogetti in quella contenuti, o, vero de cose pertinente alla Religione et stato ecclesiastico, ne usar' parolle particolari a s.mi sacramenti della chiesa o, vero dire parolle, o, sogetti de quali soferire si puotesse sinistra interpretatione c[ontr]a le cose della S.ta fede Catholica, o, che potessero indur' qualche superstitione a simplici ascoltanti ne incantesimi ne altre

3.o, no[n] possino dir' parolla alcuna o, far' atti alcuni quali siano lascivi, et corrompino, i, boni costumi ma che habbino da esser' honesti et modesti tanto nel prologo q[ua]nto in ogni parte della comedia ne meno sino habiti lascivi, come sarebbe donna vestita da homo o, simile corutelle

4.o se si fratarano nelle comedie sogieti amorosi habbino d'esser' de fine honesto, et la causa de quelli sii p[er] boni effetti de animo, et no[n] del senso, et questo se habbi da esprimere nelle prime parolle de sopra cio si dirano

5.o ch[e] non possino far' comedie inanzi al fine della messa

6. o no[n] habbino ardir' de nominar' il nome del S.r Idio et Soii Sancti in dette comedie

7. o no[n] dicano parolle quali in particolare potessino aportar' ingiuria ad alcuno

8. o no[n] habbino de far' le comedie nelle stanza ove habitano li giudei sicome p[er] il passato si ritrovino inconsideratamente haver' fatto essendo prohibito di raggione la conversatione de xtiani [christiani] co[n] giudei

9. o no[n] possino recitar' alcuna comedia se prima no[n] si trovi el sogetto d'esso visto, et sottos[cri]tto almeno da doi delli ss.ti dellegati

X.mo che quelli giorni che sono prohibiti a recitar' Comedie s'intendino prohibiti tanto in lochi, et case particolari come in publico salvo se no[n] haverano special licenza da essi S.ri o, da uno d'essi

6. ASMN, Decreti, libro 49, fo. 70^v
14 March 1580. Decree of Guglielmo Gonzaga naming Filippo Angeloni purveyor of comedians' licences in Mantua

Ser.mo Sig.r mio sempre osser.mo
Mi ritrovo haver fatto, alli comici confidenti, una spesa di molta importanza per il recitare delle comedie, con patti, et conditioni come per publico instrumento si può vedere; et già sono passati giorni, che si è principiato a recitare, per la qual occasione, si ha scosso per capara di molti Palchi, circa D. mille, da diversi Nobili di questa città. Hora mò, mi è stato rifferto dalla sig.a Vittoria, che V. ser.ma Alt.a vuole Petrolino al suo servizio non sapendo forse le obligationi che egli ha con esso meco, per li accordi fatti; il che veramente sarebbe la total ruina, et dissunione di questa compagnia et a me levarebbe, oltra il danno, l'honore, et reputatione per havere accomodato la mettà de Nobili di questa città; alli quali resteria del continuo, ogni mala sodisfatione. Per il che co' ogni riverentia vengo a supplicarla, che la si degni, et vogli favorirmi in questo bisognio, con permetere che il detto Petrolino possi restare, senza altro impedimento. Che s'io non potrò in altro corrispondere a così grato favore, m'affaticarò co' il desiderio di haver occasione per servirla sempre; et le resterò perpetuo, et obligatissimo servitore. Sono stato astretto tener, co' il detto, alcuni termini di ragione, ch'io non ho potuto far di manco, perché si diceva che egli voleva partire, anchora che egli mi affermasse non haversi obligato a V. Ser.ma Alt.a di alcuna cosa, che non si haverebbe ligato con noi. Né crederò havere fatto cosa, che habbia da disgustare in alcun conto, alla benignità et grandezza sua. Alla quale, co' vivo cuore et riverentia humilmente mi raccomando.

    Di Venetia alli 4. Gen.o 1580
    Di V. Ser.ma Altezza
    Humiliss.mo et Devot.mo
    Ser.re Hettor Tron

7. ASMO, Archivio per Materie, Comici

4 January 1580 [1581]. Ettore Tron, Venice, to Duke Alfonso II d'Este, Ferrara

Instrutti dell'informatione che ha il giocondo nostro Filippo Angelone di tutti li comici mercenari, zaratani et can' in banchi, lo eleggiamo per superiore ad essi in tutti li nostri stati, sì che alcuno di loro, o solo o accompagnato, non habbia ardire di recitare comedie o cantare in banco, vendendo ballotte o simili bagattelle, senza sua licenza in scritto, nè d'indi dipartirsi senza la med[e]s[i]ma licenza, sotto pena di essere tutti spogliati di ciò che haveranno, così comune come proprio, da esser diviso in tre parti, l'una delle quali sia applicata al fisco nostro, l'altra al Magistrato, ove vogliamo che si faccia l'essecutione sommariamente et rimessa l'appellatione, et la terza ad esso superiore; al quale concediamo facoltà di dar le sovrascritte licenze havendo però prima havuto il consenso in voce da noi, et in assenza nostra da quel loco, dal Magistrato in scritto ove è Magistrato, et nelli altri luoghi dalli giusdicenti per noi deputati, potendo egli deputar uno o più logotenenti secondo il bisogno, et di più di poter, tanto esso quanto li logotenenti, confermar le licenze col sigilo del suo ufficio della maniera che è qui inserto. Commandando a tutti li nostri ministri, così presenti come futuri, che queste nostre osservino et facciano inviolabilmente osservare. In fede di che le presenti saranno sottoscritte di nostra mano et sigillate del nostro maggio sigillo.

8. ASB, Demaniale 220/2127. MEMORIALE DI NOTIZIE ATTINENTI ALL'ARCHIVIO DELLE RR MM DEL CORPUS DOMINI Raccolte da diverse Scritture. Nel quale si tratta dell'Origine, e Privilegi del Monastero, Chiesa, Altari Reliquie, Indulgenze Obblighi di Messe Legati perpetui Crediti di Monte, Crediti diversi, Debiti, et altre cose, con le sue Tavole. IN BOLOGNA MDCC.

[p. 339, par. 107] Dell'Anno 1581 in occasione della fabrica nuova del Monasterio delle Monache del Corpus D[omi]ni li Comici, ò Comedianti principiorono à pagare à dette Monache L. Cento la settimana per tutto il Tempo che faccevano Comedie su la Salla, e parimenti pagavano li Mastri de Ponti L.20. la settimana, ma poi del 1582. essi Comici principiorono à pagare solo L.15. la settimana, e tutto questo in vigore delle Conventioni che faccevano con Monsig. Vicelegato di quel tempo, come appare da due Libri antichi rispetto ad uno chiamato Entrata, e spesa al fo. 149. e 150. e rispetto all'altro chiamato fabrica nuova del Monasterio fo. 64. quali [p. 340] sono Posti nell'Archivio del Monastero nella Scanzia Seconda n.° 7. e Scanzia Terza n° 6.

Per il che anche presentemente le dette Monache riscotano qualche cosa da detti Comedianti quando fanno Comedie, come si vede da un Libretto sopra del quale serivano tutto ciò riscotano posto nell'Archivio del Monasterio Scanzia Seconda Libro Settimo n.° 1.

[p. 902] Credito con li Comici, e Comedianti
Devano li Comedianti che recitano sù la Salla del Podestà pagare alle Monache del Corpus D[omi]ni L.4. p[er] ciascheduna Comedia che faranno.
In Vigore del Possesso che hanno queste Monache ab antiquo, stante che si trova ne Libri del Monasterio che questi Comici, ò Comedianti principiorono à pagare sino dell' Anno 1581. in occasione della fabrica nuova del Monasterio fatta da Papa Gregorio XIII. e si vede che alla prima pagavano L.100. la settimana p[er] tutto il tempo che faccevano Comedie sù la Salla, e li Maestri de Ponti pagavano L.20. la Settimana, mà poi da L.100. convennero di dare solo L.15 la Settimana, e faccevano le loro Conventioni con Monsig.^{re} Vicelegato, e ciò si vede da due libri antichi rispetto ad uno chiamato Entrata, e Spesa del Monasterio al fo. 149. 150. posto nell'Archivio del Monasterio Scanzia Seconda n.° 7., e l'altro chiamato fabrica nuova del Monasterio al fo. 64 Posto nella Scanzia Terza n.° 6.
Vi sono poi altre Memorie nell'Archivio, et in spetie una lettera del Cardinale Lodovisi scritta del 1622. 8. Gennaro alle Monache del Corpus D[omi]ni qual dice trà l'altre cose queste paroli scrivo al Cardinale Legato acciò: che faccia dare lo Scudo de Comedianti al suo Monasterio, e si vedano altri Raccordi che mostrano che le Monache dovrebbero havere un scudo p[er] ogni Comedia come si può vedere in dette Memorie quali però sono di poco momento poste nell'Archivio del Monasterio Scanzia Prima Libro ++. n.° 6.
Parimenti per provare il detto possesso vi sono in detto Archivio due libretti uno de quali hà servito dell'Anno 1585. al 1621. p[er] tenere conto di quello hanno riscono da Comedianti e l'altro principia dell'Anno [*blank space*] et hà servito sino al presente Anno 1700. e sono tutti questi due libri posti nell'Archivio del Monasterio Scanzia Seconda Libro Settimo n.° 1, e n.° 2.
Si presente esse Monache riscotano qualche cosa p[er] detto Comedie, mà si rende assai difficile, e p[er] essere questa entrata incerta quivi non si può fare altra Mentione.

9. ASMN, Gonzaga, b. 1256
   13 April 1583. Francesco Andreini, Ferrara, to Vincenzo Gonzaga, Mantua

Al Ser.mo Principe di Mantova mio S.re collen.mo. Mantova

Serenissimo Signore
Per il S. Antonio Musico di V.A.S. ò inteso l'animo suo e la sua buona intentione, intorno Alla Novella Compagnia, ch'ella brama mettere in sieme. E Per che mi trovo obligatissimo Alla gentilissima gratia di V.A.S. No[n] posso, se no[n] con mio grandiss.o dispiacere Ringratiarla del cortesissimo animo suo, d'havermi fatto degno insieme co[n] la mia consorte, d'Esser' Annoverato fra cosi degna Compagnia Poi che trovandomi obligato, et legato p[er] fede Alla compagnia de comici Gelosi, et in Particolare al clar.mo S.r Alvise Michiele Patrone della stanza di Venetia, sono astretto a no[n] potere accettare il Partito, et il volere di

V.A.S. Poi che p[er] mettere insieme questa compagnia bisogna guastarene Tre la qual cosa poi dificile, se bene, a V.A.S. ogni dificilissima cosa è facilissima, a farsi. Inoltre, che ritrovandomi in ferrara solo, no[n] posso senza il parere degl'altri compagni, Manco offerir' la compagnia de Gelosi, al servitio di V.A.S. co[n] che pregandola a tenermi co[n] la mia consorte nel' numero delli suoi minimi servitori et in sua buona gratia, li bacio, le degnissime mani, insieme co[n] mia moglie, Pregando N. S. p[er] la felicità, et esaltatione di V.A.S.

    Di ferrara, il 13. Aprile 1583
    Di V.A.S.
    Umiliss.o servitore
    Fran.co Andreini
    comico geloso

10. ASMN, Gonzaga, b. 1257, fos. 2^r–3^v
    3 April 1584. The Comici Uniti, Ferrara, to Vincenzo Gonzaga, Mantua.

Al Ser.mo Principe di Mantova Sig.r mio coll.mo. Mantova

Ser.mo Principe
Havendo noi comici uniti, umilissimi servi di V.A.S. di nuovo tornata insieme la Compagnia di Pedrolino, come già era, et anco migliorata di personaggi, famosi nell'arte comica. Et desiderando noi venire a Recitare a Mantova con buona gratia di V.A.S. umilmente la preghiamo, et supplichiamo concederne licenza si che possiamo venire che subito saremo prontissimi; noi sariamo venuti confidandosi nella bontà di V.A.S. Ma p[er] che il sig.r Filippo Angeloni musico fa ogni opera, acciò che noi no[n] ci venghiamo. Et non sapendo noi di ciò la causa. Habbiamo voluto prima farne consapevole V.A.S. A fine che la si degni trattarne con l'Altezza Ser.mo del Sig.r Duca suo Padre, et ar' si che possiamo venir' liberamente, a servirla et facendole Reverenza. Umilissima[me]nte, baciamo le degniss[im]e mani di V.A.S. pregando N. S. p[er] la sua felicità maggiore di Ferrara, il 3 d'Aprile, 1584.
    Di V.A.S.
    Umilissimi servi e devoti
    gli UNITI,

Pedrolino,	Lutio	Batista da treviso franceschino
Bertolino,	Cap.o Cardone	la s: ra giulia Brolo
Magnifico	Flaminio	isabella
Gratiano,	Giovandonato	Grillo

11. ASMN, Gonzaga, b. 1514
    7 April 1584. Battista Guarini, Padua, to Vincenzo Gonzaga, [Mantua]

Ser.mo sig.re et Patron mio Colend.mo
V.A. favorisce troppo le cose mie. et dico troppo et perche no[n] meritano tanto,

et perche la mia fortuna non vuole ch'io possa goder del favore ch'ella mi fa. Scrissi gia un'altra volta pur in risposta d'una sua lett.ra della med.a instanza; che la mia Tragicomedia Pastorale per mia somma disgratia non poteva esser all'ordine apena per tutto quest'anno, se ben il disiderio mio sarebbe stato di finirla quanto prima per poterne servire l'A.V. la quale saprà che dopo ch'io son qui non ci ho potuto mai metter mano. et manca ancora tutto il Quinto atto; et tutti i chori, et io son di cosi fatta natura nel poetare, che s'io no[n] ho tutto il cervello ben riposato no[n] posso far verso che mi compiaccia. mass.te in poema comminciato da me con molto sottilo, et esquisito gusto, intanto che ho penato tre anni a farne li quattro atti che son in essere et in essi ancora mancano alcune cose di qualche importanza. Ma tutto che l'opera fosse compitiss.a credami certo l'A.V. che non si metterebbe all'ordine in tre mese. et questo perche oltre l'esser di molte et molto lunghe parti, dal primo atto in fuori è tutta piena di novità et di grandissimi movimenti, i quali vogliono essere concertati, et con lungo studio provati et riprovati in scena. et mass.te un giuoco che va nel terzo atto ridotto in forma di ballo fatto da un choro di Ninfe, et questo è ancora nelle mani di Leone; ne la Musica e fatta, et tanto men le parole; hor vegga l'A.V. com'è poss.le di essequire mass.te in cosi breve tempo quelche disidera. Lascio stare tante altre difficoltà, la scena che va fatta con artificio insolito, le persone, che vogliono essere et di viso et di presenza, et di maniere proportionate al soggetto. nel quale come ella sa se ben si tratta di pastori, son però nobiliss.mi come quelli ch[e] derivano da ceppo divino. per modo che io non so vedere come poterla ubbidire, quando anch[e] volessi far al peggio che io sapessi. Voglio ben che V.A. sappia ch[e] ne sento un cordoglio inestimabile. Ma Patron mio Ser.mo quello che no[n] si può è degno di scus [*page torn*] et nel mio caso di compassione, perche dopo che son qui posso dire d'essere stato sempre mezzo ammalato. et per questo fra quattro o cinq. di mi pongo nelle mani dei medici. Mi consola però che forse no[n] mancaranno a V.A. dell'altr[*torn*] favole, come comedie, et anche pastorali, se ben sono state vedute. ma potrebbe per aventura trovar qualche nuova comedia non piu veduta tra i suoi me[*torn*] di Mantova dove so che sono ingegni nobiliss.mi et particolar.te il S. Curzio[*torn*] Ill.mo mio Sig.re Alle quali favole per dar piacere a gli occhi di coloro c[he] no[n] intendono o no[n] curano, o no[n] gustano l'artificio comico, si potrebbono fare intermezzi apparenti con macchine; come potrà et sapia ottimam.te fare et commandare l'A.V. et so io che in Mantova no[n] mancherann[*torn*] artefici eccellenti, et Poeti da sapere eggregiamenti trovar l'inventio[*torn*] et animarla co' loro componimenti. Et questo lodarei ch'ella facess[*torn*] mass.te in Nozze di Principessa Italiana, et particolar.te Toscana d[*torn*] la lingua nostra fiorisce. Et perche il messo di V.A. no[n] torni con le mani vuoti, le mando una mia nuova comedia, la quale se piacerà, la esshibisco in diffetto d'altra cosa che meglio sia: et la supp.o à tenerla appresso di se, ogni volta ch[e] no[n] se ne serva, percioche ella mi è cara et non vorrei di fosse veduta se non sarà recitata. Mi rallegro poi con tutto il cuore delle nozze nobiliss.e di V.A. con la

quale mi dolse di no[n] haver potuto far quest'uff.o quand'ella fu qui. et veram.te N.S. Moliti mi fe fran torto. patienza. Et qui fo fine facendo hum.ma riverenza à V.A. col pregarle ogni disiderato avenimente. Di Pad.a li 7 di Ap.le 1584.
    Di V.A. Ser.ma
    Hum.mo et divotiss.mo Ser.re
    Batt Guarini

12. ASMN, Gonzaga, b. 1162, fos. 692^r–693^v
    2 September 1585. Pirro Malvezzi, Bologna, to Vincenzo Gonzaga, Mantua

Alla Ser.ma Alt.za del S.r Prencipe di Mantova S.re et p'ron mio Col.mo

Ser.mo S.re P'ron mio Col.mo
Delli tre comici de V.A.S. m'hà comandato che io facessi opera, che sono venissero da lei, Marco Antonio Galbiati, et Giacomo Po[ns]ini [*obscured by the seal*] s'erano partiti il giorno inanzi che mi fosse resa la l'ra sua; di maniera che non mi resto luogo di poter far' officio se non con Gio: Paolo; il quale mi rispose che, essendo recitanti a bastanza in quella compagnia non poteva credere, de tal richiesta venisse im[m]ediatam.te dal desid.o di V.A.S. ma ad istanza di qualcuno di quei comici poco amico di questi, et quando pure ella n'havesse havuto di bisogno, che haveria lasciato questi se bene se gli è obligato per un'anno; et messo da banda ogn'altro rispetto per venir à servir le: pur che havesse havuto com[m]odo di poter restituir loro certa som[m]a di danari che gli hanno imprestato; al che non volli replicar altro senza la comissione di V.A.S. la quale potrà comandare quel che vorrà che si faccia perche tanto si esseguirà, si come la obbedirò sempre ad ogni minimo suo cen[n]o. conservi mi per suo devotiss.o ser.re che io per fine con la debita riverenza le bacio le ser.me mani et le prego som[m]o contento. Di Bolog.a li ii di sett.re 1585
    Di V.A.Ser.ma
    V're humilis.o et devotis.o Pirro Malvezzi

13. ASMN, Gonzaga, b. 1162, fos. 743^r–744^v
    16 December 1585. Lodovico de' Bianchi, Bologna, to Vincenzo Gonzaga, Mantua

Al Ser.mo principo di Mantua mio Sig.re Colendi.mo. In Mantua

Seren.mo Vicemcio figliolo onor.do
P[er] la grande inportunitade e superbia che va usando la Delia non sol' con me ma con quasi tuta la compagnia e poi p[er] la sua ingniorancia qual' causa che da nisuno no[n] puo escere vista ne sentita e p[er] il volere cominacie in paurire il mondo causa si che a V.A. dicho se la desidera che venando la conpagnia in Mantua veng[h]i a servirla al tuto non voglio la Delia overo me ne resterò io qua in Bologna poi che p[er] sua causa ancho se lasciaro di pigliare Adriano e

la sig.ra Silvia parteranno necessarie in la conpagnia cosi ne gli intermedi Come ne l[']altre cose e qua vi e parte che nisuno no[n] le vole ascholtare a principal mentre la Delia ciamata [chiamata] in Bolognia la goba pero V.A. pensi bene quelo che la vole si feci e ne dia aviso p[er] che io al tuto non voglio escere dove lei a modo alcuno ad ogni modo pocho mi curo di far' piu comedie ma p[er] servire a [?sr] A sono quivi chio certo non vi sarei parmi avere dito abastanza Con V.A. a la quale umile m[']inchino e bascio le serene mani pregandoli dal cielo ogni felicita e con tanto di Bologna ali 16 di decemb[re] 1585
 DVAS
 servitore lodovicho di bianchi da bolognia
 deto il dotor graciano comicho geloso

14. ASMN, Gonzaga, Autografi, busta 10, fos. 50^r–50^v
 14 January 1587. Isabella Andreini, Florence, to Eleonora de' Medici, Mantua

Alla Serenissima Principessa de Mantova, Sig:ra mia Coll:ma. In Mantova

Serenissima Signora
Se nell'Etiopia dove sono genti barbare, si trovano alcuni popoli che quantunque barbari siano, Adorano dui Dij, l'uno im[m]ortale e l'altro mortale, lo im[m]ortale come creatore di tutto l'universo, et il mortale come loro benificatore, Quanto maggiormente qui nella bella Italia giardino del mondo, dove è lume di fede, e splendori di costumi politici, si deve adorare l'alto, et im[m]ortale Dio sommo Motore dell'Universo, e nel' belliss:mo seno della Nobiliss:ma città de MANTO, V.A.S. come Dea mortale, vera donatrice di santi, e si Notabili benefitij. certo si, che far lo deve ogn'uno e poi che questo si deve à V.A.S. io che umiliss:ma e devotiss:ma serva le sono Non resto d'Adorarla, come Mia terena, belliss:ma et gratiss:ma Dea. Poi che da Lei ho riceuto il singolar' benefitio, et segnalitiss:mo favore Dell'haver' accettato, Lavinia mia figliola, per sua umilissima e devotiss:ma serva. La quale con la occasione del Sig:r Claudio Francese, suo Devotiss:mo, vengo di nuovo a ricordargliela servitrice se bene si trova in età di non poterla servire; et con mio marito vengo anch'io, come devotiss.ma di V.A.S. à pregarle dal' suppremo Dator' delle gratie, ogni grandezza, et felicissimo parto, et umilissi:te raccomandandomele in gratia, con baciarle la Degniss:ma veste: Di fiorenza il 14. di Gennaio 1587.
 Di V.A.S.
 Umiliss:ma servitrice e devota.
 Isabella Andreini comica gelosa

15. ASMN, Gonzaga, Autografi, busta 10, fos. 54^r–55^v
 5 April 1587. Isabella Andreini, Florence, to Eleonora de 'Medici, Mantua

Alla Ser.ma Prencipessa de Ma'toa Sig:ra mia Coll:ma Mantova

Serenissima signora
Con la occasione della venuta del Ser.mo sig:r Prencipe suo Degnissimo consorte qua a Fiorenza, et con la comodità Del sig:r Claudio francese suo Affetionatissimo, e devotissimo Servitore, non ho voluto mancare, di venire con questa mia a farle reverenza, con tutta quella humiltà maggiore che p[er] me sua humilissima, e Devotissima Servitrice si puote, pregando S.A.S. Degnarse di conservarmi in sua buona gratia insieme con Lavinia mia figliola, et sua humilissima Servitrice facendo anco sapere, a S.A.S. come Dal Ser:mo Gran Duca suo Degniss:o Padre, e Dalla Ser.ma Gran Duchessa, sono stata favorita, oltre a molt'altri favori d'un segnalatissimo favore Simile a quello fattomi da S.A.S. d'accettare la sorella minore di Lavinia mia figliola, p[er] sua servitrice, Della cui Gratia, e di quella, che mi fece S.A.S. Rendo gratie infinite a Iddio, et alle vostre Altezze Ser.me Alle quali prego dal'istesso Dio tutte quelle contentezze che puonno desiderare co[n] c[he] fine me li Raccomando in gratia con mio marito, et bacio la Deg:ma Veste. et li Prego felicissimo Parto. Di Fiorenza il 5. Aprile 1587
    Di S.A.S.
    Humiliss:ma e Devotiss:ma servitrice
    Isabella Andreini comica Gelosa

16. MIRTILLA. / PASTORALE / D'ISABELLA ANDREINI / COMICA GELOSA. / IN VERONA Appresso Girolamo Discepolo / 1588

Alla Illustriss. et eccellentiss. Sig. la Sig. Donna Lavinia della Rovere Marchesa del Vasto. Signora Mia Colendiss.

Io cominciai quasi da scherzo Illustrissima, & Eccellentissima Signora, ad attendere à gli studi della Poesia, e di tanto diletto gli trovai, ch'io non ho mai più potuto da sì fatti trattenimenti rimanermi, e come dal cielo mi sia stato negato ingegno atto a sì alto e nobile esercizio, non per questo mi son io sgomentata, anzi mi sono ingegnata d'assomigliarmi a quelli che nati e allevati nell'Alpi nevose o campi sterili, non però lasciano di coltivarli a tutto lor potere per renderli più che possano fecondi. È l'ingegno umano cosa troppo divina, e coloro che nell'ozio intrepidi lasciano così raro dono perire, non meritano tra gli uomini essere annoverati, però che trapassando la vita loro con perpetuo silenzio, a guisa che le bestie fanno, non sono buoni ad altro che a consumar quello che dalla natura o dalla terra è prodotto. Da sì fatta maniera di vita e costumi desiderando io d'allontanarmi, seguitai gli incominciati studi; onde m'avvenne alli giorni passati di comporre una PASTORALE, la quale io, per aventura troppo ardita, mando ora fuori con la scorta del nome di Vostra Eccellenza Illustrissima. Desiderando che ciò mi giovi a mostrarle la devozione e riverenza ch'io le porto, non intendendo che l'autorità del suo divino nome la difenda, perciò che essendo questa la prima fatica dell'ingegno mio che sia venuta in luce, desidero sentirne liberamente l'openione di ciascuno, per potere i difetti di questi e degli altri miei scritti emmendare. Accetti per tanto V.E. Illustriss. questa mia PASTORALE, che hora le appresento, con quella istessa humanità, ch'ella più volte s'è degnata (contra ogni mio merito) di prestar gratia silentio alle mie vive parole, e per non infastidirla humilmente me le inchino, bacciandole con ogni riverenza le degnissime mani, e pregandole da Dio ogni suo maggior contento, e felicità.

Di Verona il dì xxiv. di Febraro M.D.LXXXVIII. Di V.E. Illustriss. Humiliss. serva, e devota Isabella Andreini Comica Gelosa.

17. ASMN, Gonzaga, b. 2642, fos. 170^r–171^v
1 July 1588. Ottavio Lambardesco, Mantua, to Marcello Donati, Florence

Al molt'Ill.re s.r mio s.r osser.mo Il s.r Conte Marcello Donati Cons.re del ser.mo s.r [*postal tape*]tova, et Monferrato. à Fiorenza

Molt'Ill.re s.r mio s.r osser.mo
Non è ancor comparso mr. Leone da Som'o, con tutto che qsti hebrei m'havevano accertato, che mercordi passato saria stato qui, hora non san'o più certo quando venirà, dicono nond.no, che l'aspettano questa settimana che viene; Il Massaro con molt'altri hebrei, mi portarno hieri sera la qui inchiusa scrittura pregandomi à farla capetare in mano a S.A., sarà contenta V.S. se però gli parerà bene à darla a V.A.S. et io intanto starò aspettando quello mi sarà com'andato intorno à questo particolare, come faccio d'ogn'altra cosa per serv.o dell'A.S. in buona gra della quale faccio humiliss.a riverenza, et à V.S. bacio la mano, et le raccordo qlla l'ra in racc.ne delli miei lug.ni Martini, Di Mant.a il p.mo di Lugno nel 1588.

Da parte del S.r M'ro di casa mille racc.ni et baccamani
D.V.S. molt'Ill.re
S.re aff.mo
Ottavio Lambartesco

Ha l'Università degli heb: i co'l Ban: riaccettato prontam:te de fare la com'essa Comedia, ò Pastorale, come piacerà all'Alt: S. la quale puo restar sicura, ch'il desiderio che han'o unitam:e di renderla sodisfatta à pieno, non gli lasciarà mancare d'ogni diligenza possibile, per che riesca bella, e piacevole, e che non manchi di decoro.

Vero è, che desiderano che l'A.S. facci ellettione, di quella favola che piu le piacerà, si per che non s'assicurano, che si elleggesse cosa che fosse à gusto di quella, e si anco per non essere in paese mr. Leone di som'i, piu d'altro instrutto di simili sogetti, co'l quale se ne potria trattare, et senza esso malam:te se ne sapria discorrere.

Il detto mr. Leone è andato in Piemonte, e ben che si dica che sara qui la 7.na pross:a non ve ne è però certezza. Et non è parso alli heb:ri di chiamarlo, levandolo da qualche negotio che forse havesse in q'lle parti, havendo giudicato, che senza dubio, sia meglio che l'A.S. lo facci fare, volendo che egli n'habbi carico, come l'altre volte.

La sudetta ellettione, quanto piu tosto si farà, tanto meglior effetto portarirà ne recitanti, che con piu com'odo, pigliaran'o a mente le lor parti et se le faran'o piu sicure.

Saria necc:o, che fosse dato carico dall'A.S., a qualche Cavaliero, ò a qualche Gentilhomo d'authorità che havesse cura di questo fatto, con ogni diligenza, et al quale si potesse haver ricorso, per qual si voglia cosa che occorresse, et massime, nel far accettare le parti a qualche renite'te, poi che occorrendogli a valersi di Poveri, che vivono delle lor fatiche, non mancheran'o essi heb: di pagarli il tempo che perderan'o, come han' sempre fatto.

Quello che importa, e che sono i sud:i heb:i sforzati a mettere in consideratione all'A.S. si è che il giorno del 22 di 7bre, nel quale vengono com'essi, ad essere all'ordine per recitare questa favola, e una delle piu sollen'e, e principali feste, che habbiano tra loro, et non solo il 22, ma il 23 ancora, e'l 24 è sabbato, si che sara necc:o, o di anticipare al d:o tempo un giorno, overo d'aspettare alla D'nica seg:te, quando non si volesse far l'opera, manchevole di molte vaghezze, come di fochi, et di suoni, e d'altre piacevolezze, non comportate dalla legge heb:ca a farsi in simili giorni festivj.

18. ASF, Mediceo, f. 829, fo. 227^{r-v}
27 September 1591. Isabella Andreini, Bologna, to Belisario Vinta, Florence

Al Molto Ill.re sig:r mio oss:mo il Signor Cavalier Bellisario Vinta Segretario Deg:mo [torn] .mo Gran Duca di Toscana. Fiorenza.

Molto Ill.re Sig:re mio oss.mo
Dalla Ser.ma Signora Duchessa di Mantova. fù accertata V.S.M. Ill:re del desiderio, che sua A.S. ha sempre hauto di favorirmi non solo in Mantova, ma in qual si voglia altra parte p[er] dove si estende la grandezza sua p[er] sua inata bontà. hor di nuovo p[er] q.a mia facciole sapere come di fresco da S.A. sono stata fatta degna di sapere come ha ottenuto p[er] risposta. Dal Ser.mo Gran Duca, intorno alla licenza del recitare in Fiorenza che si contenta della mia Compagnia, quando però sia buona p[er] Fiorenza, e p[er]ch'io desidero sommamente, servire à quelle Altezze Serenissime. vengo con q:a mia, prima p[er] farle riverenza come Affett:mo e Devotiss:mo servitrice ch'io le sono, seconda p[er] supplicarla voglia favorirme con il favore della Ser:ma S.ra Duchessa di Mant:a mia S.ra, appresso il ser:mo Gran Duca mio S.re in farmi ottenere cosi segnalato favore di poter' venire à recitare in Fiorenza con la Com:a al tempo solito di cominciarsi nel solito salone, e la gratia della Gabella delle nostre robe usate, e p[er] quelle dell'uso della Comedia; che della segnalatiss:a gratia ch[e] mi concedirà .S.A.S. resterò con eterna memoria della grandezza e gentilezza sua; e sarò tenuta pregare il S.re Iddio. p[er] la sua sanità, lunga vita, et esaltatione, et à V.S. sarò p[er] sempre

obbligatissima, le mando la lista de tutti li personaggi che sono nella compagnia mia acciò sesti servita farla vedere al Ser.mo Gran Duca, poi che .S.A. di Mantova mi fà dire tale essere la volonta del Ser.mo Gran Duca. supplicandola p[er] ultimo poi di farmi degna, di risposta, quà in Bologna dove recitiamo, aspettando la buona gratia del Ser.mo Gran Duca nostro seg.re et baciandole le gentilissime mani, con mio marito, e tutta la Compagnia gli prego da Iddio sommo contento: Di Bologna alli 27 di Settembre 1591
    Di .V.S.M. Ill.re
    Servitrice Affett.ma
    Isabella Andreini comica

19. ASB, Legato, Expeditiones, no. 114, fo. 32^v
    14 November 1593

Conced.o licenza alla s.ra Vittoria Piissimi comica et alla sua compagnia di poter fare et recitare su la sala del s.r podestà le comedie, tragicomedie, tragedie, pastorali et altri loro virtuosi trattenimenti in tutti li giorni della settimana, fuori però che il venere et purché ne giorni di feste commandate non incomincino a recitare se non dopo il vespro, et in tutti gli altri giorni non incomincino parim[ent]e a recitare prima che siano finite di leggere tutte le lettioni publiche dello Studio. Et ciò senza inc[ors]o di pena alc[un]a. Pagando però in mano di m. Gio[vanni] Maria Monaldini cancell[ier]o alla n[ost]ra cancell[eri]a scudi trenta di m[one]ta il mese, ogni settim[an]a la rata, da distribuirsi in elem[osin]a ad arb[itri]o n[ost]ro.
    Die 14 nov.is 1593.
    O. Band.s v. leg.s
                                                                                       Tax. C. 8.
[*In the left margin:*] A dì 14. nov.re incominciarono.

20. ASF, Dogana di Firenze, serie antica, f. 223, supplica n. 318
    30 March 1594
    Ser.mo G. Duca:

La Compagnia de Commedianti di Petrolino nominati li uniti, hanno supp.to à V.A.S. p[er] havere le stanza d[e]lle Commedie, et si co[n]tentono cominc.re il di p.o di 9bre, o prima, et durare fino al p.o di quaresima, Nese[n]to buona relat.e d[e]lli strume[n]ti hanno à recitare, signifide [= significa] ch[e] la Vett.ria no[n] verrà à servire, ma un altra in suò scambio soffetiote [= sufficiente]: et p[er]ch[e] V.A.S. mi ha comand.to ch[e] io intenda da Isabella Andreini, se vuol'essere di q.a Compag.a sono stato da essa in p[er]sona, et mi ha detto ch[e] no[n] lo può fare, trovandosi promesso alla sua Compag.a et à chi V.A.S. farà fra[n] d[e]lle stanza sieno obligati dare mallevadore di cominc.re al p.o di 9mbre p[ro]seguire fino al p.o di quaresima, et pag.re à tempi debiti, acciò la Dog.a sia sicura di riscuotere: et à V.A.S. bascio hum.te la mane dio la feliciti, et contenti di Dog.a li 30. di M.zo 1594

    D. V.A.Ser.ma
    umil. S.re Fran.co Biffoli

Concedasi loro co[n] le conditioni d'oblighi et cantele [?cautele] sod.e et del pagare qua[n]to ha s'e pagato dalla compagnia che quest'anno ha servito
    L[ett]o il di 31 marzo 94

21. ASB, Legato, Expeditiones n. 114, fo. 71^v
    14 April 1594

Concediamo licenza alla S.ra Isabella Andreini Comica Gelosa, et alla sua Compagnia di poter fare, et recitare su la sala del Sig. Podestà le Comedie, tragicomedie, tragedie, pastorali, et altri loro virtuosi trattenimenti in tutti li giorni della settimana dal Venerdi in poi, et purche nelli giorni di Feste commandate non incomincino à recitare sinora dopò i Vespro, et ciò senza incorso di pena alcuna: Pagando però in mano di M. Gio: Maria Monaldini Cancell.o alla nra Cancelleria scudi trenta di moneta il mese ogni settimana la rata, da distribuirsi in elemosino a luoghi pii ad arb.o nro. Dat. Bon die 14 Aprilis 1594.
    O Band. V leg.

                                                Tax: C.8

[*in the left margin:*] A di 3 di Maggio 1594 s'incominciono à recitare loro Comedie

22. Gentile Pagani, *Del teatro in Milano avanti il 1598*, as cited in D'Ancona, 'Il teatro mantovano', pt. 3, pp. 333–4. 13 October 1594

Primo intermedio.
Dato il segno, cade la tela figurata il mare, adornata di diverse sorti di pesci, per il che si scoperse la scena affigurata la città di Napoli. In mezzo al palco stava a traverso una tela dipinta che assomigliava alla marina, sopra della quale apparse la Vittoria comediante accomodata a modo di sirena. Costei fece il prologo, il quale finito, la scena subito fu coperta d'una tela dipinta d'arbori, boschi, monti e colli ameni, ove comparsero Fetonte et Epapho contrastando insieme, dicendo Epapho potersi vantare essere figliuolo di Giove, ma che non sapeva come Fetonte potesse essere figliuolo del sole, chiamandoli chiarezza di questo. Fetonte andò a trovare Climene sua madre, addimandandola se era stato generato dal Sole: lei giurando che sì, li disse che andasse dal Sole a dimandarglielo. Così vi andò, et di lontano inginochiatosi, con la mano avanti gl'occhi, gli domandò signo, acciò conoscesse essere suo figliuolo. Egli giurando per la stigia palude li disse che sì, et che in segno di ciò domandasse ciò ch'egli voleva, et cavandosi li raggi l'accarezzò molto. Fetonte li domandò di guidare un giorno il suo carro della luce. Febo lo dissuase da ciò perchè non lo havrebbe saputo giudare, pure insistendo, glie lo dà, ongendolo prima acciò non abbrugiasse.

2.do intermedio.
La scena fu coperta tutta in un subito con tele dipinte con arbori secchi et campagne, che non parevano se non fuoco, per il gran calore. A mezo il palco comparvero i Fiumi con li urni, che in cambio d'essere pieni d'acqua s'abbrugiavano, et per ciò esclamavano a Giove di tanta distrutione. Fatte queste esclamationi, comparvero i quattro Tempi dell'anno, ciascuno dolendosi del danno che pativano per il gran calore, et poi tutti insieme inginochiati cantando invocarono Giove che li soccorresse, onde tirò il tuono, s'aperse il cielo et comparse Giove a cavallo dell'Aquila, che rispose volervi provedere. Fetonte passando sopra il carro, lamentandosi di tanta fatica et del gran pericolo in che si trovava, Giove lo saetò, et lo fece cadere dal cielo, et la madre sua comparse lamentandosi d'havere perso il figliuolo, et che le sorelle per il gran piangere si erano convertite in piante di pioppe. Et s'udiron strepiti grandi di tuoni in cielo, dopo i quali continuando i lampi et tuoni, tempestò confetti sopra il palco, che causò gran alegrezza a Relichino et Pedrolino, et molto riso alli ascoltanti.

3.o intermedio.
Comparse la tela della scena depinta che affigurava la bella primavera, uscendo una bell.ma donna vestita pomposamente sopra un carro tirato da due leoni, che cantava bell.mi versi, la quale era l'Aurora, et al suo scoprirsi, le stelle ch'erano rosseggianti in cielo, s'annichilarono. Era costei accompagnata da varij canti d'uccelli et massime de rusignoli, et simil.te de galli. Comparvero cinque Pastori con viole che sonavano per eccellenza, et con essi erano quattro villani che ballavano nizzarda et altri balli, che fecero bello vedere. Comparvero li Fiumi con li urni pieni d'acqua, che scaturivano acque odorifere, e cantando versi.

4.o intermedio.
Finito il terzo atto et la musica al solito, le tele di verdura copersero la scena, e comparsero le 4 Stagioni dell'anno, e ciascuna recitò versi in lode et ringratiamento delle racquistate sue ordinarie forze, et poi comparvero quattro Dei, i quali cantarono madrigali bell.mi, et nel finire conchiusero: andiamo andiamo, con concento sonoro più volte dicendo: andiamo andiamo. E così fu finita la comedia.

Li Comedianti che furono gli ordinarij, comparvero beniss.o vestiti, li intermedij ornati. Costa alla comunità di Milano da 2.m[ila] du[ca]ti. Gli auditori eccedevano 6.m[ila]. Vi era il senato et tutti li Maestrati con quelli di Provig.e, infinite et ben ornate Dame. Sue Ecc.ze et la casa sua s'intendono.

23. ASB, Legato, Expeditiones, no. 115, fo. 73^v
16 June 1595

Licenza a m. Francesco Andreini et compagni comici Uniti di poter ritornar a recitare in Bologna su la sala del s.r podestà il pross.o autunno le comedie, tragicomedie, tragedie, pastorali et altri loro virtuosi trattenimenti, incomincian-

do dalla sera della festa di San Petronio et seguitando per tutto il carnevale a venire. Purché non recitino li giorni di venere, mentre dura l'Advento et le feste del S.mo Natale. Pagando però in mano di m. Gio[vanni] Maria Monaldini can-cell[ier]o alla n[ost]ra cancell[eri]a in tutto 'l tempo che recitaranno scudi trenta di mon[et]a il mese, ogni settimana la rata, da distribuirsi in elemosine a luoghi pii ad arb[itri]o n[ost]ro. E ciò senza inc[ors]o di pena alc[un]a. Die 16 Junii 1595.
    M. Acq.va Arcivesc.o v. leg.o
                                                       Tax. C. 8.
[*in the left margin:*] confirmamus Han. ep. ori. Vicel.s Dat. Bon. Die 14 sept.ris 1595

24. ASMN, Gonzaga, busta 1165, fo. 623^{r-v}
    27 November 1596. Isabella Andreini, Bologna, to Vincenzo Gonzaga, Mantua

Al' Ser.mo mio Sig.or Col.mo Il Ser.mo Sig.or Duca di Mantova

Ser.mo Sig:r Duca mio S:re
Quel male il qual ci aviene per nostro difetto, è faciliss.mo da sopportare, ma intolerabile è quello che senza nostra colpa ci accade; intolerabile è adunque il male, et il graviss.mo dispiacere ch'io senti ser.mo mio S.re nel credermi poco ingratia di V.A.S. gratia da me ragionevolmente stimata quanto la propria vita poiche questo m'aviene non per lo mio, ma per l'altrui difetto: ma dato, e concesso pure sicome piace alla nemica mia sorte, ch'io sia fatta d'alcuna cosa colpevole appresso l'A.V.S., ricordisi per gratia il mio benigno signore che i principi altro non sono che Dii terreni, e sicome non è levito agli Dei il serbar sdegno, od'ira contra le cose mortali, così non è levito a voi mio terreno Dio l'essere adirato, o sdegnato contro di me sua infiniss.ma serva: Ma perche è proprio degli animi grandi il dementicarsi presto l'offese, quand'io pure l'habbia o per mia sciocchezza, o per l'altrui inganno offesa, mi giova di credere che V.A.S. non pur si sia placata, et habbia posta l'offesa inoblio, ma l'habbia interamente perdonata: delche et io, e 'l mondo tutto sarà sicuro al hora, che piacerà a l'A.V.S. di richiamarmi alla sua desideratiss.ma servitù del che con ogni affetto la prego: pregando anco Iddio che conceda à V.A., alla ser.ma moglie, e figli ogni maggior felicità: di Bologna li 27 Novemb. 1596.
    Di V.A.S.
    Humiliss.ma e Devotiss.ma serva
    Isabella Andreini

25. Rome, Archivio Capitolino, fondo Orsini, busta 108 (3), no. 754
    29 December 1597. Isabella Andreini, Florence, to Virginio Orsini, [Rome]

Ill.mo et Ec:mo S.r mio oss.mo
Letta la cortesiss:ma sua non mancai di far quello ch'a'me' s'aspettava, e perche li

S.ri otto ritengano appresso di loro il memoriale e la nota del lotto, rimando à V.E. nuova supplica in quella forma che essi S.ri hanno ordinato; e prego l'E.V. voglia p[er] sua bo[n]tà superare ogni intoppo acciò ch'io possa esser à tempo di valermene restando à l'E.V. con obligo indicibile e chi quanto in mio favore hà fatto, e di quanto per sua somma bontà desidera di fare; che è non pur caparra, ma intero pagamento di quello ch'ella deve alla grandezza del suo generoso sangue nato solo p[er] giovare e per gareggiar con le più lucide, e pretiose gemme di splendore, e di valore. e così piaccia à Dio di conservarla infinitamente com'io sò di dire il vero. con che fine senza fine me le raccomando in gratia baciandole la degniss.ma cappa: di Fiorenza li 29: Decemb. 1597
    Di V.E. Ill.ma
    Devotiss.ma ser.va
    Isabella Andreini

26. ASMN, Archivio Gonzaga, b. 1166, fos. 317^r–318^v
    9 June 1598. Datio Spinola, Bologna, to Vincenzo Gonzaga, Mantua

Al Seren.mo mio sig.or Colend.mo Il sig.or Duca di Mantova

Sereni.mo mio sig.or Colend.mo
La Compagnia di questi Comici ser.ri di V.Alt.a Seren.ma, che ella ha mandato à chiamare, sente dispiacere d'esser da me ritenuta per domane, e non poter venire à tempo à servirla conforme à l'obligo suo; et io come servitor divot.mo che le sono patisco l'istesso e maggior dispiacere, essendo sforzato di ritenergli per gusto del seren.mo sig.or Arciduca Ferdinando d'Austria arrivato quà hoggi, dove si tratterrà domane ancora. E perche tengo ordine da N.S.re di far tutti quei regali, che humanam.te mi sia possibile à S.Alt.a, che hà mostrato part.re desiderio di sentire una di q[u]esti Comedie, et io haveva già fatto mettere in punto tutto che fà di bisogno qui in Palazzo per tal'effetto: stando in ord.ne li Comici ancora quando è arrivata la commiss.e dell'Alt.a V'ra, sono stato astretto per serv.o di S.S.tà; e consolat.ne di S.Alt.a, con la confidenza che tengo nella infinita benignità di lei, esser cagione che non possino d.i Comici venir subito à servirla. Però humiliss:te la supp.co à perdonar loro, et à me insieme, condonando'l troppo ardir mio al sud.o rispetto de la sodisfattione di N.S.re, a la quale sò, esser disposta l'A.V'ra ancora, et à degnarsi di tenermi per suo vero ser.re che non essendo q[u]esta per altro, prego Dio che la conservi feliciss.a e riverent.te le bacio le mani. Di Bologna à 9. di Giugno. 1598.
    Di V.Alt.a Seren.ma
    Devotiss.o s.re
    Datio Spinola

27. ASMN, Archivio Gonzaga, b. 1725
    2 March 1601. Ercole Bellone, Milan, to Vincenzo Gonzaga, Mantua

Al ser.mo s.or mio s.or col.mo il s.or Duca di Mantoa et Monferrato

Sig.or mio sig.or col.mo
Hieri sera trovandomi à festa in casa di Don Giorgio Manrique vicino al Conte di Foentes Ecc.mo mi disse che voleva supp.re con una sua le 'ra V.A. à farle gra' di mandarle i comedianti, e piu commandava à me lo dovesse aiutare con una mia. Io le rispose q[u]ello che V.A. si puo immaginare fosse debito mio, ma non puote iscusarme di non scriverle, com'anco non hò potuto q[ue]sta mane d'inviarle il p[rese]nte corriere, havendomi S. Ecc.za mandato à dire le formali parole che trovandosi anche à letto, mi commandava, che scrivesse à V.A. quanto hò d.to di sopra in suo nome stando che proffessava d'esserle tanto servitore ch'era certo l'haverebbe scusato, se non le scriveva lui proprio, e di suo pugno, istimando tanto q[u]esta gra' com'ogn'altra che potesse ricevere p[er] adesso. Io, che vego, che q[u]esto sig.or tratta piu tosto alla soldatesca, che stare sù i pontiglij, hò accetatto il carrigo com'anco di promettere io p[er] tutte le spese, che faranno i d.ti comedianti, sì nell'andare, come nel ritorno et à buon conto hò cominciato à spendere del mio 20. ducatoni nel p[rese]nte correre, che mi saranno poi rimborsati, e della sud.a spesa che faranno i comedia'ti quando non fossero sodisfatti quì intieram.te prometto di farlo del mio supp.do V.A. humilm.te quando la si compiace che vengono subito, a farli soccorrere de denari p[er] il viaggio, dando ordine che siano messi alla mia partita che li farò sempre buoni come sarà conveniente. Sò che V.A. desidera dare ogni gusto à S. Ecc.za come lei professa di corresponderle, e per ciò non le sarò piu tedioso, salvo che p[er] fine le faccio humilissim.te riverenza. di Milano il di ii Marzo 1601.

 D.V.A. ser.ma
 humiliss.mo et oblig.mo
 ser.' Hercole Bellone

28. ASMN, Gonzaga, b. 1725
 12 March 1601. Ercole Bellone, Milan, to Vincenzo Gonzaga, Mantua

Ser.mo s.or mio s.or col.mo
Li comici che V.A. per sua benignità s'è compiaciuto mandare a qsto Ecc.mo s.or Conte di Fuentes capitorno quà sabato prossimo passato nell'hora del desinare, et io fece ch'il Capitan Cardone montò subito sù le poste, et andò à trovare S.E.za à Pavia con una mia l'ra che fù buonissima resolutione poiche l'Ecc.za sua diede subito ordine, che [torn] enesse à levare la sud.a compagnia, e la conducesse à [torn] [Pa]via, com'hà fatto, mà à fare che d.o Capitan Cardone andasse à fare q[u]est'officio vi bisogno molte parole poiche loro intendevano d'haver getato la spesa, e che la gra' che haveva fatto V.A. fosse frustratoria, il che non parse à me conveniente, et in somma ci lo fece andare, che è stato anco di gusto di tutta la compagnia, poiche S.Ecc.za ha mostrato di vederli volontieri p[er] poter goder le comedie in q[u]esti pochi giorni che si fermerà in Pavia.

A S.Ecc.za hò ripresentato con l're con quanto amore, e prontezza V.A. l'hà servito in quest'occasione assicur[*torn*][an]dola, ch'in tutte l'altre di suo gusto, e servitio no[*torn*][n] sara mai per mancar di servirla, e come sarà r[*torn*][i]tornato, reitererò l'officio in viva voce; In [*torn*] V.A. con ogni sommisione m'inchino à piedi [*torn*] [. Da] Milano il di 12 Marzo 1601.
  D.V.A. ser.ma
  humiliss.mo et oblig.mo
  ser' Hercole Bellone

29. ASM, Autografi, cart. 95, fasc. 19bis
  Ill.mo et Ecc.mo sig.re
  Gli Comici Uniti
  M[i]l[ano] die 2. Junij 1601
  P. fo: 33

Ill.mo et ecc.mo s.re
Isabella, Pedrolino, e gli istessi compagni, che furono favoriti da V.E. Ill.ma sendo chiamati da Mantova a Milano, e da Milano a Pavia per l'occasione dell'abboccamento di Mons.r Ill.mo Aldobrandino, et Altezza di Savoia con ogni debito di reverenza la supplicano à far loro grazia, che possano in Milano nella stanza solita del suo Palazzo recitar le loro honeste comedie. hanno già supplicato, ed hora di nuovo supplicano mandando messo à posta, confidano nella sua benignità, ed offerendosi prontissimi ad ogni suo cenno le pregano da N.S. felice fine d'ogni suo desiderio.
  [*diff. hand*] 1601. à 12 di Giugno.
  Faviasigli la patente nella forma solita.
  Cara

30. ASM, Registri delle Cancellerie, s. XXI, no. 25, fos. 33^v–34^r
  20 June 1601.

Don Pietro Enriquez d'Alvedo. Essendo cosa non men debita che degna, et convenevole l'aiutare, et favorire quelli che col loro virtuoso studio procurano il benefetio particolare, et sodisfattione del publico in generale, si come per quello che à noi stessi con sta fanno li Comici Uniti recitando, et rappresentando tanto virtuosam.te ciò che loro occorre, che non solo è di frutto à molti in particolare, mà risulta in tutta la presente Città in generale di non poco contento. Habbiamo p[er] ciò voluto accompagnare con la presente le virtù, et valore d'essi Comici Uniti, et concederli, sicome facciamo, che possino liberam.te, et senza alcuna contradittione recitare le loro honeste comedie tanto in publico, quanto in privato in questa Città di Milano; Con che si recitino le dette commedie in questo Palazzo nel luogo solito, che cosi se nè contentiamo p[er] degni rispetti, et che non si recitino ne i giorni di festa, ne i Venerdi, co[n] che non si doprino

habiti religiosi, ne simili ad essi, ne si mescolino cose divine, ne dicano parole dishoneste, et servando nel resto circa l'essercitio loro, et rappresentatione d'esse commedie gli ordini gia dati p[er] i precessori nostri in q.o governo che è di mostrare, et far vedere da i Deputati sopra ciò il soggetto delle cose prima di rappresentarle p[er] schivare ogni occasione di scandalo. Ordinando, et commandando con la presente à tutti gli offitiali, et ad ogn'altra p[er]sona all'auttorità nostra soggetti, che non solo ad essi Comici Uniti non diano, ne premettano darsi p[er] il sud.o conto impedimento, ne molestia alcuna, mà gli prestino ogni giusto favore, et aiuto possibile, ne alcuno manchi di essequire quanto dis.a contiene p[er] quanto stima cara la gratia n'ra. Da qui in Milano a xx Giugno 1601. sig.a El Conde de fuentes
    V.t Salazar
    Longonus

31. ASMN, Archivio Gonzaga, b. 1725
    15 July 1601. Lelio Bellone, Milan, to Vincenzo Gonzaga, Mantua

Al ser.mo Prencipe mio s.or et padron sing.mo Il s.or Duca di Mantova et di Monferrato

Ser.mo Prencipe mio s.or et padron sing.mo
Questo Ecc.mo s.or conte di Fuentes ha datto ord.ne segretam.te che si diano le mostre à tutte queste cavallerie leggiere a che fine non si sà. é per conto dell'Armada s'hanno lettere di Napoli che dicono, che sia per andare verso la Vallona à sbarcarsi et che daranno a Greci et Albanese le armi in mano volendo andare all'acquisto di s.or Martino sotto cui vi stette anco, dicono, l'Ecc.mo s.or Don Ferrante Gonzaga. et come esso s.or di Fuentes facci continuare la fabricatione delle carrette et casse per l'artiglieria dandolene molta pressia.

    S.E. non stà molto composta col s.or Condestabile de Castiglia, il quale di Spagna scrive à questi ss.ri della previsione della Città che S.M.tà non intende che s'aggravi d'allogiam.to essa Città come intendeva di fare l'E.S. di presente, volendole allogiare le due compagnie della sua guardia, per lo che hieri mandò sfuza Brivio Commiss.rio gn'le nello Tribunale della d.a provisione à farle instanza che rissolvessero sop.a detto allogiamento, et ballotando, riuscito il tutto in bianco, le fù risposto che non intendevano di farlo, ma che Il E.S. facesse conforme le dava gusto; et il tutto rifferito, delliberò d.a E.cc.za di rimandare esso Brivio à far sapere all'Vicc.rio con i dodeci di provisione che le dassero le loro ragioni iniscritto perche non intendono d'allogiare; è questo si crede per qual che nuovo ord.ne che le sij venuto di Spagna (come ce ne da inditio la d.a lettera dil s.or Cond.le) che non astringa la d.a Città al detto allogiamento, per lò che le d.e Guardie sarebbero tuttavia sopra q'ste hostarie, q'ndo Il Prencipe d'Ascole, forse per havere [?]decore de far quatrini, non le havesse domandate in magg.or parte per mettere in Monza suo feuda à riffrenare il pensiero di q'lli huomini che stavano per movere litte seco.

Del s.or Duca di Modena si và publicando che S.M.tà Catt.ca le habbi assegnato 12/m. scudi di Prato, l'anno, et ne habbi anco datto altri 4/m. l'anno a Dona Matilda sorella dil s.or Duca di Savoia per la buona servitù fatta alla ser.ma Dona Catherina sua sorella. Che 'l sud.to s.or Duca di Savoia habbi rettirato molto la sua casa dalle spese, et che se restia su'l avantaggio di mettere insieme delle [torn] et ch'habbi mandato a dimandare li comici uniti. li q[u]ali [torn]ndo pattegiare seco forse non li andarano à dar' ricreat.e, et qui à commedie non solo le và Il s.or Conte di Fuentes ma anco ve le invita il cons.e. Che è quanto m'occorre dire per hora all'A.V. acciò per fine faccio hum.te riverenza. di Milano à 15. di Luglio 1601.
  D. V.A. ser.ma
  Hum.o et fed.mo ser.re
  Pre Lelio Bellone

32. RIME / D'ISABELLA ANDREINI / PADOVANA / Comica Gelosa. / Dedicate all'Illustriss. & Reverendiss. Sig. / IL SIG. CARDINAL S. GIORGIO / CINTHIO ALDOBRANDINI. / [mark] / in Milano, / Appresso Girolamo Bordone, & Pietromartire Locarni / compagni. M. DCI. / Con licenza de' Superiori.

All'Illust.mo & Rever.mo mio Sig.re e patron col.mo Il Signor Cardinal S. Giorgio Cinthio Aldobrandini.

 Se dovessero le persone private con egual ca[m]bio pareggiare i favori de i Principi, dubbio non è, ch'essendo questa troppo faticosa, e disegual'impresa alle forzero, dovrebbono più tosto desiderar le gratie, che vedersi di quelle arricchite; non è però, che s'habbiano da porre in oblìo, perche questa sarebbe espressa ingratitudine; e non si trova cosa, che da così fatto vitio ne difenda; ond'io, che oltre ogni mio merito sono stata da V.S. Illustrissima, e Reverendissima favorita non una volta, ma molte, e molte; comech'io fin da principio sgombrassi dalla mente ogni pensiero, ed ogni speranza di poter giamai agguagliar i suoi favori: tuttavia non hò mancato di pensar meco stessa, e d'ingegnarmi per trovar cosa, ond' almeno io potessi mostrarmene ricordevole; e son'andata hor questa, ed hor quella scegliendo, nè mai mi son'appigliata ad altra, che à questa delle mie Rime; nè meno havrei havuto ardir di prenderla, conoscendo, ch'ella è troppo humile alla sua grandezza, quand'io non sapessi, che non per altro à lei hò voluto dedicarle, che perch'ella conosca, ch'io serbo memori a delle gratie ricevute, e per segno della riverenza, ch'io le porto. oltre che m'è parso ancora, non dirò convenevole; ma necessario (dovend'io à persuasione di molti mandarle alla luce del Mondo) il consacrarle non ad altrui, che à V.S. Illustriss. e Reverendiss. vero Tempio della Virtù, e dell'Honore, ed à questo fare m'hà confortata non poco il perito legislator Ligurgo, ilquale nelle sue ben composte leggi ordinò, che quei doni, che sacrificando s'offerivano à gli Iddii fossero poveri, e semplici, accioche più facilmente potessero da ciascheduno esser honorati. Dunque non sarà sconvenevole, s'à voi gran CINTHIO, che per l'altezza dello stato, e per la 'nfinita virtù altro quasi non sete, che un terreno Dio, co'l giudicio del quale si fà bello il Mondo, appresento, e sacro questo mio picciol dono; picciolo in quanto à voi mio Signore; poiche non è cosa per grande, che sia, ch'à vostri meriti contraposta non appaia picciola; ma non già tale inquanto à me, poiche nè più cara, nè più pregiata cosa haveva io da donare à V. Sign. Illustrissima, e Reverendissima; essendo questi componimenti (quali siano) parti di quel poco ingegno, ch'è piacciuto alla divina bontà di concedermì; e però da me amati in quella stessa guisa, che s'amano i propri figli; ne i quali no[n] pur si tie[n] caro il bello, e 'l buono, ma l'istesse macchie, e difetti aggradiscono, e piacciono; e se à grandezza di quelli tutto ardisce il Padre, e tenta il tutto, perche io, che sola à questi miei figli son Padre, Madre, e Nutrice non doverò tentare à grandezza, ed à gloria loro di rischiarargli à raggi divini di voi lucidissimo Sole, dallo splendor del quale possono ricever perpetuo lume? ricevagli dunque la sua benignità; e se le pareranno per avventura indegni dell'altezza de' suoi pensieri (come quella, ch'è sempre intenta à cose sublimi) iscusimi appresso di lei la materna pietà, che 'l bene della sua prole continuamente desidera; e gradisca, e lodi in me se non altro l'accorto, e saggio avvedimento, havendo con giuditio eletto alle mie debili, ed oscure compositioni un così forte, e lucido appoggio, e per fine humilissima le m'inchino.

Di Milano il dì 22. Settembre 1601.
Di V.S. Illustriss. e Reverendiss.
Devotiss serva
Isabella Andreini.

33. ASM, Autografi, cart. 94, fasc. 3
Al Po.tà di Pavia
a 12 di ott.re 1601

Ill.mo & ecc.mo S.re
Isabella Andreini Comica humiliss.a serva di V.E. Ill.ma con ogni debito di reverenza le espone, che due volte hà procurato di recordar à V.E. à bocca la promessa della lettera per Pavia, ma sempre le è stato detto esser occupata. hor essendo per partirsi humiliss.a le s'inchina, e la supplica con questo memoriale à fargliene grazia; e perche s'intende, che di questi che montano in banco in piazza publica fanno commedie, anzi guastano commedie, parimente la supplica a fare scrivere al S.r Podestà, che non consenta, che le facciano; confida nella sua benignità, e le prega da N.S. felice fine d'ogni suo desiderio.

[2ᵛ] Memoriale
D'Isabella Andreini

34. RIME D'ISABELLA / ANDREINI PADOVANA, / [Damaged] / IN PARIGI. / Appresso Claudio de Monstr'oeil nella Corte del / Palazzo al nome di Iesus. / 1603.

ALL'ILL.MO S.RE IL S.R SEBASTIANO ZAMETTI. Ill.mo mio S.re patron col.mo

Queste poche Rime, ch'io dedico à V.S. Ill.ma sono state da me fatte parte in Italia, e parte in Francia. Le fatte in Italia son quelle, che prime in ordine hanno quei brevi argomenti, e, che sono in stampa con l'altre mie. Quelle che hanno solamente: nomi, à cui sono indirizzate, qui in Parigi m'hà dettate l'affetto. Hò fatta questa unione per dichiararmi (come veramente sono) divotiss.a à i nominati, non escludendo però l'universale. Si compiaccia V.S. Ill.ma di leggerle, nè se ne sdegni, poiche non si sdegnava neanche Q. Mutio Scevola huomo celebratissimo di giuocar talvolta alla palla per sottrarsi al grave studio delle leggi. Non la pregherò à gradir la picciolezza del dono, perche quant'ella concedesse à miei preghi, tanto torrebbe alla sua benignità; dirò solo, che voglia adempieri miei difetti con la sua gratia, ed humilissima le m'inchino.

Di Parigi, il di 20. di Marzo 1603.
Di V.S. Ill.ma Divotiss.a Serva,
Isabella Andreini.

35. ASF, Mediceo, f. 917, fo. 777^{r-v}
26 August 1603. Isabella Andreini, Paris, to Belisario Vinta, Florence

Al Molto Ill.re Sig.or mio, oss.mo il Sig.or Bilisario Vinta Seg.rio di St.to di [torn] .S.A.S. A firenze

Molto Ill.re mio s:re e pron' col.mo
Alla commissione della Maestà della Regina cristianiss.a, & alla sua bontà .V.S. perdoni il mio fastidirla. ch'io sia lontana dal darle molestia ella può assicurarsene, send'io stata parecchi mesi senza scriverle di particolare, che pur m'importa; Hora non potendo far dimeno è forza, ch'io replichi queste poche righe. Saprà .V.S. che da che le mandai la lettera scritta dalla Regina à sua Altezza ser.ma in materia del far haver merito à tutta la somma di que' denari, ch'io hò sul Monte di Pietà in Firenze, tre volte ella me n'hà dimandato. Due in Parigi, e una à Monceaux, dove sono stata con la compagnia à servire; La prima, io le mostrai la lettera, che 'l S.r Cioli per ordine di .V.S. m'havèa scritta data sotto il di 14 di Marzo del corrente anno. Le altre due, e particolarmente l'ultima, che fù il mese passato le dissi, che non ne haveria havuto altro aviso: ma, ch'io ne sperava bene, confidata nella gentilezza, e nell'humanità del S.r Cav.r Vinta mio signore offeziosissimo verso chi ricorre alla sua bontà. Ella lodando la mia speranza, e maravigliandosi della tardanza mi disse, ch'io scrivessi di nuovo, e procurassi d'intender l'esito del negozio, che, s'havesse bisognato altra lettera l'haveria scritta, certiss.a d'ottener in mio benefizio quel, c'havesse dimandato. Scrivo dunque si per ubbidir alla commiss:e come perche mi sarebbe più caro di renderle palesi della grazia ottenuta, che d'affaticarla in altro scrivere, e la prego ad ordinare, che me ne sia dato ragguaglio, che ben la lettera giungera à tempo, dovendo noi star al

servizio dell'una, e dell'altra Maestà questo verno, e forse ancor più. Humiliss.a le m'inchino, e le prego da N.S. il colmo d'ogni desiderata prosperità.
Di Parigi il di 26 d'Agosto 1603
D. V.S. molto Ill.re
Servitrice aff.ma
Isabella Andreini:

Poiscritta. Facendomi .V.S. grazia di sue lettere, e dovend'io seguitar la corte le mandi con qualche mezo, ch'i'possa haverle: Non sò dove disegni d'andar il Re. qui ognun dire, ch'anderà in Provenza, e che per ottobre dev'esser in Lione. sia come si voglia; se .V.S. si compiacerà di farmene degna ben saprà come farlo, e le m'inchino di nuovo—

36. ASF, Mediceo, f. 920, fo. 513^r

7 December 1603. Isabella Andreini, Paris, to Belisario Vinta, Florence

All'Ill.mo mio S:re e pr'on col:mo il S.r Cav.r Bellisario Vinta segretario del ser.mo gran Duca di Toscana di Firenze

Ill.mo S:re e p'ron mio col.mo
La lettera di .V.S. Ill.ma data sotto l' 8.o giorno del mese passato mi fù resta il di di .S. Caterina, allaquale haverei risposto subito, s'io fossi stata in Parigi. Io era con la compagnia à Fontainebleau, dove sono stata trentasei giorni, compiacendosi l'una, e l'altra Maestà della nostra servitù, e trattenendoci con provisione di 200 D.di al mese. Subito, ch'io l'hebbi letta me n'andai a far riverenza alla Regina, e la ringraziai se non quanto doveva, almeno quanto sapeva della grazia in sua grazia ottenuta, ed ella se n'allegrò, offerendomi in ogn'altra mia occ.ne benignamente ogni favore, cosi ringrazio il ser.mo Gran Duca della concessione, e .V.S. Ill.ma della memoria, c'hà havuta d'una sua devotissima servitrice procurandole il desiderato benefizio. La Maestà del Re mostrò d'haverne pari contento con la Regina (perch'io la ringraziai in sua presenza) e s'offeri anch'egli com'ella s'era offerta dicendo, c'haveria sommamente caro ogni mio bene, ilqual bene non meno riconosco dall'offizio di .V.S. Ill.mo che dalla lettera di Sua Maestà, e dalla benignità di sua Altezza; e sicome a tutti due sono, e sarò perpetuamente obligata, cosi à tutti tre prego, e pregherò sempre da N.S. il colmo d'ogni desiderata prosperità, & humiliss.a le m'inchino.
Di Parigi il di 7 di Decembre 1603.
Di .V.S. Ill.ma
Devotiss.a servitrice
Isabella Andreini

37. PIANTO / D'APOLLO, / RIME FVNEBRI: / In morte d'Isabella Andreini, Comica / Gelosa, & Accademica Intenta / detta l'ACCESA. / *Di Gio. Battista Andreini suo figliuolo.* / Dedicato alla Sereniss. Madama /

LEONORA GONZAGA, / DVCHESSA DI MANTOVA, / E di Monferrato, &c. / Con alcune Rime piaceuoli, sopra vno SFORTVNATO / POETA dello stesso Autore, / [mark: CRESCIT OCCVLTO / VELASCUS] / IN MILANO, Per Girolamo Bordoni, & Pietromartire / Locarni. 1606. *Con licenza de' Superiori.*

Alla Sereniss. Madama / LEONORA GONZAGA, / DVCHESSA DI MANTOVA, / E DI MONFERRATO, &c. / *Giovan Battista Andreini Comico Fedele.*

Che il dolore della morte di persona cara sia il più atroce, che provi mortale, è già così noto, che non fà di mestieri, ch'io m'affatichi provarlo: nè volendo potrei: poi che bastante non è questa penna figurar la mia pena; onde perciò già cede il freddo inchiostro alle calde lagrime mie: poi, che conosce, che meglio sapranno piangere gli occhi, che spiegare egli stesso concetti à tanta angoscia conformi. Fermisi dunque questa mano, che si come degna non fù di chiudere le materne luci nell'hora estrema, così comanda il dolore ch'ella termini la cominciata impresa. Intanto non isdegni l'Altezza sua d'accettare queste mie funebri composizioni, vero parto del dolore, vere amare lagrime del mio cuore: come quella invitissima Principessa, il cui valore, è così grande, che non potendo tutto portarlo la fama, v'aggiunse il Cielo quattro nere Aquile, le quali lampeggiano gloriose nello Scudo del Serenissimo VINCENZO GONZAGA, Consorte suo, e mio Signore, à voi dunque ò saggia Leonora, à voi dico ò lucidissima Stella (alla quale si devono indirizzare tutte l'opere di coloro, che nel Mar di qual si voglia fatica honorata navigano) volgo questo lugubre, & ondeggiante mio Legno: ilquale da i flutti de i maligni sicuro (mercè sua) essendo, potrà ogn'hora con sì felice scorta solcar l'onde del mondo tranquille, e provare ogni momento i Zefiri dell'aura popolare secondi: & insieme intanta sua felice calma conoscer farà, che si come la mia cara Madre vivendo, e servendo l'Altezza Vostra se le dichiarò così sviscerata, & obligata ancella, così morendo, & amando spronò mè suo figlio à farle questo flebil dono, acciò, che la Fama ad alto suono d'ISABELLA debba dire.
Grande amor non si scorda co'l morire. Data in Milano à dì 1. Luglio. 1606.
Di V.A.S.
Servo devotissimo
Gio. Battista Andreini
Comico Fedele.

38. LETTERE / D'ISABELLA / ANDREINI / PADOVANA, / COMICA GELOSA, / ET ACADEMICA INTENTA; / NOMINATA L'ACCESA. / *Dedicate* / AL SERENISSIMO DON CARLO EMANVEL / DVCA DI SAVOIA, &c. / *CON LICENTIA DE SVPERIORI, E PRIVILEGIO.* / [mark] / IN VENETIA, MDCXII. / Appresso Sebastiano Combi.

AL SERENISSIMO D. CARLO EMANUVEL DVCA DI SAVOIA, &c.

La Natura, (Serenissimo Signore) quella nostra madre ottima, e massima vedendo di non poter perpetuar ciascun di noi stessi, come quella, che non hà altro fine, che di perpetuarci in modo che non habbiam mai fine, procurò studiosamente per altro mezo di conseguir il desiderio suo in quanto poteva; onde saviamente destò in alcuno ardentissima voglia di filgliuoli, nipoti, e pronipoti, nella vita de i quali, i Padri, gli Avi, & i Proavi, benche morti, felicemente immortali si vivono. Alcun'altro, perche godesse del privilegio della vita dopò la vita, chiamò quelle à nobilissime arti, così di essa Natura imitatrici, che molte volte hanno ardire di gareggiar mirabilmente seco; e che sia vero, ecco le vive dipinte, che ingannano gli uccelli, & ecco la statua scolpita, che innamora un giovane: ma giudicando, anzi chiaramente conoscendo questa grande, e più prudente madre, che frà tutte le cose atte à render l'huomo immortale, attissimo era il sapere, con la sua mirabil forza il fè a lui tanto commune, che eli è in lui desiderio innato. Chiamasi l'huomo mercè del sapere, Signor delle cose inferiori, famigliar delle superiori, terreno Dio, animale celeste, e finalmente, pompa, e miracolo della medesima Natura. Dimandato Anassagora, perch'era nato, disse. Per contemplar le stelle, laqual cosa non potendosi fare, se non per mezo del sapere ci fa conoscer, che ogn'uno che nasce, nasce con desiderio, di sapere; hor essend'io stata dalla bontà del Sommo Fattore mandata ad eser Cittadina del Mondo, & essendo per avventura questo desiderio di sapere nato in me più ardente, che in molt'altre Donne dell'età nostra, lequali come che scuoprano in virtù de gli studi molte, e molte esser divenute celebri, & immortali, nondimeno vogliono solamente attender (e ciò sia detto con pace di quelle che à più alti, & à più gloriosi pensieri hanno la mente rivolta) all'go, alla conochia, & all'arcolaio, essendo dico in me nato ardentissimo il desiderio di sapere, hò voluto à tutta mia possanza alimentarlo; e benche nel mio nascime[n]to la Fortuna mi sia stata avara di quelle commodità, che si convenivano per ciò fare, e benche sempre i' sia stata lontanissima da ogni quiete, onde non hò potuto dir con Scipione, che mai non mi son veduta men'otiosa, che quando era otiosa, tuttavia per non far torto à quel talento, che Iddio, e la Natura mi diedero, e perche 'l viver mio non si potesse chiamar un continuo dormire, sapend'io, che ogni buon Cittadino è tenuto per quanto può à beneficar la sua Patria, à pena sapea leggere (per dir cosi) che io il meglio, ch'i'seppi mi diedi à comporre la mia Mirtilla favola boschereccia, che se n'uscì per le porte della stampa, e si fece vedere nel Teatro del Mondo molto male in affetto, per colpa di proprio sapere (io non lo nego) ma per mancamento ancora d'altrui cortesia (e non v'ha dubbio.) Dopò sudai nella fatica delle mie Rime, e di ciò non contenta procurai di rubbar al Tempo, & alla necessità del mio faticolo essercitio alcun breve spatio d'hora, per dar opera a queste lettere, che di mandar alla luce presso gli altri miei scritti ardisco, più, perche mi confido nella benignità del Mondo, che, perch'i'creda, ch'esse vagliano; e se alcuno dicesse, che fu sempre intentione di chi mandò lettere alle stampe, d'insegnar il vero modo di scriverle, sappia quel tale, ch'io non hebbi mai cosi temerario pensiero, sapendo, ch'è solamente dato a gli huomini più intendenti l'havere, e 'l conseguir simil fine. Intention mia dunque fu di schermirmi quanto più i' poteva dalla morte: ammaestrata cosi dalla Natura; per ciò non doverà parere strano ad alcuno s'io ho mandato, e se tuttavia mando nelle mani de gli huomini gli scritti miei, poiche ogn'uno desidera naturalmente d'haver in se stesso, e 'n suoi parti, se non perpetua, almeno lunghissima vita: e per conseguirla più facilmente hò eletto di dedicar questa forse non ultima fatica à V.A.S. e benche a Principe tanto perfetto cosa men che perfetta donar non si dovesse, e benche i'm'avvegga, che queste lettere mancano tanto di perfettione quant'ella n'abbonda, nondimeno hò voluto seguir il mio proponimento, assicurandomi, che non perderò tanto per gli infiniti mancamenti d'esse, quanto acquisterò per gli innumerabili meriti suoi. Sà V.A.S. che quelli, che dedicano le fatiche loro hanno tutti diverso fine; percioche altri conoscendo, ò stimando i lor componimenti di tanta perfettione, che 'l Tempo con le sue rapine, e con le sue violenze non possa punto lor nuocere si persuadono di raccomandar all'immortalità con le opere i nomi di quelli a cui hanno voluto dedicarle. Altri nella dedicatione ad altro non intendono, che ad ubbidir alla consuetudine, poiche hoggidì non si mandano fuori quattro righe, che non habbiano con esse la dedication loro. Altri ciò fanno, perche le genti sappiano sotto qual protettione essi vivono, & altri per altre mondane occasioni mandano fuora i lor libri cosi dedicati. Hora se dimandasse alcuno a me, perch'io mandi fuori le presente mie Lettere sotto 'l chiarissimo nome di V.A.S. che dovrei, o che potrei risponderé? certo non altro che la sopradetta ragione, cioè, per conseguir più facilmente ò perpetua, ò almeno lunghissima vita; ma perpetua senza dubbio, poich'ella perpetuamente nelle sue Heroiche attioni, viverà: aggiungendo, ch'io non sapeva in qual altro modo far conoscer ad altrui, ch'io son vera, & humilissima serva, che nel sacrarle i frutti (benche senza sapore) colti ne i campi delle mie lunghe vigilie; i quali se per avventura le saran grati, reputerò d'haver non picciola parte di quella felicità, allaquale s'ingegnano tanto i mortali d'arrivare. Ricevagli dunque V.A.S. e si ricordi, ch'è non minor segno d'animo generoso il ricever con benignità i doni piccioli, che 'l donar con magnificenza i grandi, ancorche si possa con ragion dire, ch'ella più tosto doni, che riceva; essendoche queste opere mie non più mie: ma sue saranno per lei sola tenute in pregio; onde vien'a donarmi quello, che con tanta ansietà, e con si lunga fatica è stato da me procurato; & humilissimamente inchinandomi la prego con quel più vivo affetto, ch'io sò, e posso a tener tanto me per sua serva, quant'io tengo V.A.S. per mio Signore.

Di Venetia adì 14 Marzo 1607.
Di V.A. Sereniss.
Humilissima, e devotissima serva.
Isabella Andreini.

39. Fatiche / Comiche Di / Domenico / Bruni Detto / Fulvio. / Comico Di Madama Serenissima Principessa di / Piemonte. Parte Prima. Dedicate

All'Illu/strissimo, & eccellentissimo, D. / Cesare di Vandome Duca / Di Vandome, di Belforte, & / di Etampe, Governato / re di Bertagna, &c. / [*mark*] / Parigi, / Per Nicolao Callemont. / MDCXXIII.

Prologo in laude della musica

Non essendo per altro composta, nostri Signori, la comedia che per essempio dell'uman vivere e per dare diletto a gl'ascoltanti, dubbio non ha che bisogna al poeta comico giudicio di conoscere quai mezzi debba usare per giungere al suo fine, qual è di dilettare e di giovare. Per dilettare adopera diversi lenguagi, abiti ridicoli e motti arguti; per giovare dimostra prudenti vecchi, col consiglio de' quali a gl'ascoltanti insegna, introduce giovani e giovane innamorati che, con i suoi finti travagli, mostrano alla gioventù quai siano i veri, ed infine scuopre, in un bene inteso suggetto, a quanti accidenti in questa vita umana siamo sottoposti. Diletta la comedia a gl'occhi con gl'apparati, con gl'abiti e colla presenza de' recitanti, ralegra il core col riso, pasce l'intelletto con le sentenze, e per dare inefabile piacere all'udito, inanzi che si cominci e nel fine d'ogni atto, vole che si canti e suoni per alettare e dilettare, essendo che molti vogliono che maggiore diletto non si trovi ch'il suono e 'l canto. Macrobio dice che ogni anima è presa ed ogni cosa vivente alettata da' suoni musicali; e Cassiodoro dicea ch'ella placa la crudeltà, ecita la dapocagine, rende salubre l'ozio a' vigilanti, gl'odii rivolge in grazia; ed in somma, niuna cosa ritrovarsi più atta a rimovere gl'animi umani. Onde con ragione noi comici tante volte in una sola comedia abiamo introdotto la musica. Chirone, conoscendo l'iraconda natura d'Achille, li aprende la musica colla quale egli poi tenta convertire in amore l'ira che contro Agamenone avea concetta. La inesorabil crudeltà di Nerone, che non poté essere placata dall'amor della patria, dalla riverenza del precettore e finalmente dall'amor della madre, che quella non facesse per suo diletto ardere, e quello e questa morire, i suoni musicali di Terno cittaredo ebero forza di mitigarla, ed aprire la strada ad amore, fra l'ombre caliginose de' suoi innumanissimi pensieri. Lamia colla soavità del canto più che colla bellezza infiamava gl'uomini e, fra gl'altri, tanto di lei si accese Demetrio, che niuna consolazione godea maggiore che l'udire le sue dolcissime noti. Orfeo, con la divinità del suono e del canto, non solo acquistò l'amore di leggiadre ninfe, ma de' Numi infernali; ed Amfione per mezzo della musica fabrica le mura a Tebe. Onde con ragione, per placare gli animi de gl'impazienti, i comici si prevagliono della musica. Teofilo la chiamò conservatrice d'amore: e ben lo dimostrò quel gentil musico che mentre visse col suono e canto conservò l'amore di Clitenestra verso Agamenone. Riferisse Plutarco ch'un delfino, tratto dalla dolcezza del canto d'Arione, innamorato di lui, lo salvò dal mare ov'egli per timore de' marinari s'era gettato. Placa il suono del timpano la ferocità dell'elefante. Aqueta la melodia della fistula la ferità del cervo. Accese la soavità della cetra un'oca dell'amor d'un cittaredo. Liberarono, colla dolcezza del suono, Febo la Grecia e Talete Creta dalla peste. Mosse la sonora cetra d'Eumonio una cicala, la quale, cantando mentre egli sonava, fece l'ufficio d'una cora che s'era rotta. E però non è meraviglia se la musica ammolisse gl'animi umani: il che, conosciuto da' comici, tre volte ordinariamente in una comedia hano introdotto il canto. Pitagora dicea che i globi celesti fano i lor movimenti con eccellentissime voci che l'una all'altra perfettamente corispondono, ed assegnava a ciascun cielo la voce propria, e voleva ch'il sole per essere maggiore, più lucido e principale fra gl'altri pianeti, reggesse l'armonia. E Plato dicea ch'ogni cielo gode il canto d'una sirena. Gl'elementi sono quattro, e nel numero del quattro sono compresi il duplo, triplo, quadruplo, sesquialtero, sesquiterzio, diapson, disdiapson, diapente e diateseron, come dimostra il Ficino, onde tra loro compartita la gravità, la leggerezza, il freddo, il caldo, l'umido ed il secco, ne risulta perfetta armonia. Se noi consideraremo la pulsazione che deriva da' spiriti del cuore in tutto il corpo umano, conosceremo che questa altro non è che armonia, poiché mentre gl'umori del corpo insieme s'amano, si conserva l'armonia della pulsazione; subito che tra di loro nasce discordia e che l'uno supera l'altro, ella rimane alterata. Ma che diremo noi essere la comedia che musica. Tre sorti di generi ha la musica: diatonico, cromatico ed enarmonico, e tre atti ha la comedia. L'armonia è concento che nasce da due parti almeno, insieme unite, e la comedia è armonia che nasce dalle molte parti de' personaggi insieme uniti. Unisono altro non è che due voci simili insieme accompagnate, e dolce unisono è quello che nella comedia è formato da duo amanti d'un solo volere. La disonanza è distanza di suono grave ed acuto, che insieme per loro natura unir non si ponno, e nella comedia è disonanza tra l'avarizia de' vecchi e la liberalità de' giovani, che insieme per natura unir non si ponno. La musica aletta e la comedia diletta; la musica è molte voci concordi insieme e la comedia è da molte persone apresentata. La musica è d'utile, e la comedia è di giovamento. Per mezzo della musica s'espongono al canto poetiche invenzioni, e per mezzo della comedia si rapresentano sopra i teatri infiniti poemi. La musica ha bisogno di silenzio e la comedia non ricerca altro che attenzione. Eccovi dunque la comedia, perfetta musica. Or tocca a voi, Signori, mentre questi miei maggiori sono per farvi sentire il concento della lor comedia, a fare silenzio, acció che non diate a loro quel disturbo che darebbe a eccellente musico, mentre con virtuosa compagnia essercita il canto, uno che indiscretamente facesse rumore e la sua armonia impedisse.

40. Isabella Andreini, *Mirtilla*
    Act III, Scene v, lines 1721–97

Opico
Or via rendete al suon concorde il canto,
Poiché noi siamo in sì bel loco a l'ombra,
Dove Flora tra i fiori
In braccio al suo marito si riposa;
Ed ei per la dolcezza
Spira vento soave in queste fronde,

Virgil, *Eclogues*
Eclogue 3, lines 55–111

Palaemon
Dicite, quandoquidem in molli consedimus
    herba.
et nunc omnis ager, nunc omnis parturit arbos
nunc frondent silvae, nunc formosissimus annus
incipe, Damoeta; tu deinde sequere, Menalca:
Alternis dicetis; amant alterna Camenae.

E 'l mormorar de l'onde
Farà tenore al suono
Di questo cavo legno.
Or tu comincia Filli,
E poi segui Mirtilla;
Cantate dunque a prova,
Che 'l cantar a vicenda aman le Muse.

Filli
Dotta Calliopea,
Madre di quel buon trace,
Ch'ogn'animal più fero e più fugace
Con la sonora voce a sé traea,
Inspira, o diva, a questa voce mia
Soave melodia.

Damoetas
Ab Iove principium, Musae: Iovis omnia plena;
ille colit terras, illi mea carmina curae.

Mirtilla
O de le Muse padre,
Vien oggi nel mio canto e nel mio core,
Nel mio cor che si sface
De' tuoi studi non men che de la face
Del mio nemico Amore.
Così le prime sue membra leggiadre
Vesta la figlia di Peneo sdegnosa
Per esserti pietosa.

Menalcas
Et me Phoebus amat; Phoebo sua semper apud
  me
munera sunt, lauri et suave rubens hyacinthus.

Filli
Quattro e sei pomi accolti in un sol ramo
Serbo a la mia capanna e gli destino
Al mio vago pastor che cotant'amo.

Damoetas
Malo me Galatea petit, lasciva puella,
et fugit ad salices, et se cupit ante videri.

Mirtilla
Una fromba da me con bel lavoro
Fatta di seta e di fin or contesta,
Sarà don di colui che amo e adoro.

Menalcas
At mihi sese offert ultro, meus ignis, Amyntas,
notior ut iam sit canibus non Delia nostris.

Filli
Quanti spargo sospiri e quanti lai,
Perché 'l mio crudelissimo pastore
Pietoso del mio mal si mostri omai.

Damoetas
Parta meae Veneri sunt munera: namque notavi
Ipse locum, aëriae quo congessere palumbes.

Mirtilla
Chi non sa quante volte ho questi colli,
Per isfogar la mia angosciosa pena,
Fatti del pianto mio tepidi e molli?

Menalcas
Quod potui, puero silvestri ex arbore lecta
aurea mala decem misi: cras altera mittam.

Filli
Igilio mi donò due tortorelle
l'altr'ieri, e Clori per invidia quasi
morissi, tanto eran vezzose e belle.

Mirtilla
Due panieri di fior Alcon mi diece,
E Amaranta già di sdegno folle
Volse, per non vederli, altrove il piede.

Filli
L'empir il ciel di strida, ohimè che vale
E 'l crescer acqua co 'l mio pianto a
    l'acqua,
Se non m'acquista fede al mio gran male?

Mirtilla
Amo Uranio crudele e non me 'n pento,
Che la beltà, ch'a tutti gli occhi piace,
Mi fa lieta gioir d'ogni tormento.

Filli
La neve al sole si dilegua, e 'l foco
Strugge la cera, e a me lo sdegno e l'ira
D'Uranio il cor consuma a poco a poco.

Mirtilla
Giovan l'erbe agli agnelli, a l'api i fiori;
A me sol giova contemplar d'Uranio
Nel vago viso i bei vivi colori.

Filli
Dimmi, ninfa, qual è quell'animale
che ne l'acqua si crea poi vive in fiamma
e tuo sarà questo dorato strale.

Mirtilla
Dimmi qual pesce in ocean s'asconde
Che tremar face chi lo tocca a pena
e due caprette avrai bianche e feconde.

Damoetas
O quotiens et quae nobis Galatea locuta est!
partem aliquam, venti, divum referatis ad auris.

Menalcas
Quid prodest, quod me ipse animo non spernis,
Amynta,
si dum tu sectaris apros, ego retia servo?

Damoetas
Phyllida mitte mihi: meus est natalis, Iolla;
cum faciam vitula pro frugibus, ipse venito.

Menalcas
Phyllida amo ante alias: nam me discedere flevit,
et longum 'formose, vale, vale' inquit, 'Iolla'.

Damoetas
Triste lupus stabulis, maturis frugibus imbres,
arboribus venti, nobis Amaryllidis irae.

Menalcas
Dulce satis umor, depulsis arbutus haedis,
lenta salix feto pecori, mihi solus Amyntas.

Damoetas
Pollio amat nostram, quamvis est rustica,
    Musam:
Pierides, vitulam lectori pascite vestro.

Menalcas
Pollio et ipse facit nova carmina: pascite taurum,
iam cornu petat et pedibus qui spargat harenam.

Damoetas
Qui te, Pollio, amat, veniat, quo te quoque
    gaudet;
mella fluant illi, ferat et rubus asper amomum.

Menalcas
Qui Bavium non odit, amet tua carmina, Maevi,
atque idem iungat vulpes et mulgeat hircos.

Damoetas
Qui legitis flores et humi nascentia fraga,
frigidus, o pueri, fugite hinc, latet anguis in herba.

Menalcas
Parcite, oves, nimium procedere: non bene ripae
Creditur; ipse aries etiam nunc vellera siccat.

Damoetas
Tityre, pascentis a flumine reice capellas:
ipse, ubi tempus erit, omnis in fonte lavabo.

Menalcas
Cogite ovis, pueri: si lac praeceperit aestus,
ut nuper, frustra pressabimus ubera palmis.

Damoetas
Heu heu! Quam pingui macer est mihi taurus in ervo!
idem amor exitium pecori pecorisque magistro.

Menalcas
His certe—neque amor causa est—vix ossibus haerent.
Nescio quis teneros oculus mihi fascinat agnos.

Damoetas
Dic, quibus in terris (et eris mihi magnus Apollo)
Tris pateat Caeli spatium non amplius ulnas.

Menalcas
Dic, quibus in terris inscripti nomina regum
nascantur flores, et Phyllida solus habeto.

Opico
Non più ninfe amorose, a me conviene
terminar queste vostre
amorose contese:
Lite non sia tra voi, dove è cotanta
Parità di valore; e io vi giuro
Per gli altri dei ch'a mio giudizio siete

Palaemon
Non nostrum inter vos tantas componere lites:
et vitula tu dignus et hic—et quisquis amores
aut metuet dulcis aut experietur amaros.
claudite iam rivos, pueri: sat prata biberunt.

Pari ne la beltà, pari nel canto.
Ben vi dirò che faticate invano,
poi ch'ognuna di voi
Uranio segue e ama
E pur v'è noto omai
Ch'Ardelia egli sol ama, Ardelia cura:
dunque non sia tra voi discordia o figlie,
ma lasciate d'amar chi voi non ama.

    41. Florence, Biblioteca Nazionale, Magliabecchi, VII, 15

    ALLA SER:MA MADAMA / CRISTIANA de LORENO / GRAN DVCHESSA di TOSCANA, / SIGNORA MIA COLENDISS:MA

CANZONE
Quando scendeste ad'illustrare il mondo
Venere con le gratie in sen' v'accolse,
E ne suoi veli avvolse
Le membra pargolette,
E con viso giocondo
Il cinto di beltade a sè disciolse
E à voi legollo, indi le schiere elette
De i propitij celesti, et almi Numi
Pieni di gioia, e festa
Girorno à terra i lumi,
E dissero hoggi à questa
Pegia Fanciulla à gara ogn'un di noi
Infonda lieto tutti i pregi suoi.

Ne di donna le mamme v'allattaro,
Ma come al folgorante Giove piacque
Le tremanti, e dolci acque
Del famoso Hippocrene
In latte si cangiaro
Per darvi gli alimenti, e si compiacque
Tanto del vostro bello il sommo bene
Ch'ogni virtute in quell'humore ascose,
E col latte suggeste
Quant'ei saggio ripose
Nell'onda, o don celeste
A null'altra concesso, don ch'appieno
V'hornò di vago, e casto il volto, e 'l seno.

E crescendo con voi cresciuta è tanto
Virtù, senno, valor, gratia, e beltate,

Ch'ad'ogn'altra involate
Con sua vergogna, e scorno,
Di gloria il pregio, e 'l vanto;
O fortunata, anzi felice etate
In cui nasceste, o lieto, o caro giorno,
Sovra ogni merto il vostro altier' s'estolle
Come d'altezza avanza
Gran Monte un picciol colle;
Di Dio l'alma sembianza
In voi riluce qual lume per vetro
E per voi si fà chiaro il mondo tetro.

Prefissa meta il ciel, la terra, e 'l mare
Hanno, ma quale ingegno
Porrà termine, o segno
A i merti vostri tanti.
Per voi convien ch'impare
Ad'aggrandirse il mondo, acciò piu degno
Volo spieghi la Fama, Apollo canti
Le vostre lodi, scendino le stelle
A coronarvi il crin per che non serra
Gemme si ricche, e belle
In sè la madre terra
Ch'in giro poste, e 'n ricco, e bel lavoro
Sien degne di toccar le chiome d'Oro.

Già destinata al bel paese tosco
Degna Regina il gallico valore
Mostrò l'invitto core
E con pompa reale
Venne giocondo vosco;
Che potrà dir qual gioia, e qual dolore
La bella Francia in un sol punto assale.
God'ella che la sua leggiadra prole
Sia giunta à Rege invitto,
S'affligge poscia, e duole
E batte il seno afflitto,
Poi che girare in altra parte il piede
La sua più cara, e bella figlia vede.

Quando solcaste lieta il seno ondoso
Del gran Nettun con l'incavato pino,
Venne ogni Dio marino
E le Nereidi, e Theti

Dal fondo loro erboso,
E gli occhi alzaro al bel viso divino
Dolce cantando, et uscir fuora lieti
Guizzando i pesci, e quanti Numi ascosi
Stan nel'onda spumosa,
O ne gli Antri muscosi,
A voi Reale sposa
Guidando in schiera amorosetti balli
Offriro Conche, Perle, e bei Coralli.

E s'al gran tosco Rege non v'havesse
Consorte eletta il cielo, e i merti vostri
De i loro salsi chiostri
V'havrian creata Dea,
Ma 'l Fato no 'l concesse;
E poi che vi donaro i marin Mostri
Con doglia loro a la famosa Alfea
Ella con volto allegro in sen vi prese
E con voci gioconde
Al ciel gratie ne rese,
Verdeggiaron le sponde
Cigni s'udir che con leggiadri modi
Volar ferono al ciel le vostre lodi.

Hora il bel Arno la tranquilla feonte
Al venir' vostro alza dall'onde fuori,
Coronata di fiori
L'alma Flora v'abbraccia,
Vengon dal vicin Monte
Ad'inchinarsi à voi Ninfe, e Pastori,
Trabocca altrui per gli occhi, e per la faccia
La soverchia dolcezza; del suo petto
Ogn'un Tempio vi face,
Col festivo diletto
Vola la santa Pace,
Suona la bianca Fama l'aurea tromba
E, MEDICI, e LORENO il ciel rimbomba.

Canzon degna non sei
Di gire inanzi à lei,
Vanne à la Fama, e humil la prega ch'ella,
Le dica ch'io le son devota ancella.

    Di .V.A.S.
    Humiliss:a e devotiss:a serva
    Isabella Andreini comica gelosa

Alla Ser:ma Madama Christiana de Loreno
Gran Duchessa di Toscana.
Signora mia colendiss:ma

EPITALAMIO
D'amor l'aria sfavilla;
Nel vago ondoso mare
L'alma fronte tranquilla
Cinta d'alga Nettuno lieto scopre;
Par che la terra ogni suo studio adopre
Nel mostrarsi di frutti, e fiori adorna,
Flora gioconda appare;
Con chiome vive, e chiare
Colui che 'l mondo aggiorna
Sorge tutto ridente
Da la dorata porta d'Oriente.

Dal dì che fur disgiunti
I confusi Elementi
Non furo insieme aggiunti
Più fortunati Sposi, il sommo Giove
Sopra di questi ogni sua gratia piove;
Così gli Dei de la celeste corte
Stieno à suoi voti intenti,
Ond' i cor più contenti
Trapassi la lor sorte,
Ne più desire, o spene
Gli resti di goder di maggior bene.

Il superbo Pavone
Spiega l'occhiute piume,
E de la sua Giunone
Con larghe ruote il carro in terra adduce,
Al lampeggiar de la celeste luce
Lascian Driadi, e Napee Selve, e cristalli,
Sovr'ogn'human costume
Nettare corre il fiume,
Risuonan Monti, e Valli
Di voci alte, e gioconde,
E spiran gratie i Boschi gli Antri, e l'onde.

Ecco dal terzo cielo
Venere santa, e pia

Che d'amoroso zelo
Fiammeggia, e Giuno abbraccia, e par che diche
Spente, deh, sien trà noi le guerre antiche;
Godon le Sfere, e par che qui rimbombe
L'angelica armonia,
Ogni dolor s'oblia,
Baciano le colombe
I bei Pavoni in segno
Che spenta è tra le Dee l'ira, e lo sdegno.

Venere ha seco Amore
Amor vero, Amor santo
Che del più puro ardore
Ch'habbian le stelle ha in man sacrata Face
Ch'ogni più freddo core avampa, e sface,
Hor tù dispiega Amor le tue bell'ali
A te signor s'aspetta
Di far dolce vendetta
Di lei, che Fiamme, e strali
Sprezzò sdegnosa, atterra;
Doma quel cor che ti fè un tempo guerra.

Himeneo vieni a noi
E'n questo dì beato
Lega gli eccelsi Heroi
D'indissolubil nodo, il ciel' s'inbruna
Splende in vece di Sol, la bianca Luna,
Vieni ch'è tempo homai, vien che lui miro
Solo à gli scetri nato
Pender dal volto amato,
Vedi che di desiro
Arde di cor la rosa
Ch'ha nel candido sen la bella Sposa.

Tù Dio tù pungi, e scalda
La vaga giovinetta
Ch'è quasi pura falda
Di neve pe 'l timor che la circonda,
Col fiammeggiante vel la chioma bionda
Coprile, onde lo Sposo homai gioisca
Del bel che si l'alletta,
La celeste Angioletta
L'alma beltade offrisca
Al suo cupido Amante,

Ne tenga l'alma più dubbia, e tremante.

Gioite, homai gioite,
Ecco danzando scende
Da le sponde gradite
D'Elicona Himeneo di persa cinto
Di latte, e minio il bel viso dipinto,
Sgombra santo Himeneo la fredda tema
Che con Amor contende,
Dolce battaglia attende
Lo Sposo, hor seco prema
La Verginella il letto
A gli assalti d'amor per campo eletto.

Se 'l bel furor divino
Hoggi mi scopre il vero
Dal alvo peregrino
Verrà d'Heroi si generosa Prole
Ch'altra simil giamai non vide il sole;
Per cui rinoverassi in ogni parte
Il bel vivere primiero,
Del Regio sangue altero
Saran le glorie sparte
Si ch'ogni estremo lido
Sentirà rimbombar la fama, e 'l grido.

Di generoso ardire
Havrai Canzone il vanto,
Ben ch'eguale al desio non s'erga il canto.

    Di .V.A.S.
    Humiliss:a e devotiss:a serva
    Isabella Andreini comica gelosa

42. Correspondence between Isabella Andreini and Erycius Puteanus

a. EPIST XIX. Ticinum. ISABELLAE ANDRAEINAE, Academica Intentae (*Erycii Puteani epistolarum fercula secunda* (Milan, 1602), 41)

Nae tu mihi animo defectum Naturae supples, ANDRAEINA, virilis gloriae non capax tantu[m], sed consors: imò tu sexum tuum linquens, ipso virtutis nisi in virum te transformas. Quod si à viro virtus dicenda, felicior tu viro, quae mulier fructum virtutis procreas: si verò à virtute vir, tibi proemium melioris nominis debetur, quae munia melioris nominis, viri inquam, obis. vir igitur es; & vir quoque diceris, si ANDRAEINAE nomen examinas. Ego quantum te laudo, tantum accuso ignaviam nostram, qui ne nominis quide[m] dignitatem ampliùs tuemur. FVIMVS TROES. Nunc descissimus paullatim, animìque neglecto cultu, ne dicam spreto, formae fortunaéque vanissimis delitiis fastum profitemus. Haec doleo, sed te amo, quòd da[n]nata nobis studia & vota amas. Die Lunae Orationem hîc publicè habiturus sum, *De Munere meo publico*. Vtinam propitiam tuam Suadam experiar, & audacter ac feliciter dicam! utrumque subdifficile, sive apud haec ingenia, quibus difficulter satisfacias? sive meâ naturâ, qui timidior, sive verecundior sum. Commasculabo animum, & conabor inter paucos viri nomen retinere. Vale cum CALENO tuo, ac Antalogistam tuu[m] saluta.

Mediolani, v. Eid. Nouemb. [M]. [D].CI.

Epistle 19. Pavia. To Isabella Andreini, Accademica Intenta.

Truly in my opinion you supply a defect of Nature, Andreina—you, who are not only capable of male glory but in fact an equal partner in it. No, more; abandoning your own sex, you transform yourself by the labour of virtue into a man. Now if the word virtue [*virtus*] derives from the word man [*vir*], then you are more fruitful than a man—you who, although a woman, bear the fruit of virtue. But if the word man derives from the word virtue, then the reward of the better name, meaning the name of man, is due to you who perform the offices belonging to the better name. Therefore you are a man. And indeed you are called a man by name, if you examine the name Andreina. And on a par with my praises of you, I measure my own worthlessness—I, who do not defend even the dignity of the name very well. We were Trojans once. Now we have declined little by little and, while the cultivation of the mind is neglected, not to say shunned entirely, we declare our arrogance with the most vain ornaments of fortune and appearance. These things I lament but you I love, because you love the studies that our age has condemned and dedicated to death. On Monday, I am to give a public speech here entitled, 'On My Public Office'. Would that I might have recourse to your Persuasion and that I might speak boldly and felicitously! Each of these things is rather arduous for me, either because of the strength of my mind, which can be satisfied only with difficulty, or because of my nature, which makes me rather timid or, more precisely, shy. I shall screw up my courage, however, and attempt to retain the name of man among a few persons at any rate. Milan. 9 November 1601.

b. Isabella Andreini to Eyricius Puteanus (Reulens, *Erycius Puteanus et Isabelle Andreini*, 24–5)

Molto Ill.re Sig.or oss.mo

La penna di VS si debb'essere poco stancata, poich'ella nel viaggio dello scrivere ha consumato poco spatio di carta; non dirò già come VS dice, che la sua lettera a me car.ma sia giunta vota e scarica, perchè quanto inchiostre esce della sua

dottiss.ma penna, si può con ragione dire che sia tant'oro, e tante note tante gemme; non ha dunque da credere ch'io le sprezzi, essendo che l'oro e le gemme son cose da tenersi molto care et particolarmente da me, che come donna ramo gli ornamenti e so che ne più belli, ne più ricchi ricever posso di quelli che vengono da VS alla quale bacio con mio marito le mani pregandole da Dio somma felicità. Faccia un baccia mano al Sr Jacopo suo amico, e mio S.re. Di Pavia, li 14 di novemb. 1601. Di VS Ill Affe.ma ser.ce
    Isabella Andreini

Most Illustrious and Respected Sir,
Your pen must have been a little tired, since it in the course of writing consumed little space on the page; I will not say, as you do, that your letter, to me most dear, arrived both empty and depleted, because however much ink comes from your most learned pen, one can rightly call it so much gold, and so many notes, so many gems; do not then think that I spurn them, as gold and gems are things to keep very dear and particularly by me, since, as a woman, I covet ornaments and I know that none more beautiful, none more rich could I receive than those which come from you, whose hands I kiss, with my husband, praying to God to give you complete happiness. Kiss the hand of Mr Jacopo, your friend and my patron. From Pavia, 14 November 1601. Your most affectionate servant,
    Isabella Andreini

c. Isabella Andreini to Erycius Puteanus (Reulens, *Erycius Puteanus et Isabelle Andreini*, 25–6)

Molto Ill.re Sr mio oss.mo
Se 'l volere si cangiasse in potere e 'l desiderio in effetto, mi darebbe il cuore di render gratie per lodi, Sr Ericio mio, se VS fosse così verace nel lodarmi com'è ingegnoso nel rinovar la lode, me felice; ma ohime! ch'io sono tanto lontana da questa desiderata felicità! Quanto è lontano l'effetto dall'opinione! So ben io fermamente che quando la virtù non si fosse prima denominata dall'huomo, che bisognerebbe c'hora ella comminciasse, poi che voi vir veramente virtuosissimo meritate che la virtù de voi si nomini. Oh! foss'io quella famosa Teano, moglie di Pitagora, che tanto seppe, o quell'altra greca Teano che parimente tante degne cose scrisse, perchè s'io fossi tale, come voi dite, all'hora m'ingegnerei di scriver di voi, e so che 'l nobil soggetto mi darebbe tal occasione, ch'io per aventura comporrei versi alti e celebri e quali sariano forse meritevoli di quelle eccelse lodi delle quali vi piace d'honorar al presente quelli da me composti, ma quale io sono procurerei nondimeno di cantar il gran lume nostro, chiaro sol di virtù, non curando il restar abbagliata dalla soverchia luce, quand'io non fossi per hora data alla fatica delle mie Lettere, le quali come diversi di stile, non lasciano ch'io possa invocare a vostra contemplatione le Muse; ma forse spaventate anch'esse per così

alta materia, ricuserebbero il venire, e pur ch'Apollo medesimo non temesse, pur sia che vuole, so ch'un giorno vorrò piu tosto parlando di voi scoprirmi ignorante, che tacendo ingrata. Non viva inforse VS di farmi gratia delle sue lettere, assicurandola ch'io non posso haver cibo più caro che quello de i frutti del suo sapere. Ho inteso dell'oratione ch'è per fare, e mi rallegro seco certa che n'acquistera grandi.ma lode si come fa in tutte l'attioni sue, e come aviene dal suo bellissimo elogio nelle mie rime, il quale è celebratissimo da chiunque lo vede. Il chieder Suada è dunque soverchio a colui che tien Pito nella bocca. Termino col foglio, salutandola caramente con mio marito e 'l Sr Gio: Paulo. Ho scritto un'altra a VS le piacera darmene aviso salutando il Sr Jacopo per me. Di Pavia, li 19 novemb. 1601. Di VS Ill Affe.ma ser.ce

    Isabella Andreini

My Most Illustrious and Respected Sir,
If one could change want into power and desire into fact, it would give me the heart to return thanks for praises, my Mr Erycius; and were you so true in praising me as you are ingenious in renewing the praise, I would be happy. But, alas, I am so far from this desired happiness! How far is the fact from the opinion! I know full well that, if virtue were not previously named by man, it would be necessary to do so now, since you, *vir*—truly most virtuous—deserve that your virtue be named. Oh! Would that I were that famous Theano, wife of Pythagoras, who knew so much, or that other Greek Theano who likewise wrote such worthy works, because, if I were such as these, as you say I am, then I would seek to write of you. And I know this noble subject would give me such inspiration that I should, with good fortune, compose high and celebrated verses that might be worthy of the excessive praise which you now take pleasure in bestowing on those I have already composed. But such as I am, I will be able, nevertheless, to sing of our great light—our radiant sun of virtue—not worrying that I shall be blinded by the brilliance of such dazzling light, were I not at the moment working on my Letters which, so different in style, do not permit me to call forth the Muses to your contemplation. But perhaps they too, frightened by such a high subject, would refuse to come. And as long as Apollo himself did not fear, come what may, I know that one day I shall rather display my ignorance in speaking of you than my ingratitude in keeping silent. Do not hesitate, sir, to make me the gift of your letters, resting assured that I could not have food more dear than the fruits of your wisdom. I heard about the oration that is to be made, and I rejoice with you, certain that you will receive great praise from it, as is given to all your actions, and as results from your most beautiful encomium in my *Rime*, which is highly praised by whoever sees it. Suada, therefore, is not necessary for him who holds Pito in his mouth. I end my letter with the page, greeting you dearly, together with my husband and Mr. Giovan Paolo [Fabbri]. I have written another letter to you; let

me know you received it and greet Mr Jacopo for me. From Pavia, 19 November 1601. From your most affectionate servant,
    Isabella Andreini

d. EPIST. V. Ticinum. ISABELLAE ANDRAEINAE, Academica Intentae
(*Erycii Puteani epistolarum fercula secunda*, 17–19)

Tantam facundiam, tantas litteras in feminam cadere! Ubi robustior ille sexus, qui in chartis pallet, in pulpitis sudat, in studijs consenescit? Ecce litteris nunc quoque Amazones sunt, & Pe[n]thesileam suam habe[n]t. Annon sic meritò te appellem ANDRAEINA, & τοὶς ἀνδρὸὶ opponam? Feminis à Naturâ insitum, loqui: tibi verò, benè loqui. quo sit, ut corrigendo muliebre vitium, virilem virutem superes. Platoni olim, ut in prodigio est, mel suum apes, velut divinae facu[n]diae indices, in os inserverunt: tibi verò Gratiae ipsae, *non montem Hymettum* (Valerij verbis utor) *thymi flore redolentem, sed Musarum Heliconios colles omni genere Doctrinae virentes, Dearum instinctu depastae, maximo ingenio dulcissima alimenta summae eloquentiae instillasse videntur*. Scribis acutè accuratéque: dicis extempore, sed quasi scripseris; eâ ubertate & copiâ, ut cùm nihil addi possit, nihil supersit; eo gestu, ut loqui ipsos digitos; eâ voce, ut *intùs canere Sirenum concordiam* putem; eâ deniq felicitate & successu, ut nutu arbitrióque tuo
    —*pleni modereris frena theatri*.
Quoties te audivi, inscitiam & infantiam eorum deprehendi, qui se doctos disertos'que profitentur: ac meipsum quoque, cui dicendi partes in publico sunt, puduisset tituli mei; nisi tu eum elegantissimo carmine (elogium sive augurium prome[n]s) adservisses. Ego augurium interpretor, quod tu elogium esse voluisti: & sic elogij luce circumfusus, tueor dignitate[m] nominis mei, velut augurio promissam. Tu verò beata, ò Suada, ò Musa, cui jam immortalitas parta! Tua enim, dum vivis, scripta in pretio sunt, & leguntur; ac, dum vivis, aliorum quoque de te monumenta habes, & posteritati tuae coepisti interesse. Ejà Ejà: lege, & legere; imò excitare, ut scribendo scribentium praeconia superes: excitare, ut posterorum accessuram admirationem augeas. Te nobis Natura ipsa, temporìsque pater: tu te posteris dabis. quod'que te admiramur, tuae industrie, & simul benignae Naturae acceptum ferimus; sed quòd posteri admirabuntur, in te unam redundabit. Quo te vehementiùs hortor & rogo, ne minùs scribendo teipsam posteris, quàm dicendo benignitatem Naturae nobis commendes. MYRTILLAM Eclogam, & nunc EPIGRAMMATA vidimus: plura emolire: ut liberis foecunda, libris quoque evadas. Ergò *Epistolares lucubrationes*, queis Comicas omnes delitias, Tragicas divitias, & quicquid elegantiarum est, inclusisti, de manu prome, ut in manus multorum veniant: nos heredes, & deinceps posteri erunt, tu tamen semper domina. Aliter enim se Fortunae ludibria, aliter haec ingenij monumenta habent: illa, post te alium atque alium possessorem sortientur: haec nunquam tua esse desinent, etiam cùm videbuntur desijsse. Est etiam quod jure quodam

amplius à modestiâ tuâ exigimus; ut, proemio ingenii publicè sumpto, ostendas te non ingrato feculo tam praeclaris ac lucule[n]tis dotibus illuxisse. Jtaque laurum carpe, & te[m]pora venustam'que illam χρυσῆς' Ἀφροδίτης venustatem inumbra. ita enim futurum, ne dum verborum nectare audientium sensum mulces, vultus igneo nitore & oculorum radijs accendas. Nec renue. Posteri ipsi iniquè laturi, quòd promereri Phoebarum hunc honorem potueris, non adsumpseris: nos malè audituri, quasi praemium inviderimus. Cogita ò Suada, ò Musa, & teipsam, nos, posteros'que cogita; me quidem ingenij, & eloquij tui miratorem & cultore[m] aeternum habitura. Sic carmen hoc habe, no[n] ut ipsum (impolitum enim est;) sed ut animum inspicias. Vale. Mediolani, Postridie Eidus Decembr. [M].[D].CI.

AD ISABELLAM ANDRAEINAM, SECVLI NOSTRI SULPICIAM,
Florem illibatum populi Suadaéque medullam ENCOMIASTICON.

    Ter dilecta Jovi, cui tres tria munera quondam
    Contribuere Deae, Cypris, Tritonia, Juno;
    Carmine te facili dicam, tua munera dicam.
    Cypris, natalem creperi cum luminis auram
    Libares, medio spumantis gurgite Pomi
    Emergens, vultum'que tibi, cilium'que, comam'que
    Flore venustatis tinxit; Geniumque Leporum
    Omnibus inspersit me[m]bris: Venus altera ut esses;
    Alma Venus, sed casta, & casti mater Amoris.
    Mox, ubi conspexit neglecta crepundia Pallas,
    Indidit ingenij vires, & femina Fama,
    Pierio facilem perfundens nectare mentem,
    Pierio facilem perfundens nectare linguam,
    Nectare, quâ prisci durares Suada Theatri.
    Pennato sequitur gressu Saturnia Juno,
    Nubilis indignans sine conjuge virginis annos
    Labi: felicem thalamum, taedas'que jugales,
    Et tabulas ornat: carmen canit ipse Hymenaeus.
    Duceris à caro, & numerò foecunda marito
    Multiplici pateris Lucinae prole labores.
    Constans connubij vinclum! Tu conjuge digna:
    Te pariter conjux, cui pignora cara dedisti.
    Nunc ternae veterem Divae posuére furorem,
    Quas'que Paris peperit rixas, feliciter aufers.
    Tu nova dicéris Cypris, Tritonia, Juno:
    Casto coniugio, Sophiâ, vultus'que decore.

Epistle 5. Pavia. To Isabella Andreini, Accademician of the Intenti.

That such eloquence, that such learning should fall to the part of a woman! Where does that sex which is mighty in writing, which sweats in public declamation, which grows old in literary studies—where does it show itself stronger than in you? Behold, now there are Amazons of learning, and they have their own Penthesilea! Shall I not call you by the name Andreini with good reason, and compare you to men? It has been implanted in women by nature to be able to speak, but in you to be able to speak well, whence it arises that by correcting a feminine vice you surpass even the virtue of the male. Once, as an omen of the future, bees put their honey into Plato's mouth, as though they were signifying the presence of divine eloquence. But the Graces themselves seem to have instilled in your great character the sweetest nourishment of the highest eloquence—the Graces, who 'not on Mt. Hymettus, redolent with flowering thyme' (I am quoting Valerius) 'but on the Heliconian hills, growing green with every kind of learning, feed on the inspiration of the goddesses'. You write with accuracy and acuity; you speak extemporaneously, but as if you had composed it—with such richness and fullness that, when nothing can be added, nothing remains unaddressed—with such gestures that I could imagine your fingers themselves were speaking—with such a voice that I could suppose that the harmony of the Sirens sang within you—with such propriety and, finally, success, that by your nod and authority, you can hold the reins of a full theatre. As often as I have heard you, I have perceived the ignorance and childishness of certain persons who profess themselves to be learned and well spoken; and I myself, who have a part in public speaking, would have been ashamed of my own title, had you not protected it with your most eloquent song. I interpret as an augury that which you wished to call a panegyric, and I can protect the dignity of my name as though that dignity were promised by an augury. You are truly blessed, O Persuasion, O Muse—you, who already have a share of immortality. For while you are yet alive, you have monuments of your own creation and monuments created in your honour by others as well, and you have begun to live among posterity. Come, come; read out loud and be read by others. No, spur yourself on to surpass in your writing the praises of writers. Spur yourself on to increase the admiration of coming posterity. Nature herself and father time have given you to our age, but you will give yourself to posterity. What we admire in you, we owe to your own industry and at the same time to benign Nature, but what posterity will admire in you will redound to you alone. For which reason I exhort and beg you the more vehemently, to commend yourself no less to posterity by writing than by speaking you commend to us the kindness of Nature. We have seen the *Mirtilla* eclogue and now your *Rime*. Bring out more, so that fertile with children as you are, you may also become fertile with books. Accordingly, you have enclosed for me from your own hand epistles that they might come into the hands of many, compositions in which every comic delight, tragic riches, and everything elegant reside. Our age is your heir, and hereafter posterity will be, but you will nevertheless be the mistress of all. For worldly goods are one thing, but these monuments of intellect are another. The former will fall to the lot of one or another owner after you, but the latter will never cease to be your own, even when they seem to do so. There is also that which we justifiably demand more fully from your modesty; namely, that by publicly taking up the prize of intellect, you might show that you have illuminated a not ungrateful age. Therefore take the laurel, and shade with it your temples and that lovely loveliness of golden Aphrodite. For so it will be, that while you delight the senses of your audience with the nectar of words, you will not burn them with the fiery glow of your face and the rays of your eyes. And do not object; posterity itself will bear it badly that you deserved this Phoeban honour but did not take it. And they will hold our age in bad repute, as if we had begrudged you this honour. Consider, O Persuasion, O Muse, both yourself and our age and the people who will be hereafter—you, who will have in me, at any rate, an eternal admirer and devotee of your intellect and eloquence. Thus, accept this poem—not in order to inspect it for itself (for it is unpolished), but in order to inspect the mind of its author. Farewell. Milan. 14 December 1601.

> To Isabella Andreini, Sulpice of our Age,
> The faultless flower of the people and quintessence of Persuasion.

> Thrice favoured of Jove, on whom three Goddesses have bestowed
> Three gifts from heaven—the goddesses Venus, Minerva, Juno.
> I shall sing of you in a facile poem, I shall sing of your gifts,
> Which the goddesses have bestowed—the goddesses Venus, Minerva, Juno.
> Venus, emerging from the crest of the wave in the foaming Pontus,
> Tinted your face, your eyebrows, and your hair with the flower of loveliness
> While you were tasting the newborn breeze of dusky light.
> She sprinkled talent and charm over all your limbs so that you might be
> A second Venus—bountiful Venus, but chaste, and the mother of chaste Love.
> Shortly after, when Athena caught sight of the rattle you neglected,
> She gave you the strength of intellect and the seeds of Fame,
> Infusing your nimble mind with Pierian nectar,
> Infusing your nimble tongue with Pierian nectar;
> Your mind, so that the Muse of ancient Lyceum might continue to exist there,
> Your tongue, so that the Persuasion of ancient theatre might continue to exist there.
> Saturnian Juno follows on winged step, indignant
> That a virgin's years are slipping by without a husband.
> She prepares the wedding chamber, the conjugal torches

And the tables for the feast; Hymenaeus himself sings the song.
May you be led in marriage by a kind husband and, soon fecund,
May you labour with numerous offspring in libations to Lucina.
O, the firm bond of marriage! You are worthy of your husband,
And he is equally worthy of you, he to whom you have given dear pledges.
Now the three goddesses have put aside their ancient fury;
The strife which Paris caused among them, you felicitously carry away.
You will be called a new Venus, Minerva, Juno;
You will be called Wisdom, decorous of face and chaste in marriage.

e. Epist. XI. Isabellae Andreinae. Ticinum (Reulens, *Erycius Puteanus et Isabelle Andreini*, 33–4, from *Epistolarum Bellaria*)

Scribendi desiderium, et simul argumentum mihi e litteris tuis crescit: decrescit stilus et eloquentia. Tantum videlicet a animo manus discrepat, ut illum excitari ad respondendum, hanc retardari sentiam ab eadem tua Suada. Animus enim modestiam tuae scriptionis, manus elegantiam aemulatur. Modestiam, quam imitari (liceat dicere) possum: elegantiam quam non possum. Sic igitur excitare me profiteor, ad id quod possum; retardari in eo, quod non possum. Scribere enim ad te cupio, et non cupio: cupio, ne officio desim; non cupio, ne infantià peccem. Et tu tamen ut scribam, eloquentiae mihi laudem impertis Desine: scriam, ut deinceps infantiam meam accuses, officium non desideres. Vale. Mediolani. XV. Kal. Jan. 1601.

Epistle 11. To Isabella Andreini. Pavia.

My desire to write, and at the same time the things I have to write about, grows greater because of your letters. However, my ability to write and my eloquence grow less. So far indeed is my hand out of pace with my mind, that while I feel the latter spurred on to respond, I feel the former held back from responding, both things by the same cause—your persuasion. For my mind strives to imitate the modesty of your writing, while my hand strives to imitate the elegance—a modesty which (may it be permitted to me to say) I can imitate, but an elegance which I cannot. Accordingly, I declare that I am spurred on to that which I can do, but that I am held back in that which I cannot do. For I wish to write to you, and I do not wish to. I wish to, lest I be found wanting in my duty, but I do not wish to, lest I give offence by my inability to express myself. And nevertheless, to get me to write, you say that I have some claim to praise for eloquence. Say so no longer. I will write in order that, though you charge me with incompetence in expressing myself, you will not find me wanting in my duty. Farewell. Milan. 18 December 1601.

f. Isabella Andreini to Erycius Puteanus (Reulens, *Erycius Puteanus et Isabelle Andreini*, 26)

Ill.re Sr mio oss.o
Se dalle mie lettere cresce in VS il desiderio di scrivermi scema in me dalle sue, non per mancamento d'amore ma per difetto di sapere. Tutte le ragioni hanno da persuadere VS allo scrivere, ma particolarmente queste due: che scrivendo ella indora le carte della sua infinita virtù et ammaestra me che vivo tanto desiderosa d'apprendere. Io poi per tutte le ragioni non doverei scrivere, e per questa principalmente che quanto più scrivo, tanto più scuopro l'ignoranza mia. Che farò io dunque? S'io scrivo mi dimostro ignorante, s'io non iscrivo mi dimostro mal creata, pur di due mali eleggo il minore, che sarà lo scrivere, poi ch'è meglio, al giuditio mio, il dimostrarsi ignorante per difetto d'educatione, che mal creata per rustica natura. Del Sr Lipsio dottissimo non mi burlo io, ma temo che 'l suo perfetto gusto non trovi insipidi, amari od aspri i putti del mio mal colto ingegno. Hora è giunto un messo del Ser.mo di Mantova, il quale è venuto per noi onde non posso più lungamente scrivere. VS mi scusi: di Mantova, a Dio piacendo, supplirò a quanto mancò al presente. Mi conservi VS in sua gratia, e m'ami poi ch'io come ammiratrice delle sue virtù lo merito. Mio marito, il Sr Gio. Paulo et io salutiamo VS pregandole le buone feste, il buon anno et ogni altro bene. Di Pavia, li 24 decem. 1601.

    Di VS Ill.mo Aff. ser.ce
    Isabella Andreini

My Most Illustrious and Respected Sir,
If, from my letters, the desire arises in you to write me, it is less in me because of yours—not for lack of love, but out of ignorance There is every reason to persuade you to write, but particularly these two: that in writing you gild the paper with your infinite virtue and you teach me, who wants so much to learn. I, then, have every reason not to write, and for this principally: that the more I write, the more I show my ignorance. What then shall I do? If I write, I show myself to be ignorant, if I do not write I show myself to be ill-bred; of the two evils, I choose the lesser—that is, to write, since it is better, in my mind, to show oneself ignorant by defect of education, rather than ill-bred because of base nature. I do not joke about the most learned Mr Lipsius, but I fear that his perfect taste might find the offspring of my ill-cultivated wit dull, bitter, or sharp. Now a messenger of the most Serene Duke of Mantua has arrived, who has come for us, and so I cannot write any longer. Your Lordship, excuse me: from Mantua, God willing, I will make up for what I cannot do now. Keep me in your graces and love me, since I, as admirer of your virtue, deserve it. My husband, Mr Gio. Paolo [Fabbri], and I send our regards to you, wishing you happy holidays, a happy new year, and every other good thing.

From Pavia, 24 December 1601.
Most illustrious, from your most affectionate servant,
Isabella Andreini

g. Isabella Andreini to Erycius Puteanus (Reulens, *Erycius Puteanus et Isabelle Andreini*, 26–7)

Ill. S.r mio os.mo

Potess'io così render cambio di virtù, come rende cambio d'amore! Le cose naturali sono sempre facili, l'amare è cosa naturale adunque l'amare è sempre facile, e più facile diventa ancor l'amare quand'altrui ha del continuo in mente oggetto amabilississimo come il Sr Ericio, vero erario del tesoro incorruttibile della virtù. Se la penultima mia hebbe valore di ristor l'animo vostro e di risanar il corpo, non fu perche ella fosse, come VS dice, Hygia dea della sanità, ma perchè voi sete di così buona natura, ch'ogni picciolo medicamento v'è salubre; comunque si sia, le mie verranno sempre a servirvi senza aspettar d'esser provocate, basterà solo che voi usando la solita cortesia rendiate il cambio alle mie. Ma, che dico di cambio? Il cambio s'intende delle cose eguali, il che non può seguire tra le sue e le mie, poi che le mie sono piene d'ignoranza, e le sue sono l'istessa sapienza, e mai non giungono a me, che non mi sieno apportatrici di nuovo bene, onde non sarà da maravigliarsi s'io lo procurerò a tutto mio potere, e poi che VS dice d'essermi tenuto della sanità e della vita, impieghi l'una a l'altra dispensandomi quelle gratie ch'io tanto bramo; starò aspettando con desiderio i nuovi frutti del suo bellissimo ingegno, per satiar la fame dell'imparare, in tanto rendo i saluti a VS con mio marito e 'l Sr Gio. Paulo pregandole da Dio sommo contento. Di Mantova, li 4 febb. 1602.

Di VS Ill.re
Aff. ser.ce
Isabella Andreini

My Most Illustrious and Respected Sir,

Would that I could repay your virtue as you repay my love! Natural things are always easy; love is a natural thing, and therefore love is always easy, and becomes still easier when one has always in mind a most lovable object like Mr Erycius, true receptacle of the incorruptible treasury of virtue. If my penultimate letter had the power to restore your spirit and heal your body, it was not because it was, as you say, Hygia, goddess of health, but because you are of such good nature that every small medication does you good; in any case, my letters will come to serve you without waiting to be asked; it will be enough for you, using courtesy alone, to exchange yours for mine. But why do I speak of exchange? Exchange occurs between equal things, and that cannot be between your letters and mine, since mine are full of ignorance, and yours are knowledge itself; and they never arrive that they do not bring me some new good thing, and so it will not be surprising if I were to seek it with all my powers, and since you say you are obliged to me for health and life, use the one and the other, giving me those rewards that I so covet; I will be anxiously awaiting the new fruits of your most excellent wit to satiate my hunger for learning. In the meantime, I send you greetings with my husband and Mr Gio. Paolo [Fabbri], asking God for your complete contentment. From Mantua, 4 February 1602.

Most illustrious and serene, from your most affectionate servant,
Isabella Andreini

h. EPIST. LVI. Mantuam. ISABELLAE ANDRAEINAE, Academicae Intentae (ASM, Autografi 151; *Erycii Puteani epistolarum fercula secunda*, 90–1)

O Suada! ut amer, sinamme laudari. laudare tamen facilius poteris, quàm amare: cùm laus ad gratiam saepè profecta, immerentem quoque ornet; Amor no[n] possit nisi è vero proficisci. Eo te ingenio & benignitate novi, ut laudare & amare quemcumque velis: eo tame[n] judicio & prudentia, ut non nisi dignum. unde qui merebitur, hunc laudabis & amabis: qui non merebitur, hunc no[n] amabis; et si verboru[m] aliquo lenocinio laudabis, ne despicere videare. Digno igitur Laudem Amorem'que tribuas; indigno Laudem eloquio fingas, verum è pectore Amorem nunquam promas. ita facilius Artem, quàm Naturam ad fucum detorquemus, quòd autem laudamus, Arte fieri; quòd amamus, Naturâ, planum est: & sic difficiliorem Arte Naturam esse; cùm laudare quemcumque Arte possis, amare Naturâ non possis, nisi pectus tibi commoveat, & de Virtutis suae igni scintillam adspiret. Quid igitur? facilè tu amare? facilius ego censeo laudare. At delitias etiam facis, voves'que, ut aequè Virtute ac Amore possis respondere. Respondes verò; nisi alio à fonte tuu[m] velis, alio amore[m] meum derivare. Virtutis tu me causâ amas, & ego te Virtutis. parem Amorem habemus: ergò & Virtute[m]. REVOCO, revoco, & discindo hunc ambitiosi σοφίσματος nodum. Imparem Amorem habemus, & imparem Virtutem. ego quippe Amore vinco, tu Virtute. Sic igitur triumphum hunc agamus, ego Amoris, tu Virtutis. Vale. Mediolani, Eidibus Febr. [M].[D].CII.

Epistle 56. To Isabella Andreini, Accademica Intenta, Mantua

O Persuasion! On the condition that I am loved do I allow myself to be praised. Albeit to praise will have been easier for you than to love, inasmuch as praise often arises from a desire to flatter, and may decorate also the undeserving, but love cannot arise except genuinely. I know your character to be of such temper and natural kindness as to praise and to love whomsoever you wish; but yet to be of such judiciousness and prudence as not to do so unless the person is deserving. Accordingly, him who is deserving you will praise and love, but him who is not deserving you will not love even if you praise him with some ornamentation of words so as not to appear to despise him. On the worthy man, then, you bestow praise and love, but in the case of the unworthy man you feign praise with eloquence, but you never send true love out of your heart. Thus it is that we bend art to falsehood more easily than nature. To the extent that we praise, this is accomplished by art. But to the extent that we love, this is, by nature, unaffected. And accordingly nature is more difficult than art, since you can praise anyone whosoever by art, unless your heart be moved and you breathe forth a spark from the fire of its virtue. What then? Do you think it is easy to love? I think it is easier to praise. But you are having fun at my expense, and vow that you can reciprocate virtue as much as you can love. You reply in accord with truth when you say this, unless you wish to derive your love from one source and mine from another. You love me because of my virtue, and I love you because of your virtue. Our love for one another is equal, and so too our virtue. No, I take it back, I take it back, and I cut this knot of over-eager sophistry. Our love for one another is not equal, and neither is our virtue. For my love is greater than yours, and your virtue is greater than mine. Thus therefore do we achieve this triumph, I of love, you of virtue. Farewell. 13 February 1602.

i. Isabella Andreini to Erycius Puteanus (Reulens, *Erycius Puteanus et Isabelle Andreini*, 27–8)

Ill.re S.r mio oss.mo
Egli è pur vero, che fatto novello Gordio co' i favori che continuamente vi piace di farmi stringere così forte il nodo dell'obligo mio, che come il nodo dell'antico solo fu sciolto dalla spada d'Alessandro, così questo solo sarà sciolto dalla falce di morte. O Sr Ericio mio! Dunque chiamate beni le mie lettere, le quali per esser così mal composte come vuol la necessità del tempo a cui le rubbi, tremano a venir nelle mani d'huomo che tanto intende! Io certo arrossisco nell'intendere come voi non solo degnate le mie lettere della vostra lettura (alla quale senza dubbio non l'esporrei se non m'affidasse più la vostra bontà che non mi sgomenta la mia ignoranza), ma ancora le comunicate ne i vostri per voi fortunatissimi paesi agli amici.

Voglia Dio, che l'autorità del saper vostro tanto mi giovi, che passando la mia fama nei freddi del settentrione, non s'agghiacci le penne, ma perchè temo di così fatta sventura? L'ardente desiderio che la mia fama accompagna per farmi in tutti i miei detti ammiratrice dell'infinita vostra virtù, non basta ad assicurarmi da qual si voglia induratissimo gielo? Oltre che sapendo gli amici vostri il vostro valore et essend'ella da quello portata, è forza che voli sicura in quelle parti, dove per voi veggo spuntar nuovo Olivo e fabricarsi altra Athene; ma non sia, ch'io entri ne vostri meriti che veramente divini non hanno da essere scritti da penna mortale. Sr Ericio, quando mi fu dato di conoscervi, io n'elessi patrone e non amico, ne poteva amico eleggervi poi che solo tragli eguali si mantien l'amicitia, la qual uguaglianza non è tra noi, poichè voi con l'altezza del vostro ingegno toccate il cielo, et io con la bassezza del mio mi giaccio in terra; e se pure alcuna volta surgo, è solo quando mi porgete l'aiuto vostro, e quando penso alle vostre virtù, le quali mi fecero l'altra sera formar questo sonetto, ch'io vi mando prima che sia aggiunto con altri alle Rime che si ristamperanno in breve. Siate contento di gradir non il dono, ma l'animo della donatrice, ch'è tutto vostro. Siate servito poi di presentar con mille saluti quest'altro sonetto al mio Sr Gherardo, al quale per fretta non lo mandai scritto come si conveniva. Il Sr Gio. Paulo e mio marito vi rendono duplicati i saluti ringratiandovi della memoria che di loro tenete; le compositioni mandatemi oltre modo mi son care e rendo gratie a quel pensiero, che nacque in voi d'illustrarmi con la loro dedicatione. Io non havendo altro che dedicarvi vi dedico la mia pronta volontà, e per fine senza fine vi bacio la mano pregandovi da Dio ogni contento. Di Mantova, li 6 di marzo 1602.

    Di VS Ill Affe.ma ser.ce
    Isabella Andreini

My Most Illustrious and Respected Sir,
It is certainly true, that having become a new Gordius through the favors that it continuously pleases you to make me tie so strongly the knot of my obligation that, just as the knot of the ancient one was loosened only by the sword of Alexander, so too this knot will only be loosened by the scythe of death. O, Mr Erycius! Then you call my letters good, which are so badly composed because they want the necessary time of which they are robbed, trembling to come into the hands of a man who so understands! I certainly blush from the understanding that you not only honor my letters by your reading (to which without doubt I would not offer them if I did not trust your kindness more than my dismay at my ignorance), but what's more you communicate them to your friends in your regions, which are most fortunate because of you.

    God willing, that the authority of your knowledge be of such use to me, that passing my fame in the cold climate of central Italy, my quills do not freeze. But why do I fear the occurance of such misadventure? Is not my ardent desire, which together with my fame makes me in everything I say an admirer of your infinite virtue, enough to keep me from the hardest ice? And in addition to your friends knowing your worth, and you being carried by that, it is because of this that I fly safely to those places where because of you I see a new olive tree grow, a new Athens built. But I can't go into your merits, which are truly divine and can't be described by mortal pen. Mr Erycius, when it was my privilege to meet you, I elected you to be my patron and not my friend. Nor could I choose you as a friend since only among equals can friendship be sustained, which equality is not between us, since you with the height of your intellect touch the heavens, and I with the lowliness of mine lie on earth. And even if at times I raise up, it is only when you offer me your aid and when I think about your virtues, which caused me the other evening to write this sonnet, which I send to you before it is gathered with the other poems in my *Rime*, which will be reprinted soon. Be content to accept not the gift, but the spirit of the giver, who is all yours. Please present with a thousand greetings this other sonnet to my Mr Gherardo, to whom for lack of time I did not write as I should have. Mr Giovan Paolo [Fabbri] and my husband offer you greetings redoubled, thanking you for the memory you keep of them. The compositions you send me are extraordinarily dear to me, and I offer thanks for the thought that originated in you to make me more illustrious by dedicating them to me. I, having nothing else to dedicate to you, dedicate my ready willingness, and finally without end I kiss your hand, praying God for your every contentment. From Mantua, 6 March 1602.

Your most illustrious, from your most affectionate servant,
Isabella Andreini

j. Isabella Andreini to Erycius Puteanus (Reulens, *Erycius Puteanus et Isabelle Andreini*, 28–9)

Ill. S.r mio oss.mo

Piacesse a Dio, che 'l dolore c'ho del male di VS si potesse cambiare in salute, che certo non havereste bisogno ch'Esculapio s'affatticasse per voi, essendo che sareste più sano dell'istesso Apollo. Ma perch'io non possa far questo, ho io da procurar di consolarmi con parole? Certo no, si perch'io non son atta a farlo, come ancora, perchè farei grandissimo torto alla sua prudenza, alla quale è noto, che poi che gli accidenti delle cose non vengono per lo più conformi alla volontà nostra, è forza che noi disponiamo la nostra volontà in conformità degli accidenti che avvengono. La sanità è uno de' beni della Fortuna, onde per lo contrario diremo che l'infirmità sia uno de' suoi mali. Ma perchè la Fortuna è sempre minor dell'huomo savio, possiamo concludere, che uno de suoi effetti, ch'è tanto minor di lei, sia tale, ch'appresso alla saviezza dell'huomo egli sia nulla. Ecco dunque che 'l Sr Ericio, savissimo tra i savii, benchè sta aggravato dal male, non è molestato da cosa alcuna.

Non rispondo all'altra sua, ch'io ricevei prima di questa, perchè le sue lettere son tali, che la risposta haverebbe di bisogno di grandissimo studio, et io non posso attendervi, contendendolo i giorni in che siamo, che chiamano al altre cure, e vietandolo ancora il non sentirmi a mio modo, rispetto alla quadragesima che m'ha sbattuta assai. Se poi la buona voluntà e 'l obligo, che all'altrui cortesia si tiene, possono far ch'altro componga bene, io dirò con VS che 'l sonetto, ch'io feci per VS sia veramente bello com'ella scrive. Mio marito bacia le mani di VS desiderandole da Dio ogni contento, il che faccio anch'io con tutto il cuore; qui termino per non fastidirla con la lunga lettura. Di Mantova, il dì primo d'Aprile 1602.

Di VS Ill.re Affe.ma ser.ce
Isabella Andreini

My Most Illustrious and Respected Sir,
Would to God that the sorrow I have regarding your illness could be exchanged for health, since you would have no need for Esculapius to labour on your behalf, since you would be healthier than Apollo himself. But since I am unable to do this, must I console myself with words? Certainly not, as much because I am not suited to do it, as it is because I would insult your prudence by which you know that since things do not always happen according to our wishes, it is necessary that we should dispose our wishes to conform to the incidents that happen. Health is one of the good things of fortune, and so we say to the contrary that infirmity would be one of the bad things. But because fortune is always lesser than a wise man, we may conclude that anything she does which is so much beneath her is such that next to the wisdom of man it is nothing. Therefore, it is the case that Mr Erycius, wisest among the wise, although he suffers illness, he is assailed by a thing of no account.

I am not responding to your other letter, which I received before this one, because your letters are such, that the answer would require great attention, and I cannot give it because these days fight against it, calling me to other cares; and also my not feeling my usual self prohibits it because the Lenten season has worn me out. If then, goodwill and the obligation that one has to another's kindness, help one to compose well, I will say together with you that the sonnet I made for you is truly beautiful as you yourself write. My husband kisses your hands, desiring for you from God every contentment, which I also do with all my heart; here I will end in order not to tire you with a long letter. From Mantua, 1 April 1602.

Your most illustrious, from your most affectionate servant,
Isabella Andreini

k. Isabella Andreini to Erycius Puteanus (Reulens, *Erycius Puteanus et Isabelle Andreini*, 29)

Ill.re S.r mio oss.mo
Vengo con queste poche righe a romper il lungo et noioso silentio che passa da molti giorni in qua tra di noi, il quale non voglio che più lungamente si vanti di privarmi del cibo soave de' suoi nobilissimi concetti, che sono stati (sua merce) per tanto tempo dati per esca nutritiva all'anima mia, la quale se non fosse per se stessa immortale saria (mi dubito) morta per così lungo digiuno. Ho ben io scritto e da Mantova, e da Verona, a VS et a Sr Gherardo per ricever gratia com'è lor costume, e dall'uno e dall'altro, ma convien che le mie sieno andate in sinistro non potendo io argomentar in loro mancamento d'amore o di creanza. Passò il Sr Sadeler per Verona, e seppi che in Milano alloggiò con VS onde con tal occasione mi venne pensiero d'un intaglio di sua mano, e subito mi feci rittrarre, e sarà mandato a Vinetia, e ben ch'io habbia cavalieri, che mi favoriscono, sapendo quanto VS gli sia amico, e quanto l'amiticia possa ne' cuori virtuosi, la prego caldamente a scrivere una lettera al suditto, pregandolo a servirmi subito, accioch'io

possa come sarò a Milano metterlo nelle mie rime, che si ristamperanno tosto ch'io giunga. Non son più lunga, le bacio la mano e la prega a tenermi in sua gratia et a salutar in mio nome il Sr Calderone. E NS la feliciti. Di Brescia, li 18 di Giugno 1602.
 Di VS Ill.re Affe.ma ser.ce
 Isabella Andreini

My Most Illustrious and Respected Sir,
I write these few lines to break the long and unpleasant silence that has been between us for many days, which I do not want to allow to continue longer, depriving me of the sweet food of your most noble conceits, which have been (thanks to you) for so long given as food to my soul which, if it were not itself immortal, would be (I fear) dead from such a long separation. I have written from Mantua and from Verona to you and to Mr Gherardo [Borgogni] in order to receive thanks, as is your custom, from you and from him, but it happened that my letters went awry, because I can't formulate my arguments about love and manners. Mr [Raffaello] Sadeler came through Verona, and I learned that in Milan he stayed with you and so on such occasion the thought came to me to have an engraving made by him, and I immediately had my portrait done, and it will be sent to Venice, and even though I have other gentlemen who would do me the favour, knowing how good a friend you are of his, and how much weight friendship has in virtuous hearts, I ask you fervently to write a letter to the above-named asking him to oblige me in this right away, so that I can, when I am in Milan, put it in my *Rime*, which will be reprinted as soon as I arrive. I won't go on. I kiss your hand and ask you to keep me in your graces and to greet Mr Calderone in my name. And may our Lord give you every happiness. From Brescia, 18 June 1602.
 Most illustrious sir, from your most affectionate servant,
 Isabella Andreini

l. Isabella Andreini to Erycius Puteanus (Reulens, *Erycius Puteanus et Isabelle Andreini*, 29–30)

Ill.re S.r mio oss.mo
Se la penna potesse esser tanto pronta quanto è il desiderio, a pena giunta haverei salutato il S.r Ericio; ma perchè è impossiile, convien che la sua benignità scusi la mia tardanza, la quale è veramente degna di scusa, poi che non m'avanza tempo di respirare, non che di visitar i miei carissimi amici e padroni, con lettere. Noi siamo il più delle volte chiamati da SAS fuori della città, e quando non andiamo fuori, bisogna servir qui, tanto che sempre siamo in volta, onde a gran fatica ho potuto far questi sonetti, ch'io mando per segno d'amore a VS et ho anchor mandati al Sr Gherardo mio. Ho cercato della sua lettera e non l'ho trovata, havendola io lasciata con altre di VS a Mantova tra quelle cose ch'io bramo di preservar dall'ingiuria

del tempo il più che sarà possibile, benchè in tutti i luoghi sono dal tempo sicure le cose ch'escono dell'intelletto nobilissimo del Sr Ericio; poichè teme il tempo dell'opere sue non meno che l'opere altrui temano del tempo, per la qual cosa egli s'affretta, ancor che vecchio e zoppo, di fuggir da loro per non esser abbattuto e vinto. E senza più, bacio a VS la mano con mio marito, e 'l Sr Gio Paulo. E NS la conservi. Di Torino, li 14 d'Agosto 1602.
    Di VS Ill.re Affe.ma ser.ce
    Isabella Andreini

My Most Illustrious and Respected Sir,
If one's pen could be as prompt as one's desire, I would have greeted Mr Erycius upon my arrival; but because it is impossible, his goodness must excuse my tardiness, which is truly worthy of excuse, since I do not have time enough to breathe, let alone to visit my dearest friends and patrons with letters. We are most of the time called by his most serene highness outside the city, and when we do not go away, there is need to serve here, such that we are always busy, and so only with great effort I have been able to compose these sonnets, which I send as a sign of love to you and have also sent to my Mr Gherardo. I have looked for your letter and I have not found it, having left it with others of yours in Mantua, among those things that I desire to preserve from the ravages of time as much as possible, although in all places the things that come from the most noble intellect of Mr Erycius are safe from time; since time fears for his own work no less than the works of others fear time, for which reason he hastens, even if old and lame, to flee from them in order to not be beaten and conquered. And without further ado, I kiss your hand along with my husband and Mr Gio. Paolo [Fabbri]. And our Lord keep you. From Turin, 14 August 1602.
    Most illustrious sir, from you most affectionate servant,
    Isabella Andreini

m. EPIST. LXXVIII. Ticinum. IS. ANDRAEINAE, Academicae Intentae.
(Erycii Puteani epistolarum fercula secunda, 117)

Animum impedire stili languor non potuit, quominùs scriben di fervorem demonstrare[m]. Ita enim excitatus suavissimis tuis litteris sum, ut relactantem manum in scriptionis obsequiu[m] coëgerim. Tuis litteris: & simul adolescentis hujus petitione, qui commendari à me voluit, & mercit; rogavit, & obtinuit. Cur autem commendari? ut specimen Comici studij daret, & in numerum sive Collegium vestrum adoptaretur. Adolescens est dicendi non ignarus, qui aliàs etiam ora hominum & pulverem publicum non exhorruit. Nisi fallor, *ex hoc ligno Mercurius fiet*. De Epistolis tuis, invitissimus audivi, sepositas eas esse. Cave, per omnes Musas.

καὶ γὰρ αἰσχύνην φέροι
πρᾶγμ' ἐς χέρας λαβόντ' ἀπώσασθαι τόδε

Etenim dedecus adfert, acceptum in manus negotium abucere. Iterùm, cave, si cothurnu[m] Euripidis aestimas, à quo moneris. Vale. Mediolani, XVIII. Kal. Ia[n]. [M]. [D]CII.

Epistle 78. To Isabella Andreini, Accademica Intenta, Pavia.

Sluggishness of pen could not impede my mind to the extent that I should demonstrate the less my eagerness to write. For I was so spurred on by your most urbane letters, that I have forced my resisting hand into the duty of writing—by your letters, and at the same time by the petition of this young man who wished me to write him a letter of recommendation, and who deserved, asked, and has obtained what he asked for. Why did he wish a letter of recommendation? That he might present you with an example of his comic studies, and be adopted into your number, or more exactly your college. He is a young man who is not ignorant of the art of speaking, who on other occasions also has not been affrighted by the faces of men and the dust of the public stage. Unless I am deceived, *from this material is Mercury sprung*. With regard to your letters, I have heard most unwillingly that they have been put aside—beware, by all the Muses!

> It would be a cause for reproach if I should refuse this business
> after taking it into my hands. [Euripides, *Hecuba*, lines 1241–2]

Again, beware, if you revere the tragic boot of Euripides, by whom you are warned. Farewell. Milan, 15 December 1602.

Bibliography

ALLEN, MICHAEL J. B., *Marsilio Ficino and the Phaedran Charioteer* (Berkeley and Los Angeles, 1981).
—— *The Platonism of Marsilio Ficino: A Study of his Phaedrus Commentary, its Sources, and Genesis* (Berkeley and Los Angeles, 1984).
ALLEN, PAUL C., *Philip III and the Pax Hispanica, 1598–1621: The Failure of Grand Strategy* (New Haven and London, 2000).
AMADEI, FEDERIGO, *Cronaca universale della città di Mantova*, 3 vols. (Mantua, 1956).
ANDREINI, FRANCESCO, *L'alterezza di Narciso* (Venice, 1611).
—— *Le bravure del Capitano Spavento* (Venice, 1607, 1609, 1615, 1624), ed. Roberto Tessari (Pisa, 1987). Translated into French as *Les Bravachieries du Capitaine Spavente* (Paris, 1608).
—— *Il felicissimo arrivo del serenissimo D. Vittorio Principe di Savoia insieme col serenissimo D. Filiberto suo fratello nella famosa città di Torino descritto in verso sdrucciolo da Francesco Andreini comico geloso, detto il Capitano Spavento* (n.p., n.d).
—— *L'ingannata Proserpina* (Venice, 1611).
—— *Nuova aggiunta alle bravure del Capitano Spavento* (Venice, 1614).
—— *Ragionamenti fantastici posti in forma di dialoghi rappresentativi* (Venice, 1612).
ANDREINI, GIOVAN BATTISTA, *La Ferinda* (Paris, 1622).
—— *La ferza* (Paris, 1625).
—— *La Florinda* (Milan, 1606).
—— *La Maddalena lasciva e penitenti* (Mantua, 1617; Milan, 1620, 1652).
—— *Il pianto d'Apollo* (Milan, 1606).
—— *Lo schiavetto* (Milan, 1612; Venice 1620); ed. Laura Falavolti (Turin, 1982).
ANDREINI, ISABELLA, *Fragmenti d'alcune scritture* (Venice, 1620, 1625, 1627, 1647; Turin, 1628).
—— *Lettere della signora Isabella Andreini . . . aggiuntovi di nuovo li raggionamenti piacevoli dell'istessa . . . di nuovo ristampate, & con ogni diligenza ricorrete* (Venice, 1625, 1652).
—— *Lettere d'Isabella Andreini e fragmenti di alcune scritture* (Turin, 1621, 1628, Venice, 1663).
—— *Lettere d'Isabella Andreini padovana, comica gelosa, et academica intenta; nominata l'Accesa* (Venice, 1602, 1607, 1610, 1617, 1625).

ANDREINI, ISABELLA, *Mirtilla* (Verona, 1588, 1599; Ferrara, 1590; Bergamo, 1594; Venice, 1598, 1602, 1616; Milan, 1605); ed. Maria Luisa Doglio (Lucca, 1995). Translated into French as *Myrtille bergerie* (Paris, 1602).

—— *Rime* [parte prima] (Milan, 1601; Paris, 1603, 1605; Naples, 1696).

—— *Rime . . . parte seconda* (Milan, 1605).

ARIOSTO, LUDOVICO, *Orlando furioso*, trans. Guido Waldman (Oxford, 1983).

ARISTOTLE, *The Poetics*, trans. James Hutton (New York, 1982).

ARTUSI, GIOVAN MARIA, *L'Artusi, overo Delle imperfettioni della moderna musica* (Venice, 1600; Bologna, 1968).

—— *Seconda parte dell'Artusi overo Delle imperfettioni della moderna musica* (Venice, 1603; Bologna, 1968).

ASCOLI, ALBERT, *Ariosto's Bitter Harmony: Crisis and Evasion in the Italian Renaissance* (Princeton, 1987).

ATLAS, ALLAN, *Renaissance Music: Music in Western Europe, 1400–1600* (New York, 1998).

[BALDINI, BACCIO], *Discorso sopra la mascherata della genealogia degl'Iddei de' gentili* (Florence, 1565).

BALESTRIERI, LINA, *Feste e spettacoli alla corte dei Farnese* (Parma, 1981).

BARBIERI, NICOLÒ, *La supplica, discorso famigliare a quelli che trattano de' comici* (Venice, 1634; Bologna, 1636); ed. Ferdinando Taviani (Milan, 1971).

BARTOLI, FRANCESCO, *Notizie istoriche de' comici italiani che fiorirono intorno all'anno MDC fino a' giorni presenti*, 2 vols. (Padua, 1781).

BASCHET, ARMAND, *Les Comédiens italiens à la cour de France sous Charles IX, Henri III, Henri IV et Louis XIII* (Paris, 1882).

BENEDETTI, GIOVANNI, *Notizie e documenti intorno la vita di Francesco Settimani fiorentino e cavaliere di S. Stefano* (Florence, 1875).

BESUTTI, PAOLA, 'Da *L'Arianna* a *La Ferinda*: Giovan Battista Andreini e la "comedia musicale all'improviso" ', *Musica disciplina*, 49 (1995), 227–76.

—— 'The "Sala degli Specchi" Uncovered: Monteverdi, the Gonzagas and the Palazzo Ducale, Mantua', *Early Music*, 27 (1999), 451–66.

BLANCHARD-ROTHMULLER, CATHERINE ANNE, *Leone Ebreo de' Sommi's Four Dialogues on Stage Presentations: A Translation with Introduction and Notes* (AnnArbor, 1973).

Breve descritione della barriera fatta in Mantova il primo maggio 1594 in occasione dell'arrivo da Roma dell'Illustr. et Eccellentiss. Sig. Duca di Nevers padre del Sig. Carlo Gonzaga principe di Nevers et Duca di Rethel (Mantua, 1594).

Breve descrittione delle feste fatte dal serenissimo Sig. Principe di Mantova nel giorno natale della serenissima Infanta Margherita, et nella venuta delli serenissimi principe di Savoia nella città di Casale per veder detta signora, et il Sig. Principe prima della lor partita per Mantova (Casale, 1611).

BROWN, HOWARD MAYER, 'Emulation, Competition, and Homage: Imitation and Theories of Imitation in the Renaissance', *Journal of the American Musicological Society*, 35 (1982), 1–48.

—— 'The Geography of Florentine Monody: Caccini at Home and Abroad', *Early Music*, 9 (1981), 147–68.
BRUNI, DOMENICO, *Fatiche comiche* (Paris, 1623).
BRUNO, A., *Gabriello Chiabrera e Isabella Andreini (estratto dal Bullettino della Società Storica Savonese, Anno I. N. 1)* (Savona, 1891).
BULFINCH, THOMAS, *Myths of Greece and Rome*, comp. Bryan Holme (New York, 1979).
BURATTELLI, CLAUDIA, *Spettacoli di corte a Mantova tra Cinque e Seicento* (Florence, 1999).
CACCINI, GIULIO, *Le nuove musiche e nuova maniera di scriverle (1614)*, ed. H. Wiley Hitchcock (Madison, Wis., 1978).
CALORE, MARINA, 'Amori pastorali: poesia e musica nell'Italia padana', in Francesco Passadore (ed.), *La musica nel veneto dal xvi al xviii secolo* (Adria, 1984), 23–40.
CAMILLO, GIULIO, *L'idea del teatro dell'eccellent. M. Giulio Camillo* (Florence, 1550).
CAMPORI, G., and SOLERTI, ANGELO, *Luigi, Lucrezia e Leonora d'Este* (Turin, 1888).
CANAL, PIETRO, *Della musica in Mantova: notizie tratte principalmente dall' Archivio Gonzaga* (Mantua, 1881; Bologna, 1977).
Capitolationi fatte tra N. S. Papa Clemente ottavo, et il S. D. Cesare da Este, nella pace & accommodamento delle cose di Ferrara, & suo ducato (Ferrara, 1598).
CARDAMONE, DONNA, *The* Canzona villanesca alla napolitana *and Related Forms, 1537–1570* (Ann Arbor, 1981).
CAROSO, FABRITIO, *Il ballarino* (Venice, 1581).
—— *La nobiltà di dame* (Venice, 1600); translated into English as *Courtly Dance of the Renaissance* by Julia Sutton, music transcribed and ed. F. Marian Walker (New York, 1995).
CARTER, TIM, 'Artusi, Monteverdi, and the Poetics of Modern Music', in Nancy Kovaleff Baker and Barbara Russano Hanning (eds.), *Musical Humanism and its Legacy: Essays in Honor of Claude V. Palisca* (Stuyvesant, NY, 1992), 171–94.
—— 'Lamenting Ariadne?', *Early Music*, 27 (1999), 395–405.
CASTAGNA, RITA, *Mantova nella storia e nell'arte* (Florence, 1979).
CAVICCHI, A., 'Lettere di musicisti ferraresi: Lodovico Agostini (1534–1590)', *Ferrara viva*, 4 (1962), 185–210.
CHATER, JAMES, '"Un pasticcio di madrigaletti"? The Early Musical Fortune of *Il pastor fido*', in Angelo Pompilio (ed.), *Guarini, la musica, i musicisti* (Lucca, 1997).
CHIABRERA, GABRIELLO, *Canzonette, rime varie, dialoghi*, ed. Luigi Negri (Turin, 1964).
—— *Le maniere de' versi toscani* (Genoa, 1599).
—— *Scherzi e canzonette morali* (Genoa, 1599).

CINI, GIOVAN BATTISTA, *La vedova commedia di M. Giovambattista Cini, Rappresentata a honore del serenissimo arciduca Carlo d'Austria nella venuta sua in Fiorenza l'anno MDLXIX* (Florence, 1569).

Claudio Monteverdi: studi e prospettive. Atti del convegno, Mantova 21–24 ottobre 1993, ed. Paola Besutti, Teresa M. Gialdroni, and Rodolfo Baroncini (Florence, 1998).

CLOULAS, IVAN, *Catherine de Médicis* (Paris, 1979).

CLUBB, LOUISE GEORGE, *Italian Drama in Shakespeare's Time* (New Haven, 1989).

COCHRANE, ERIC, *Florence in the Forgotten Centuries 1527–1800* (Chicago and London, 1973).

COMI, SIRO, *Ricerche storiche sull'Accademia degli Affidati e sugli altri analoghi stabilimenti di Pavia* (Pavia, 1792).

Comici dell'arte: corrispondenze, ed. Siro Ferrone, Claudia Burattelli, Domenica Landolfi, and Anna Zinanni, 2 vols. (Florence, 1993).

COPENHAVER, BRIAN P., *Hermetica* (Cambridge, 1992).

CROCE, GIULIO CESARE, *La libraria, convito universale, dove s'invita grandissimo numero di libri tanto antichi, quanto moderni, ritirati tutti in un sonetto, opera non men utile, che dilettevole* (Bologna, 1592).

CUSICK, SUZANNE, 'Gendering Modern Music: Thoughts on the Monteverdi–Artusi Controversy', *Journal of the American Musicological Society*, 46 (1993), 1–25.

—— ' "There was not one lady who failed to shed a tear": Arianna's Lament and the Construction of Modern Womanhood', *Early Music*, 22 (1994), 21–41.

—— 'Re-voicing Arianna', *Early Music*, 27 (1999), 436–50.

D'ANCONA, ALESSANDRO, *Origini del teatro italiano*, 2 vols. (Turin, 1891).

—— 'Il teatro mantovano nel secolo XVI', *Giornale storico della letteratura italiana*, 5 (1885), 1–79; 6 (1885), 1–52 and 313–51; 7 (1886), 48–93.

DENORES, GIASON, *Apologia contra l'auttor del Verato* (Padua, 1590).

—— *Della rhetorica*, 3 vols. (Venice, 1584).

—— *Poetica* (Padua, 1588).

Descrittione della mascherata delle bufole, fatta nell'inclita città di Fiorenza da suoi ill. Duca, et Principe, per honorar la presenza della serenissima altezza di Carlo Arciduca d'Austria (Florence, 1569).

Descrizione del canto de sogni mandato dall'illustrissimo & eccellentissimo S. Principe di Fiorenza, & di Siena il secondo giorno di febraio 1565 in Fiorenza (Florence, 1566).

Descrizione delle pompe e feste fatte ne la città di Pisa per la venuta de la S. Madama Christierna de l'Oreno Gran Duchessa di Toscana (Florence, 1589).

Discorso in materia de suo Teatro (Venice, 1552).

DORRON, CLAUDE, *Discours des choses mémorables faittes à l'entrée du Roy de France et de Pologne en la ville de Venize remarquées par Claude Dorron*

parisien. Envoyé à la Royne mère du Roy et Régente de France en son absence (Lyons, 1574).
DUCHARTRE, PIERRE LOUIS, *The Italian Comedy*, trans. Randolph T. Weaver (New York, 1929).
DURANTE, ELIO, and MARTELLOTTI, ANNA, *Cronistoria del concerto delle dame principalissime di Margherita Gonzaga d'Este* (Florence, 1979).
ELLIOTT, J. H., *Europe Divided 1559–1598* (New York and Evanston, Ill., 1968).
Entrata del Christianiss. Re Henrico III di Francia, et di Polonia, nella città di Mantova, con gli sontuosissimi apparati et feste fatte da sua Eccellentia, per ricever Sua Maestà Christianissima (Venice, 1574).
Entrata reale fatta in Milano dalla serenissima regina, D. Margarita d'Austria sposata al potentiss. rè di Spagna D. Filippo III (Milan and Cremona, 1599).
ERENSTEIN, ROBERT, 'Isabella Andreini: A Lady of Virtue and High Renown', in *Essays on Drama and Theatre: Liber Amicorum Benjamin Hunningher* (Amsterdam, 1973), 37–49.
L'Età della riforma cattolica (1559–1630), vol. 10 of *Storia di Milano* (Milan, 1957).
EVANGELISTA, ANNA MARIA, 'Il teatro dei comici dell'arte a Firenze', *Biblioteca teatrale*, 23–4 (1979), 70–86.
—— 'Le compagnie dei comici dell'arte nel teatrino di Baldracca a Firenze: notizie dagli epistolari (1576–1653)', *Quaderni di teatro*, 6 (1984), 50–72.
FABBRI, PAOLO, *Monteverdi*, trans. Tim Carter (Cambridge, 1994).
I fabii comedia di Lotto del Mazza calzaiuolo fiorentino, recitata in Firenze l'anno 1567 nel Palazzo ducale doppo 'l battesimo della illustrissima S. Leonora primogenita del illustriss. S. Principe di Firenze e di Siena, et della serenissima principessa la Regina Giovanna d'Austria (Florence, 1567 [1568]).
FACCIOLI, EMILIO (ed.), *Mantova: le lettere*, 3 vols. (Mantua, 1959–63).
FALAVOLTI, LAURA, *Attore: alle origini di un mestiere* (Rome, 1988).
FAUSTINI, AGOSTINO, *Dalle historie di Ferrara che seguono l'altre del Sig. Gasparo Sardi* (Ferrara, 1646).
FELDMAN, MARTHA, 'The Academy of Domenico Venier, Music's Literary Muse in Mid-Cinquecento Venice', *Renaissance Quarterly*, 44 (1991), 476–512.
La felicissima entrata della serenissima regina di Spagna, Donna Margherita d'Austria, nella illustrissima città di Ferrara . . . descritta dal cavallier reale (Ferrara and Venice, 1598).
FENLON, IAIN, '*In destructione turcharum*: The Victory of Lepanto in Sixteenth-Century Music and Letters', in Francesco Degrada (ed.), *Andrea Gabrieli e il suo tempo* (Florence, 1987), 293–317.
—— 'Lepanto: The Arts of Celebration in Renaissance Venice', *Proceedings of the British Academy*, 63 (1987), 201–36.
—— *Music and Patronage in Sixteenth-Century Mantua* (Cambridge, 1980).
—— 'Music and Spectacle at the Gonzaga Court, c. 1580–1600', *Proceedings of the Royal Musical Association*, 103 (1976–77), 90–105.

FENLON, IAIN, 'Preparations for a Princess: Florence, 1588–89', in Fabrizio della Seta and Franco Piperno (eds.), *In cantu et in sermone: For Nino Pirrotta on his Eightieth Birthday* (Florence, 1989), 259–81.

Le feste et trionfi fatti dalla Signoria di Venetia nella felice venuta di Henrico III Christianissimo Re di Francia e di Polonia (Paris, BNF, MS ital. 799 (10475; Mazarin), transcribed in Nolhac and Solerti, *Il viaggio in Italia di Enrico III, Re di Francia e le feste a Venezia, Ferrara, Mantoa e Torino* (Turin, 1890), 275–306.

Feste nelle nozze del serenissimo D. Francesco Medici Granduca di Toscana, e della sereniss. sua consorte la Signora Bianca Cappello (Florence, 1579).

FICINO, MARSILIO, *De vita coelitus comparanda*, vol. 3 of *De vita libri tres* (Venice, 1498); translated into English and edited as *Three Books on Life* by Carol V. Kaske and John R. Clark (Binghampton, NY, 1989).

FOLLINO, FEDERICO, *Compendio delle sontuose feste fatte l'anno M.DC.VIII. nella città di Mantova per le reali nozze del serenissimo prencipe D. Francesco Gonzaga, con la serenissima infante Margherita di Savoia* (Mantua, 1608).

—— *Descrittione dell'infirmità, morte, et funerali del sereniss. sig. il Sig. Guglielmo Gonzaga* (Mantua), 1587.

—— *Descrittione delle solenni cerimonie fatte nella coronatione del Sereniss. Sig. il Sig. Vincenzo Gonzaga IIII Duca di Mantova e di Monferrato II* (Mantua, 1587).

FORTUNA, SIMONE, *Le nozze di Eleonora de' Medici con Vincenzo Gonzaga* (Florence, 1868).

Frammenti storici dell'Argo ticinese, ed. Giovanni Vidari, 2 vols. (Pavia, 1886).

FRANGIPANI, CORNELIO, *Tragedia* (Venice, 1574).

FROMSON, MICHELE, 'A Conjunction of Rhetoric and Music: Structural Modelling in the Italian Counter-Reformation Motet', *Journal of the Royal Musical Association*, 117 (1992), 208–46.

—— 'Imitation and Innovation in the North-Italian Motet, 1560–1605' (Ph.D. diss., University of Pennsylvania, 1988).

[GABRIELLI, FRANCESCO], *Infirmità, testamento, e morte di Francesco Gabrielli detto Scappino, composto, e dato in luce à requisitione de gli spiritosi ingegni, con l'intavolatura della chitarriglia spagnola, sue lettere, e chiaccona* (Verona, Padua, and Parma, 1638).

—— *Il triomph et la comedia fatta nelle nozze di Lipotoppo, con Madonna Lasagna, con tutte le sorti d'istrumen de suoni, & canti, che furno a dette nozze, & li servidori che portorno la colatione* (Venice, 1586).

GAETA BERTELÀ, GIOVANNA, and PETRIOLI TOFANI, ANNAMARIA, *Feste e apparati medicei da Cosimo I a Cosimo II: mostra di disegni e incisioni* (Florence, 1969).

GAGLIANO, MARCO DA, *La Dafne* (Florence, 1608).

GALLICO, CLAUDIO, 'Emblemi strumentali negli "scherzi" di Monteverdi', *Rivista italiana di musicologia*, 2 (1967), 54–73.

GARZONI, TOMASO, *La piazza universale di tutte le professioni del mondo, e nobili et ignobili* (Venice, 1585, 1595).

GIUSTINIANI, VINCENZO, *Discorso sopra la musica*, trans. Carol MacClintock (Musicological Studies and Documents, 9; Rome, 1972).

GORDON, MEL, *Lazzi: The Comic Routines of the Commedia dell'Arte* (New York, 1983).

GRAFTON, ANTHONY, *Commerce with the Classics: Ancient Books and Renaissance Readers* (Ann Arbor, 1997).

—— *Defenders of the Text: The Traditions of Scholarship in an Age of Science, 1450–1800* (Cambridge, Mass., 1991).

—— and JARDINE, LISA, *From Humanism to the Humanities: Education and the Liberal Arts in Fifteenth- and Sixteenth-Century Europe* (London, 1986).

[GRAZZINI, ANTON FRANCESCO], *Descrizione degl'intermedii rappresentati colla commedia nelle nozze dello illustrissimo ed eccellentissimo Signor Principe di Firenze e di Siena* (Florence, 1566).

GREENBLATT, STEPHEN, *Renaissance Self-fashioning: From More to Shakespeare* (Chicago, 1980).

GRENDLER, PAUL, *Schooling in Renaissance Italy: Literacy and Learning, 1400–1600* (Baltimore, 1989).

GRILLO, GIOVAN BATTISTA, *Breve trattato di quanto successe alla Maestà della Regina D. Margherita d'Austria N. S. dalla città di Trento fine d'Alemagna, e principio d'Italia fino alla Città di Genova* (Naples, 1604).

GUALTEROTTI, RAFFAELLO, *Descrizione del regale apparato per le nozze della Serenissima Madama Cristiana di Loreno moglie del Serenissimo Don Ferdinando Medici III. Granduca di Toscana* (Florence, 1589).

—— *Feste nelle nozze del serenissimo Don Francesco Medici Gran Duca di Toscana; et della sereniss. sua consorte la Sig. Bianca Cappello* (Florence, 1579).

GUARINI, BATTISTA, *Compendio della poesia tragicomica, tratto dai duo Verati, per opera dell'autore del Pastor Fido, colla giunta di molte cose spettanti all'arte* (Venice, 1601).

—— *Il pastor fido*, ed. M. Guglielminetti (Milan, 1971).

—— *Il Verrato ovvero difesa di quanto ha scritto M. Giason Denores* (Ferrara, 1588).

—— *Il Verato secondo* (Florence, 1603).

GUARINI, MARCANTONIO, *Compendio historico dell'origine, delle chiese e luoghi pii della città e diocesi di Ferrara* (Ferrara, 1621).

GUARINO VERONESE, *Epistolario di Guarino Veronese*, ed. R. Sabbadini, 3 vols. (Venice, 1915–19).

GUAZZI, ELEUTERIO, *Spiritosi affetti a una e due voci. Cioè arie madrigali & romanesca da cantarsi in tiorba in cimbalo & chitariglia & altri istromenti con l'alfabetto per la chitara spagnola. Libro primo* (Venice, 1622).

GUNDERSHEIMER, WERNER L. (ed.), *The Italian Renaissance* (Toronto, Buffalo, and London, 1993).

HAAR, JAMES, *Essays on Italian Poetry and Music in the Renaissance, 1350–1600* (Berkeley and Los Angeles, 1986).

HAAR, JAMES, 'The *Madrigale arioso*: A Mid-Century Development in the Cinquecento Madrigal', *Studi musicali*, 11 (1983), 203–19.

HANKINS, JAMES, 'The Myth of the Platonic Academy of Florence', *Renaissance Quarterly*, 44 (1991), 429–75.

—— *Plato in the Italian Renaissance*, 2 vols. (Leiden, 1990).

HANNING, BARBARA RUSSANO, 'Apologia pro Ottavio Rinuccini', *Journal of the American Musicological Society*, 26 (1973), 240–62.

—— 'Glorious Apollo: Poetic and Political Themes in the First Opera', *Renaissance Quarterly*, 32 (1979), 485–513.

—— 'Monteverdi's Three Genera: A Study in Terminology', in Nancy Kovaleff Baker and Barbara Russano Hanning (eds.), *Musical Humanism and its Legacy: Essays in Honor of Claude V. Palisca* (Stuyvesant, NY, 1992), 145–70.

—— *Of Poetry and Music's Power* (Ann Arbor, 1980).

HARRÁN, DON, 'Doubly Tainted, Doubly Talented: The Jewish Poet Sara Copio (d. 1641) as a Heroic Singer', in Irene Alm, Alyson McLamore, and Colleen Reardon (eds.), *Musica franca: Essays in Honor of Frank A. D'Accone* (Stuyvesant, NY, 1995), 197–231.

—— 'Investigation through Interrogation: The Case of Female Poets and Feminist Poetry in the Sixteenth-Century Madrigal', *Recercare*, 7 (1995), 5–46.

—— 'Salamone Rossi as a Composer of Theater Music', *Studi musicali*, 16 (1987), 95–131.

—— *Salamone Rossi: Jewish Composer in Late Renaissance Mantua* (Oxford, 1999).

HARTMANN, ARNOLD, Jr., 'Battista Guarini and *Il Pastor Fido* (1590)', *Musical Quarterly*, 39 (1953), 415–25.

HARTT, F., *Giulio Romano* (New Haven, 1958).

HELLER, WENDY, 'Reforming Achilles: Gender, *Opera seria* and the Rhetoric of the Enlightened Hero', *Early Music*, 26 (1998), 562–81.

HILL, JOHN WALTER, *The Life and Works of Francesco Maria Veracini* (Ann Arbor, 1979).

HOLFORD-STREVENS, LEOFRANC, '"Her eyes became two spouts": Classical Antecedents of Renaissance Laments', *Early Music*, 27 (1999), 379–93.

IBERTI, ANNIBALE, *Relatione de' ricevimenti fatti in Mantova* (Mantua, 1598).

INGEGNERI, ANGELO, *Danza di Venere pastorale di Angelo Ingegneri* (Vicenza, 1584).

—— *Della poesia rappresentativa & del modo di rappresentare le favole sceniche* (Ferrara, 1598); ed. Maria Luisa Doglio (Ferrara and Modena, 1989).

JORDAN, CONSTANCE, *Renaissance Feminism: Literary Texts and Political Models* (Ithaca, NY and London, 1990).

KING, MARGARET L., 'Book-Lined Cells: Women and Humanism in the Early Italian Renaissance', in Patricia H. Labalme (ed.), *Beyond their Sex: Learned Women of the European Past* (New York, 1984), 66–90.

KIRKENDALE, WARREN, *The Court Musicians in Florence during the Principate of the Medici* (Florence, 1993).

—— *Emilio de' Cavalieri, 'Gentiluomo romano': His Life and Letters, his Role as Superintendent of all the Arts at the Medici Court, and his Musical Compositions* (Florence, 2001).

KONSTAN, DAVID, *Broken Columns: Two Roman Epic Fragments*, trans. David R. Slavitt (Philadelphia, 1997).

KRISTELLER, PAUL OSKAR, *Marsilio Ficino and his Work after Five Hundred Years* (Florence, 1987).

LASSO, ORLANDO DI, *Canzoni villanesche and villanelle*, ed. Donna G. Cardamone (Recent Researches in the Music of the Renaissance, 82–3; Madison, Wis., 1991).

LA VIA, STEFANO, 'Concentus Iovis adversus Saturni Voces—magia, musica astrale e umanesimo nel IV intermedio fiorentino del 1589', *I Tatti studies: Essays in the Renaissance*, 5 (1993), 111–56.

LAWNER, LYNNE, *Harlequin on the Moon: Commedia dell'Arte and the Visual Arts* (New York, 1998).

LEA, KATHLEEN M., *Italian Popular Comedy: A Study in the Commedia dell'Arte, 1560–1620*, 2 vols. (Oxford, 1934; repr. New York, 1962).

Lettere di scrittori italiani del secolo XVI, ed. G. Campori (Bologna, 1877).

LEUCHTMANN, HORST, *Orlando di Lasso: Sein Leben* (Wiesbaden, 1976).

MCCLARY, SUSAN, *Feminine Endings: Music, Gender, and Sexuality* (Minneapolis, 1991).

MACCLINTOCK, CAROL (ed. and trans.), *Readings in the History of Music in Performance* (Bloomingon, Ind., 1982).

MACNEIL, ANNE, 'The Divine Madness of Isabella Andreini', *Journal of the Royal Musical Association*, 120 (1995), 195–215.

—— 'Music and the Life and Work of Isabella Andreini: Humanistic Attitudes toward Music, Poetry, and Theater during the Late Sixteenth and Early Seventeenth Centuries' (Ph.D. diss., University of Chicago, 1994).

—— 'A Portrait of the Artist as a Young Woman', *Musical Quarterly*, 83 (1999), 247–79.

—— 'Weeping at the Water's Edge', *Early Music*, 27 (1999), 406–18.

MACROBIUS, *Commentary on the Dream of Scipio*, ed. and trans. William Harris Stahl (New York, 1952).

MAFFEI, SCIPIONE AGNELLO, *Gli annali di Mantova* (Tortona, 1675).

MATTEI, PIETRO [Pierre Matthieu], *Histoire de France* (Paris, 1606); translated into Italian as *Della perfetta historia di Francia* by Alessandro Sanesio (Venice, 1625).

MALHERBE, F., *Œuvres de Malherbe*, ed. L. Lalanne, 6 vols. (Paris, 1862).

MAMONE, SARA, *Firenze e Parigi: due capitali dello spettacolo per una regina Maria de' Medici* (Milan, 1987).

—— *Il teatro nella Firenze medicea: problemi di storia della spettacolo* (Milan, 1981).

MANCINI, FRANCO, MURARO, MARIA TERESA, and POVOLEDO, ELENA, *I teatri di Venezia*, vol. 1, pt. 1 of *I teatri del Veneto*, 4 vols. (Venice, 1985–96).

—— *I teatri del Veneto*, 4 vols (Venice, 1985–96).

MANZUOLI, NICOLÒ, *Rime, e prose di diversi auttori in lode del sereniss. prencipe Nicolò Donato raccolte da Nicolò Manzuoli* (Venice, 1620).

MAROTTI, FERRUCCIO, and ROMEI, GIOVANNA, *La professione del teatro*, vol. 2 of *La commedia dell'arte e la società barocca* (Rome, 1991).

MAYLENDER, MICHELE, *Storia delle accademie d'Italia* (Bologna, 1927).

MECONI, HONEY, 'Does Imitation Exist?', *Journal of Musicology*, 12 (1994), 152–78.

[MERENDA, G.], *Historia della città di Ferrara* (Rome, BAV, Barb. lat. 4948).

MERULO, CLAUDIO, *Canzoni d'intavolatura d'organo di Claudio Merulo da Correggio a quattro voci, fatte alla francese, Libro primo* (Venice, 1592).

MILLER, ROARK, 'The Composers of San Marco and Santo Stefano and the Development of Venetian Monody (to 1630)' (Ph.D. diss., University of Michigan, 1993).

I modi: The Sixteen Pleasures, an Erotic Album of the Italian Renaissance, ed. and trans. Lynne Lawner (Evanston, Ill., 1988).

MONALDINI, SERGIO, 'Il teatro dei comici dell'arte a Bologna', *L'Archiginnasio*, 90 (1995), 33–164.

MONSON, CRAIG, 'Disembodied Voices: Music in the Nunneries of Bologna in the Midst of the Counter-Reformation', in id. (ed.), *The Crannied Wall: Women, Religion, and the Arts in Early Modern Europe* (Ann Arbor, 1992), 191–210.

MONTEVERDI, CLAUDIO, *The Letters of Claudio Monteverdi*, ed. Denis Stevens (rev. edn., Oxford, 1995).

—— *The Operas of Monteverdi* (English National Opera Guide 45, ed. Nicholas John; London, 1992).

—— *Tutte le opere*, ed. G. Francesco Malipiero ([Vienna], n.d).

MURARO, MARIA TERESA, *Gran Teatro La Fenice* (Venice, 1996).

—— *Scenografie di Pietro Gonzaga* ([Venice], 1967).

—— *Studi sul teatro veneto fra Rinascimento ed età barocca* (Florence, 1971).

—— *Venezia e il melodramma nel Seicento* (Florence, 1976).

NAGLER, ALOIS MARIA, *Theatre Festivals of the Medici 1539–1637* (New Haven and London, 1964).

NEGRI, CESARE, *Breve narratione del soggetto de gli Intermedij del Sig. Camillo Schiafenati, rappresentati nell'Armenia pastorale del Sig. Gio. Battista Visconte* (Milan, 1602).

—— *Le gratie d'amore* (Milan, 1602; facs. edn. New York, 1969).

NERI, ACHILLE, 'Gli "intermezzi" del "Pastor fido"', *Giornale storico della letteratura italiana*, 5 (1888), 405–15.

NERI, FERDINANDO, *Il Chiabrera e la Pléiade francese* (Turin, Milan, and Rome, 1920).

NEWCOMB, ANTHONY, 'Alfonso Fontanelli and the Ancestry of the Seconda Pratica Madrigal', in R. L. Marshall (ed.), *Studies in Renaissance and Baroque Music in Honor of Arthur Mendel* (Kassel and Hackensack, NJ, 1974), 47–70.

—— 'Courtesans, Muses, or Musicians? Professional Women Musicians in Sixteenth-Century Italy', in Jane Bowers and Judith Tick (eds.), *Women Making Music: The Western Art Tradition, 1150–1950* (Urbana and Chicago, 1986), 90–115.

—— *The Madrigal at Ferrara, 1579–1597*, 2 vols. (Princeton, 1980).

New Grove Dictionary of Opera, ed. Stanley Sadie (London, 1992).

NOLHAC, PIERRE DE, and SOLERTI, ANGELO, *Il viaggio in Italia di Enrico III re di Francia e le feste a Venezia, Ferrara, Mantova e Torino* (Turin, 1890).

OSSI, MASSIMO, 'Claudio Monteverdi's Concertato Technique and its Role in the Development of his Musical Thought' (Ph.D. diss., Harvard University, 1989).

—— 'Claudio Monteverdi's *Ordine novo, bello et gustevole*: The Canzonetta as Dramatic Module and Formal Archetype', *Journal of the American Musicological Society*, 45 (1992), 261–304.

OVID, *Heroides*, trans. Mary Innes (Harmondsworth, 1955).

—— *Metamorphoses*, trans. Mary Innes (London, 1955).

PALISCA, CLAUDE V., 'The Artusi–Monteverdi Controversy', in *Studies in the History of Italian Music and Music Theory* (Oxford, 1994), 54–87.

—— *The Florentine Camerata* (New Haven, 1989).

—— *Girolamo Mei: Letters on Ancient and Modern Music to Vincenzo Galilei and Giovanni Bardi* ([Rome], 1960, 1977).

—— *Humanism in Italian Renaissance Musical Thought* (New Haven, 1985).

—— *Studies in the History of Italian Music and Music Theory* (Oxford, 1994).

PANDOLFI, VITO, *Il teatro del rinascimento e la commedia dell'arte* (Rome, 1969).

—— (ed.) *La commedia dell'arte: Storia e testo*, 6 vols. (Florence, 1988).

PAOLUCCI, ANTONIO, and MAFFEZZOLI, UMBERTO, *Sabbioneta: il teatro all'antica* (Modena, 1993).

[PARFAICT, FRANÇOIS and CLAUDE], *Histoire de l'ancien théâtre italien, depuis son origine en France, jusqu'à sa suppression en l'année 1697* (Paris, 1767).

PARISI, SUSAN, 'Ducal Patronage of Music in Mantua, 1587–1627: An Archival Study', 2 vols. (Ann Arbor, 1989).

PASQUALI, MARTA, and FERRETTI, MARINA, 'Cronotassi critica dei Legati Vicelegati e Governatori di Bologna dal sec. XVI al XVIII', *Atti e Memorie della Dep. di Storia Patria per le provincie di Romagna*, 23 (1972), 117–301.

PASSIGNANI, GIOVANNI, *Descrittione degl'intermedii fatti nel felicissimo palazzo del Gran Duca Cosimo et del suo illustrissimo figliuolo principe di Firenze et di Siena: per honorar la illustriss. presenza della sereniss. altezza dello eccellentissimo Arciduca d'Austria* (Florence, 1569).

PAVONI, GIUSEPPE, *Diario descritto da Giuseppe Pavoni delle feste celebrate nelle solennissime nozzi delli serenissimi sposi, il Sig. Don Ferdinando Medici & la Sig. Donna Christina di Loreno Gran Duchi di Toscana* (Bologna, 1589).

—— *Entrata della sereniss.ma Gran Duchessa sposa, nella città di Fiorenza* (Bologna, 1589).

PERSIA, FERRANTE, *Relatione de' ricevimenti fatti in Mantova alla Maestà della Regina di Spagna dal Sereniss. Sig. Duca, l'anno MDXCVIII del mese di Novembre* (Mantua and Ferrara, 1598).

PETRACCONE, ENZO, *La Commedia dell'arte—storia, tecnica, scenari* (Naples, 1927).

PICOT, EMILIO, *Gli ultimi anni di G. B. Andreini in Francia* (Pisa, 1901).

PIRROTTA, NINO, *Music and Culture in Italy from the Middle Ages to the Baroque* (Cambridge, Mass., 1984).

—— 'Scelte poetiche di Monteverdi', *Nuova rivista musicale italiana*, 2 (1968), 10–42, 226–54; translated into English as 'Monteverdi's Poetic Choices' in *Music and Culture in Italy from the Middle Ages to the Baroque* (Cambridge, Mass., 1984), 271–316.

—— and POVOLEDO, ELENA, *Music and Theatre from Poliziano to Monteverdi*, trans. Karen Eales (Cambridge, 1982).

PITTORRU, F. *Torquato Tasso* (Milan, 1982).

PLATO, *Euthyphro, Apology, Crito, Phaedo, Phaedrus*, trans. Harold North Fowler (Cambridge and London, 1982).

PORCACCHI, TOMASO, *Le attioni d'Arrigo terzo Re di Francia e di Polonia* (Venice, 1574).

PRIZER, WILLIAM F., 'The Frottola and the Unwritten Tradition', *Studi musicali*, 15 (1986), 3–38.

Prosatori latini del Quattrocento, ed. Eugenio Garin (Milan, 1952).

PRUNIÈRES, HENRY, 'Monteverdi and French Music', *The Sackbut*, 3 (1922), 98–110.

—— 'Monteverdi e la musica francese del suo tempo', *Rassegna musicale*, 2 (1929), 483–93.

—— *La Vie et l'œuvre de Claudio Monteverdi* (Paris, 1926), translated into English as *Monteverdi: His Life and Work* by Marie D. Mackie (London, 1926; Westport, Conn., 1974).

PUTEANUS, ERYCIUS, *Epistolarum fercula secunda* (Milan, 1602).

PUTNAM, MICHAEL C. J., 'Virgil and History', lecture presented at the University of Chicago, 9 January 1995.

QUINT, DAVID, *Origin and Originality in Renaissance Literature: Versions of the Source* (New Haven, 1983).

RABB, THEODORE K., *The Struggle for Stability in Early Modern Europe* (New York, 1975).

Raccolto delle feste fatte in Fiorenza dalli ill.mi et ecc.mi nostri signori e padroni il Sig. Duca, et il Signor Principe di Fiorenza et di Siena, Nella venuta del serenissimo

Arciduca Carlo d'Austria per honorarne la presenza di sua altezza (Florence, 1569).

RADCLIFF-UMSTEAD, DOUGLAS, *The Birth of Modern Comedy in Renaissance Italy* (Chicago and London, 1969).

REHM, RUSH, *Marriage to Death: The Conflation of Wedding and Funeral Rituals in Greek Tragedy* (Princeton, 1994).

Relatione dell'arrivo in Spagna della serenissima regina d'Austria con solenne ricevimento fattole dal catholico rè N. S. nella insigne città di Valenza, et sposalitio celebrato nella chiesa maggiore di quella città (Verona, 1599).

REULENS, CHARLES, *Erycius Puteanus et Isabelle Andreini: lecture faite à l'Académie d'Archéologie le 3 Février 1889* (Antwerp, 1889).

REYNOLDS, CHRISTOPHER, 'The Counterpoint of Allusion in Fifteenth-Century Masses', *Journal of the American Musicological Society*, 45 (1992), 228–60.

RICHARDS, KENNETH, and RICHARDS, LAURA, *The Commedia dell'arte: A Documentary History* (Oxford, 1990).

RIGON, FERNANDO, *The Teatro Olimpico in Vicenza* (Milan, 1989).

RINUCCINI, OTTAVIO, *L'Arianna tragedia rappresentata in musica* (Mantua, 1608).

—— *La Dafne d'Ottavio Rinuccini rappresentata al serenissimo Duca di Parma dalla serenissima Granduchessa di Toscana* (Florence, 1604).

ROCKE, MICHAEL, *Forbidden Friendships: Homosexuality and Male Culture in Renaissance Florence* (New York, 1996).

ROMANO, REMIGIO. *Prima raccolta di bellissime canzonette musicali, e moderne, di autori gravissimi nella poesia, & nella musica* (Vicenza, 1618, 1622).

—— *Seconda raccolta di canzonette musicali; bellissime per cantare & sonare, sopra arie moderne* (Vicenza, 1620).

—— *Terza raccolta di bellissime canzoni alla romanesca. Per suonare, e cantare nella chitara alla Spagnuola, con la sua intavolatura. Con altre canzonette vaghe, & belle* (Vicenza, 1620, 1622).

—— *Nuova raccolta di bellissime canzonette musicali, e moderne, di auttori gravissimi nella poesia, & nella musica* (Venice, 1623, 1625).

—— *Ressiduo alla quarta parte di canzonette musicali. Di auttori gravissimi nella poesia et nella musica* (Venice, 1626).

ROMEI, ANNIBALE, *I discorsi* (Venice, 1585); translated into English as *The Courtiers Academie: Comprehending seven severall days discourses: wherein be discussed, seven noble and important arguments, worthy by all gentlemen to be perused . . . Originally written in Italian by Count Hannibal Romei, a Gentleman of Ferrara, and translated into English by IJ* [John Kepers] (London, 1598); ed. Alice Shalvi (London, 1968).

RONCHINI, AMADIO, *Lettere d'uomini illustri conservate nell'Archivio di Parma* (Parma, 1853).

ROSSI, BASTIANO DE', *Descrizione del magnificentissimo apparato e de' maravigliosi intermedi fatti per la commedia rappresentata in Firenze nelle felicissime nozze degl'illustrissimi ed eccellentissimi signori il Signor Don Cesare d'Este, e la Signora Donna Virginia Medici* (Florence, 1585).

Rossi, Bastiano de', *Descrizione dell'apparato e degl'intermedi, fatti per la commedia rappresentata in Firenze, nelle nozze de' serenissimi Don Ferdinando Medici e Madama Christina di Loreno, Gran Duchi di Toscana* (Florence, 1589).

Ruggiero, Guido, *Binding Passions: Tales of Magic, Marriage and Power at the End of the Renaissance* (New York and Oxford, 1993).

Sala, Torello, *Dizionario storico biografico di scrittori, letterati ed artisti dell'Ordine di Vallombrosa*, 2 vols. (Florence, [1929]).

Sansovino, Francesco, *Venezia città nobilissima et singolare* (Venice, 1581).

Sardi, Gasparo and Faustini, Agostino, *Libro delle historie ferraresi* (Ferrara, 1646).

Saslow, James, *Ganymede in the Renaissance: Homosexuality in Art and Society* (New Haven, 1988).

—— *The Medici Wedding of 1589: Florentine Festival as* Theatrum mundi (New Haven, 1996).

—— *The Poetry of Michelangelo: An Annotated Translation* (New Haven, 1991).

Scala, Flaminio, *Il teatro delle favole rappresentative* (Venice, 1611); ed. Ferruccio Marotti (Milan, 1976); translated into English as *Scenarios of the commedia dell'arte* by Henry F. Salerno (New York, 1967).

Scalini, Marcello, *Breve discorso intorno alle solennità fatte in Turino alli dodeci di maggio nel battesimo del serenissimo prencipe di Piemonte, Filippo Emanuelle primo genito del Serenissimo Carlo Emanuelle Duca di Savoia, et di Donna Catherina Infante catolica di Spagna* (Milan and Parma, 1587).

Schiafenati, Camillo, *Breve narratione del soggetto de gli intermedii del Signor Camillo Schiafenati, quali havrannosi a rappresentar nella egloga pastorale del Sig. Gio. Battista Visconte intitolata l'Arminia, alla presenza della serenissima Infante Donna Isabella, & del Sereniss. Arciduca Alberto d'Austria* (Milan, 1599).

Schrade, Leo, *Monteverdi, Creator of Modern Music* (New York, 1950).

Smith, Winifred, *The Commedia dell'Arte* (New York, 1964).

Solerti, Angelo, *Gli albori del melodramma* (Milan, 1904; Bologna, 1976).

—— *Ferrara e la corte estense nella seconda metà del secolo decimosesto: i discorsi di Annibale Romei gentiluomo ferrarese* (Città di Castello, 1891).

—— *Musica, ballo, e drammatica alla corte medicea dal 1600 al 1637* (New York and London, 1968).

—— and Lanza, Domenico, 'Il teatro ferrarese nella seconda metà del secolo XVI', *Giornale storico della letteratura italiana*, 9 (1891), 148–85.

Sommi, Leone de', *Quattro dialoghi in materia di rappresentazioni sceniche*, ed. Ferruccio Marotti (Milan, 1968), translated into English as 'Leone Ebreo de Sommi's *Four dialogues on stage presentations*' by Catherine Anne Blanchard-Rothmuller (Ann Arbor, 1973).

La sontuosissima entrata della Serenissima Margherita d'Austria Regina di Spagna, et del Serenissimo Arciduca Alberto d'Austria in Ferrara (Verona, 1598).

SPELTA, ANTONIO MARIA, *La curiosa, et dilettevole aggionta del Sig. Ant. Maria Spelta, cittadino pavese, all'historia sua* (Pavia, 1602).

—— *Historia* (Pavia, 1597).

STAMPA, GASPARA, *Selected Poems*, ed. and trans. Laura Anna Stortoni and Mary Prentice Lillie (New York, 1994).

[STRIGGIO, ALESSANDRO], *La favola d'Orfeo rappresentata in musica il carnevale dell'anno M.D.CVII, nell'Accademia de gli Invaghiti di Mantova* (Mantua, 1607).

STRUNK, OLIVER, *The Baroque Era*, rev. Margaret Murata; vol. 4 of *Source Readings in Music History*, ed. Oliver Strunk (New York, 1998).

SUTHERLAND, N. M., *The French Secretaries of State in the Age of Catherine de Medici* (London, 1962).

TASSO, TORQUATO, *Aminta* (Venice, 1581); ed. Claudio Varese (Milan, 1985).

—— *Gerusalemme liberata* [1581]; translated into English and edited as *Jerusalem Delivered* by Ralph Nash (Detroit, 1987).

TAVIANI, FERDINANDO, 'Bella d'Asia: Torquato Tasso, gli attori e l'immortalità', *Paragone/letteratura*, 35 (1984), 3–76.

—— *La fascinazione del teatro*, vol. 1 of *La commedia dell'arte e la società barocca* (Rome, 1969, 1991).

—— and SCHINO, MIRELLA, *Il segreto della commedia dell'arte: la memoria delle compagnie italiane del XVI, XVII e XVIII secolo* (Florence, 1986).

TESTAVERDE MATTEINI, ANNAMARIA, *L'officina delle nuvole: il teatro mediceo nel 1589 e gli* Intermedi *del Buontalenti nel* Memoriale di Girolamo Seriacopi, vol. 11/12 of *Musica e teatro: quaderni degli Amici della Scala* (Milan, 1991).

TOMLINSON, GARY, 'Madrigal, Monody, and Monteverdi's "Via naturale alla immitatione"', *Journal of the American Musicological Society*, 34 (1981), 60–108.

—— *Metaphysical Song: An Essay on Opera* (Princeton, 1999).

—— *Monteverdi and the End of the Renaissance* (Berkeley and Los Angeles, 1987).

—— *Music in Renaissance Magic: Toward a Historiography of Others* (Chicago, 1993).

TOSCAN, JEAN, *Le Carnaval du langage: le lexique érotique des poètes de l'équivoque de Burchiello à Marino (XVe–XVIIe siècles)* (Lille, 1981).

TROIANO, MASSIMO, *Discorsi delli trionfi, giostre, apparati, e delle cose più notabile nelle sontuose nozze dell'Illustrissimo et Eccellentissimo Sig. Duca Guglielmo primo genito del generosissimo Alberto quinto* (Munich, 1569).

—— *Die Münchner Fürstenhochzeit von 1568: Massimo Troiano: Dialoge*, ed. Horst Leuchtmann (Munich, 1980).

VALERINI, ADRIANO, *Oratione d'Adriano Valerini veronese, in morte della divina Signora Vincenza Armani, comica eccellentissima* (Verona, [1570]).

VASARI, GIORGIO, *Descrizione dell'apparato fatto nel tempio di S. Giovanni di Fiorenza per lo battesimo della signora prima figliuola dell'illustrissimo, et eccellentissimo S. Principe di Fiorenza et di Siena Don Francesco Medici, et della serenissima Reina Giovanna d'Austria* (Florence, 1568).

VIGENÈRE, B. DE, *La Sumptueuse et Magnifique Entrée du très-christien Roy Henry III de ce nom, Roy de France et de Pologne, gran Duc de Lithuanie, & en la cité de Mantoue, avec le portraits des choses les plus exquises* (Paris, 1576).

VIGILIO, GIOVAN BATTISTA, *La insalata: cronaca mantovana dal 1561 al 1602*, ed. Daniela Ferrari and Cesare Mozzarelli (Mantua, 1992).

VIRGIL, *Eclogues, Georgics, the Aeneid*, trans. H. Rushton Fairclough (Cambridge, Mass. and London, 1986).

Vocabolario degli Accademici della Crusca (Venice, 1612).

WALKER, D. P., *Music, Spirit, and Language in the Renaissance*, ed. Penelope Gouk (London, 1985).

——— *Les Fêtes du mariage de Ferdinand de Médicis et de Christine de Lorraine, Florence 1589*, i: *Musique des intermèdes de 'La Pellegrina'* (Paris, 1968).

——— 'La Musique des intermèdes florentins de 1589 et l'humanisme', in *Les Fêtes de la Renaissance* (Paris, 1956), i. 133–44.

WALLER, MARGUERITE, 'The Empire's New Clothes: Refashioning the Renaissance', in Sheila Fisher and Janet E. Halley (eds.), *Seeking the Woman in Late Medieval and Renaissance Writings: Essays in Feminist Contextual Criticism* (Knoxville, Tenn., 1989), 160–83.

WALTERS, SUZANNA DANUTA, *Material Girls: Making Sense of Feminist Cultural Theory* (Berkeley, 1995).

WATKINS, GLEN, and LAMAY, THOMASIN, 'Imitatio and Emulatio: Changing Concepts of Originality in the Madrigals of Gesualdo and Monteverdi in the 1590s', in Ludwig Finscher (ed.), *Claudio Monteverdi: Festschrift Reinhold Hammerstein zum 70. Geburtstag* (Laaber, 1986), 453–88.

WEINBERG, BERNARD, *A History of Literary Criticism in the Italian Renaissance*, 2 vols. (Chicago, 1961).

WERT, GIACHES DE, *Opera omnia*, xiv, ed. Carol MacClintock ([Rome], 1973).

WHENHAM, JOHN, 'A Masterpiece for a Court', in *The Operas of Monteverdi*, ed. N. John (London, 1992).

WILSON, BLAKE, '*Ut oratoria musica* in the Writings of Renaissance Music Theorists', in *Festa musicologica: Essays in Honor of George J. Buelow* (Stuyvesant, NY, 1995), 341–68.

WISTREICH, RICHARD, 'Hearing a Lost Voice—Monteverdi's *Ogni amante è guerrier* (1638) and a Veteran Warrior-Singer', paper presented at the Conference on Medieval and Renaissance Music, York, England, July 1998.

WOODS, MARJORIE C., 'Rape and the Pedagogical Rhetoric of Sexual Violence', in Rita Copeland (ed.), *Criticism and Dissent in the Middle Ages* (Cambridge, 1996), 56–86.

—— 'Rhetoric in the Medieval Classroom, with Some Modern Applications', paper presented at the Congreso Internacional de Retórica en México, 20–4 April 1998.

YATES, FRANCES A., *The Art of Memory* (Chicago and London, 1966).

—— *Astraea: The Imperial Theme in the Sixteenth Century* (London, 1975).

—— *Giordano Bruno and the Hermetic Tradition* (Chicago and London, 1964).

ZORACH, R., 'Gallia Fertilis and Antique Cybele', paper presented at the Sixteenth-Century Studies Conference, Toronto, 22–5 October 1998.

Index

abduction, *see* rape
Académie de Poésie et Musique 62
Accademia degli Affidati 78n
Accademia degli Intenti (Pavia) 56, 74, 78, 91, 252, 291, 305
Accademia degli Intrepidi 77, 252
Accademia degli Invaghiti 164
Accademia della Crusca 52
 Vocabolario 51, 61
Accademia Filarmonica 77, 252
Accademia Olimpica 8n
Accesa, *see* Andreini, Isabella.
Accolti, Marcello 21, 235–6
Achilles 92, 94, 151–4
Acquanegra, Christoforo 218
Agostini, Lodovico 214
Agucchia, Giovan Paolo 258
Ahi serpentella 172
air de cour 135
Alberghini, Angelica 213
Albizi, Camillo 220–1
Aldobrandini, Cinzio 244, 253, 257, 288–9
Aldobrandini, Ippolito (Clement VIII) 78, 148n, 231, 241–2, 245, 249
Aldobrandini, Margherita
 marriage to Ranuccio Farnese (1600) 22, 249–50
Aldobrandini, Pietro 2, 79, 242–5, 249, 251–3, 286
alfabeto notation 27, 71, 172
Alighieri, Dante 160
 Inferno 37, 160
allegory 16, 52, 55–6, 58–60, 75, 158, 168

Allen, Michael J. B. 60
allusion, *see* imitation
alms, payment of 10, 190, 226, 255, 258, 271–2
alternation, singing in 33, 39–43, 140–1
 see also competition, singing in
Ambra, Francesco d'
 La cofanaria 189
Ambrosini, Pietro 217
Amici, Diomede 228
Ammirato, Scipione 230
Andreini family 47–8, 80, 85, 88, 148, 164, 173
Andreini, Antonio 187
Andreini, Domenico 48n, 259
Andreini, Francesco (Evangelista Deuchino) 4–8, 10, 17–18, 30–1, 41, 47–50, 78, 163, 172–3, 187, 199, 214, 231, 235, 238, 252, 259–63, 272–3, 282, 307, 316–20, 322
 Le bravure del Capitano Spavento 18, 30, 41, 259, 261–3
Andreini, Giovan Battista (Lelio) 1, 4–5, 7, 10, 23, 30, 43, 48–50, 133, 146–7, 163–6, 169–70, 172–5, 182n, 199, 238, 258–9, 262, 291–2
 L'Adamo 166
 Amor nello specchio 164
 La campanazza 164
 La centaura 164
 La divina visione 166
 Due commedie in commedia 169
 Li duo Leli simili 164

Andreini, Giovan Battista (Lelio) (*cont.*):
  La Ferinda 163–4
  La Florinda 166, 259
  La Maddalena 7, 166
  La Maddalena lasciva e penitente 166n, 174
  Il pianto d'Apollo 48n, 259, 291
  Lo schiavetto 1, 13, 43, 147, 164–76, 181–4, 262
  La sultana 164
  La Tecla 166
Andreini, Isabella Canali (Accesa) 4–5, 10, 30–3, 36–8, 42–4, 46–51, 53, 55–6, 59–64, 67–9, 71–5, 77–83, 87, 89–99, 103–4, 111, 116–23, 125–7, 134–7, 163, 173, 178–82, 184–6, 196, 214, 222–3, 226–8, 230, 232, 235–7, 240–1, 246, 249, 251–63, 273, 276–81, 283–4, 288–92, 294, 296, 302, 305–23
  'Amorosa mia Clori' 104
  'D'amor l'aria sfavilla' 64, 303–5
  'Care gioie che le noie' 178–81, 184
  death of 4, 30–1, 43, 48–9, 258, 292
  'Deh girate luci amate' 178–81
  'Ecco l'Alba ruggiadosa' 63, 67–9, 71, 74
  'La forza d'Amore' 37–9, 55, 74–5
  Fragmenti d'alcune scritture 262–3
  'Io credèa che tra gli Amanti' 63, 68–9, 71–2, 74, 173, 184
  Lettere 30, 37–8, 55–6, 74–5, 254, 259–63, 292–4, 309–13
  Mirtilla 33–4, 37–46, 53–4, 62, 71, 75, 78n, 83n, 93, 122–3, 134, 223, 227, 235, 241, 246, 254, 258, 262, 277, 293, 296–300, 309
  'Movèa dolce un zefiretto' 63, 135–40
  'Ove sì tosto voli sogno?' 96, 98–9, 103–4
  La pazzia d'Isabella 32–4, 46–7, 51, 56–8, 61–2, 68, 73, 75, 185, 226, 249
  'Per lo soverchio affanno' 96–7
  'Quando scendeste ad'illustrare il mondo' 64–6, 300–2
  'Quella bocca di rose' 97–9, 104–11
  Rime 55, 63, 68, 70–1, 78, 93, 97–8, 116–17, 119, 121, 252–3, 255–8, 288–90
  Rime . . . parte seconda 256, 258
  'S'alcun sia mai, che i versi miei negletti' 121, 278
Andreini, Lavinia (suor Fulvia) 48, 222, 241, 247, 276–7
Andreini, Pietro Paolo 48n, 238
Andreini, Virginia Ramponi (Florinda) 4–5, 7, 11, 13, 23, 30, 71, 80–1, 127, 130, 132–3, 141–2, 147–50, 161–2, 163–6, 168–70, 172–5, 178, 181–3, 185, 213, 259
Angelone, Filippo 7, 204, 234, 247, 271, 273
Anguillara, Giovanni dell' 156
Antinori, Giovanni 213–14
Antonazoni, Giovan Maria 257
Aquinas, Thomas
  Summa theologica 94
Aragona, Blaseo d' 242–3
Arbisso, Anna d' 235
Archilei, Vittoria 16, 19, 21
Archinto, Orazio 193
Arcimboldi, Giovanni 193, 198, 269
Arco, Livia d' 244
aria 15–16, 27, 29–30, 167, 169–70, 172–4, 181
Ariosto, Ludovico 87, 213
  Orlando furioso 34, 51, 84n, 87, 89, 92, 95, 190

Index

Ariosto, Orazio 225
Aristotle 2
   Ars rhetorica 155
   Poetics 144–7
Arlecchino, *see* Martinelli, Tristano
Armani, Vincenza 4, 14, 33–7, 40, 64, 88n, 91, 133, 190, 193, 267
Arona, Francesco d' 199
Arrighi, Gostantino 19
Arrivabeni, Lelio 232
Artusi, Giovan Maria 77, 83–6, 88, 90–6, 99, 104, 116, 125, 148–9, 186, 244, 250, 256
Asso, Martino da 198
Athena, *see* Pallas Athena
Augustine 143–4, 158
   Confessions 144
Augustus 53
Aurelia romana 5, 228, 234, 239
Austoni, Giovan Battista 229
Austria, Albert of 78, 79n, 82–3, 242, 244–6, 248
   marriage to Isabella of Spain (1599) 22n, 78
Austria, Barbara of 189, 195
   marriage to Alfonso II d'Este (1565) 189
Austria, Catherine of
   marriage to Carlo Emanuele of Savoy (1590) 227
Austria, Charles of 193, 242
Austria, Eleonora of 79, 148n, 188, 237
Austria, Ernst of 236
Austria, Ferdinand of 83, 202–3, 242, 284
   marriage to Anna Caterina Gonzaga (1582) 212
Austria, Giovanna of 18, 192, 202
   marriage to Francesco de' Medici (1565) 189
Austria, Giovanni of 10n, 13, 196, 202

Austria, Margherita of 78–9, 81, 83, 88, 243–6
   marriage to Philip III of Spain (1598) 22, 78, 81, 88, 147–8, 164
Austria, Maximilian II of 188–9, 200, 203, 210, 254, 257
Austria, Rudolph II of 198, 200

Baïf, Jean-Antoine de 62
Baldovini, Emilio 228, 239
ballo, balletto, see dance
Bandini, Ottavio 235
Baratti, Claudio 228
Barbarigga, Concordia 228–9
Barberino, Alessandro 237
Barbieri, Nicolò 55, 61
Bardi, Giovanni de' 12, 34, 47, 52–4, 56, 213–14, 216, 221, 225–6, 239, 250
Bargagli, Scipione
   La pellegrina 46–7, 52, 56, 225–6
Basile, Adriana 90
Basilea, Simone 5, 203
bass 41, 43, 71, 104, 130, 134
   see also ground bass; instruments, musical
Bavaria, Albrecht IV of 187, 203
Bavaria, Maximilian of 241
Bavaria, Wilhelm V of 203, 241
   marriage to Renée of Lorraine (1568) 192
Beato, Gabriel 208
Bellamano, Franceschina 40
Belli, Girolamo 217
Bellone, Ercole 242–3, 245–6, 251, 284–6
Bellone, Lelio 252, 254–5, 287–8
Belloni, Nicolò 247–8, 251
Bendidio, Anna 194, 201, 203
Bendidio, Isabella 194, 203
Bendidio, Lucrezia 194, 202–3
Bentivoglio, Cornelio 201, 203

346 Index

Bentivoglio, Isabella 201
Bentivoglio, Lucrezia 201
Bentivoglio, Ulisse 227
Bentivoglio, Vittoria 202
Bevilacqua, Ercole 199, 229
Bianchi, Lodovico de' (Dottor
  Graziano) 5, 17–18, 19n, 200,
  216–17, 220, 222, 226, 273, 275–6
Biffi, Carlo 24, 26
Biffoli, Francesco 266, 281
Boethius 55
  De institutione musica 55
Bon, Altobello 263
Bonarelli, Guidubaldo 77, 252
Bonrizzo, Alvise 196
Bordone, Girolamo 78, 257–8
Borgogni, Gherardo 321–22
Borromeo, Pirro Visconte 213–14,
  228, 233
Borsato, Francesco 208
Boschetti, Zan Battista 195
Boussu, Marie de 253
Braga, Jacomo 240
Brancaccio, Giulio Cesare 198, 202,
  205–8, 214
Brown, Howard Mayer 33, 173n, 185
Brunetti, Domenico 178
Bruni, Domenico 18n, 55, 235–6, 263,
  294
  Fatiche comiche 294–5
Bucintoro 12
Buonarotti, Michelangelo 37, 60,
  86n, 95n, 167, 189, 250
  Tancia 167, 169
Buoncompagni, Girolamo 216
Buontalenti, Bernardo 53, 193, 221,
  226, 234

Caccini, Giulio 31, 71, 173–4, 184,
  214, 233, 250, 256
  Amor ch'attendi 172
  *Le nuove musiche e la nuova maniera
  di scrivirle* 170–1

Il rapimento di Cefalo 173, 250
Tu c'hai le penne Amore 71, 170–5,
  178, 181, 184
Caccini, Settimia 173
Calzoni, Gabrielle 218
Camillo, Giulio 14, 159
  Discorso in materia del suo teatro 14,
  159
camerata 12, 52
Canal, Pietro 214
canario, see dance
Canigiani, Bernardo 192, 194, 199,
  201–3
Canovaro, Gabriele 229
cantastorie 13, 43n
canto alla francese 72–4, 134–5
  see also *canzone alla francese*;
  canzonetta alla francese; style,
  French
canzone 27, 65, 172
  a ballo 167
  alla francese 134, 141, 172
canzonetta 33, 43–4, 49, 62–4, 68, 71,
  73, 75, 103, 134–5, 170, 172, 174,
  178, 181–2, 184, 186
  alla francese 22, 33, 51, 61–2, 72–3,
  134, 140, 181
  morale 63
  see also *scherzo*
Capello, Bianca 223
  marriage to Francesco de' Medici
  (1579) 203
Capello, Silvan 235
Cappella, Martianus 54
Capponi, Francesco 200
Carbone, Ludovico 84
Cardi, Fortunato 254
carnival 5n, 8–11, 24, 96, 169, 173
Caro labbro vermiglietto 71
Caroso, Fabritio 250
  Il ballarino 22
  La nobiltà di dame 22, 250
Carracci, Agostino 123–4

Index

Carter, Tim 132, 146
Case del Mandragola 81
Castagna, Giovan Battista 5, 228
Castiglione, Baldassare 232
catharsis 53, 144–5, 149
Cattaneo, Claudia 252
Cattaneo, Federico 220, 224–5
Cattaneo, Primocerio 227
Cattaneo, Valeriano 238
Cavalieri, Emilio de' 5, 21–2, 226, 231, 233, 235–6, 239, 246, 249
Cavalli, Orazio 209
Cavriani, Cesare 208–11, 213, 227, 229, 233
Cavriani, Ottaviano 229, 234, 240
Cecchini, Flaminia 255
Cecchini, Pier Maria 11n, 18n, 228, 247, 253
Ceruto, Antonio 190–1
Chalcidius 54
Charlemagne 60
Chiabrera, Gabriello 62–4, 67–8, 73, 134–5, 140, 185, 250
 'Amorosa pupilletta' 135–7
 Lament of Europa ('Cari paterni regni') 143, 159–60
 intermedi for *L'idropica* 143, 159–60, 250, 261
Chieppio, Annibale 230–2, 243–4, 254, 259
chorus 12–13, 15, 140–2, 151, 158, 168–9, 274
ciaccona, see dance
Cicogna, Pasquale 238
Cicognini, Cosimo 223
Cifra, Antonio 178
Cignardi, Ferrante 251
Cincinnati, Daniele 210–11
Cini, Giovan Battista 189, 193
Cizzuolo, Anteo 219
Cicero 55, 141, 159n
 Rhetorica ad Herennium 149

citizenship, *see* community
Claudio francese 222, 230, 276–7
Clement VIII, *see* Aldobrandini, Ippolito
Clermont, Charles Henri de 194
Cochran, Eric 52
comedy 1, 3, 9, 13, 18, 23, 27, 32, 35, 46, 55–6, 58, 62, 74–5, 123, 128, 133, 163–70, 174, 190–4, 197–9, 201–4, 206–8, 212, 214–15, 217, 220–1, 224–6, 229, 231–2, 234–5, 237, 243, 245, 247–50, 253–7, 260, 278–82, 285–6, 289, 295–6
Comesari, Santino
 Il ballo di donne turche 168
comica gelosa, comico geloso 4, 6, 27, 35, 273, 276–8, 281, 288–9, 291, 302, 305
coming of age 86, 96n, 110, 133, 145, 153–4, 158, 161, 184–6
commedia erudita 2
commedia vulgare 2
commitment 6–8
 by contract 5–8, 10, 236
 see also community, citizenship; obligation
community 53, 92, 152–6, 175
 citizenship 3, 62, 78, 80, 84, 86, 88, 164, 252, 254
 competition 4, 66
 performing in 2, 32–76
 singing in 33, 38–46, 75, 134, 181, 184–6
concerto delle dame, see *concerto delle donne*
concerto delle donne 7, 80, 87, 206, 209–10, 214, 216–17, 233
Concini, Giovan Battista 213, 217, 226
Confidenti, Compagnia de' 5, 9–10, 196, 205–7, 209–10, 212, 239, 246, 248, 255, 258
contest, *see* competition

Conosciuti, Leonardo 203–4, 212
Contarini, Giulio 243
Contarini, Iacopo 223, 227
contrasto 134
Cornacchia, Pietro Martire 265, 267
Corteccia, Francesco 18, 189
Cortesei, Valentino (Capitano Cardone) 236
Cortile, Ercole 198–9
Costantini, Antonio 13, 146, 149, 261
Council of Ten 11, 203, 210, 213, 218
Cozzi, Federico 213
Cremasco, Lodovico 244
Cueva, Gabriel de la 192–3
Cusano, Cardinal 21–2
Cusick, Suzanne 85–7, 92, 94, 129n, 130, 156

dance 21–4, 29, 152, 134, 143n, 168–9, 194, 198, 205, 211, 230, 232–3, 236, 250, 282
  balletto 22, 151
  ballo 128, 140–1
  calata 168–9
  canario 21–3, 182, 236
  ciaccona 27, 29–30
  galliarda 169
  sfessania 169
  villan di Spagna 168
daughter 48, 57, 93, 95, 130n, 151–3, 161, 173, 192, 219, 222, 229, 233, 242
death 11, 27, 29–30, 43, 48–9, 70, 79n, 95, 110–11, 143, 144n, 150–1, 153–5, 157–61, 163–4, 168, 177, 185, 188–9, 191, 193–6, 198, 200–3, 208, 219, 221, 223, 225, 228, 231, 233, 235, 237–9, 241–5, 247, 250, 255, 257–63
decorum 15, 36, 84, 110, 125, 145, 154, 158, 162
Deh, Florinda gratiosa 71, 172

Delia, *see* Rocca Nobili, Camilla
Denores, Giason 148–9, 155, 220, 227
  Della rhetorica 155–6
Desiosi, Compagnia de' 234–5, 238–41
Deuchino, Evangelista, *see* Andreini, Francesco
Dido 34, 144–5, 190
diplomacy 6, 88, 91
divine madness 2, 46, 49, 51, 55–6, 58–63, 74–5, 121–2, 167, 185
dominance 59, 61, 88, 95–6, 98–9, 185
Donati, Marcello 205, 209–10, 213–15, 227, 265, 278
Donato, Giovanni 215
Donato, Nicolò 235
Doni, Giovan Battista 24
Donne, Sebastiano dalle 223
Dori, Giorgio 192
Dottor Graziano, *see* Bianchi, Lodovico de'
dramma per musica 3, 184
Duke's comedians 2, 77–8, 80, 165

Easter 6n, 8, 77–8
education 84, 86, 94, 96n, 150, 186
Effrem, Muzio 174
Elizabeth I of England 193
eloquence 36, 46, 49, 51, 74, 84, 87, 92–4
emulation, *see* imitation
eroticism 58, 122–3, 125
  see also homoeroticism
Este family 95
Este, Alfonso II d' 8, 10n, 30, 80, 188–9, 195, 197, 199, 201–8, 210, 212, 218–22, 239–41, 253
  marriage to Lucrezia de' Medici (1560) 188
  marriage to Margherita Gonzaga (1579) 203

Este, Bradamante d' 199, 203
Este, Cesare d' 79, 188, 220–1, 223, 240–4
Este, court 7, 30, 214
Este, Ercole II d' 188
Este, Ippolita d' 237
Este, Leonora d' 208, 231
    marriage to Carlo Gesualdo (1594) 236
Este, Lucrezia d' 193, 210, 219, 242
Este, Luigi d' 194, 200, 203–6, 212–3, 221
Este, Marfisa d' 203–4, 212

Fabbri, Giovan Paolo 5, 219, 229, 231, 257, 275, 308, 314, 316, 319, 322
Fabbri, Paolo 146, 182n
Falavolti, Laura 164
Fall of Phaethon, *see* intermedi
fame 1, 31, 34–5, 49, 77, 122, 164–5
Farnese family 257
Farnese, Alessandro 207, 221, 233
Farnese, Margherita 208–15
    marriage to Vincenzo Gonzaga (1581) 10, 206–8
Farnese, Ottavio 187
Farnese, Ranuccio 212, 233
    marriage to Margherita Aldobrandini (1600) 22
Faruffino, Giovan Stefano 298
Fedele, Cassandra 87, 93
Fedeli, Compagnia de' 1, 4, 10n, 23, 31, 128, 133, 164–5, 172–4, 228, 239, 258, 261
Fedele, Flaminio 228, 239
Fedele, Lutio 5, 228, 273
Fedini, Giovanni
    Le due persilie 19
Ferrara, devolution of 3, 79, 129, 148n, 241

Ferrari, Benedetto
    L'Andromeda 11
Ferrari, Cristoforo 252
Ficino, Marsilio 53–4, 58–61, 72
    Commentary on Plato
    De vita coelitus comparanda 122, 159n
ficta, see *musica ficta*
Fiesoli, Marietta di Lorenzo de' 199
figures of words 85, 144–5, 186
Fiorini, Ippolito 244
Fintler, Giorgio 213
Flaminia romana 4, 19n, 33–5, 51, 190–2, 267
flauto dolce, *see* musical instruments
Florinda, *see* Andreini, Virginia Ramponi
Follino, Federico 64, 129–30, 143, 146, 148–50, 155–62, 229, 253, 260–1
    Compendio 64, 157
Fontanelli, Alfonso 225
Fonteny, Jacques de 260
Fortunio, *see* Petignoni, Rinaldo
frame 20, 38–9, 52–3, 71, 88, 92, 125, 141, 152, 158, 184–6
France, Charles IX of 188, 196
France, court of 3, 48, 163, 173
France, François II of 188
France, Henri II of 1
France, Henri III of 11–12, 15, 43, 195–8, 200, 226
France, Henri IV of 3, 79, 146, 173, 226, 236, 249, 256–7
France, Renée of 198
Frangipani, Cornelio
    Tragedia 11–16, 35, 43, 144, 146, 197, 265, 268
Fuentes, Count of 2, 77, 238, 240, 250–2, 254, 259, 285–8

Gabrielli, Francesco (Scapino) 9,
  11n, 24, 26–31, 223
  Aria di Scapino ('*I più rigidi cori*')
    27, 29–30
  Barzelletta di Scapino 71, 173
  *Infermità, testamento, e morte di
    Francesco Gabrielli* 27, 29
  Scapinata 71, 173
Gabrielli, Giovanni (Sivello) 9, 224,
  237, 240
Gagliano, Marco da 144, 261
Galassi, Cesare 228
Galbiati, Marco Antonio 275
Gallico, Claudio 72n, 135
Garzoni, Tomaso 14, 16, 20, 35–6, 40,
  46, 55, 133, 238
  La piazza universale 14–15, 55, 61n,
    238
Gatico, Camillo 215
Gazamini, Paolo 229
gaze 98, 116
Gelosi, Compagnia de' 1, 3–14,
  16–19, 21, 30–6, 43, 46–9, 52,
  55–6, 62, 64, 90n, 128, 144,
  165–6, 173, 182, 268, 272–3
gender 20, 37, 39, 60–1, 84n, 86,
  91–3, 95–126, 174–5, 178, 181,
  185–6, 194–208, 210–14, 218,
  220–1, 224, 226–8, 231, 233,
  235–6, 239, 250, 306–23
  see also representation
Ghirlenzoni, Lelio 233
Ghivizzani, Alessandro 174
Ghizzolo, Giovanni 178
gift 34, 44, 52–3, 58–9, 61, 91, 133,
  153, 161n
  divine 58–9, 61, 66
  of harmony and rhythm 52–3, 147
Giglioli, Girolamo 244
Giulio Romano 160–1
Giusti, Giusto 234
Giustiniani, Vincenzo 188, 198

Gondi, Giovan Battista 257
Gondi, Girolamo 257
Gonzaga, Anna Caterina
  marriage to Ferdinand of Austria
    (1582) 212
Gonzaga, Cesare 190–1
Gonzaga, court 3, 7, 48, 62, 78–80,
  127–62, 164, 225
Gonzaga, Eleonora 237
Gonzaga, Eleonora Anna Maria 245
Gonzaga, Fabio 243
Gonzaga, Ferdinando 20–1, 129, 133,
  164n, 259–60, 262
Gonzaga, Ferrando 206, 219
Gonzaga, Ferrante 218, 287
Gonzaga, Francesco 164, 221, 255,
  258–9, 262
  marriage to Margherita of Savoy
    (1608) 4, 185
Gonzaga, Gian Vincenzo 231
Gonzaga, Guglielmo 9–10, 148n,
  187–8, 190–2, 196–8, 201, 203–5,
  208–10, 212–14, 216–20, 222–3,
  271
Gonzaga, Lodovico 239
Gonzaga, Margherita 163, 203–4,
  206, 212, 215, 217, 230, 238–9,
  241, 248, 252, 257, 259, 261
Gonzaga, Massimiliano 35, 191
Gonzaga, Vespasiano 223
Gonzaga, Vincenzo 2–4, 6–7, 10n,
  17, 48, 73, 77–80, 82–3, 128–30,
  133, 148, 163–5, 173, 182, 188,
  204–25, 227, 229–35, 238–48,
  250–5, 258–62, 272–3, 275,
  283–5, 287, 292
  marriage to Eleonora de' Medici
    (1584) 6, 17, 216
  marriage to Margherita Farnese
    (1581) 10, 208
Goretti, Antonio 83, 148, 244
Grafton, Anthony 144

Grana, Giacomo 194, 200
Grandi, Adriano 252
Graziano, *see* Bianchi, Lodovico de'
Grazzini, Anton Francesco (Il Lasca)
   Descrizione degl'intermedi 189
   La gelosia 18
Great Panathenaea 32
Greenblatt, Stephen 89–90, 130
Grillo, Giovan Battista
   Breve trattato di quanto successe 82
Grimani, Marino 238, 259
ground bass 13
Gualterotti, Raffaello 226
Guarini, Alessandro 247
Guarini, Anna 206, 242
Guarini, Battista 81–4, 110, 148, 206, 210, 212, 215, 218–19, 221, 223, 230–3, 239, 273, 275;
   Il pastor fido 79, 81, 99, 123n, 110–11, 147–9, 162, 215, 217–18, 221, 227–8, 230–33, 242–45, 247, 274
   L'idropica 128, 143, 159–60, 215, 261
Guarini, Taddea 228
Guarino Veronese 84, 86–7, 89, 91, 93–4, 110, 125, 144
   educational system of 84–5, 94, 96, 144, 158
Guazzi, Eleuterio 71–2
   Io credèa che tra gli amanti 72, 173, 184
   Spiritosi affetti 71n, 72
Guerrieri, Giovan Battista 214
Guidiccioni, Laura 90, 226, 239
Guidoboni, Guidobono 216, 219, 230–2, 235
Guisoni, Ferrante 201

Harmony of the Spheres 14, 16, 33, 36–8, 51–3, 55, 75, 125, 159n, 186

Harò, Count of
   wedding of (1594) 11, 17, 19–20, 237
hermeticism 14, 37, 52, 159
Hitchcock, H. Wiley 174
Holford-Strevens, Leofranc 128
homoeroticism 58, 111
homosexuality 96
honour 1, 7, 15, 30–1, 41, 49, 53, 68, 155–6, 163, 166–7, 175, 288
humanism 12, 51–2, 54–5, 84–8, 91–6, 110, 122, 125–6, 128–32, 144, 149–50, 157, 162, 184, 186

Iberti, Annibale 245
imitation 7–8, 33–5, 37–8, 40, 44, 49, 51–2, 54–6, 58–9, 62–3, 74, 91, 93, 96, 104, 110, 123, 125, 162, 134–5, 140–2, 145, 163, 185–6
improvisation 12n, 14, 36–7, 43, 64, 133–4, 186
Ingegneri, Angelo 2–4, 30, 41–2, 165, 218, 243
   Della poesia rappresentativa e del modo di rappresentar le favole sceniche 2, 30, 41, 42, 83n, 243
instrumentalists 12, 42, 168–9, 232, 236
instruments, musical 9, 12, 24–9, 36, 38–44, 71, 134–5, 140–1, 168, 170, 178, 223, 234
   arpicordo 178
   bass 27
   bonacordo 27
   chitarrone 134–5, 140–2
   clavicembalo 134–5, 140–2
   flauto dolce 24, 41, 43–4
   flute 41, 209
   guitar (*chitariglia*) 27, 64, 71, 169, 232; Spanish (*chitarra alla Spagnola*) 4, 24, 27, 29, 71, 169–70, 173

instruments, musical (*cont.*):
  harp 27
  harpsichord 134
  lute 24, 27, 40–41, 43–4, 64, 168–70; played with a virtuosic hand 36, 40, 44, 181
  lyre 68, 72
  mandola 27
  panpipe 41–2
  pastoral 41
  theorbo 27, 71
  trombone 27, 234
  trumpet 12, 15, 197
  viola 27
  violin 27, 134–5, 142, 234
intellect 36–7, 46, 51, 87
intermedi 12, 16–20, 32–5, 46–7, 52–3, 56, 276, 281–2, 146, 169, 189–90, 193, 208–9, 212, 215, 217, 220–6, 237, 243–5, 247–8, 250, 253–4, 261
  apparenti 18, 274
  Fall of Phaethon (1594) 17, 19–20, 281–2, 237
  for *L'idropica* (1608) 128, 143, 159–60, 261
  Mercury and Philology (1598) 81–2, 245
  non apparenti 18
invention 18, 27, 34, 104, 132, 145, 165, 281–2
irrationality 38
  see also women, *in extremis*
Isachino da Mantova (Massaro) 278
Ivanovich, Christoforo 9

Kirkendale, Warren 21

Laderchi, Giovan Battista 217, 228
Laghi, Andrea di 229
Lambardesco, Ottavio 265, 278

lament 20, 33–4, 38, 67, 69, 127–62, 163, 165, 176, 185, 190, 260
Lamento d'Arianna, see Monteverdi, Claudio, *Lamento d'Arianna*
Lamento della ninfa, see Monteverdi, Claudio, *Lamento della ninfa*
Lamento dell'ingrata, see Monteverdi, Claudio, *Lamento dell'ingrata*
Lampugnano, Giulio Cesare 198
Lanci, Cornelio 199
Landi, Antonio
  Il commodo 18
Lasso, Orlando di 43, 190, 192
Leandro, *see* Pilastro, Francesco
Legati, Giovanni 19
Lelio, *see* Andreini, Giovan Battista
Lent 5n, 8
Licino, Giovan Battista 222
licenza 185
licence 5, 7, 22, 157, 190, 194–6, 198, 201–5, 213, 215–16, 218–25, 227–30, 234–41, 247–8, 251–2, 255, 258–9, 268–70, 279–81, 282–3, 286–7, 289
  see also commitment
Livizzano, Carlo 192
Locarni, Pietromartire 78, 257–8
Lombardi, Bernardino 228, 239
Loredan, Pietro 193
Lorraine, Christine of 3, 192, 225, 227, 230, 237, 240–1, 246, 250, 258, 300–5
  marriage to Ferdinando de' Medici (1589) 5, 16–17, 32, 37, 39, 47, 61, 64–6, 74–5
Lorraine, Renée of 194
  marriage to Wilhelm V of Baveria (1568) 192
Luzzara, Carlo 218
Luzzaschi, Luzzasco 180, 193–4, 212, 233, 244, 246, 253, 260

Machiavelli, Lucrezia 194, 200
Machiavelli, Nicolò
  La mandragola 18
  Clizia 18
Macrobius 295
  Commentary on the Dream of Scipio 55
  Saturnalia 55
Madri della Cantelma 48, 241, 247, 259
madrigal 13, 16, 18, 36, 43, 81, 94, 98–9, 103–4, 110–11, 184
Maggi, Ottaviano 13, 196–7
Magli, Giovan Gualberto 164, 260
Magni, Carlo 255, 260
Magno, Giovanni 260
Malatesta, Pandolfo 1–3, 164–6, 172, 262
male voice, *see* gender
Malherbe, François de 22
Malvezzi, Cristofano 19, 217, 221, 226
Malvezzi, Pirro 218–20, 235, 275
Mamei, Pietro Antonio 229
Mancini, Franco 9, 11n
Manelli, Francesco
  L'Andromeda 11
Manfredi, Mutio 230
Manuzio, Aldo 206
Marenzio, Luca 43, 205, 210, 226
Marino, Giovan Battista 56, 185
Marliani, Ercole 220, 262
marriage to death 151–5, 158–61, 168, 185
Martelli, Camilla 192
Martinelli, Angelica 206
Martinelli, Caterina 260–1, 182n
Martinelli, Drusiano 9–10, 206, 233–4
Martinelli, Tristano (Arlecchino) 7, 9, 11, 20, 23–4, 81, 164n, 187, 237, 240, 247, 249, 256–7, 259, 282

Massaro, *see* Isachino da Mantova
Mattei, Pietro [Matthieu, Pierre] 2, 53, 250
Mazzo, Lotto del 192
McClary, Susan 86, 89n, 92, 110
Medici family 3, 47–9, 52–3, 88, 163
Medici, Carlo de' 240
Medici, Caterina de' 133, 188
  marriage to Ferdinando Gonzaga (1617) 262
Medici, Claudia de' 258
Medici, Cosimo I de' 47, 187, 192, 194, 196, 200
  marriage to Eleonora de Toledo (1539) 18
Medici, Cosimo II de' 5, 21, 164, 167, 232
Medici, court 18, 46, 49–50, 52–4, 56, 61, 147, 167, 232
Medici, Eleonora de' 3–4, 48, 88, 147–8, 163, 190, 192, 206, 221–2, 230, 232, 241, 247–50, 256, 260–1, 276, 279, 292
  marriage to Vincenzo Gonzaga (1584) 6, 17, 148, 215–17
Medici, Ferdinando de' 3, 21, 163, 187–8, 200–1, 210, 213, 217, 222–3, 226, 228–30, 233, 236–7, 240–1, 246–7, 257–8, 261, 279–80, 291
  marriage to Christine of Lorraine (1589) 5, 16–17, 32, 37, 39, 47, 62–3, 65, 82, 130, 134, 173, 181, 185
Medici, Filippo de' 202
Medici, Francesco de' 237, 239
Medici, Francesco Maria de' 18, 192, 196, 202–4, 206–10, 213–14, 216–17, 222–3
  marriage to Bianca Capello (1579) 203

Medici, Francesco Maria de' (cont.):
  marriage to Giovanna d'Austria
    (1565) 189
Medici, Giovanni de' 188–9, 237,
  250, 255, 262
Medici, Giovan Paolo de' 195
Medici, Isabella de' 200
Medici, Lorenzo de' 246
Medici, Lucrezia de'
  marriage to Alfonso II d'Este
    (1560) 188
Medici, Margherita de' 230
Medici, Maria de' 3, 23, 48, 79, 88, 163,
  173, 196, 249–50, 256–7, 290–1
  marriage to Henri IV (1600) 3,
    249–50
Medici, Virginia de' 192, 220–1
  marriage to Cesare d'Este (1586)
    220–1
Medici, Virginio de' 232
Melfi, Giuseppe 228
memory 13–14, 24, 149–50, 159, 162,
  186
Mentre vivo lontano 172
Mercurius Trismegistus 14
Mercury and Philology, *see* intermedi
Merulo, Claudio 12–16, 43, 144, 197,
  233, 257, 268
metamorphosis 14, 35
Michiel, Alvise 6, 8–9, 214, 272
Minaggio, Dionisio
  The Feather Book 25, 183
Mirandola, Federico Pico da 237
Miroglio, Federico 206, 215, 227
Mocenigo, Aloisio 13, 196–7
Mocenigo, Alvise 193, 202
Molza, Tarquinia 90, 202, 214, 220
Monaldini, Giovan Maria 280–1, 283
Monasterio Corpus Domini 10,
  207–8, 210–11, 271–2
monetary units 187
Monte di Pietà (Florence) 48, 240,
  257, 290

Monteverdi, Claudio 7, 14, 24, 31, 40,
  42–5, 62, 73–4, 77–8, 80–6, 92,
  99, 104, 110, 127, 129–44, 146–9,
  156, 161–2, 164, 168, 174, 182,
  184, 210, 217, 233, 238–9, 244,
  252–4, 256, 260–1
  Amorosa pupilletta 135–7
  Arianna 7, 13–14, 40, 81, 127–33,
    141–3, 146–7, 149–64, 167–8,
    173, 182n, 184–5, 260–1
  Canzonette à tre voci 43–5, 182,
    217
  Cruda Amarilli 85, 99, 110–11
  Il ballo delle ingrate 7, 128, 130,
    132, 140, 143n, 261
  Io mi son giovinetta 110
  L'incoronazione di Poppea 29, 156n
  Lamento d'Arianna ('Lasciatemi
    morire') 20, 71, 127–34, 142–3,
    146–7, 150, 153, 155–8, 161–2,
    168, 172–3, 185–6
  Lamento della ninfa ('Amor',
    dicea') 20
  Lamento dell'ingrata ('Ahi troppo è
    duro') 130–4, 140–3, 167, 173,
    181, 184
  O Mirtillo 110
  Orfeo 19, 163–4, 184, 260, 256
  Ottavo libro de madrigali 74
  Scherzi musicali 72–3, 134–5, 142
  Si come crescon alla terra i fiori
    44–5
Monteverdi, Giulio Cesare 7, 72
  Il rapimento di Proserpina 7, 173,
    262
Monteverdi, Leonora Camilla 256
Monteverdi, Massimiliano Giacomo
  258
moresca 35
Moro, Paolo 210
Music of the Spheres, *see* Harmony of
  the Spheres
musica ficta 16

Nani, Antonio 229
nature 34, 39, 53, 68, 88–94, 121–2, 125–6, 150n, 293–4, 305–6, 315–16
Negri, Cesare 196, 198, 233
  Le gratie d'amore 22–3, 79n
Negro, Giulio Santo Pietro del
  Mov'èa dolce un zefiretto 135–40
neoclassicism 1–2, 12, 14, 20, 33–4, 37, 52–3, 62–3, 67, 85, 87, 90, 91n, 128, 133, 149–50, 153–4, 157, 159n, 182, 295–6, 300–23
neoplatonism 2, 37, 49, 52–6, 58–61, 75, 121–2
Neri, Filippo 21
Newcomb, Anthony 87, 90n
Nobili, Flamino de' 5
Nobili, Orazio de' 5, 199, 203, 228, 239
Nobili, Vittoria de' 5, 239
Nogarola, Isotta 86–7, 89, 91
Nolffi, Guido 228
Nora fiorentina 5, 228, 239

obligation 6–10, 75, 80, 83n, 272–3, 278–80, 283
ode 63, 67, 69, 73
Olivo, Luigi 215, 219–20, 227
Ongarino, Francesco 242
opera 11, 20n, 54, 110, 147, 154n, 156, 184, 186
  reale 3
oral process 13, 71
oratory 4, 35, 61, 84, 87–8
Orlandi, Santi
  Amorosa mia Clori 104
ornamentation 27, 44, 72, 134, 139, 157, 307
Orologgi, Giuseppe 156
Orsini, Isabella 199
Orsini, Virginio 266, 283
Osanna family of printers 157
Osmo, Jacopo d' 10, 208–9

ottava rima 13, 16, 166n, 169
Ovid 35
  Heroides 150, 156, 161
  Metamorphoses 150

Pagani, Gentile 266, 281
Paganini, Silvio 256
Palace of Civic Affairs (Savona) 62
Palazzo della Ragione (Mantua) 35
Paleologa, Margherita 189
Palisca, Claude 21
Palladio, Andrea 8n, 182
Pallas Athena 15–16
Pallavicino, Benedetto 77, 222, 253
Panciatichi, Vincenzo 250
Pantalone, *see* Pasquati da Padova, Giulio
Panzanini, Gabrielle 5, 203
Pasquati da Padova, Giulio (Pantalone) 4, 196, 217, 224, 268
pastoral 3, 18, 33, 35, 37, 41, 62, 81–2, 84, 111, 122, 148, 274, 277–8, 280–2
pastoralism 37–46, 58, 60, 53–4, 62, 64, 75, 96, 173, 186, 293–4, 300–5
Patrizi, Francesco 202
patron 4–6, 8, 13, 17, 88, 95, 160, 162, 182
  natural 47
patronage 3–4, 47, 49, 80, 88, 90, 95, 163–4, 167
Pauli, Margherita 233
Pavoni, Giuseppe 32–3, 46–7, 61–2, 72, 226
  Diario 32–3, 49, 51, 57, 61, 73–4, 130
Pax Hispanica 4
Pedrolino, *see* Pellesini, Giovanni
Pellegrina, Lodovica 223
Pellegrini, Vincenzo
  Canzona detta la Serpentina 172
  Canzoni de intavolatura d'organo fatte alla francese 172

Pellesini, Giovanni (Pedrolino) 4,
    8–11, 20–4, 79, 83n, 200, 206–8,
    215, 217, 236–7, 240, 248, 251–2,
    257, 270, 273, 280, 282
Pellini, Giovanni 208
Penthesilea, *see* women, amazonian
Pepoli, Ercole 262
Peri, Jacopo 19, 217, 241, 246
    Dafne 173
Persia, Ferrante 81, 245
Petignoni, Rinaldo (Fortunio) 195–6,
    230, 236
petrarchism 44, 95–6, 116, 121, 125
Peverara, Laura 204–6, 208, 212–13,
    244, 250
Phaedran charioteer 58–60, 76,
    185–6
Piazza, Diego de la 199–200
Piccolomini, Alessandro 221
Piisimi, Vittoria 4–5, 8–11, 13–16,
    18–20, 32–3, 36, 46–7, 59, 91,
    185, 198–9, 204, 206–7, 226, 228,
    234, 237, 239, 270, 280
    La cingana 32, 34, 46–7, 56, 226
Pilastro, Francesco (Leandro) 228–9,
    231, 234, 236–8
Pimentel, Alonso 194
Pimentelli, Diego 252–3
Pino, Bernardino 214, 216
Pirrotta, Nino 17, 47n, 135
plague 11, 160n
Plato 54–5, 59, 149, 156, 159n
    Laws 54
    Phaedrus 37, 54–5, 58–60
    Timaeus 37, 53, 55
Plautus 89
Pléiade, see Académie de Poésie et
    Musique
poesia per musica 63, 68, 72, 95
Polini, Pavia di 229
Poliziano, Angelo 84, 87, 93, 110,
    125

Pomponazzi, Aurelio 216–17, 234,
    242, 248
Ponsini, Giacomo 275
Ponte, Nicolò da 219
Ponti, Diana 227, 238, 240–1
Pontremoli, Girolamo da 161
Porcacchi, Tomaso 265, 267
Porphyry 53
possession 61
    see also divine madness
Preti, Baldassare de 192
Priuli, Girolamo 191
prohibitions against comedians 5–6,
    8
prologue 13, 17, 19–20, 53, 81, 83n,
    155–7, 185, 201, 247, 295
prophesy 2, 60, 30
proportion 14–15, 55
Prosperi, Bartolomeo 232
Puteanus, Erycius 36, 77–8, 83–4, 87,
    89, 91–4, 98, 104, 110, 116, 121,
    125, 127, 186, 250, 253–6, 305–23

Quintus Roscius Gallus 55

Radavil, Giorgio 231
rape 122, 128, 153–4, 159, 185
    of Europa 159–60
    of Oreithyia 58–60, 75
Rasi, Francesco 74, 239
recitative 43, 130, 133, 140, 147, 186
Rehm, Rush 128, 151, 154–5
Rena, Orazio della 225
representation 1, 11, 16–17, 20, 33–4,
    56, 60, 85, 88, 94, 104, 110–11,
    121, 128, 144, 146, 151–4, 156–7,
    159–62, 165, 168, 170, 173, 184,
    186
    of gender 20, 37, 95–126
    of wind 39–40, 42, 75
rhetoric 12, 15–16, 36, 51–2, 71–2,
    84–6, 88, 91–2, 94, 96, 99–100,

104, 116, 125, 128, 141, 145,
  149–50, 154–7, 162, 186
Ricasoli Rucellai, Orazio 221
  Platonic dialogues 52
Ricio, Antonio 6–7, 208, 214
Rincio, Marcello 265, 269
Rinuccini, Ottavio 85, 128, 174, 203,
  225–6, 241, 246, 249, 258, 260–1
  Arianna 81, 127, 129, 141, 146–7,
    150–1, 153, 155–7, 161–2, 261
  Il ballo delle ingrate 128, 130–4,
    140–3, 261
  Dafne 173, 241, 246, 249, 258, 261
  Euridice 146, 249
Rocca, Guido 229
Rocca, Michele della 233
Rocca Nobili, Camilla (Delia) 17–18,
  220, 275–6
Rogna, Luigi 34, 190–1
Romano, Remigio 71, 172–3
Romei, Annibale 219
Roncagli, Silvia 4, 18, 220, 276
Ronsard, Pierre de 62–4, 67, 69
Rosa, Ercole 218
Rossetti, Stefano 19
Rossi, Bastiano de' 47, 52, 54, 220, 229
  Descrizione dell'apparato 47, 64
Rossi, Carlo 146–7, 239, 259–60
Rossi, Girolamo de' 220
Rossi, Salomone 174–222
Rovere, Francesco Maria della 193,
  198
  marriage to Livia di Ippolito della
    Rovere (1599) 246
Rovere, Guidobaldo della 198
Rovere, Lavinia della 277
Rubini, Nicolò 178
Russano Hanning, Barbara 54

Sadeler, Raffaello 116, 118, 320–21
Sala degli Specchi (Mantua) 127,
  146n, 261

sala delle commedie 52, 261
Salimbeni, Girolamo 5, 228, 231,
  236–9
Salone Margherita 79, 244
Salviati, Antonio Maria 219–20
Salviati, Lionardo 221
San Giorgio, Teodoro 191, 197, 204,
  213
Sanchez, Francesco 246
Sanseverino, Barbara 195, 199, 201
Sansovino, Francesco 8–9
Santissima Annunziata (Florence)
  48, 50
Sanvitale, Leonora 199
Saracini, Claudio 178–9, 184
  Care gioie che le noie 178–9, 181,
    184
  Seconde musiche 178–9
Saracini, Sinolfo 201
Sarnis, Camillo 228
Savoy, Carlo Emanuele of 2, 99, 157,
  188, 206, 222, 227, 248–9, 260,
  286, 292
Savoy, court 150, 161
Savoy, Margherita of 78–9, 83, 88,
  145, 155, 261
  marriage to Francesco Gonzaga
    (1608) 4, 78, 81, 88, 127, 130n,
    155, 164
Scala, Flamino (Flavio) 5, 30, 57–8,
  187, 196, 254, 261–2, 273
Scamozzi, Vincenzo 223
Scapino, *see* Gabrielli, Francesco
Scarpetta, Giuseppe 225, 228, 239–40
scenario 14, 30, 134, 140, 151–2, 166,
  184
scherzo 71, 134–5, 139–42, 172–3, 178,
  182
Schiafenati, Camillo 79, 248
Scolari, Giovan Battista 192
Scotto, Honorio 227
seconda prattica 73, 77

self-fashioning 49, 89–90, 95, 116, 125, 130
Seneca 156n
Senesi, Alessandro 258
Serguidi, Antonio 202, 210
Simone bolognese 267
Socrates 54, 58
soliloquy 15, 19, 30, 37, 53, 128
  see also prologue
Sommi, Leone de' 190, 214, 224, 230, 274, 278
  Quattro dialoghi in materia di rappresentazioni sceniche 19
song, celestial 38–9, 41, 49, 72, 76, 174, 184, 168
  see also divine madness; Harmony of the Spheres
sonnet 5n, 36, 40–1, 55, 62, 77n, 98–9, 121, 123n, 178
Sorgga, Aurelia 228
Spagnolo, Giulio 224–5
Spain, Isabella of 246–8
  marriage to Albert of Austria (1599) 22, 78–80, 244
Spain, Philip II of 1, 79, 243–5
Spain, Philip III of 242, 246, 255
  marriage to Margherita of Austria (1598) 22, 78, 81, 88, 147–8
Spanish guitar, *see* musical instruments
Spano, Donat'Antonio 104–9
  Quella bocca di rose 97–9, 104–9, 111
Spelta, Antonio Maria 256
Spinola, Datio 242, 266, 284
Stampa, Gaspara 90, 121
  'Or sopra il forte e veloce destriero' 98–9
stanza delle commedie (Venice) 6, 8, 280
Statius
  Achilleid 86n, 153

Stella, Giulio Cesare 242
Striggio, Alessandro 11, 19, 85, 164–5, 189, 193, 216–17, 221–2, 240, 260–2
  Il sacrificio d'Ifigenia 128, 143, 151, 153, 158–9, 164, 261
  Orfeo 163–4, 184, 260
Strozzi, Giovan Battista 18
Strozzi, Giulio 210, 244
style 3, 11–12, 20–2, 24, 36, 43, 47, 51, 55–6, 61–4, 68, 71–4, 89, 96, 99, 104, 111, 121, 125, 130, 133–5, 140–1, 145, 147, 149, 167, 173–4, 178, 184, 186
  Aristotelian 2, 52, 81, 147, 149, 162
  Ciceronian 35, 49, 84n, 85n, 149
  elegant and wise 46, 51, 84
  French 3, 22, 33, 49, 62, 72–4, 133–5, 182
  Italian 23, 30, 74
  Petrarchan 44, 95–6, 116, 121, 125
  Roman 2, 5, 49
  submission 51, 59, 61, 76, 86, 95–6, 98–9, 111, 130, 185
Sullam, Abram 231
Summo, Faustino
  Discorsi poetici 81
Sutton, Julia 22

tagliacanzone 24
Tasso, Torquato 110, 201, 217, 220–1
  Aminta 111, 122–3, 195, 206
  Gerusalemme liberata 84n, 89, 95, 126
Tassone, Ferrante Estense 217, 240
Tassoni, Ercole 201
Taviani, Ferdinando 111
Teatro di Baldracca 238
Teatro del Castello 82, 245
teatro di musica 11
Teatro Grimani 29

Index

Teatro Michiel 8–10, 182, 207
Teatro Olimpico 8n
Teatro di Sabbionetta 223, 227
Teatro Tron 8, 10–11, 22, 182, 207
Teatro degli Uffizi 46–7, 52, 239, 250, 256
Tedesco, Michele 224
Terracina, Laura 95
terza rima 43
terzina 33, 43–4
Tettone, Rinaldo 233
theatre 1, 11, 14, 19–20, 30, 55–6, 63, 71, 77–80, 82–3, 116, 121, 125, 182, 184, 293, 309–13
Theatre of Memory 14, 159
Thiene, Giulio 199, 201
Toledo, Eleonora de 187–8, 200
    marriage to Cosimo I de' Medici (1539) 18
Tomlinson, Gary 58–9, 122
Torelli, Marsilio 254
Toresana de Bugatis de Bellinis, Veronica 260
Torre, Pietro Paolo 103–4
    Ove sì tosto voli sogno? 96, 98–9, 103–4
tragedy 3, 12, 18, 33–4, 35n, 56, 128, 145–7, 149, 156, 166, 190, 199, 280–2
tragicomedy 3, 18, 34, 81–2, 84n, 148–9, 217, 250, 274, 280–2
Treaty 250–2
Treaty of Antwerp 4n
Treaty of Cateau-Cambrésis 1
Treaty of London 4
Treaty of Vervins 4n, 77–9, 242, 249–50
Trissino, Agosto 196, 205–6, 216, 218
Troiano, Massimo 192–3
Trombetti, Giovan Battista 228, 239
Tron, Ettore 8, 207, 270
Trotti, Borso 193

Trotti, Ercole 242
Turco, Annibale 212–13
Turino, Lanfranco 205

Udine, Hercole 259
Uniti, Compagnia degli 5, 202, 215–18, 221–2, 229, 233, 235–8, 240, 252, 273, 286–7, 282
Urbani, Oratio 204, 206–10, 213–14, 216
Urban VII, *see* Castagna, Giovan Battista

Valerini, Adriano 4, 18, 35–6, 203, 220, 224, 229, 275
valour 33–4, 37, 46, 49, 51, 61, 74–5, 144, 163
Vargnano, Scipione 246
varietà 28, 34, 36
Vasari, Giorgio 189–90
Vecchi e Cusana, Marchesa Giulia de' 22
Vecchi, Orazio 43
Vegi, Carlo 228, 239
Vendramini, Francesco 223, 227
Venier, Domenico 40
Venier, Sebastiano 202
versi sciolti 13, 16
Verzellino, Giovanni Vincenzo 62
via naturale alla immitazione 133, 142, 147, 162
Viani, Antonio Maria (Vianino) 243, 247–8, 260–1
Viani, Camillo 243, 247–8, 260–1
Vigianti, Giulio 228, 239
Vigliega, Antonio de 245
villan di Spagna, see dance
villanella 24, 27
villanescha 27, 205
Vinta, Belisario 48, 199, 202, 216, 223, 225, 230, 233, 241, 249, 257–8, 279, 290–1

Virgil 54, 159n, 296
  Aeneid 54n, 144–5
  Eclogues 34, 37–9, 296–300
virtue (*virtù*) 1–3, 31, 33–4, 38, 46n, 49, 51, 53, 58–9, 61, 63, 66, 74, 84, 89, 91–2, 94–5, 125, 127, 288, 306–23
  ingested in a drink 51
Visconte, Giovan Battista 248
  Arminia 79
Vizani family 32
Vizani, Giasone 226
Vizani, Pompeo 226

Wert, Giaches de 7, 43, 214, 221–2, 230
  Tirsi morir volea 110–16, 125
women
  amazonian 13, 87, 309–13
  heroic 34, 87–8, 95, 110
  in extremis 85, 128, 144–5, 158
  representation of 2, 81, 86, 89, 91–3, 111, 116, 121–2, 126–7, 153, 169–70, 175–6, 178, 184–6: as goddesses 16, 81, 145, 151, 160–2, 309–13; as sibyls 37, 60–1; as sirens 16–17, 53, 56, 63

Zametti, Sebastiano 290
zanni 24, 49, 202–3, 209, 211, 239, 249, 255–6
Zarlino, Gioseffo 12, 268
Zibramonte, Aurelio 203, 205, 211, 213
Zirolani, Hercole 217